YOHANAN A.P. GOLDMAN, Ph.D. (1989) in Theology, University of Fribourg, Switzerland, is Privat-Docent at the University of Fribourg and a Member of the Editorial Board of the *Biblia Hebraica Quinta*.
ARIE VAN DER KOOIJ, Ph.D. (1978) in Theology, University of Utrecht, is Professor of Old Testament Studies at Leiden University, The Netherlands, Secretary of the International Organization for the Study of the Old Testament (IOSOT) and Chief Editor of *Vetus Testamentum*.
RICHARD D. WEIS, Ph.D. (1986) in Religion, Claremont Graduate University, is Professor of Old Testament Theology and Dean of the Seminary at United Theological Seminary of the Twin Cities, in Minnesota, USA.

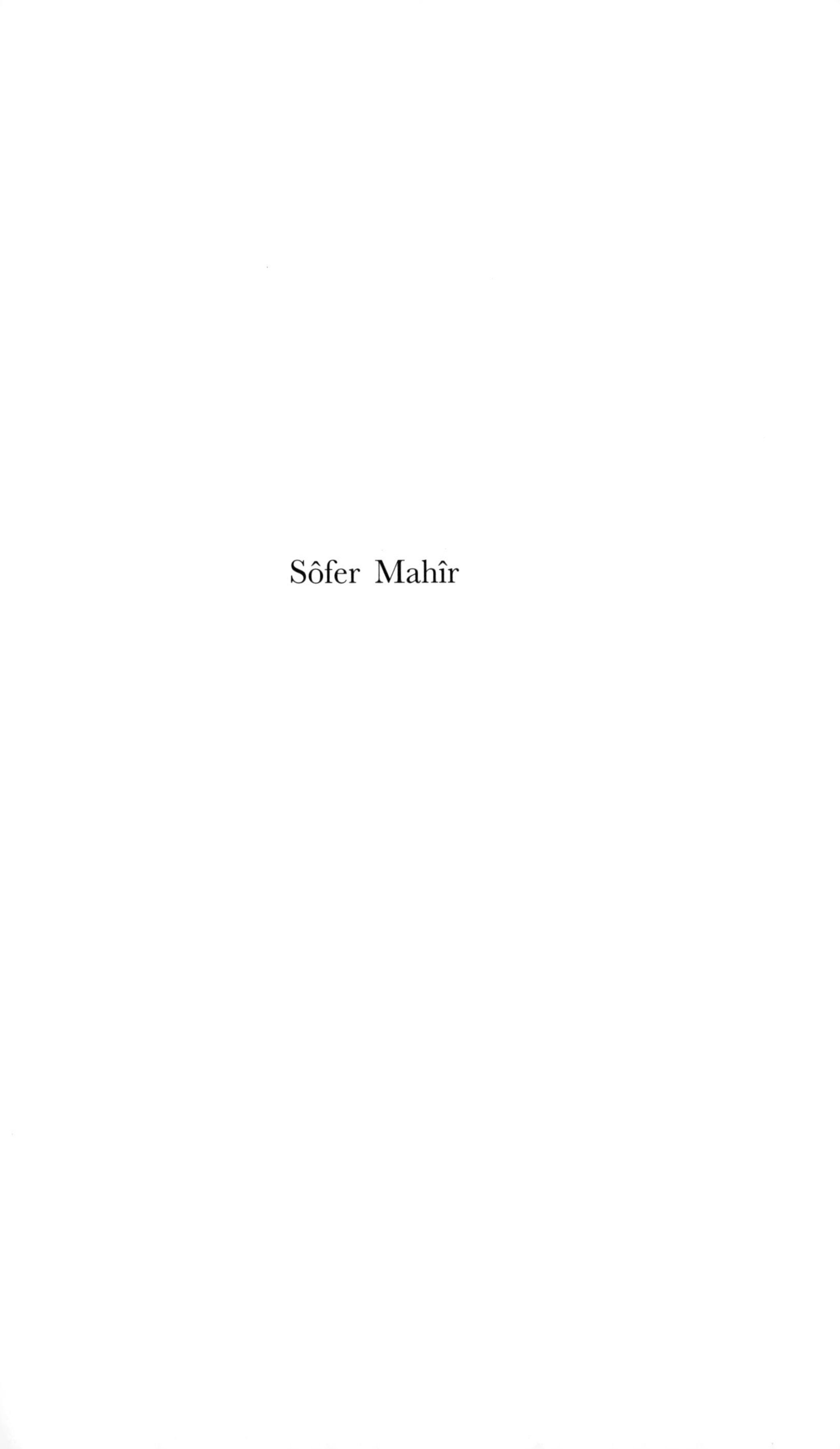

Sôfer Mahîr

Supplements
to
Vetus Testamentum

VOLUME 110

Adrian Schenker O.P.

Sôfer Mahîr

Essays in Honour of Adrian Schenker Offered by Editors of *Biblia Hebraica Quinta*

Edited by

Yohanan A.P. Goldman, Arie van der Kooij and Richard D. Weis

BRILL
LEIDEN • BOSTON
2006

This book is printed on acid-free paper.

Library of Congress Cataloging-in-Publication data

Sôfer mahîr : essays in honour of Adrian Schenker / offered by the editors of Biblia Hebraica quinta ; edited by Yohanan A.P. Goldman, Arie van der Kooij, and Richard D. Weis.

p. cm. — (Supplements to Vetus Testamentum, ISSN 0083-5889 ; v. 110)

Includes bibliographical references and index.

ISBN 90-04-15016-1 (hardback : alk. paper)

1. Bible O.T.—Criticism, Textual. 2. Bible. O.T.—History. 3. Bible. O.T.—Versions. I. Schenker, Adrian, 1939– II. Goldman, Yohanan, 1952– III. Kooij, Arie van der, 1945– IV. Weis, Richard D. V. Series.

BS410.V452 vol. 110
[BS1136]
221.4'46—dc22

2005058638

ISSN 0083-5889
ISBN 90 04 15016 1

PRINTED IN THE NETHERLANDS

CONTENTS

PREFACE

With this volume we seek to honour our colleague and friend, Adrian Schenker, particularly as the one who presides over the Editorial Committee of the international project, *Biblia Hebraica Quinta* (*BHQ*). The essays herein have been written by editors who are involved in the project – each on the book which he or she is editing for *BHQ*.

Adrian Schenker is not only a biblical exegete and theologian, but also an outstanding scholar in the field of textual criticism of the Old Testament. He developed his expertise under the stimulating guidance of a master in the field, Dominique Barthélemy. His own first major and masterly contribution to this field consisted of two publications containing the edition of hexaplaric fragments of the Psalms (1975 and 1982), the first of which was based on his dissertation as well as his Habilitationsschrift. These studies testify to a most accurate way of dealing with textual evidence – with a sharp eye for details which is typical of all his publications.

In the seventies, Adrian Schenker was an assistant in the Hebrew Old Testament Text Project (HOTTP; 1970–1979) of the United Bible Societies. This experience with experts in the field such as Dominique Barthélemy, Hans Peter Rüger and James Sanders afforded him, and other younger scholars as well, an excellent opportunity to become more acquainted with the pecularities and intricacies of the field. He was the one who was responsible for the text of the Preliminary Reports of the HOTTP.

In later years Adrian Schenker published a number of very stimulating contributions pertaining to the textual criticism of the Old Testament, as well as to Septuagint studies, such as his articles on the LXX of Jeremiah and on 1 Esdras. His scholarship as a textual critic covers a broad range of areas, as is evident from his acquaintance with less well known fields such as the study of Karaite sources.

In the beginning of the nineties a new UBS project was started as a branch out of the HOTTP roots. This aimed at a new edition of the Hebrew Bible, the *Biblia Hebraica Quinta*. In view of his expertise it was only natural that Adrian Schenker was to become one of the members of the Editorial Committee, and subsequently was elected to be the president of that committee. The biblical book he is preparing for *BHQ* is that of Kings. In recent years he has produced two major studies on this book in which he deals with the relationship between the Septuagint and the Masoretic text. Both works are most stimulating, opening up new and exciting vistas on the textual history of Kings. The innovative part of these and his other contributions to the study of Kings is that variant readings attested by the Septuagint not only are treated as isolated readings, but more particularly are studied on the literary level.

Adrian Schenker is a remarkable scholar and a fine person. On behalf of the whole *Quinta* team we offer this volume to him in great appreciation of his work and his role as 'wise father' of the project.

The Editors
Yohanan Goldman
Arie van der Kooij
Richard Weis

LIST OF CONTRIBUTORS

Robert Althann, Pontifical Biblical Institute.

Piet B. Dirksen, Leiden University.

Natalio Fernández Marcos, Philological Institute, CSIC, Madrid.

Anthony Gelston, University of Durham (retired).

Agustinus Gianto, Pontifical Biblical Institute.

Yohanan A. P. Goldman, University of Fribourg.

Innocent Himbaza, University of Fribourg.

Phillipe Hugo, University of Fribourg.

Arie van der Kooij, Leiden University.

Johan Lust, University of Leuven (retired).

David Marcus, Jewish Theological Seminary of America.

Carmel McCarthy, University College, Dublin.

Gerard J. Norton, Dominican Priory Institute, Tallaght.

Martin Rösel, University of Rostock.

Magne Saebø, The Norwegian Lutheran School of Theology (retired).

Rolf Schäfer, German Bible Society, Stuttgart.

Jan de Waard, University of Amsterdam and University of Strasbourg (retired).

Richard D. Weis, United Theological Seminary of the Twin Cities.

INTRODUCTION

The essays offered in this volume cover a great variety of topics and issues in the field of textual criticism and the textual history of the Hebrew Bible, the Old Testament. The contributors open up lines of reflection based on their experience as editors of the *Biblia Hebraica Quinta*. Some of them focus on the text of M, either in the sense of modern literary approaches which add to our understanding of the Hebrew text (Althann, Gianto), or by dealing with particulars of the Leningrad Codex, M^L (McCarthy, Marcus, Norton, Rösel, Saebø). A few contributors provide an assessment of the textual situation of a given book, including a characterization of textual witnesses (Fernández Marcos, Lust, Rösel, Weis, and to some extent Himbaza and Hugo). Closely related to that, several contributions are concerned with translation technique (Gelston, Himbaza, De Waard), or more particularly with an evaluation of variant readings (Dirksen, Van der Kooij, Rösel). Other topics treated include: the relationship between textual history and canonisation (Goldman), differences between *BHQ* and *BHS* (Marcus), and the interaction between literary, or redactional analysis and textual criticism (Schäfer, Weis).

The contributions are presented in alphabetical order according to the names of the authors. R. Althann, editor of Job, deals with characteristics of Classical Hebrew poetry (such as ellipsis and metonymy) which are helpful for a better understanding of the Hebrew text (M) of Job. He argues that new efforts to understand the Hebrew text – such as the one presented in this essay – are of great significance for the evaluation of variant readings and the text critical issue of 'correcting' the Hebrew text.

P. B. Dirksen discusses particular cases in the new critical apparatus to the text of Canticles. Having finished his role as editor, he now plays the part of the user of the new edition by evaluating readings in the apparatus. The instances dealt with in detail concern cases where G differs from M and S, cases where S differs from M and G, cases where G and S agree against M, as well as cases where G and S differ from M and from each other.

In his essay on 'the genuine text of Judges' N. Fernández Marcos offers his 'provisional conclusions on the text history and critical restoration of the book' of Judges. The essay contains, first of all, a presentation and characterization of the textual witnesses of the book including a very useful discussion of G (which is still lacking in the edition of Göttingen). In the section on the history of the text he argues that 'the Hebrew text underlying G, T, S and V belongs to the Masoretic tradition'. It is his contention that this also applies to the evidence from Qumran, including 4QJudg[a] which is not to be considered a witness of a literarily different and shorter text of Judges. Furthermore, he rightly observes that the absence of evidence and current witnesses supporting a non-Masoretic Hebrew text constitutes the main problem for restoring a critical edition of the book. Finally, the author deals with the issue of an eclectic edition – as proposed by the Oxford Hebrew Bible project – in comparison with a diplomatic one (*BHQ*).

A. Gelston, who is preparing the new edition of the book of the Twelve, draws the reader's attention to several 'factors that had a limiting effect on the ancient translators' understanding of the Hebrew text'. These factors are the phenomenon of homonyms, the matter of vocalization, i.e., the way the underlying unvocalized Hebrew text was read, and the matter of confusion between distinct verbs with two consonants in common. For all three factors he discusses a number of examples.

Like Althann, A. Gianto focuses on the literary and stylistic aspects of the Hebrew text, in his case the text and story of Daniel 2.

Y. Goldman, editor of Qohelet, deals with the matter of the book's canonisation in early Judaism. After presenting the rabbinic sources attesting a strong opposition to the canonical status of the book in this milieu, and discussing the nature of such opposition, he suggests that M represents a text which has been corrected at some points (7:19; 7:23–24; 8:1) in order to create a book that could be accepted as canonical among 'the disciples of the sages'. Thus M Qohelet represents a 'témoin d'un compromis théologique'.

I. Himbaza, who just has started his work as editor of Leviticus, provides the reader with detailed information about the way in which the sacrificial terminology in Leviticus 1–7 has been handled in the textual witnesses.

The contribution of Ph. Hugo offers an instructive presentation of the history of research concerning the Old Greek of the books of

Kings. The essay is meant to put the work of A. Schenker, the actual editor of Kings for *BHQ*, into perspective.

A. van der Kooij, who is responsible for the new edition of Isaiah, discusses a number of variant readings in Isaiah which are attested by two or more Qumran MSS. After a brief discussion of some examples of different types of readings, several cases where multiple Qumran biblical MSS attest the same variant reading against M are dealt with. Based on an evaluation of the evidence, he concludes that "while in a few cases shared readings in Qumran MSS testify to a better text, in many cases the combined evidence turns out to be of a secondary nature in comparison to M".

J. Lust offers a discussion of some major issues concerning the Hebrew text of the book of Ezekiel. After a survey of the most important textual sources – Qumran and G – and the way the state of the text is evaluated in commentaries, he deals with the crucial matter of which Hebrew text should be the aim of the textual critic – the proto-M text, or the pre-M text. He argues that M and G testify to two different redactional stages of the book – M being the longer text – which implies that most of the important differences between M and G do not pertain 'to the domain of textual criticism, but rather to that of literary criticism'. He also summarizes his view on the longer pluses in M. Finally, he turns his attention to the issue of the Hebrew language of the book (LBH) and the intriguing matter of the double name, which in most cases can be considered to be part of the early tradition.

D. Marcus provides the reader with a discussion of points of difference between the new edition, *BHQ*, and previous editions, in particular *BHS*, based on his work as editor of Ezra-Nehemiah. The points, which are illustrated with examples from the forthcoming edition of Ezra-Nehemiah, concern the following areas: (1) the availability of new resources, (2) the comparison with other Tiberian MSS, (3) the representation of the Masorah, (4) the inclusion of 1 Esdras as a constant witness, and (5) the circumscribed use of suggestions for textual emendation.

C. McCarthy, editor of the book of Deuteronomy, turns the spotlight on the Mm and Mp notes of two major Masoretic witnesses, M^{L} and the Madrid Codex M1 (M^{M1}). Based on a detailed comparison, she reaches the conclusion that 'a certain number of the Mm and Mp notes accompanying Deuteronomy in M^{M1} differ in varying ways from those contained in M^{L}'. She further concludes not only "that any given Masoretic manuscript is incomplete without its own particular Masorah, one should also insist that one must not try to put on one manuscript the clothes that properly belong to another!".

G. Norton also focuses on the nature of M^L, by dealing with the layout of the manuscript as far as the text of the Psalter is concerned. The layout of this part of the codex is marked by gaps within the lines which are not to be considered as *setumot*, as would be the case in prose texts. The question is raised which factors might have contributed to these intralinear gaps in the presentation of the Psalter. He argues that these gaps are not to be seen as sense gaps, or the like, but that they are of an ornamental nature, at least most of them. Two categories of ornamental line gapping can be distinguished, the one plus two arrangement, and the zig-zag. However, in other cases (e.g., in Psalms with alphabetic acrostics) other factors seem to be involved. He concludes with regard to the presentation of Psalms in *BHQ* that there is no reason to try to reproduce the gaps in a modern edition.

M. Rösel provides the reader with a characterization of the most important witnesses to his book, Numbers: M^L, Qumran witnesses – in particular $4QNum^b$, Smr and G. The characterization is based on a selection of chapters (chs. 22–24). As for M^L attention is given to several aspects, especially the Masorah. His discussion of a number of variant readings in $4QNum^b$, Smr and G illustrates the fact that each textual witness should, first of all, be assessed in its own right as well as that each reading should be evaluated individually. Some variants may be due to context, others turn out to be interpretative – the latter indicating that reception history is part of the textual history of a book.

M. Saebø offers a detailed discussion of the use of the *paseq* in M^L Esther. His conclusion is that the *paseq* has various functions, related first of all to the specific meaning of words, and is meant as an aid to a correct understanding and reading of the text. It also indicates an element of emphasis, in this way contributing to a particular interpretation of the Hebrew text.

R. Schäfer, editor of Lamentations, offers an illustration of a dialogue between textual criticism and structural analysis of a poetical text, Lamentations 1. As far as the textual witnesses are concerned, 4QLam is of particular significance. In light of this witness he offers a reconstruction of the original text of v. 7 and of vv. 16–17, and argues that the poetical structure of the reconstructed text of the chapter is more balanced and harmonious ('ein stimmigeres Bild') than the structure of the text according to M.

J. de Waard, editor of Ruth as well as of Proverbs, deals with lexical ignorance as reflected in the ancient versions of Proverbs. Two examples are being discussed, the rare word קָרֶה and the *hitpael* of the root גלע.

Finally, in an instructive essay R. Weis provides the reader insight into the method he employs in preparing the new edition of the book of Jeremiah. In view of the complicated textual situation the first step to be taken concerns parallel redaction critical analyses of each pericope in M and G. The next step consists of an analysis of translation technique in the versions, primarily in G, which is necessary to establish the respective *Vorlagen* with any degree of probability. Based on these two steps, constituting the preparatory work, one should proceed to the consideration and evaluation of individual textual variations. He illustrates this method of analysis using Jeremiah 37–38 (G, 44–45). As is argued on the basis of examples, the method applied is very helpful in distinguishing between 'redactional' and 'transmissional' variant readings, the former of which do not belong to the field of textual criticism.

Taken together, these essays constitute an ensemble which, compared to the situation as reflected by *BHS*, testifies to the wide variety of new data and trends in the field of textual criticism. The editors of the volume take great pleasure in offering this ensemble to Adrian Schenker, the president of *BHQ*. It is their wish that, in the years to come, he may continue to guide and stimulate the work for the new edition in the manner of 'the waters of Shiloah that flow gently'.

Yohanan Goldman
Arie van der Kooij
Richard Weis

REFLECTIONS ON THE TEXT OF THE BOOK OF JOB

Robert Althann

A critical edition of the book of Job requires the presentation of the most important ancient witnesses to the text, especially of the pre-Tiberian Hebrew witnesses, of the Old Greek, the Vulgate, the Peshitta, the Targum and relevant material from the Dead Sea scrolls. In the case of Job we are fortunate to have critical editions of the text of important witnesses available in published form.[1] These authorities must be weighed and in particular, the relationship between M and G needs to be clarified. The difficulty here is well known. The Greek Job is about one-sixth shorter than the Hebrew Job, which is also true for the Coptic Sahidic version and for the Vetus Latina.[2] How are we to explain such a difference? Did the Greek translator(s) work from a Hebrew text different from that reflected in the Hebrew text that we know, or is there another explanation? N. Fernández Marcos in a paper read at the Colloquium Biblicum Lovaniense in 1993 argued that the differences should be attributed mainly to the Greek translator's techniques. When the translator was faced with a text he could not understand he engaged in paraphrase with the aim of producing an intelligible Greek text. At the same time the translation could be quite literal, where the text was understood.[3] It can be seen that the use of the Greek text of Job for 'correcting' the Hebrew one would be a hazardous undertaking. Before we engage in corrections to the Hebrew text we need to make a new effort to understand it.

---

[1] Cf. J. Ziegler (ed.), *Job* (*Septuaginta: Vetus Testamentum Graecum* XI/4; Göttingen, 1982); F. A. Gasquet, et al. (eds.), *Biblia Sacra iuxta Latinam Vulgatam Versionem*, vol. 9, *Libri Hester et Iob* (Rome, 1951); L. G. Rignell (ed.), *The Old Testament in Syriac according to the Peshitta Version*, II/1a, *Job* (Leiden, 1982); D. M. Stec, *The Text of the Targum of Job: An Introduction and Critical Edition* (AGJU 20; Leiden, 1994); J. P. M. van der Ploeg and A. S. van der Woude (eds.), *Le targum de Job de la Grotte XI de Qumrân* (Leiden, 1971). See also D. N. Freedman, A. B. Beck and J. A. Sanders (eds.), *The Leningrad Codex: The Facsimile Edition* (Grand Rapids, 1998).

[2] Cf. N. Fernández Marcos, "The Septuagint reading of the book of Job," in W. A. M. Beuken (ed.), *The Book of Job* (BETL 114; Leuven, 1994), 251–266, esp. 251–252.

[3] Fernández Marcos, "Septuagint reading," 254 and *passim*.

The twentieth century has in fact provided us with new tools with which to tackle the apparently refractory text of Hebrew Job. Lexicography has benefited from the finds at Ras Shamra-Ugarit and elsewhere.[4] There has also been progress in our understanding of Classical Hebrew grammar and of the characteristics of Hebrew poetry due at least in part to researches into the literature of the ancient Near East.[5] Research has been accompanied by much discussion and we are still in the early stages of our endeavour to achieve a complete analysis of Classical Hebrew poetry.[6] In what follows we will consider some passages in Hebrew Job in the light of their literary characteristics.

Job 14:3
אף־על־זה פקחת עינך   ואתי תביא במשפט עמך

And do you open your eyes upon such a one,
and bring *me* into judgment with you?

There is here an abrupt change of person from the first to the second stich, with "such a one" being paralleled by "me". G, V and S all reject this change and read instead the third person. Yet the technique of the abrupt change of person is common in Northwest Semitic literature and is often used as a means of drawing the audience's attention to something that should affect them personally.[7]

[4] Consult *HAL* and *DCH*.

[5] See the investigations of Y. Avishur, *Stylistic Studies of Word-Pairs in Biblical and Ancient Semitic Literatures* (AOAT 210; Kevelaer, 1984); J. L. Kugel, *The Idea of Biblical Poetry: Parallelism and Its History* (New Haven, 1981); W. L. Michel, *Job in the Light of Northwest Semitic*, vol. 1 (BibOr 42; Rome, 1987); M. O'Connor, *Hebrew Verse Structure* (Winona Lake, Ind., 1980); W. G. E. Watson, *Classical Hebrew Poetry: A Guide to Its Techniques* (JSOTSup 26; Sheffield, 1986). Consult also the pioneer labour of M. Dahood, especially *Psalms* I–III (AB 16–17A; Garden City, 1966–1970). Volume III includes the "Grammar of the Psalter," pp. 361–456, prepared together with T. Penar. Several of Dahood's students published dissertations on Old Testament poetic books. See particularly A. C. M. Blommerde, *Northwest Semitic Grammar and Job* (BibOr 22; Rome, 1969); A. R. Ceresko, *Job 29–31 in the Light of Northwest Semitic* (BibOr 36; Rome, 1980); E. Zurro, *Procedimientos iterativos en la poesía ugarítica y hebrea* (BibOr 43; Rome, 1987).

[6] For discussion of the method of M. Dahood, see J. Barr, "Philology and Exegesis: Some General Remarks, with Illustrations from Job 3," in C. Brekelmans (ed.), *Questions disputées d'Ancien Testament: Méthode et théologie* (BETL 33; Leuven, 1974), 39–61, and the bibliography in E. R. Martinez, *Hebrew-Ugaritic Index II with an Eblaite Index to the writings of Mitchell J. Dahood* (*SubBi* 4; Rome, 1981), 137–139. Consult also R. Althann, *Studies in Northwest Semitic* (BibOr 45; Rome, 1997).

[7] Cf. S. Gevirtz, "On Canaanite Rhetoric: The Evidence of the Amarna Letters from Tyre," *Or* 42 (1973), 162–177.

Job 23:2
גם־היום מרי שׂחי ידי כבדה על־אנחתי

Today also my complaint is defiant,
My hand is heavy upon my groaning.

G and S change the suffix of ידי to the third person, understanding a reference to the Almighty. Nevertheless, the first person suffix would fit the context if Job were trying to suppress his groaning.[8] In that case we would have an instance of metonymy, with "groaning" representing "groaning mouth".

Job 3:20
למה יתן לעמל אור וחיים למרי נפשׁ

Why does *he* give light to the tormented
And life to the bitter of soul?

There is no real textual problem here, but the verb does raise a question. יתן in fact seems to lack a subject. The reference is clearly to the Almighty and some translations offer a passive, "Why is light given to the tormented?", following the example of G and V.[9] The subject does in fact emerge, though only in v. 23, and is, as we expected, God. There is here then an example of the literary device known as 'delayed identification' or 'delayed explicitation'. The identity of the subject is deliberately delayed to heighten suspense and compel attention.[10]

Job 34:6b
אנושׁ חצי בלי־פשׁע

My *wound* is incurable, though I am without transgression.

The ancient versions support the חצי, literally, "my arrow", of M, yet commentators have often found it awkward here. M. Pope translates, "Wounded with his darts", reading חִצָּיו and parsing the suffix as third person.[11] Others emend the text to מַחֲצִי, "my wound".[12] On

[8] Consult E. Dhorme, *A Commentary on the Book of Job* (Nashville, 1984), 343–344.

[9] See S. R. Driver and G. B. Gray, *A Critical and Exegetical Commentary on the Book of Job* (ICC; Edinburgh, 1921), 2:21.

[10] On this literary technique, see Watson, *Poetry*, 336.

[11] M. Pope, *Job: Introduction, Translation, and Notes* (AB 15; Garden City, 1973), 256. See too N. Habel, *The Book of Job: A Commentary* (Philadelphia, 1985), 475.

[12] For instance G. Fohrer, *Das Buch Hiob* (KAT 16; Gütersloh, 1963), 464.

the other hand Driver and Gray render, "my arrow(-wound)", referring to 6:4 "the arrows of the Almighty are present in me".[13] This is surely correct for here again we see metonymy.

Another literary practice not always easy to identify is ellipsis or the omission of a word or phrase that must then be restored by the hearer (or reader). There are many different approaches to this subject, some semantic, others syntactic. Cynthia Miller has studied this phenomenon in Ugaritic literature and her findings may be considered relevant to other Northwest Semitic literature. She gives the following description of her approach to syntactic ellipsis,

> Ellipsis involves constructions in which a speaker (or writer) omits one or more elements from a clause, thus creating a structural hole or gap. The hearer (or reader) must restore the missing components in order to comprehend the sentence.[14]

The question is then how to recognize what has been omitted.

Miller draws attention to four features of ellipsis,

> First, the second line is structurally incomplete as a verbal sentence; the operation of ellipsis has produced a structural hole in the line. Second, the constituent structures of the two lines otherwise correspond exactly – subject, verb, prepositional phrase – and the constituents are in the same order in both lines. Third, the two verbs involved in ellipsis need not have the same number or gender. Finally, ellipsis occurs out of the second line.[15]

The salient feature of ellipsis is a structural hole in the surface syntax. Ellipsis operates across coordinate structures, that is, two conjuncts which together former a larger structure. Constituents may be deleted, that is, ellipsis is possible, only when they are lexically identical in both conjuncts. Ellipsis operates across coordinate structures in which the conjuncts have constituent strings that correspond in linear order. Miller considers that the syntactic arrangement of the two conjuncts is critical to ellipsis. Further, ellipsis usually takes place at the periphery of the clause.[16]

---

[13] Driver and Gray, *Job*, 1:295.

[14] Cynthia L. Miller, "Patterns of Verbal Ellipsis in Ugaritic Poetry," *UF* 31 (1999), 333–372, esp. 333.

[15] Miller, "Patterns," 337.

[16] Miller, "Patterns," 342–343.

For certain types of ellipsis M. O'Connor employs the term, 'gapping'. He explains, "Gapping we shall limit to ellipses which obscure the structure of one of the clauses involved, creating a structure which can only be analyzed in comparison with another".[17]

The following possible instances of ellipsis are taken from the Elihu speeches.

Job 34:30
מִמְּלֹךְ אדם חנף ממקשׁי עם

Lest the godless rule,
Or those who ensnare the people.

G omits the verse, while Theodotion translates, βασιλεύων ἄνθρωπον ὑποκριτὴν ἀπὸ δυσκολίας λαοῦ, "causing a hypocrite to be king, because of the waywardness of the people", apparently vocalizing מַמְלִךְ. V renders, *qui regnare facit hominem hypocritam propter peccata populi*, understanding the verse the same way. It is not our intention to comment on the different vocalization of the consonantal ממלך, but rather to try and explain M. The verse is frequently the subject of emendation. Habel comments that "This verse seems to be corrupt and missing at least one verb".[18] There is also the question of how it is linked to its context.[19] Dhorme omits חנף on the grounds that it overloads the text.[20] The problem then is in part stichometric, whether there are two stichs in the verse or only one. *BHS* in fact reads only one stich. If, however, the verse is allowed two stichs, the distribution of words is 3+2 and the syllable count 7+5, a normal pattern. The content of the second stich parallels אדם חנף, while a verb is found only in the first stich, yielding an example of incomplete parallelism, often described as the ballast variant. If in parallelism a component of the first stich is missing from the second, then at least one of the components in the second stich must be longer.[21] Here the five syllables of ממקשׁי עם balance the four syllables of אדם חנף of the first stich. The verse taken by itself then conforms to the canons of Classical Hebrew poetry.

---

[17] O'Connor, *Hebrew Verse Structure*, 126.

[18] Habel, *Job*, 476.

[19] The verse is omitted by Fohrer (*Hiob*, 465) on the grounds that it is an explanatory gloss to vv. 24–26. Driver and Gray (*Job*, 1:300, 2:262–263) also omit the verse in their translation and comment that the Hebrew text is dubious.

[20] Dhorme, *Job*, 524.

[21] See Watson, *Poetry*, 343.

There remains the question of whether v. 30 illustrates the phenomenon of ellipsis. The parallelism suggests that the verb of the first stich also qualifies the second. At the same time ממקשי עם can be taken as simply in apposition to אדם חנף in which case no grammatical ellipsis need be supposed.

Job 36:17
ודין־רשע מלאת דין ומשפט יתמכו

And of judgment on the wicked you are full,
Judgment and justice take hold of you.

Opinions on this verse diverge greatly and already the ancient versions do not adhere to the traditional Hebrew text. The translation above is based on that of Driver and Gray who find a difficulty in the omission of the suffix on the verb in the second stich.[22] The pronominal object is, however, frequently omitted if clarity is not affected, and this seems to be the case here.[23] It is not necessary to posit ellipsis since the omission of the suffix here conforms to Classical Hebrew usage.

Job 36:19
היערך שועך לא בצר וכל מאמצי־כח

Will your riches be equal to it without affliction,
Or all your exertions of strength?

The meaning of the noun שוע is uncertain and the ancient versions do not offer much help. It may be 'riches' in view of שוע "opulent" in 34:19,[24] or also possible is 'cry for help'.[25] The presence of כח in the second stich seems to favour 'riches' (or 'power') which also yields good parallelism, albeit incomplete. וכל מאמצי־כח balances שועך and illustrates the ballast variant. There is no parallel to the other words of the first stich, and so the eight syllables of the second correspond to the three syllables of שועך. The word pattern of the verse is 4+3

[22] Driver and Gray, *Job*, 1:312, 2:278.

[23] Cf. P. Joüon, *Grammaire de l'hébreu biblique* (Rome, 1923) §146i.

[24] See the discussion in Driver and Gray, *Job*, 2:279; F. Zorell, *Lexicon Hebraicum et Aramaicum Veteris Testamenti* (Rome, 1968), 829b. The sense may also be 'powerful', cf. M. Dietrich and O. Loretz, "Ugaritisch *ṯʿ/ṯʿy* und hebräisch *šwʿ*," *UF* 19 (1987), 33–36.

[25] Cf. BDB, 1002b; *HAL*, 1340b. Some emendation is then practised, see Dhorme, *Job*, 548.

and the syllable count 10+8. Ellipsis would seem to be present. וכל מאמצי־כח is not in apposition to שׁוּעֲךָ yet shares the other words of the first stich, as also the suffix of שׁוּעֲךָ.

These brief comments show how research into the characteristics of Classical Hebrew poetry may shed light on biblical texts. The endeavour to arrive at a fuller understanding of the words of Scripture is well illustrated in the work of Adrian Schenker who has so often led the way in text-critical, exegetical and theological research. To him this essay is respectfully dedicated.

SEPTUAGINT AND PESHITTA IN THE APPARATUS TO CANTICLES IN *BIBLIA HEBRAICA QUINTA*

Piet B. Dirksen

As is the case for most of the Old Testament, the textual critic of Song of Songs is almost totally dependent on the ancient versions. Hebrew sources offer no help. Only in one case does a Masoretic manuscript offer an interesting (though not convincing) alternative reading, viz., in 8:6, whereas the Qumran material is limited to two small fragments, which do little to help solve text-critical problems.

The readings of the versions are recorded in the critical apparatus of *BHQ* in so far as (in the judgment of the editor) they "arguably, but not necessarily" represent a Hebrew text differing from the lemma derived from M^L. Inclusion of a reading in the apparatus, therefore, only indicates that it is worth considering, in light of the little textual material we have. Actually, the editor will most likely include a number of cases, possibly most of them, while not believing for a single moment that the alternative reading is any challenge to M. In recording these readings he abstains from standing in between the text and the user.

Thus the user of the edition is called upon to evaluate the readings of the apparatus. In the present article this is done by the *BHQ* editor himself, though not in that capacity but rather as an interested user, that is, so to say, from the other side. This is partly to satisfy his own curiosity and partly to present his considerations to other users of this text. Only the readings of the two major witnesses that cover the whole of Canticles, G and S, will be dealt with.

Cases which involve only the vocalization are, strictly speaking, not of text-critical interest since the Masoretic vocalization is an interpretation of the consonantal text. Venerable though it may be, it is subject to challenge on the basis of another interpretation of that text, certainly when that interpretation is as old as G or S.

First, those readings of G will be considered in which it deviates from M without support from S, then those of S in which it deviates from M without support from G, thirdly those readings in which G and S agree against M, and finally those cases in which both versions differ from the Hebrew in a different way.

The way in which lemma and alternative readings are presented below is not determined by consistency but by readability. The readings of the other versions have only incidentally been mentioned. The apparatus commentary for Canticles in *BHQ* may give some additional information. The signs > and < stand for "is translated/read as" and "is derived from" respectively.

1. G Differs From M + S

Variations in Vocalization

1:2, 4 (cf. G + S at 4:10): דֹּדֶיךָ, "your love" > דַּדַּיִךְ "your breasts" (+ V): Almost universally the vocalization of M is followed. One of the few exceptions is E. A. Livingstone, who holds that original "breasts" was changed to "love" for anti-anthropomorphic motives.[1]

5:13 (S missing) מִגְדְּלוֹת "towers (of perfumes)" > φύουσαι = מְגַדְּלוֹת "bringing forth (perfumes)", which relates to כערונת read as a plural: This reading, also found in V and T, is accepted by many, e.g., Horst in the apparatus of *BHS*, Würthwein,[2] NRSV ("yielding fragrance"). *CTAT* gives two reservations:[3] (1) (following Ehrlich): beds of spices bring forth the ingredients, not the final product, the perfumes. The question, however, is whether such a sharp distinction between the plant and the product is justified; compare בֹּשֶׂם, which means both balsam tree and balsam as spice. Unfortunately מֶרְקָחִים occurs only here. (2) The parallelism with v. 13b suggests that in v. 13a the second clause refers to "his cheeks" and not to "beds". It is, however, noteworthy that in vv. 13b, 14a, b, the second clause begins with a participle. In favour of M *CTAT* quotes Gerleman, who thinks of the "Salbkegel", known from Egypt.[4] Following this lead, Keel translates "Wie Türme von Salben".[5] Yet, the "towers" of M remain

[1] E. A. Livingstone, "'Love' or 'Breasts' at Song of Songs i 2 and 4? The Pre-Masoretic Evidence," *Studia Patristica* 30 (1997), 8–11.

[2] E. Würthwein, "Ruth, Das Hohelied, Esther," in *Die fünf Megilloth* (HAT 18; Tübingen, 1969), ad loc.

[3] D. Barthélemy, *Critique textuelle de l'Ancien Testament*, vol. 5 (OBO 50/5; Fribourg & Göttingen, forthcoming), ad loc. (cited from a copy of handwritten notes kindly provided by the author). (*CTAT* 5)

[4] Ibid.; G. Gerleman, *Ruth/Das Hohelied* (BKAT 18; Neukirchen-Vluyn, 1965), ad loc.

[5] O. Keel, *Das Hohelied* (ZBK 18; Zürich, 1986), ad loc.

doubtful, whereas the rendering of G makes good sense, and with the participle (see above) is consistent with vv. 13b, 14.

7:9 בְּתָמָר > בַּתָּמָר, "in the palm tree" (S indet): This is indeed the likely vocalization, certainly after v. 8, and is accepted generally in commentaries and translations.

8:2 מִיַּיִן הָרֶקַח, "from wine, (i.e.) spice" > מִיֵּין הָרֶקַח, "from wine of spices": Whether the second word is understood as in apposition, or as in the construct state, the meaning is 'spiced wine'. According to Gesenius-Kautzsch, the second word is "*sicherlich*" meant to be in construct state.[6] This may seem the most probable alternative, but in view of the different use of the apposition in Hebrew, we cannot be sure.

8:5 יְלָדַתְךָ > יֹלַדְתֶּךָ (+ σ', V; S indet): With the alternative vocalization the last clause is a repetition of the previous clause, although it is accepted among others by Horst in the apparatus of *BHS*, Gerleman,[7] REB, NRSV. The Masoretic vocalization gives a continuation (". . . there your mother conceived you, there she conceived, bore you", cp. 5:6) and seems preferable.

Addition

In the following cases the obvious explanation for an addition is assimilation, or amplification: 1:3 "more than any spice" (< 4:10); 1:4 "to the scent of your myrrh" (< 1:3); 2:10, 13 "my dove" (cf. 2:14; 5:2; 6:9); 3:1 "I called him but he did not answer me" (< 5:6); 5:2 "on the door" (cf. Judg 19:22); 5:8; 8:4 "by the powers and by the forces of the field" (< 2:7; 3:5); 6:6 "your lips are like a crimson thread and your mouth is lovely" (< 4:3); 6:11 "There I will give you my breasts" (< 7:13); 8:5c "(who conceived) you" (< v. 5b).

Although the possibility is not *a priori* to be excluded that in the *Vorlage* of G the alternative reading formed part of the Hebrew text, the number of cases makes this improbable. In one case, however, it can be argued that the plus goes back to the Hebrew *Vorlage*: in 2:9 G has the addition ἐπὶ τὰ ὄρη Βαιθηλ, which translates "on the Beter-mountains" of 2:17. In that verse, however, G has ἐπὶ ὄρη κοιλωμάτων, which according to Gerleman indicates ("offenbar") that in

[6] W. Gesenius and E. Kautzsch, *Hebräische Grammatik* (Leipzig, 1896), §131, n. 1.
[7] Gerleman, *Ruth/Das Hohelied*, ad loc.

this case G did not take the plus from 2:17, but translated a Hebrew *Vorlage*.[8] That may have been the case, but we can go no further than that. In the other cases the Greek of the addition is identical to that of the source. For 1:10 see below under "Stylistic Adaptation".

Omission

2:10 וּלְכִי־לָךְ: These two words may have been omitted as superfluous after the (mis)reading of לָךְ as לְכִי at the beginning of the line although this omission does not occur in v. 13.

2:15 שׁוּעָלִים[2] (+ 4QCant[b], V[Mss]): This is an obvious case of haplography.

3:11 בְּנוֹת צִיּוֹן : An omission in G is more likely than a (later) addition in M. Garbini omits these two words.[9]

4:1 "from the mountain Gilead" > "from Gilead": The omission can be explained as an assimilation to 6:5. For the reverse see below under S at 6:5.

5:6 חָמַק : The verb occurs only once more, in Jer 31:22, as a *hitpael*. G has παρέρχομαι, which is a normal translation of עָבַר, so that חָמַק is the missing word. One might be excused for suspecting עָבַר to be an explanatory gloss to חָמַק,[10] but the reverse is out of the question. Probably an enforcement is intended: "he turned away, disappeared" (cp. 8:5).

Stylistic Adaptation

1:10 The exclamation is preceded by τί, "what!", which translates מָה in 4:10; 7:7. It does not fit in well with the comparison in this verse.

4:1, 2; 6:5, 6 כְּעֵדֶר, "as a flock of goats" / "ewes" > "as flocks . . ." (4:1, 2 + V; 6:5 + V[mss]; 6:6 + α', σ', V[mss]): 4QCant[a,b] (apart from S) are strong support for M's singular form.

[8] Ibid.

[9] G. Garbini, *Cantico dei Cantici: Testo, traduzione, note e commento* (Brescia, 1992), 150.

[10] A. Piras, "At ille declinaverat atque transierat (Cant 5,2–8)," *ZAW* 106 (1994), 489, n. 15.

7:5 שַׁעַר, "gate" > "gates": The eyes of the girl are compared with pools beside the gate of the "crowded city" (?) of Heshbon. G's plural form might have been prompted by the plural "pools", but M's singular is a more natural indication of the location of the pools.

Misreading / Misinterpretation

1:4 מָשְׁכֵנִי, "draw me" > "they drew you": The Masoretic accentuation wants us to read: "Draw me; after you we will run", which is hardly meaningful. G's reading is an attempt to redress this. The verb could easily be read as a defective plural perfect; more substantial was the change in suffix. Generally, however, the accentuation is disregarded, and the following "after you" connected with the first word, "Draw me after you", which makes perfect sense.

1:10 "Your cheeks are beautiful with earrings (בַּתֹּרִים) . . . with strings of jewels (בַּחֲרוּזִים)" > "as earrings (כַּתֹּרִים) . . . as strings (כַּחֲרוּזִים) . . ." (+ V): In contrast to the Hebrew, this reading hardly makes sense.

2:10 לְךָ > ἐλθέ, which presupposes לְכִי: The last two words of the line leave no doubt about the Hebrew as a *dativus ethicus*, cp. 2:13. G's rendering may have been prompted by the preceding imperative.

2:13 לכי: G's misunderstanding in 2:10 seems here to be shared by M itself. The Kethib, "go", is accepted by G in keeping with 2:10. There can, however, be no doubt that the Qere is correct as a *dativus ethicus*. The Qere is supported by 4QCant[b] and presupposed by S (also V and T).

4:6, 14 הַלְּבוֹנָה > הַלְּבָנוֹן (+ α' in v. 6; + V in v. 14): This is an easily made scribal error, perhaps the more so after "mountain" / "hill" (v. 6) and "trees" (v. 14).

4:8 אֲמָנָה > πίστεως: This case has no text-critical relevance, but is interesting as one of the examples that a version has misunderstood a geographical or a proper name and translated it as a noun or – as here – on the basis of the root; cf., e.g. 6:4 (G + S).

4:10 שְׁמָנַיִךְ, "(the scent of) your oils" > שַׂלְמֹתַיִךְ (". . . of your garments"): This is a misreading, probably under the influence of v. 11.

5:11 כֶּתֶם פָּז > χρυσίον καὶ φαζ: G apparently has not understood the second Hebrew word, "fine gold", which stands in apposition to "gold".

7:11 תְּשׁוּקָתוֹ, "his desire" > ἡ ἐπιστροφὴ αὐτοῦ (+ V): V renders *conversio*, which seems to presuppose תְּשׁוּבָתוֹ. It is possible that this holds good also for G's rendering. Both this noun and the verb ἐπιστρέφω often render a form of the root שׁוּב. It is, however, hard to see how this reading mistake has happened.

8:1 כְּאָח > אָח (+ V): G's reading, which hardly differs in meaning from M, can be explained as haplography.

8:10 אָז > אֲנִי: This is probably a misreading, more easily made after אֲנִי in v. 10a.

Various Changes

Two deviations from the Hebrew are hard to explain. They offer no challenge to the Hebrew.

4:9 "you have stolen my heart" > "you have stolen our hearts" (twice).

8:5 מִן הַמִּדְבָּר > λελευκανθισμένη, "whitened": In 3:6 G offers a normal translation.

2. *S Differs From M + G*

Vocalization

1:4 הֱבִיאַנִי, "he took me" > הֲבִיאֵנִי, "take me" (+ σ'): Although the imperative itself makes sense (parallel to v. 4a), this change necessitates the emendation from "his chambers" into "your chambers" (see below under "*Misreading*"), which all but rules out this alternative reading. However, this combination of two emendations is accepted by, among others, Horst in the apparatus of *BHS*, Würthwein[11] and REB; for M compare 2:4.

5:16 וְכֻלּוֹ > וְכֵלָיו: For M compare 4:7.

7:6 וְדַלַּת > plural, "the tresses (of your head)" (+ V): This translation makes good sense, although it is probably based on the reading of the Hebrew as a plural, וְדַלֹּת. In Hebrew the singular is more likely, understood as denoting the (flowing) hair in its totality, although the word occurs only here (apart from Isa 38:12 as "thrum"). In a

[11] Würthwein, "Das Hohelied," ad loc.

translation the plural may indeed do justice to the poetical language, e.g., REB/NRSV: "flowing locks".

7:6 כָּאַרְגָּמָן, "like the purple(. A king . . .)" > כְּאַרְגְּמַן, "as the purple (of a king.") (+ α', σ', V): V. 6b is difficult. For a survey especially of Jewish exegesis see *CTAT*.[12] The problem is not solved by reading here a construct state instead of an absolute state.

7:7 אַהֲבָה > אֲהֻבָה ? (+ σ'^Ms^, V): It is not clear whether S (ܪܚܡܬܐ, "loved one") read a passive participle or interpreted "love" as "loved one", as *abstractum pro concreto*. There can be no doubt that the loved one is here referred to, but that may well be expressed by "love"; compare 2:7; 3:5; 8:4, where "love" refers to loved one(s), and see *CTAT*.[13] There is no reason for an emendation as proposed by Horst in the apparatus of *BHS* and Würthwein.[14]

8:13 לְקוֹלֵךְ > לְקוֹלְךָ: S has misread or misinterpreted the whole verse, with unclear syntax, "those who are dwelling in the gardens and listening to your [m. sg.] voice, let me hear [f. sg. impv.]".

Addition

5:1 The words "I have come to my garden" are repeated after "bride". The repetition itself would be possible (cf. 1:5, 16; 4:8; 7:1), but its mere possibility is no challenge to the combined strength of M and G (+ V).

6:5 "from Gilead" > "from the mountain of Gilead" (+ La, T): The addition can be explained as an assimilation to 4:1. For the reverse see under G at 4:1.

7:4 S adds "that graze among the lilies": This is an assimilation to 4:5.

Omission

4:14 כָּל־עֲצֵי, "all trees (of frankincense)" > . . . ܩܝܣܐ ܕ, "wood (of frankincense)": This comes down to the omission of "all".

[12] Barthélemy, *CTAT* 5, ad loc.
[13] Barthélemy, *CTAT* 5, ad loc.
[14] Würthwein, "Das Hohelied," ad loc.

No reason or cause can be given for the omission in 5:13 of מִגְדְּלוֹת מֶרְקָחִים and in 8:13 of חֲבֵרִים.

Transposition

1:4 "we will exult and rejoice": The two verbs often occur together in different order, S always following the order of M, except here. M has G on its side, but S is supported by 6QCant, although whether by accident or by some text-historical connection is unclear. We can go no further than saying that there were two traditions with respect to word order.

2:13 "my darling, my fair one": S stands alone in the transposition of these two words.

Misreading / Misinterpretation

1:12 עַד־שֶׁהַמֶּלֶךְ בִּמְסִבּוֹ, "While the king is around (, my nard gave its fragrance)" > ...ܥܡ ܡܠܟܐ ܒܡܣܒܗ: This is either a misreading (עִם הַמֶּלֶךְ) or a free rendering, though not far off the mark.

4:6 אֵלֶךְ לִי > ܙܠ, "go": The omission of לִי, which does not fit the imperative, indicates that S has misinterpreted the Hebrew (in combination with misreading it?).

4:11 ...כַּלָּה דְּבַשׁ > כֹּל הַדְּבַשׁ, "All honey and milk are under your tongue": "All" hardly makes sense here.

Stylistic Adaptation

2:1 "lilies of the valleys" > "...valley" (+ ε', T): It is probably just a matter of idiom. Payne Smith mentions that the same form as here in S also occurs in *Opuscula Nestoriana*.[15]

3:11 "and on the day of his joy" > "on the day...": Since "the day of his joy" is the same as "his wedding day", omission of the copula is an obvious stylistic adaptation, which is found also in modern translations.

4:13 נְרָדִים > ܢܪܕܘܣ (+ V): The singular seems more natural than the plural (cp. v. 14 and 1:12).

[15] R. Payne Smith, *Thesaurus Syriacus* (Oxford, 1879–1901), 4345; G. Hoffmann (ed.), *Opuscula Nestoriana* (1880).

4:16 "and eat its . . . fruits" > ". . . from the fruits of . . .": This is an obvious stylistic adaptation.

5:1 רֵעִים > רֵעַי (+ G[Mss], La) and דּוֹדִים > דּוֹדַי (+ La): דּוֹדִים can mean "beloved ones" (in Canticles elsewhere only singular, e.g., 5:2) and "love" (e.g., 4:10). Some translations opt for the first meaning in parallelism to רֵעִים, which creates a *parallelismus membrorum* between the two clauses, e.g., TOB ("compagnons . . . chéris") and BJ ("amis . . . mes bien-aimés"); most have the second meaning, e.g., REB ("till you are drunk with love") and NRSV ("and be drunk with love"). S has the first meaning and in a stylistic adaptation gives the two words a first person plural suffix over against strong support for the lemma without suffix. For the rest, the translation of the verse belongs to exegesis, not to text-criticism.

5:2; 6:9 "my dove, my perfect one" > "my dove, the perfect one" (= "my perfect dove"): The fact that the same difference occurs twice suggests that it is not a reading mistake. The difference in meaning is slight and seems to be stylistically motivated.

5:11 כֶּתֶם, "(his head is) gold" > כְּכֶתֶם, "like gold" (+ σ'[-Ms]): It could be a case of dittography, but more probably it is a stylistic adaptation, cf. v. 14 and 7:3 (also other witnesses), 5 (other witnesses). For the reverse see 8:10. There is some fluidity in the use of the preposition "like" in the versions, and in general it is difficult to credit these cases with any text-critical merit.

5:14 "his arms are golden rods": > ". . . like golden rods": See v. 11.

7:4 צְבִיָּה, "(twins of) a gazelle" > ". . . gazelles": This is a small stylistic adaptation which does not change the meaning.

8:9 לוּחַ, "(we will put up against her) a plank (of cedar)" > ". . . planks . . ." (+ σ', La, V): The plural makes good sense (cf. NIV, "we will enclose her with panels of cedars"), but so does the singular. This stylistic adaptation is no challenge to the lemma text.

8:10 "(my breasts are) like towers" > "towers" (+ G[Ms]): See 5:11.

Interpretation

5:8 "What will you tell him?" > "tell him": This seems to be a free translation to express the meaning of the Hebrew, cf. NRSV, "tell him"; REB, "I charge you . . . to tell him".

8:5 four times second m. sg. suffix > second f. sg. suffix ("awakened you" / "your mother conceived you" / "she bore you"): The consistency points to another interpretation: the girl is not speaking to her young man, but the other way round.

8:11 "he gave" > "I gave": The change is difficult to explain. The third person as referring to Solomon is obviously what is meant.

Various Cases

1:7 כְּעֹטְיָה: "(Why should I be) like one who is veiled": To give meaning to this text, a number of scholars assume that being veiled refers to being a prostitute (cf. Gen 38:14). Garbini indeed translates "una prostituta".[16] Murphy thinks of covering herself as a disguise.[17] Others, e.g., Gerleman[18] and NAB, emend to כְּטֹעִיָּה, "as a wandering woman", with an appeal to α', σ', S, V. This meaning fits the context well, and the emendation is tempting, but the question is whether the versional rendering is based on an alternative Hebrew text or is just a meaningful guess. The second possibility is plausible in view of the support lent to M by G and 6QCant.

5:5 "my hands dripped with myrrh" > "my hand dripped . . .": The change might have been prompted by misreading יָדַי as יָדִי (the hand which opened the door?).

5:13 הַבֹּשֶׂם > plural (+ V): The same change occurs in 6:2, where it is not recorded in the apparatus, since only *seyame* is involved and there is no support as in 5:13. This twofold occurrence suggests a conscious choice. The plural makes good sense, but so does the singular.

6:10 כַּנִּדְגָּלוֹת: The meaning of this word is not known, but there is no reason to doubt its genuineness. It occurs also in 5:10, and the root also in 2:4. S renders ܪܘܪܒܢܝܬܐ, "great ladies", "princesses", which was apparently derived from the root גדל.[19]

---

[16] Garbini, *Cantico dei Cantici*, 143.

[17] R. E. Murphy, *Song of Songs* (Hermeneia; Minneapolis, 1990), ad loc.

[18] Gerleman, *Ruth/Das Hohelied*, ad loc.

[19] See P. B. Dirksen, "Canticles," in A. Schenker, et al. (eds.), *General Introduction and Megilloth* (*Biblia Hebraica Quinta* 18; Stuttgart, 2004), 62* ad loc.

6:11 "(to look) at the blossoms of the valley" > ". . . at the blossom of the valleys" (+ ἄλλος): The reason or cause is not clear, but it has nothing to recommend itself over against the Hebrew.

7:7 בַּתַּעֲנוּגִים, "(loved one) in delights": The M reading hardly makes sense. Some exegetes maintain M, as Krinetski: "O Liebe in Wonnen".[20] Most emend the text by reading בַּת תַּעֲנוּגִים, "daughter of delights" (α', S), which then is in apposition to "love/loved one", cp. בְּנֵי תַּעֲנוּגָיִךְ, "children of your delight", Mic 1:16, and בֵּית תַּעֲנֻגֶיהָ, "her pleasant houses", Mic 2:9. Haplography would explain the Hebrew text. The only – unanswerable – question which remains is whether S and α' have seen a different Hebrew text or by good luck read the text of M by dittography as emended.

3. G and S Agree Against M

Vocalization

2:4 הֱבִיאַנִי > הֲבִיאֻנִי: This reading relates to the following case.

2:4 וְדִגְלוֹ > וְדַגְּלוּ: The imperative may have been prompted by that of the previous case ("take me") and/or by those of v. 5 ("strengthen me"; "refresh me"). The meaning of the Hebrew word is uncertain, but even then, there is nothing to recommend this interpretation.

4:8 אִתִּי, "with me" > אֵתִי "come" (twice; + V): The interpretation of this passage is uncertain, but this hardly affects this detail. Both readings make good sense, and one can understand that an unvocalized consonantal text would give rise to the two readings. Gerleman, opting for M, points to the chiasmus: adverbial phrase – "come" (תָּבוֹאִי) / "come down" (תָּשׁוּרִי) – adverbial phrase.[21] To this may be added that the two well established imperfect forms fit in better with two adverbial phrases ("with me . . .") than with two imperatives. The variant reading is preferred, for example, by Würthwein, Garbini, and NAB ("Come from Lebanon, my bride").[22] A translation as that of NIV, "come with me" (twice), seems to have it both ways.

---

[20] G. Krinetzki, *Kommentar zum Hohenlied: Bildsprache und Theologische Botschaft* (BBET 16; Frankfurt am Main, 1981), ad loc.

[21] Gerleman, *Ruth/Das Hohelied*, ad loc.

[22] Würthwein, "Das Hohelied," ad loc.; Garbini, *Cantico dei Cantici*, ad loc.

4:10 דֹּדַיִךְ, "your love" > דַּדַּיִךְ, "your breasts" (twice; + V): See above, G at 1:2. In contrast to the overwhelming majority REB translates here: "How beautiful are your breasts . . .".

5:1 בְּשָׂמִי > בְּשָׂמַי: Both readings make good sense, and we might be hesitant if we had an unvocalized text before us. For the plural see 4:10, 14; 8:14.

5:13 כַּעֲרוּגַת > כַּעֲרוּגֹת (+ α', σ', V): The plural has 6:2 on its side, and is preferred by most commentaries and, e.g., NRSV, REB. With the plural "cheeks," the plural "beds" is attractive.

7:13 דֹּדַי, "my love" > דַּדַּי, "my breasts": See 4:10.

8:2 רִמֹּנִי > רִמֹּנַי: The plural "my pomegranates" is preferred, for example, by NRSV and REB. Perhaps the suffix belongs to the whole collocation, "my pomegranate juice" (so Würthwein: ". . . von meinem Granatapfelsaft").[23]

8:9 טִירַת > טִירֹת (+ V, T): The singular "battlement" seems quite adequate.

Misreading / Misinterpretation

4:16 בְשָׂמָיו, "(that) its [the garden's] perfumes (may spread)" > בְּשָׂמַי: "My perfumes" expresses what is meant, though without M's poetical merit.

5:1 יַעְרִי, "my honeycomb": G has "my bread"; S has "my sweetness". This either means that S "translated" the metaphor, or, more likely, did not know the Hebrew word and made a meaningful guess on the basis of the context. Also σ' and V did not recognize the word.

5:10 מֵרְבָבָה, "(distinguished [?]) among ten thousand" > plural: The agreement (G, ε', V, S, T) is impressive, but the Hebrew (supported by the Hexaplaric witnesses) need not be doubted. Perhaps we have here a poetical adaptation.

6:4 "(You are beautiful as) Tirza (. . . comely as Jerusalem)": We know nothing about the beauty of Tirza, but its place here in parallelism to Jerusalem cannot be doubted. It is striking that all the

[23] Würthwein, "Das Hohelied," ad loc.

versions, G, α', σ', θ', ε', V, S, T, have misunderstood the word (cp. 7:1), and "translated" it on the basis of the verb רָצָה.

Various Cases

2:14 "in the clefts of the rock" > "... cleft ..." (+ σ'): This is probably a small change to get (supposedly) a smoother meaning, cf. 3:6 below, and G at 1:4 above.

2:17 סֹב > שׁוּב (+ V): M is confirmed by 4QCant[b]. The agreement between the three versions is noteworthy. However, with respect to ἀπόστρεψον of G we may have some doubt since the Greek verb in most cases translates the verb שׁוּב although it sometimes translates סָבַב. Since it is hard to see how the three (or perhaps the two) versions could have made the same improbable reading mistake (ס > שׁ), and since there is no reason to assume interdependence, we must assume that the three/two versions accidentally agree in the same interpretation of the Hebrew.

3:6 "like columns (of smoke)" > "... a column ..." (+ σ', V): This is probably an (understandable) stylistic adaptation, cf., e.g., NRSV: "like a column of smoke" and 2:14 above.

4:9 מִצַּוְּרֹנָיִךְ, "of your necklace" > מצואריך (+ α', σ', ε', V): The lemma, supported by 4QCant[b], is a *hapax legomenon* and is usually translated by "necklace", but how then is עֲנָק to be translated? NRSV, for example, has "with one jewel of your necklace". All versions suppose the almost identical and well-known word for "neck". This is followed by, for example, Würthwein ("mit einer Kette von deinem Hals"). The emendation seems at least plausible, on the basis of both meaning and support.[24]

4:12 גַּל > גַּן: The lemma, "heap of stones" or "wave" (in OT only plural), does not make sense, and the rendering "garden" of G, S, and V is followed in most commentaries and translations. Some scholars defend M (e.g., Lys, who translates גַּל with "source", and Gordis, who translates with "[a sealed] spring"), but this is hardly convincing.[25] Although it is difficult to see how a *nûn* could be misread

[24] Ibid.

[25] D. Lys, *Le plus beau chant de la création: Commentaire du Cantique des Cantiques* (Paris, 1968), ad loc.; R. Gordis, *The Song of Songs and Lamentations: A Study, Modern Translation and Commentary* (New York, 1974), ad loc.

as as a *lāmed*, a repetition of "a closed garden" seems very much in the line of the writer.[26]

6:6 הָרְחֵלִים > הַקְּצוּבוֹת: This is an assimilation to 4:2.

7:5 "Your eyes are the pools of Hesbon" > ". . . like the pools . . .": See S at 5:11.

7:10 שִׂפְתֵי יְשֵׁנִים, "the lips of sleeping people" (+ α', V): Some scholars, such as Gerleman, Keel, and Barthélemy, maintain M.[27] Doubts, however, remain. G and S agree in that they read the first word as שְׂפָתַי, "my lips", and the second word as the copula (instead of *yôd*) followed by "teeth" (G) or "my teeth" (S). There remains some doubt as to a possible poetical role of the "sleeping," but the support for the emendation is impressive, and the case for it is strengthened by its making good sense. Emendations vary in that some have "my lips and teeth" (e.g., Rudolph, Krinetzki) and others just "lips and teeth" (e.g., Würthwein).[28]

8:2 תְּלַמְּדֵנִי, "she/you teach(es) me": This expression is not clear. Gerleman thinks of an erotic connotation.[29] G and S replace it by "and to the chamber of her who bore me", for which see 3:4; this rendering is followed by NRSV. Some other commentators emend to תֵּלְדֵנִי, "who conceived me" (without relative pronoun, and imperfect with perfect meaning?). The addition of G and S gives good sense, but it is hard to think of a way in which M would have developed from this reading.

4. G and S Differ From M and From Each Other

1:3 שֶׁמֶן תּוּרַק: This is a *crux interpretum*.[30] G (as also α', ε', V, T) seems to render the participle מוּרָק, "poured out", "emptied", which is accepted by, among others, Würthwein,[31] and NIV ("Your name

[26] For repetition as a literary device see Gerleman, *Ruth/Das Hohelied*, 159.
[27] Gerleman, *Ruth/Das Hohelied*, ad loc.; Keel, *Das Hohelied*, ad loc.; Barthélemy, *CTAT* 5, ad loc.
[28] W. Rudolph, *Das Buch Ruth, Das Hohe Lied, Die Klagelieder* (KAT 17; Gütersloh, 1962), ad loc.; Krinetzki, *Kommentar zum Hohenlied*, ad loc.; Würthwein, "Das Hohelied," ad loc.
[29] Gerleman, *Ruth/Das Hohelied*, ad loc.
[30] See Dirksen, "Canticles," 64* ad loc.
[31] Würthwein, "Das Hohelied," ad loc.

is like perfume poured out"). It remains a tempting emendation, but its meaning still leaves some doubt. S, with "(ointment of) myrrh", might lend support to a *mêm* as the first letter, but its rendering may also be a pure guess.

1:4 "The king brought me into his chambers" > G has ". . . his chamber": The change from plural to singular is more easily made than the other way round, perhaps so much so that it is easier to assume a change from plural to singular than the reverse. Moreover, M is supported by 6QCant, α', σ', ε', and V. S also has a singular form but with the second person masculine suffix, which was prompted by the misinterpretation of the Hebrew verb (see above under "Vocalization"): "bring me into your chamber, O king".

2:14 הַמַּדְרֵגָה: The meaning of this word is unknown. G has τοῦ προτειχίσματος, "fortress wall", which elsewhere translates בִּנְיָן, חוֹמָה, or חֵל, and hardly makes sense here. S has ܕܣܝܓܐ, "(of) the fence/hedge". Salkind may be right that this is based on the root *gdr*.[32] The translation does, however, not give a likely alternative.

2:17; 4:6 וְנָסוּ, "(the shadows) have fled": Opinions differ as to whether this verse refers to the morning or to the evening. In the first case the "fleeing of the shadows" is clear; in the second case it must refer to the disappearing of the shadows when it gets darker. The translation of S (and V) is the same as for נָטָה in Jer 6:4; Pss 102:12; 109:23, where it refers to the lengthening of the evening shadows. It is difficult to say whether S and V were influenced by these verses or consciously made this choice on the basis of the second interpretation mentioned above. This is the only place where G has "move away" in connection with shadows.

4:1, 3; 6:7 לְצַמָּתֵךְ, "your veil" (for the meaning cf. Isa 47:2): This expression makes perfect sense. The word has, however, not been understood by G and S, which both seem to have derived it from the verb צָמַת, "to put to silence".[33]

4:1; 6:5 שֶׁגָּלְשׁוּ: This is a *hapax legomenon.*[34] The versions offer no solution.

---

[32] J. M. Salkind, *Die Peschitta zu Schir-Haschirim textkritisch und in ihrem Verhältnisse zu MT und LXX untersucht* (Leiden, 1905), 23.
[33] See also Dirksen, "Canticles," 60* ad loc.
[34] See Dirksen, "Canticles," 60* ad loc.

6:12 "Ammi-nadib": The meaning of this name – as the rest of v. 12a – has puzzled the ancient versions as well as later exegetes. The Hebrew is still a riddle for us, but the versions offer no solution. Instead they confirm the Hebrew text.

7:1 כִּמְחֹלַת הַמַּחֲנָיִם, "as the dance of Mahanaim": We know nothing about a special dance connected with Mahanaim, if indeed we have the geographical name here (cf. 6:4). Some follow the versions in translating as a noun, e.g., Murphy with "dance of the two camps".[35] The guesses of the versions presuppose M.

8:6 שַׁלְהֶבֶתְיָה: The form of the word is strange; to read it as two words ("a flame of Jahwe" > "a mighty flame", accepted by Rudolph and Snaith,[36] for example) offers no convincing alternative in spite of 2 Kgs 1:12; Job 1:16. Some scholars suppose a corrupt text here. Both G and S seem to translate the present text: G with "her flames", S with "and a flame".

8:13 הַיּוֹשֶׁבֶת, "you who dwell (in the gardens)": The girl is spoken to, as is confirmed by the feminine suffix in "your voice" and the form of the imperative. G and S both read a masculine form: G singular, S plural (cf. La[169] "*qui sedent*"). It is possible that these two forms have been prompted by v. 12b ("Solomon/the keepers"), but the Hebrew is unassailable.

Concluding Remarks

When we look at the critical apparatus of Song of Songs in *Biblia Hebraica Quinta* as far as G and S are concerned, what can we say in conclusion? First, it has to be said in general that in cases where only the vocalization is at stake, we have to choose between the honoured tradition of M and an early interpretation of the consonantal text. This choice depends not on the authority of the textual witness, but on exegesis. On that basis the alternative reading is the likely one in 5:13 and 7:9; M is probably correct in 8:5; 8:2 is uncertain. In the other cases the alternative offers no challenge to M.

---

[35] Murphy, *Song of Songs*, ad loc.

[36] Rudolph, *Das Hohe Lied*, ad loc.; J. G. Snaith, *Song of Songs* (Grand Rapids, 1993), ad loc.

Where the variant readings concern the consonantal text, our choice is nearly always a matter of probability on the basis of various considerations. If, for example, a versional deviation shows a certain pattern, as in Canticles the additions in G do, then they have less force than in incidental cases. We have to consider the strength of the witnesses; G has more authority than S, and S has to have a very strong case to stand up against M + G. A striking instance of a lonely stance of S in Canticles is 7:7 (though with support of α'). A versional rendering will seldom have text-critical relevance if it can be explained on the basis of M with respect either to form (e.g., haplography), or to meaning (e.g., as a smoothing out of the text, or a misunderstanding of it). Of course, there also is the important question whether the Hebrew text itself suggests any text-critical problem. Considerations will differ from case to case, and there is often room for a subjective assessment as is illustrated by the differences between the commentaries.

The Hebrew text of Canticles offers relatively few textual problems. There are some cases where its meaning is not clear to us, but these need not be text-critical in nature, e.g., 6:12. Where G and/or S deviate from M, the latter, with very few (possible) exceptions, holds out against these two versions. In some cases the reading of one or both of the versions is equal to M, but if M offers no problem, there is no reason to challenge it.

There are only a few cases where the versions seem to support a possible or likely alternative to M, viz. 1:3, 7; 4:9, 12; 7:7, 10.

Scholarly research may sometimes not lead to surprising results, but that does not render it unnecessary. Being engaged through a number of years in the preparation of the first volume of the "Quinta" to appear had the bonus of the many cordial contacts with the members of the editorial comittee and fellow editors. It is with pleasure that I dedicate this article to Professor Adrian Schenker, who decidedly yet amiably, coached this group.[37]

[37] I am indebted to Dr. Richard Weis, New Brighton, MN, for reading through a draft of this article and correcting the English at a number of points, and also suggesting some stylistic improvements.

THE GENUINE TEXT OF JUDGES

Natalio Fernández Marcos

The last decade has been a watershed for literary studies on the book of Judges from rhetorical, sociological, feminist or postmodern perspectives, while, on the other hand, text critical studies do not really abound. Several years of work on the text of Judges for the *Biblia Hebraica Quinta* (*BHQ*) lead me to a certain number of provisional conclusions on the text history and critical restoration of the book. I shall also allow myself a number of pertinent comments on the relationship between textual and literary criticism and the relevant approach of an eclectic, critical edition of Judges.

1. *The Witnesses*

As far as the *Hebrew* witnesses are concerned it can be said that the Masoretic Text (M) of Judges has been relatively well preserved except for Judges 5. The three major Tiberian codices – Leningrad (M^L), Aleppo (M^A) and Cairo (M^C) – have been collated anew. Thanks to the new photographs and transparencies, some graphic errors in M^L have been detected and corrected in text (4:11; 8:26) as well as in its Masorahs (3:27). The Masorah magna and parva have been incorporated into the edition, English translations provided, and the Hebrew *sîmanîm* identified. A new stichometry based on the Hebrew accents has been proposed for 5:20, 22, 24–25, 29–30 and 9:7–15. M has two significant haplographies in 16:13–14 and 19:30 (two and a half lines fallen out by *homoioteleuton*), already detected in *BHK*[3] and *BHS*. In both cases the genuine Hebrew text has been restored by conjecture from the Old Greek (G), a different text from the previous editions that were based on *Codex Vaticanus*, a witness of the καίγε-revision and not of G.

Besides the Tiberian manuscripts the Hebrew evidence of Qumran has been collated: 1QJudg, 4QJudg[a], 4QJudg[b] and 4Judg[c].[1] Some of

[1] D. Barthélemy and J. T. Milik (eds.), *Qumran Cave 1* (DJD I; Oxford, 1955),

the Qumran witnesses support M. On the other hand, 4QJudg[a], the most important fragment containing Judg 6:2–6, 11–13, is the only extant witness that does not include vv. 7–10. The editor, J. Trebolle, thinks that it preserves a different, pre-Deuteronomistic, shorter form of the book. However, I maintain that this omission was left out by accident or was abbreviated for other purposes.[2] It is not possible to state that this fragment represents a shorter or a different edition of Judges based solely on this variant, neither G or La give reason for a shorter text anywhere in the book.

Late material from the Cairo Genizah and from the medieval manuscripts collated by Kennicott and De Rossi have not been included regularly as witnesses since it has been shown that, with few exceptions, their variants do not go back before the Masoretic text.[3]

The main problem of the *Greek* text of Judges is the lack of a critical edition in the series of Göttingen. Moreover, Rahlfs' manual edition printed the texts of the *Codices Alexandrinus* and *Vaticanus* in the upper and lower part of the page respectively, giving the misleading impression that they go back to two different translations. It should be emphasized that G for Judges can be traced back to a single

62–64; E. Ulrich, et al. (eds.), *Qumran Cave 4, IX, Deuteronomy, Joshua, Judges, Kings* (DJD XIV; Oxford, 1995), 161–169, and M. Bernstein, et al. (eds.), *Wadi Daliyeh II and Qumran Cave 4, XXVIII* (DJD XXVIII; Oxford, 2001), 231–233. See also H. Eshel, "A Second Fragment of XJudges," *JJS* 53 (2002), 139–141; E. Puech, "Notes sur le manuscrit de Juges 4Q50[a]," *RQ* 82 (2003), 315–319, and E. Puech, "Les manuscrits 4QJudges[c] (= 4Q50[a]) et 1QJudges (= 1Q6)," in P. W. Flint, E. Tov, and J. C. VanderKam (eds.), *Studies in the Hebrew Bible, Qumran and the Septuagint: Essays presented to Eugene Ulrich on the occasion of his Sixty-Fifth Birthday* (Leiden, in press).

[2] N. Fernández Marcos, "The Hebrew and Greek Text of Judges," in A. Schenker (ed.), *The Earliest Text of the Hebrew Bible: The Relationship between the Masoretic Text and the Hebrew Base of the Septuagint Reconsidered* (SBLSCS 52; Leiden, 2003), 1–16. A. Rofé and Y. Amit think of it as a transmission failure at an early stage while R. Hess and R. O'Connell are inclined towards an intentional abbreviation; cf. A. Rofé, "Historico-Literary Aspects of the Qumran Biblical Scrolls," in L. H. Schiffman, E. Tov and J. C. Vanderkam (eds.), *The Dead Sea Scrolls Fifty Years After Their Discovery 1947–1997* (Jerusalem, 2000), 30–39, esp. 36, n. 29; Y. Amit, *The Book of Judges: The Art of Editing* (Leiden, 1999), 251; R. S. Hess, "The Dead Sea Scrolls and Higher Criticism of the Hebrew Bible: the Case of 4QJudg[a]," in Stanley E. Porter and Craig A. Evans (eds.), *The Scrolls and the Scriptures: Qumran Fifty Years After* (JSPSup 26; Sheffield, 1997), 122–128; R. H. O'Connell, *The Rhetoric of the Book of Judges* (VTSup 63; Leiden, 1996), 147, n. 178. D. I. Block defends the important rhetorical function of this paragraph within the whole book; cf. D. I. Block, *Judges, Ruth* (NAC; Nashville, 1999), 254.

[3] M. Goshen-Gottstein, "Hebrew Biblical Manuscripts: Their History and Their Place in the HUBP Edition," *Bib* 48 (1967), 243–290 and J. A. Sanders, "The Hebrew University Bible and *Biblia Hebraica Quinta*," *JBL* 118 (1999), 518–526, esp. 520.

translation. The studies of O. Pretzl, I. Soisalon-Soininen, B. Lindars, W. R. Bodine and J. Targarona have confirmed this assertion on the basis of the similarities, not only the disagreements, of the different texts.[4] The Greek tradition can be stratified in four groups of manuscripts using the sigla of Brooke-McLean's edition: the Antiochene recension (KZglnw + dptv); the καίγε-revision (Befijqrsuza$_2$); the Hexaplaric recension (AGabcxSyh) and a mixed group (MNyb$_2$). However, the restoration of G is extremely difficult since no group of manuscripts is free from horizontal, particularly Hexaplaric, contamination. On the other hand, I am convinced that the Greek text can only be used for text critical purposes when the stage nearest to G has been attained. Consequently, my edition of Judges for the *BHQ* is based on a critical, point by point restoration, verse by verse, of G following the criteria of textual criticism and the characteristics of every group. I am not sure that I have *achieved* the genuine restoration in each case, but there is agreement among scholars that the Antiochene text, particularly in its early stage, when it is supported by La, may preserve the closest text to G. Fortunately, we have at our disposal the current text of La in the *Codex Lugdunensis*. This is an important conclusion, since most of the general statements on the Greek text of Judges, including its literal interpretation, have been based on the text of *Codex Vaticanus*, which, as is well known nowadays, does not represent the Old Greek.

It is my intention to check these results, based on the edition of Brooke-McLean, against the collations of all the material in the Septuaginta-Unternehmen of Göttingen, especially the new evidence from the papyri.[5] But I think that, with a few exceptions, this consultation will not change the image of the text history outlined here.

[4] Full references in S. P. Brock, C. T. Fritsch and S. Jellicoe, *A Classified Bibliography of the Septuagint* (Leiden, 1973) and C. Dogniez, *Bibliography of the Septuagint 1970–1993* (VTSup 60; Leiden, 1995).

[5] Pap 968 on Judg 1:10–19 and the new fragments from Judges published by R. A. Kraft, "Some Newly Identified LXX/OG Fragments Among the Amherst Papyri at the Pierpont Morgan Library in New York City," in S. M. Paul, R. A. Kraft, L. H. Schiffman and W. W. Fields (eds.), *Emanuel: Studies in Hebrew Bible, Septuagint, and Dead Sea Scrolls in Honor of Emanuel Tov* (Leiden, 2003), 551–570. These fragments from the fifth century C.E. follow in general the text of group AGabcx. It seems that among the new folia of the *Sinaiticus* discovered in the Monastery of Saint Catherine, there is something of Judges, Cf. P.-M. Bogaert, "Septante," in *DBSup*, 588–589; Ἱερὰ Μονὴ καὶ Ἀρχιεπισκοπὴ Σινά, *Τὰ Νέα Εὑρήματα τοῦ Σινά* (Athens, 1998), 141.

With regard to the *Targum* (T) I would say with Goshen-Gottstein that it belongs rather to the history of exegesis than to the text history.[6] For Judges I rely on the standard edition to the Former Prophets (Yemenite tradition) by A. Sperber, the edition of E. Martínez Borobio for the fragments in Babylonian tradition and, especially W. Smelik's monograph.[7] T of Judges exhibits, in general, a literal translation of a text that is very close to M, with occasional glosses and midrashic expansions (cf. Judges 5, Deborah's song, and 11:39, Jephthah's daughter). The *Sitz im Leben* of the translation is a school setting, not a liturgical one, and Smelik places the date of the full version in the second century C.E. The text of this Targum was never fixed, so that parallel targumic traditions existed alongside each other. The agreements with S seem to be the result of contextual exegesis or similar translation techniques. Even when the Targum agrees with G, S and V, it should be considered that they may share common exegetical traditions. They are independent translations with indirect links with regard to each other. Special attention should be paid to the translation techniques of T of Judges concerning the names of God, the change of the Hebrew singular collective into plural, the actualization of geographical names, the clarification of obscure passages, the regular additions specifying action, the emphasis on divine trascendence and monotheism, and, occasionally, the midrashic additions.

For the *Peshitta* (S) I rely on the Leiden edition by P. B. Dirksen and his and others' studies on the transmission of the Syriac text. This edition based on ms 7a1, the *Codex Ambrosianus* in Milan, although not critical, can confidently be used for text critical purposes. According to Dirksen, the *Vorlage* of the Peshitta was closer to M than the *Vorlage* of G. But each textual case has to be discussed on its own merits within the framework of the evidence as a whole. The text critic has to be very cautious since the agreements with G, T and V may be due to the same translation technique or exegetical tradition (for example, the translation of metaphors), common Jewish exegesis, accidental agreement, guessing of the meaning through the

[6] M. H. Goshen-Gottstein, "The Textual Criticism of the Old Testament: Rise, Decline, Rebirth," *JBL* 102 (1983), 365–399, esp. 393, n. 93.

[7] A. Sperber, *The Bible in Aramaic*, vol. 2, *The Former Prophets According to Targum Jonathan* (Leiden, 1959); E. Martínez Borobio, *Targum Jonatán de los Profetas Primeros en tradición babilónica*, vol. 1, *Josué-Jueces* (Madrid, 1989), and W. F. Smelik, *The Targum of Judges* (Leiden, 1995).

context, implicit content which is made explicit, and assimilation to parallel passages. Only four variants may be of interest for the restoration of the Hebrew text of Judges (2:7; 14:4; 15:20 and 18:29). In my opinion, of the five cases of agreement between G and S that may indicate, according to Dirksen,[8] a Hebrew text underlying the two versions different from M, only one (13:12) may substantiate a different, preferred, *Vorlage*. Concerning the variants of other Syriac manuscripts Dirksen concludes that "only in a very small number of cases the difference between two readings is of interest to the textual critic".[9] In Dirksen's words, "the importance of the Peshitta seems to be that in some cases where it agrees with the LXX, it may suggest a Hebrew reading different from the one found in the Masoretic text. On the other hand, where it agrees with the Hebrew, it testifies to the early date of the present text".[10]

As it has been shown, the *Old Latin* (La) of Judges is an important witness to restore G and occasionally also the genuine Hebrew reading. Besides the current edition of the *Codex Lugdunensis* by U. Robert, I rely also on the edition of the Marginal Glosses by T. Ayuso Marazuela together with A. V. Billen's monograph.[11] The text of La regularly follows the Antiochene text in Judges. When both texts agree they represent normally G. Moreover, in several cases the genuine Greek reading has survived only through La. In a few cases the reading of La is to be preferred to the rest of the extant witnesses, including the Hebrew. However, La must be used with great caution, due to the inner-Latin corruptions and the variety of horizontal contaminations and influences experienced throughout its transmission.

Jerome's Latin translation known as the *Vulgate* (V) supplanted La in the West. His Hebrew *Vorlage* was closer to, but by no means identical, to M. He seems to have assumed that the current Hebrew text of his time was identical with that underlying the LXX. Between his theory and practice of translation Jerome shows conflicting views,

---

[8] P. B. Dirksen, *The Transmission of the Text of the Peshitta Manuscripts of the Book of Judges* (Leiden, 1972), 107–108.

[9] P. B. Dirksen, "The Ancient Peshitta MSS of Judges and their Variant Readings," in P. B. Dirksen and M. J. Mulder (eds.), *The Peshitta: Its Early Text and History* (Leiden, 1988), 127–146, esp. 146.

[10] Dirksen, *The Transmission of the Text*, 108.

[11] U. Robert, *Heptateuchi partis posterioris versio latina antiquissima e codice Lugdunensi* (Lyon, 1900), 105–155; T. Ayuso Marazuela, *La Vetus Latina Hispana. II El Octateuco* (TECC 6; Madrid, 1967), 279–305 and A. V. Billen, *The Old Latin Texts of the Octateuch* (Cambridge, 1927).

but the translation of Judges abounds in free renderings.[12] The versions of the Psalter and the Prophets were an early product, but apparently later – Joshua and Judges belong to the concluding parts – Jerome turned more and more toward the translation *sensus de sensu*, in spite of his statement in the Letter 57 (to Pammachium), that for the biblical texts it was preferable to translate *verbum e verbo*. In Judges the free renderings of idiomatic verbal constructions are very frequent. V freely deviates from Hebrew vocabulary and syntax; it shows a tendency to clarify obscure passages and to identify a more precise meaning from the context. Consequently, before assuming a different Hebrew *Vorlage* based on V, the characteristics of the translation must be considered. One should bear in mind that many variants, when they agree with G, may be directly dependent upon La. These circumstances are reflected in the great number of cases in the apparatus or commentary, where the Latin translation is defined or characterised as 'paraphrastic' or 'free translation'. For the text of V the critical edition of the Benedictines of S. Girolamo in Rome is at our disposal.[13]

2. *The History of the Text*

The Masoretic Text of Judges, for the most part, has been transmitted free of major corruptions. As will be shown in the apparatus commentary most of its readings should be preferred to the variants of the ancient versions or to the numerous conjectures suggested by previous editors or commentators. This does not mean, however, that the textual critic has little work to do in this book. Each variant has to be discussed and weighed in every case, and some readings of the versions should be preferred as genuine. There are at least two haplographies by homoioteleuton in M than can be restored on the basis of G (16:13–14 and 19:30). Notwithstanding, the retroversion proposed by *BHS* in 20:3 is not accepted for lack of a textual basis.

For the restoration of the genuine text the importance of G, especially when it is followed by La, should be emphasized. Moreover, in some cases as in 1:16 (*cum eo Amalec*) the original reading in all

[12] B. Kedar, "The Latin Translations," in M. J. Mulder (ed.), *Mikra* (Assen/Maastricht & Philadelphia, 1988), 299–339, esp. 322–323 and 326.

[13] F. A. Gasquet, et al. (eds.), *Biblia Sacra iuxta latinam vulgatam versionem*, vol. 4, *Libri Iosue Iudicum Ruth* (Rome, 1939), 215–360.

probability has been preserved only in La.[14] Sometimes, an addition or variant reading of G may be supported by a Hebrew *Vorlage* that is not attested. But even in the case that it were attested it does not follow that it should be preferred to M, since most of the additions of G seem to be secondary, facilitating glosses against the sober style of M (cf. 3:26; 4:6). Most of the G pluses in chs. 20–21 tell us more about the history of exegesis of these chapters than they do about the original Hebrew of the passages. However, in some cases the supposed *Vorlage* of G or other versions has been preferred and indicated in the apparatus.[15]

M of Judges as printed in *BHK*[3] and *BHS* can be improved in different aspects: the correction of some graphic errors in M[L] through the collation with the main Tiberian manuscripts; the inclusion of the Masorah parva and magna with the identification of the corresponding *sîmanîm*; a series of conjectures introduced in the apparatus of these Bibles have been eliminated for lack of textual support. Some of these conjectures are due to considerations of literary criticism rather than textual criticism (11:14; 13:6, 15; 14:5); others are exegetical or translation variants rather than textual (11:31). Hence the frequent advice in the apparatus commentary "retain M against *BHK*[3] and *BHS*".

The Hebrew text underlying G, T, S and V belongs to the Masoretic tradition. 1QJudg, 4QJudg[b] and 4QJudg[c] also support M. There could be doubts with regard to 4QJudg[a] with the striking omission of 6:7–10 and three small variants in connection with the Greek tradition. But scholars are divided on the interpretation of these variants. The editor thinks that 4QJudg[a] represents an older pre-Deuteronomistic stage of the text. Others maintain that it is an accidental transmission failure at an early stage favoured by its location between two *parašiyyôt* or an intentional abbreviation. I adhere to the second position: 4QJudg[a] is a manuscript that has not been carefully copied, with omissions and interlinear corrections. Moreover, I contend that there is not sufficient evidence for postulating a literarily different, shorter text of Judges based on 4QJudg[a] and a presumed shorter text of G and La. G of Judges cannot be qualified

[14] See also 2:7 and 5:31.

[15] See 3:28; 4:13, 20; 5:5, 13; 8:16; 12:7; 13:12, 21; 16:14; 18:24; 19:11, 30 and 20:45. Interestingly, in 9:46 G and La preserved the reading "Baal", corrected to "El" in M for theological purposes.

as a shorter, but rather a slightly expanded, secondary text in general.

This is where we are faced with the main problem of restoring an eclectic and critical edition in Judges: the absence of evidence and current witnesses supporting a non-Masoretic Hebrew text. T and S follow closely M as does V. The Latin translation of Judges is free and paraphrastic; it therefore seems to deviate in a lot of cases from M. However, a close scrutiny reveals that these deviations must be interpreted as stylistic renderings of M due to an idiomatic translation technique instead of the literal interpretation of La. Jerome with a more intelligible and classical Latin improves stylistically the vulgar Latin of La. Consequently, most of the V deviations in the book of Judges are characterised in the apparatus as 'paraphrastic', 'free translation'.

In other words, in contrast with the procedure adopted by most of the commentaries of the nineteenth and twentieth centuries, it has become evident that the use of the other witnesses to correct M is rarely justified, since it is precisely M which has preserved the great majority of the preferred readings. G is the main source of variant readings. In some cases the preferred reading has been restored when it is supported by G and/or La and/or other ancient versions. This preferred reading is recorded in the apparatus and can be accepted or rejected by the reader, since the retroversion is still a risky task. We need only to remember that there are twenty-two Greek equivalents in G for the Hebrew מָעוֹז (Judges 6:26), while ὑπόστασις ζωῆς is a *hapax legomenon* for מִחְיָה in 6:4, and δικαστήριον (+ τοῦ Βάαλ) is also a *hapax* as a translation of the proper name יְרֻבַּעַל in 6:32.

Besides, if these retroverted variants were introduced into the edited text, the result would be a compound text that confused evidence from Hebrew manuscripts with data from heterogeneous sources such as retroversion from the versions and other origins. It also has become apparent that the majority of the Greek variants, within their own context, are due to features of translation: slight additions to smooth the text, harmonizations with parallel passages, doublets, glosses, exegetical facilitations before obscure passages or stylistic improvements.[16] In most of the cases the readings of G do not rely on a different *Vorlage* but they concentrate on difficult words and obscure passages and can be explained by M. Consequently, all the witnesses

[16] A better Greek compared with the hebraisms of *Codex Vaticanus*.

of Judges go back to a Hebrew *Vorlage* that is slightly different from, but typologically similar to, M. The original Greek translation was very literal with regard to grammar and syntax, but not as literal as it would appear through the lenses of the καίγε-revision present in *Codex Vaticanus*. In contrast to this literal aspect in syntax, the Greek vocabulary of Judges is very rich. There is not sufficient evidence to restore a genetic stemma different from M. At present the procedure adopted by the *BHQ* project seems to me not only the most feasible, but also the most acceptable, if we do not want to mix M with fragmentary glimpses of heterogeneous sources. However, the text critical restoration of the genuine or uncorrupted text is still theoretically the unrenounceable goal of textual criticism. Moreover, as limited as the task of the text critic in the book of Judges may appear, there is a wide scope for application of text critical criteria to the individual variants of different procedence, in order to trace the history of the text, its transmission and interpretation. This critic may also keep an eye open on the literary growth of the book in order to ascertain whether this development can shed light on some aspects of textual criticism.

3. An Eclectic Edition of Judges?

Like many other scholars who specialise in textual criticism I wonder if there is still any reason to edit a single manuscript, in this case the Leningrad Codex, when critical editions have been the norm since the ninteenth century in the realm of Classical studies and modern philology; and in the field of Biblical studies in the Greek Old Testament, in the New Testament and even in Patristics. Is the Hebrew Bible so different as to justify the exception in the transmission and restoration of ancient texts? Criticism in the Italian school represented principally by such well-known scholars as G. Garbini, P. Sacchi, B. Chiesa, A. Catastini and G. Borbone give us enough food for thought.[17] As a critical editor of Greek texts brought up in the discipline of Classical philology, I have asked myself the same

[17] For the main bibliography see P. G. Borbone, "Orientamenti attuali dell'ecdotica della Bibbia ebraica: Due progetti di edizione dell'Antico Testamento ebraico," *Materia Giudaica* 6 (2001), 28–35 and G. Regalzi, "L'edizione critica della Bibbia ebraica: Giona come esempio," in G. Regalzi (ed.), *Le discipline orientalistiche come scienze storiche* (Studi Semitici 18; Roma, 2003), 99–106.

question while preparing the edition of Judges – an unavoidable question for anyone involved in the present state of biblical textual criticism. The challenge of an eclectic edition of the Hebrew Bible has been taken up in the Oxford Hebrew Bible (*OHB*), a project of R. S. Hendel.[18] Consequently, I have asked myself what the difference would be between the edition of Judges according to the criteria of the *BHQ* and the projected edition of the *OHB*. Wisely, the *OHB* does not renounce the printing of the Leningrad Codex in parallel columns against the closest text to the original restored in its consonantal form.[19] There would be, no doubt, some differences in the consonantal text: the omission by haplography in chapters 16 and 19 of the Leningrad Codex should be restored, as well as ten to fifteen preferred readings against M, according to text critical criteria as would be reflected in the apparatus of the *BHQ*. The omission of 6:7–10 in 4QJudg[a] does not belong to an original stage of the book but it constitutes an accidental or intentional abbreviation. The numerous variants of G and La in the last chapters of Judges, in my opinion, are also of secondary character; they belong rather to the history of exegesis, not to the book's text history.[20] Why is it that in our attempt to put together a true critical edition, we get so little help from the witnesses of Judges?

Here lies the central point of the Hebrew text transmission. It is true, as Sacchi emphasizes, that with the edition of the Leningrad Codex we give priority to a text of a medieval manuscript.[21] But interestingly enough, not only have the Qumran discoveries attested a plurality of texts in some biblical books, they also have reinforced the value of M in others. As far as the text of the medieval Tiberian manuscripts is concerned, in some books it has been confirmed as basically current already in the Second Temple period.[22] Therefore

[18] R. S. Hendel, *The Text of Genesis 1–11: Textual Studies and Critical Edition* (Oxford, 1998).

[19] Borbone, "Orientamenti attuali," 34.

[20] Some scholars like J. Trebolle think that they preserve a different literary stage of the text.

[21] P. Sacchi – B. Chiesa, "La *Biblia Hebraica Stuttgartensia* e recenti studi di critica del testo dell' Antico Testamento ebraico," *Hen* 2 (1980), 201–220, esp. 211.

[22] E. Tov, "The Biblical Texts from the Judaean Desert – An Overview and Analysis of the Published Texts," in E. D. Herbert and E. Tov (eds.), *The Bible as Book: The Hebrew Bible and the Judaean Desert Discoveries* (London, 2002), 139–166. According to E. Tov (pp. 155–156) fifty-two per cent of the Qumran biblical texts in the Torah, and forty-four per cent in the other books are Proto-Masoretic, while four and a half per cent in the Torah and three per cent in the other books are close to the presumed *Vorlage* of G.

the analogy with the transmission of the Classical texts must be nuanced. There is particular care for the transmission of the Hebrew text, first among the scribes, later among the Masoretes. The examples taken from the Masorahs magna and parva are very different from the *scholia* in the transmission of Homer or Aeschylus. The comparison between the procedures of the Alexandrian philology with the Homeric corpus and the process of selection and transmission of the Hebrew text adopted by the rabbis cannot be extended to the field of textual criticism. The standardization of the Hebrew text is not the result of an intentional critical activity in order to get a better recension.[23]

In the case of Judges it is difficult to restore a current text different from the Leningrad Codex when the witnesses of a non-Masoretic text are so scanty; in fact, not one is typologically different. The restoration of a consonantal text through retroversion would be highly problematic, artificial or anachronistic in the event that the reconstructed text were provided with vowels and accents. On the other hand, I think that the goals of the *BHQ* and the *OHB* are not as different as they might appear at first sight. Neither of them renounces the restoration of the true reading, the reading closest to the original once the literary development of the book has been completed. The main difference lies in the way the evidence is presented and the layout of the page. *BHQ* insists that the base of the reconstruction has to be documented. There is no change or conjecture admitted without textual support. Conjectures based on literary or exegetical considerations are expressly excluded. Text criticism and philological approach are exercised in different ways, hopefully not applied mechanically, but with art and common sense in order to attain the preferred, genuine reading. For practical reasons this preferred reading is left in the apparatus. The reader, in view of all the testimonies adduced, can evaluate it and eventually reject it as arbitrary. However, I would insist that the text critical purposes of both projects are not so different apart from the layout of the page.[24] In my opinion, the decision not to introduce the preferred variants into the text of M^L

[23] J. van Seters, "The Redactor in Biblical Studies: A Nineteenth Century Anachronism," *JNSL* 29 (2003), 1–19, esp. 8–11.

[24] For a more detailed evaluation of both editions cf. R. D. Weis, "*Biblia Hebraica Quinta* and the Making of Critical Editions of the Hebrew Bible," *TC: A Journal of Biblical Textual Criticism* 7 (2002), n.p., on-line: http://purl.org/TC/vol07/Weis2002.html.

does not come from the respect of the tradition of a sacred text, but from text critical reservations about mixing heterogeneous evidence that has its own transmission in a language different from the Hebrew. Moreover, in some books this is difficult to attain without having first achieved a text critical restoration of G.

There is a set of questions that will continue to divide scholars in the textual criticism of the Hebrew Bible such as the value of the medieval manuscripts, the Babylonian and Palestinian tradition, or the Cairo Genizah fragments for the restoration of the Hebrew text. However, there is agreement on the importance of the Qumran documents and the ancient versions, particularly G. Perhaps it is not so difficult to agree on a common methodology in text criticism of the Hebrew Bible, in spite of the different kinds of editions projected according to the different readers or addressees. Given the complicated text transmission of most of the books, some kind of compromise has to be assumed in each of the options. Even the *OHB* does not renounce the printing of the Leningrad Codex as a guide for the current text and as a practical anchorage for those books or chapters where the non-Masoretic witnesses are lacking.

I would like to add some general considerations drawn from the evolution of the theory of textual criticism in non-biblical areas. Recently it has been realized that in Classical philology the strictures of the Lachmanian theory have been corrected or smoothed in different ways. In the field of the Germanic studies the method of Lachman can hardly be applied to the medieval texts, where the manuscript tradition reflects different redactions. For French medieval texts the polemic between the followers of Lachman and Bédier is developing a new approach because it is practically impossible to determine which is the closest text to the original since the process of writing has not crystallized in fixed text but in a plurality of succesive readings or stages of such text.[25]

Perhaps such texts (anonymous medieval compositions), more like the biblical literature than the author's literature of the Classical heritage, have something to teach us, so that in the future it is not recommended to have just a single edition of the Hebrew Bible. Taking into account the fluidity of text for some biblical books in the period

[25] See the volume of *Arbor* (June 1994) devoted to Text Criticism in the different languages, especially pp. 36, 92–93 and 110–112.

ca. 300 B.C.E.–100 C.E., a plurality of editions is advisable according to the particular problems inherent to every book: synoptic editions for books with literary different redactions; eclectic editions when the extant material allows it; a Tiberian manuscript with different kinds of apparatuses when the most part of the extant evidence belongs to the Masoretic tradition. In the three cases the aim of textual criticism – to go back as far as the textual evidence allows[26] – is maintained.

May these reflections contribute to honour Adrian, a sensitive friend and passionate scholar of the Biblical text traditions, with the wish that he may continue in this leading position für viele Jahre.

[26] A. van der Kooij, "The Textual Criticism of the Hebrew Bible before and after the Qumran Discoveries," in Herbert and Tov, *The Bible as Book*, 167–177, esp. 174.

SOME DIFFICULTIES ENCOUNTERED BY ANCIENT TRANSLATORS

Anthony Gelston

A few months before taking early retirement from teaching in the University of Durham in order to devote more time to research I received an invitation from Adrian Schenker, whom I had not previously met, to edit the Twelve Prophets in the *Biblia Hebraica Quinta.* This is a great privilege, and has enabled me to spend the early years of my retirement in the work of textual criticism of the Hebrew Bible, and thus bring a large part of a lifetime's research and study to fruition. It gives me great pleasure to offer this essay as a tribute to Adrian, the leader of the *BHQ* project, in gratitude for his friendship and support, and in appreciation of his profound scholarship.

One of the salutary features of *BHQ* is the evaluation of all the extant witnesses for each case under consideration. Too often in the past the versions have been quarried in a haphazard way to throw supposed fresh light on passages in the traditional Hebrew text that appear to raise difficulties. Undoubtedly the versions do throw light on some passages, but the need constantly to evaluate the versions has convinced me much more than I had previously realized that the great majority of variations between the Hebrew Bible and the ancient versions originated within the versions themselves rather than deriving from a variant Hebrew *Vorlage.* Many of the characterizations of the versions used in the apparatus of *BHQ* serve to indicate the extent to which variations arose in the process of translation.

Like many university teachers of the Hebrew Bible it fell to my lot to teach elementary Biblical Hebrew to generations of students who were beginners in the subject. In my second year language classes I often used to ask the students to look at a passage of the Hebrew Bible that they had not previously studied, and of which no advance notice was given. The purpose of this was to develop the students' skills in interpreting an unfamiliar passage of Hebrew text, and their confidence in tackling this task. An unexpected by-product of this exercise for myself was the insight I gained into how the ancient translators might go astray when tackling the task with considerably fewer aids than the modern student.

One obvious source of difficulty was the task of deciphering the handwriting of the Hebrew text itself. Not infrequently individual letters were misread, and the difficulty of deciphering some of the Masoretic notes in the Leningrad Codex has brought home to me again the similar difficulties that must often have confronted the ancient translators. A few years ago I published a short study of such misreadings reflected in the LXX of Amos, but this was only a small sample of the cases that could be adduced.[1]

In the present article I attempt to draw attention to several other factors that had a limiting effect on the ancient translators' understanding of the Hebrew text. The first is the phenomenon of homonyms, words of identical form but quite different meaning, of which a number are recognized in modern dictionaries of biblical Hebrew. By examining how the ancient translators handled a small sample of these we may gain some insight into the difficulties they faced when having to decide which of two homonyms known to them occurred in a particular passage.

A second factor concerns the lack of vocalization in biblical Hebrew texts, beyond the partial use of vocalic consonants, at the time when the ancient versions were translated. Not infrequently the consonantal text of a particular word could be vocalized in more than one way, yielding different meanings. No doubt the traditional vocalization, later recorded by the Masoretes, is much older than their time, and it is debatable to what extent it had already become traditional at the time when the ancient translations were made. Once again an examination of cases where the ancient translators evidently vocalized the traditional consonantal text in a different way from what became the traditional vocalization throws some light on the extent to which the vocalization had already become traditional and was known to the translators. Here again the experience of exposing students in language classes to an unpointed text helped to highlight the kind of problems faced by the ancient translators.

A third factor was also suggested by a difficulty commonly experienced by students who had just completed a basic course in the grammar of biblical Hebrew. I found that they frequently did not

[1] A. Gelston, "Some Hebrew Misreadings in the Septuagint of Amos," *VT* 52 (2002), 493–500.

know where to turn in the dictionary to find the root of a particular word confronting them in the text. It proved helpful to draw up a brief résumé of the more difficult problems thrown up by the "irregular" verbs, such as the tendency for an initial נ to disappear, and the need to recognize an original ו or י as the third root letter in the verbs commonly designated ל״ה. Confusion between distinct verbs with two consonants in common and with similar meanings is all too easy, and once again an examination of how this was handled by the ancient translators has proved instructive.

It is not always practicable to distinguish clearly between these three factors. Some pairs of words are homographic, in that they are indistinguishable in form in a consonantal text, but not truly homonymic since they are consistently distinguished in vocalization, e.g. בָּקָר means 'cattle' but בֹּקֶר means 'morning'. Some words are partially homonymic, but become distinct, sometimes even in the consonantal text, in some of their forms. The two nouns און considered below are homonymic when written with a suffix or the plural ending, but vocalized distinctly in the absolute singular, while the two verbs קרא considered below are generally distinguished in the infinitive construct as קְרֹא and קְרַאת. A lack of vocalic consonants in the Hebrew *Vorlage* used by the translators may also sometimes have led to a greater confusion between similar roots.

All three of these factors could profitably be treated comprehensively, but neither space nor time allow this here. In the present article a few examples are offered in each category, although some might be placed in more than one category, in order to illustrate the kind of problem the ancient translators faced. Full details of the renderings of all the versions are given in a few cases; in others only the versions which diverge from M are noted. The examples presented here all come from the Twelve Prophets, with only occasional reference to evidence from other parts of the Hebrew Bible. The treatment is thus of an introductory and illustrative nature, but it is hoped that the evidence presented will be sufficient to draw attention to some of the real difficulties encountered by the ancient translators, to enable us to gain a more sympathetic understanding of the reasons for some of their renderings, which seem to us obviously incorrect, and at the same time to increase our respect for the positive aspects of their achievement, considering their lack of many of the aids enjoyed by the modern student.

Some of the cases discussed in this article are listed among many similar cases on pp. 122–5 and pp. 143–4 of my *Peshitta of the Twelve Prophets*,[2] and are included here by permission of Oxford University Press.

Homonyms

The first example is fully homonymic and will repay a thorough analysis. It consists of the word חרם, of which there are two nouns identical in form, the commoner meaning 'ban' and the other 'net'. Each occurs in two passages in the Twelve, the noun meaning 'ban' in Zech 14:11 and Mal 3:24, and that meaning 'net' in Mic 7:2 and Hab 1:15–17 (the word occurring three times in this last passage). How do the versions compare in recognizing the appropriate sense in each passage?

It can be said at once that each of the main versions recognizes that there are two nouns with distinct meanings. All the versions recognize the sense 'ban' in Zech 14:11. G renders ἀνάθεμα, V *anathema*, S ܚܪܡܐ (cognate with the Hebrew word), and T the interpretative קטלא (= 'killing'). The same sense is recognized in Mal 3:24, although the renderings here are much freer apart from V, which again uses *anathema*. T renders גמירא (= 'complete', with כלייה = 'destruction' understood), and S ܐܒܕܢ (= 'destruction'). G uses the adverb ἄρδην (= 'utterly', 'entirely'), which bears an interesting correspondence to T's rendering. There is, however, no doubt that all the versions have recognized this word correctly in both passages.

The same cannot be said of the word meaning 'net'. The three occurrences in Hab 1:15–17 are recognized by G, which uses two words (ἀμφίβληστρον [twice] and σαγήνη), by V (*sagena*), and by S (ܡܨܝܕܬܐ). T is more problematic. It uses the cognate חרמא in v. 15, but then uses זינא (= 'weapon') in v. 16 and משריתא (= 'camp', 'soldiers') in v. 17. This inconsistency may possibly have a textual basis in v. 17, where 1QpHab reads חרב, or it may rest on exegetical considerations. At all events T recognizes the meaning of the word at its first occurrence in v. 15.

Mic 7:2 is the most interesting of these passages. G misread the preceding verb (via √ צור rather than √ צוד), and then probably

[2] A. Gelston, *The Peshitta of the Twelve Prophets* (Oxford, 1987).

guessed at a translation for חרם to suit this new context (using ἐκθλιβῄ). The other versions all seem to have interpreted the word as 'ban', although the meaning 'net' seems more obviously appropriate in conjunction with the verb צוד (= 'hunt'), itself in parallel with the verb ארב (= 'lie in wait'). S and T render the word respectively in the same way as in Mal 3:24, while this time V resorts to the interpretative *mortem*. Surprisingly even Aquila and Symmachus[3] seem to have used the term ἀνάθεμα (the word in Syh is ܚܪܡܐ, as used by S in Zech 14:11). In mitigation of this interpretation it may be conceded that חרם (= 'ban') could be construed in this context as 'hunt to destruction', yielding a sense not dissimilar to the renderings of G, S and T in Mal 3:24. This may have led the translators to jump to the conclusion that the word here was the commoner חרם (= 'ban'), in spite of their evident knowledge of the other חרם (= 'net') in Hab 1.

The next example is the partially homonymic pair of nouns און. The semantic range of אָוֶן covers such concepts as 'disaster', 'wickedness', 'nothingness' or 'idolatry', while the less common אוֹן means either 'strength' or 'wealth'.

אָוֶן occurs eight times in the Twelve (all in the absolute form), apart from the expression לֶחֶם אוֹנִים (= 'bread of mourning') in Hos 9:4, which is regarded by some as from a separate root and will be left out of account here. Not surprisingly there are some differences of interpretation among the versions, but in most cases the word has been clearly recognized. Only in Hos 10:8 has it been confused with the place-name "On" in G and S (and by implication in T). This rendering recurs in Hab 3:7 in S alone. In no case is the word confused with אוֹן (= 'strength').

It is the rendering of the two occurrences of אוֹן that is of particular interest. Both occur in Hosea 12. In v. 4 באונו stands in contrast to בבטן, and the meaning 'strength' is recognized by οἱ λ′ (ἰσχύς), V (*fortitudo*), S (ܒܥܘܫܢܗ) and T (חוקפא). G, however, renders with κόπος, clearly confusing the word with אָוֶן, from which it is indistinguishable in its suffixed form here, and which it renders with κόπος in four of the eight passages in which אָוֶן occurs in the Twelve.

In v. 9 Aquila (ἀνωφελὲς), V (*idolum*), and S (ܣܪܩܐ) all confuse the word with אָוֶן, despite the vocalization making the identity of

[3] This is the only one of these four passages for which any Hexaplaric witnesses are extant.

the word quite plain in this instance, and despite their having correctly identified it five verses earlier. G here uses ἀναψυχή, which does not correspond to any of the regular meanings of either noun, although Macintosh[4] draws attention to the meaning 'to be at rest, at ease' in the cognate Arabic √ *'wn*. Only T recognizes the meaning 'power' (אונים) in this passage.

This is a good example of a case where the translators may have been uncertain whether they were dealing with one word or two, given the wide semantic range of אָוֶן. Apart from G[5] they all show awareness of the meaning 'strength' in Hos 12:4, but only T recognizes it five verses later. The distinction in the Masoretic vocalization evidently did not help them to distinguish between the two nouns.

Turning now from nouns to verbs we may note first the homonymous verbs קרא, of which one is very common and means 'call', 'proclaim' or 'recite', and the other is much rarer and means 'meet', 'encounter', or 'happen'. The second occurs only twice in the Twelve, and in Zech 2:7 its meaning is correctly recognized in all the versions. In its other occurrence in Amos 4:12, however, the versions are divided in their interpretations. Here G and S render it 'call upon' (ἐπικαλεῖσθαι / ܩܪܐ), while the later Greek translations and V recognize the sense 'meet' and T paraphrases too freely to allow its identification of the verb to be determined. Curiously the versions are divided again in their interpretation of the first verb in Hos 11:7, where Aquila, Theodotion and S recognize the meaning 'call', but Symmachus, T, and implicitly V translate 'meet' and G misinterprets the word as a noun. It is to be noted that 'call upon' does make sense in Amos 4:12, while Hos 11:7 is a difficult passage in which it is understandable that the ancient translators were divided in their interpretation.

Another interesting case is that of the homonymous verbs ענה, a very common verb meaning 'answer' and a less common one meaning 'be bowed down' or 'be afflicted'. The second occurs in three passages in the Twelve, but in only one, Zech 10:2, is the sense recognized by all the versions (except T, which paraphrases). In Nah 1:12, where the verb occurs twice, it is interpreted correctly by V and T, but confused with the verb meaning 'answer' in G and S. In Zeph 3:19 the verb is identified correctly in V, S and T, but in

[4] A. A. Macintosh, *Hosea* (ICC; Edinburgh, 1997), 496.

[5] G does, however, recognize אוֹן in Job 40:16, rendering it with δύναμις.

G it is confused with the preposition למען, which is related to the verb meaning 'answer'. In view of this it is surprising to find that in the clause repeated at the beginning of Hos 5:5 and 7:10 G, S and T all identify the verb as 'be afflicted', although the sense 'answer' seems more appropriate. V translates the two passages differently: *respondebit* in 5:5, but *humiliabitur* in 7:10. This is a good illustration of the kind of difficulties faced by the ancient translators, where they sometimes assumed too readily that they were dealing with the commoner of two verbs, although they were aware of both, and where they sometimes had to make a guess which of the two was more likely in a particular context.

The next example continues to divide modern translators. In addition to the common verb משל (= 'rule'), there is another verb משל, cognate with the noun משל meaning 'parable' or 'byword', which occurs twice in the Twelve, at Mic 2:4 and Hab 2:6, and is recognized there by all the versions. The verb occurs in Joel 2:17, where the Revised Version translates 'rule' in the text, but 'use a byword' in the margin. The latter sense seems the more appropriate in the context, and is adopted by the REB and the NRSV, but the ancient versions all translate 'rule'. It must be admitted that 'rule' makes good sense in this context, even if parallelism suggests that a reference to a byword is the more probable interpretation. This then must be regarded as a case, not of mistranslation, but of the need for a decision between two possible identifications of the verb.

As a final example in this section we may consider the two homonymous verbs גאל. In addition to the very common verb meaning 'redeem' there is another meaning 'be defiled', or 'desecrate' in the active themes. The second verb occurs three times in Malachi 1, twice in v. 7 and once in v. 12, where its meaning is correctly recognized in all the versions. At Zeph 3:1, on the other hand, all the versions identify the verb as 'redeem', despite the apparent contradiction with the context, which comes out particularly sharply in V's rendering: *vae provocatrix et redempta civitas*.

Differences of Vocalization

In this section we consider a number of cases where the same consonantal text could be vocalized in two or more different ways, and where the rendering of one or more of the versions reflects a vocalization different from that of the Masoretes.

A simple example is מנחה, where the word מנוחה meaning 'rest' occurs in Mic 2:10 with *scriptio plena*, and is recognized in all the versions, but recurs in Zech 9:1 with *scriptio defectiva*, where it is mistaken in G and S for the more common מִנְחָה meaning 'gift' or 'offering'. The correct meaning is recognized here by 8ḤevXII gr, Aquila and V, while T offers a paraphrase introducing the Shekinah.

A similar example is מִטָּה meaning 'bed', which is recognized by all the versions in Amos 6:4, and by Aquila, Symmachus and V in Amos 3:12, but mistaken in the latter passage for the more common מַטֶּה meaning 'staff' or 'tribe' by G, S and possibly T. (Theodotion seems to render it in the sense of the previous word.)

The next example too consists of a pair of homographs, both of which are quite common nouns, but are clearly distinguished by the Masoretic vocalization. רַע is an abstract noun meaning 'evil', and רֵעַ is a concrete noun denoting a 'neighbour' or 'colleague'. Ignoring cases where רַע is an adjective the noun occurs twelve times in the Twelve, and in each of them its meaning is correctly recognized by the versions. רֵעַ occurs thirteen times, in eight of which (implicitly in one, the second instance in Zech 14:13) it forms a contrast with איש in the idiom "a man and his neighbour" or the like. In all of these, and in four of the remaining five occurrences, it is likewise correctly identified in the versions. In one single passage, Hos 3:1, it is mistranslated "evil" by G and S. It may be observed that taken in isolation the expression "loving evil" makes reasonable sense in the context, and may not have seemed evidently erroneous to someone reading only the consonantal text.

The remaining examples in this section concern homographs more complex than the mere use of pairs of alternative nouns. G twice mistakes the common word הִנֵּה meaning 'behold' for הֵנָּה, the third person feminine plural pronoun 'they' – at Hab 2:13 in company with V and S, and at Mal 1:13 in company with S alone.

Another example involving a completely different syntax is G's misvocalization of לִבְנוֹת meaning 'to build' in Mic 7:11, recognized by all the other versions, as the noun לְבֵנָה meaning 'brick' or 'tile'.

A slightly different example involves the failure to recognize the preposition מן when attached to the noun it governs. In Mic 7:12 occurs the phrase וְיָם מִיָּם, where the noun in both words is clearly ים meaning 'sea'. G, however, misvocalizes the first as יוֹם meaning 'day' (possibly involving a metathesis, since it does not render the copula) and the second as מַיִם meaning 'water'. Theodotion transposes the first with the previous word, but also renders it "water". In Zech 9:10 occurs the similar phrase מִיָּם עַד־יָם, where G again misvocalizes the first word as מַיִם.

The final example in this section is even more complex. There are no less than three nouns עד, two vocalized עַד and meaning respectively 'eternity' and 'prey', and the third vocalized עֵד and meaning 'witness'. The situation is complicated further by the preposition עַד meaning 'until' or 'as far as' and the adverb עוֹד meaning 'still' or 'again'. G misvocalizes עַד (= 'eternity') as עֵד (= 'witness') in Amos 1:11 and Mic 7:18, and עַד (= 'prey') as עֵד (= 'witness') in Zeph 3:8, the last in company with S and possibly T. Symmachus and V, however, confuse it here with עַד (= 'eternity'). G also misvocalizes עוֹד as עַד (= 'until') in Mic 1:15, while G, V and T all vocalize the preposition עַד as עוֹד in Hag 2:19 in assimilation to the עוֹד at the beginning of the verse. In this last instance S omits the word altogether.

Confusion of Roots

A case of particular interest is to be found in three distinct roots with two letters in common (שׁ and מ). The semantic range of אשׁם is fairly wide and covers the concepts of 'incur guilt', 'be in the wrong', 'acknowledge guilt', 'suffer punishment', and 'atone'. The verb occurs eight times in the Twelve, and the noun אשׁמה once (in Amos 8:14). The verb שׁמד occurs nine times and means 'destroy'. The verb שׁמם occurs seven times, and its two cognate nouns שׁממה and שׁמה respectively eleven and five times. The basic meaning of the verb is to 'be desolate', with the active meaning 'devastate' in the *hifil* and the passive meaning 'be made uninhabited' in the *nifal*. The two nouns both denote 'desolation'. It is clear at the outset that there is some overlap of meaning between the two roots שׁמד and שׁמם, and that in some contexts אשׁם too can approximate to a similar meaning.

G consistently uses ἀφανίζειν for the verb שׁמם and ἀφανισμός for the nouns שׁממה and שׁמה (although it renders שׁממה by the verb once in Joel 2:20). For שׁמד it uses ἐξαίρειν in six cases, ἐξολεθρεύειν in Hag 2:22, and εἰς τέλος to render the infinitive absolute in Amos 9:8. In Mic 5:13 it uses ἀφανίζειν, although it is unlikely that this should be attributed to any confusion of the roots שׁמד and שׁמם,

since the same equivalence occurs in twelve passages in other parts of the Hebrew Bible.

It is when we turn to G's renderings of אשם that we find the most interesting phenomena. The renderings of the verb in Hos 4:15 (ἀγνόει), Hab 1:11 (καὶ ἐξιλάσεται), and Zech 11:5 (μεταμέλοντο) and of the noun in Amos 8:14 (τοῦ ἱλασμοῦ) indicate recognition of the correct root and its normal range of meaning. In Hos 13:1 it renders ויאשם by καὶ ἔθετο αὐτὰ, suggesting confusion with the root שׂים, although the translators may simply have been trying to make sense of a difficult text (e.g. by also adding the object αὐτὰ). In the remaining four passages (Hos 5:15, 10:2, 14:1, and Joel 1:18), however, G uses ἀφανίζειν (as it does also in Prov 30:10). Here it is difficult to resist the suspicion that the translators were confusing the roots אשם and שׁמם.

Another possible explanation would of course be that G had a *Vorlage* different from M in these passages. It has indeed often been argued that the versions reflect a *Vorlage* נָשַׁמּוּ in Joel 1:18. T's rendering here (צדיאו) also uses the root it commonly uses to render the Hebrew √ שׁמם. It is pertinent to note, however, that נָשַׁמּוּ does occur in the previous verse (17), where G renders it by ἠφανίσθησαν and T by צדיאו. G and T may therefore have been influenced by the recent occurrence of נָשַׁמּוּ in v. 17, and jumped too quickly to the conclusion that the same verb had recurred in v. 18. V (*disperierunt*) and S (ܣܦܘ) also render freely in v. 18, although neither of them use words they use for שׁמם in v. 17 or elsewhere in the Twelve. There is therefore little evidence here to support the suggestion of a Hebrew *Vorlage* נָשַׁמּוּ, and it is much more likely that the reason for the rather free renderings of the versions is to be found in the unusual subject of the verb (the herds), with an element of assimilation to the previous verse in the case of G and T.

In the case of the other three passages where G uses ἀφανίζειν to render אשם the other versional evidence in favour of M is overwhelming. In the first two the later Greek versions use πλημμελεῖν, which is their regular equivalent for אשם (and which G itself uses in thirteen passages outside the Twelve). In the third Symmachus renders μεταμελήσει, which obviously reflects תאשם. In all three S and T also render by their usual equivalents for אשם. V admittedly renders freely (*deficiatis, interibunt*, and *pereat*), but none of these are words V uses to render the roots שׁמד and שׁמם, and there is no evidence therefore that V confused אשם with either of them. In fact V uses a much wider vocabulary in its renderings of each of these Hebrew roots than any of the other versions, and it may well be that the context was felt to demand a more general rendering 'perish' than the specific 'suffer punishment'. On the semantic range of אשׁם in the Hosea passages see the comments of A. A. Macintosh.[6]

Reviewing the evidence as a whole the most likely explanation of G's use of ἀφανίζειν to render אשׁם in these four passages remains a confusion of the roots אשׁם and שׁמם on the part of the translators.

Genuine ambiguity arises in the next example, which involves confusion between the roots בושׁ (= 'be ashamed') and יבשׁ (= 'dry up'). In particular both verbs have a *hifil* הובישׁ, which could be derived by translators from either verb. In Hos 13:15 M reads וְיֵבוֹשׁ, which clearly belongs to the √ בושׁ. The versions, however, all translate as if they had read וְיוֹבִישׁ from the √ יבשׁ. The *scriptio defectiva* reading ויבשׁ of 4QXII[c] allows for either vocalization, and may well have been the consonantal text read by the translators. The context would also suggest the √ יבשׁ. In Joel 1:12 both הובישׁה and הובישׁ could derive from either root, although the general context and the presence of יָבֵשׁוּ in the verse suggest that the appropriate root is יבשׁ. V, however, translates both as though they derived from בושׁ, and is joined in this interpretation of the second by G and λ′, where S and T paraphrase. The same ambiguity arises in Zech 10:11, where only G recognizes the appropriateness of the √ יבשׁ, while V, S and T all mistakenly derive the word from the √ בושׁ.

The next example concerns confusion between the two roots ישׁב (= 'sit' or 'dwell') and שׁוב (= 'return'). שׁוב is mistaken for ישׁב by G in Hos 9:3, where it may have been influenced by יֵשְׁבוּ earlier in the verse, and in its first occurrence in Hos 11:5, although it is recognized in its second occurrence at the end of the verse. שׁוב is also mistaken for ישׁב by G and S in Zech 9:12. The cognate noun משׁובה is wrongly derived by G from the √ ישׁב in Hos 11:7 and 14:5. On the other hand ישׁב is mistaken for שׁוב by S in Mal 3:3.

The *nifal* participle נורא of ירא (= 'to fear') occurs six times in the Twelve, and in five cases (Joel 2:11, 3:4, Hab 1:7, Mal 1:14, 3:23) G renders it with the adjective ἐπιφανής, evidently confusing the word with the √ ראה (= 'to see'). The same confusion underlies its rendering in Zeph 2:11 with the verb ἐπιφανήσεται, in which it is

[6] Macintosh, *Hosea*, 214–215, 389, and 555.

followed uniquely by S (ܐܬܟܠܝ), although S recognizes the word in the other five passages. G also confuses the noun מארה and the *nifal* participle נארים from the √ ארר (= 'to curse') in Mal 3:9 with the √ ראה, although it recognizes the noun in Mal 2:2 and the verb in Mal 1:14 and twice in Mal 2:2.

Conclusion

Reviewing these cases as a whole we may observe the evident difficulty the ancient translators experienced from time to time in deciding which was the appropriate vocalization of a word or the correct identification of a homonym or a root in a particular context. In many cases they show awareness in other passages of the word whose identification they have mistaken. This in turn suggests that what became the traditional vocalization may not have become fixed at the time when the earliest translations, particularly G, were made, or at least that the translators were not aware of it if it were fixed. Their *Vorlage* may also in some cases have had fewer vocalic consonants than M. It is no accident that far more variants of this nature, particularly those involving the confusion of similar roots, are to be found in G than in the other versions. It seems reasonable to conclude that its translators had a less comprehensive understanding of biblical Hebrew than those of the later versions. While the possibility of coincidence must not be overlooked, the fact that S follows G in more of these mistaken vocalizations or identifications than any other version confirms the impression often noted before of the spasmodic influence of G on the translators of S. Bearing in mind, however, the relative lack of linguistic resources available to the ancient translators, it is remarkable that they achieved as much accurate interpretation as they did.

NOTES FROM A READING OF DANIEL 2

Agustinus Gianto

While preparing a critical edition of the Book of Daniel, the present writer becomes increasingly aware that a number of textual problems can be explained, if not always resolved, by considering the literary and stylistic aspects within each textual tradition itself. This paper will share some of this experience as a gesture of participation in a volume honoring Adrian Schenker, an accomplished textual critic and an insightful theologian.

A cursory reading of Daniel 2 will show that this chapter, more than any other part in the book, is composed mainly of direct speech, either in dialogue or monologue. Apart from the formulaic 'X said,' the narrative parts are found in two verses at the beginning (vv. 1–2) and end of the chapter (vv. 48–49) and in the middle (vv. 12–23). While the opening and closing verses can be considered as an introduction and conclusion of the chapter, those found in the middle, namely vv. 12–23, require more attention. Some commentators consider these verses, with the exception of v. 12, as a secondary insertion.[1]

The preponderance of dialogue in Daniel 2 suggests this chapter can be read as a drama, that is, as a story whose plot proceeds mainly through the dialogues between the characters. In one way or another several recent commentaries assume that reading when

[1] Commentators who consider vv. 13–23 a later insertion are, among others, A. Lacocque, *Le livre de Daniel* (Paris, 1976), 46; L. Hartmann and A. DiLella, *The Book of Daniel* (AB; New York, 1978), 139; P. Davies, *Daniel* (OTG; Sheffield, 1985), 46; J. J. Collins, *Daniel* (Hermeneia; Minneapolis, 1993), 153 and P. Redditt, *Daniel* (NCBC; Sheffield, 1999), 50. See also T. J. Meadowcroft, *Aramaic Daniel and Greek Daniel: A Literary Comparison* (Sheffield, 1995), 161–197. Their argument is based on the incongruence between v. 16, where Daniel is said to have seen the king, and v. 25, where he was introduced to the king by Arioch. Some commentators do not take this as a difficulty, see E. Lucas, *Daniel* (AOTC; Leicester, 2002), 71. For his part, W. Heaton, *The Book of Daniel* (TBC; London, 1956), 128 thinks that vv. 14–23 develop the wisdom theme beyond the needs of the story. He suspects that here the writer's own point of view enters, and for that reason the storyline is broken. N. Porteous, *Daniel* (OTL; London 1965), 43, while admitting the awkwardness of Daniel's twice seeing the king, prefers to take vv. 14–24 as part of the text and emend it on the basis of Theodotion and the S text. This will be commented on when discussing Act Two below.

dealing with Daniel 2.[2] This essay will explore the burrows dug by others and see how the basic feature of a dramatic text – a growing conflict and its resolution – is manifested. Reading Daniel 2 as a drama can reveal some facets of the text that otherwise would remain unnoticed.

The plot or the storyline in a drama proceeds by groups of situations which come out of the dialogue between the characters. These groups of situations are generally called acts, whose smaller units are labelled as scenes, a detail which will be useful especially for the analysis of vv. 14–24 below. In a dramatic text the groups of situations are arranged in such a way as to show the rise of a conflict and how this conflict becomes more articulate until it reaches its highest point, the climax, only to resolve itself. At this point the divergent situations resolve themselves, and the drama comes to a conclusion. This is basically the classical description of a dramatic plot. This structure also applies to a composition like Daniel 2 whose plot proceeds along these lines:

Act One, vv. 1–13: TENSION: Nebuchadrezzar and the court magicians
Act Two, vv. 14–24: CRISIS AND CLIMAX: God's revelation to Daniel;
Scene 1, vv. 14–16: Daniel and Arioch
Scene 2, vv. 17–18: Daniel and his companions
Scene 3, vv. 19–23: Daniel and his God
Scene 4, v. 24: Daniel and Arioch
Act Three, vv. 25–45: DENOUEMENT: Daniel and Nebuchadrezzar
Scene 1, vv. 25–28, Daniel's interrogation by the king
Scene 2, vv. 29–36a Daniel's recounting of the dream
Scene 3, vv. 36b-45 Daniel's interpretation
Act Four, vv. 46–49: CONCLUSION: Nebuchadrezzar's confession.

The division into acts and scenes is based on the main characters and the distribution of key expressions like חוא (*pael* or *hafel*) 'to manifest' + the dream, with or without the word signifying the interpretation, ידע (*hafel*) 'to make known' + somebody + the dream or its interpretation; גלא 'to reveal' + the mystery. The dramatic move-

[2] W. S. Towner, *Daniel* (Interpretation; Atlanta, 1984), 31 divides the chapter into five scenes: (1) The king's dream and the ordeal of the magicians (vv. 1–12); (2) Daniel's intervention, disclosing the secret of Daniel's power (vv. 13–23); (3) Daniel's proclamation to the king and the miracle of the recovery of the dream (vv. 24–30); (4) the dream and its interpretation (vv. 31–45); (5) the denouement, and the king's praise (vv. 46–49). Reddit, *Daniel*, 50–51, adopts this structure for his exposition.

ment starts in Act One with a growing tension that reaches its climax in Act Two, and then resolves itself in Act Three, which functions as a denouement, and ends in Act Four. The use of the adverb באדין (v. 14) or אדין (vv. 17, 19), meaning 'then', marks the transition from one scene to the next, or as in v. 25, אדין signals the beginning of Act Three.

There is an instructive coincidence between the placing of the *petuḥah* and *setumah* in the Leningrad Codex with the dramatic plot above. The sign for a *petuḥah* is placed before v. 14 (beginning of Act Two),[3] v. 17 (beginning of Scene 2, Act Two), v. 29 (beginning of Scene 2, Act Three) and v. 46 (beginning of Act Four). After v. 24 there is a *setumah*, thus marking it off from a separate unit that starts in v. 25, that is, the beginning of Act Three.

Act One, vv. 1–13: Nebuchadnezzar and the Court Magicians

In vv. 1–13 there is an accumulation of the key expressions חוא (*pael* or *hafel* with no distinction of sense) and its synonym ידע (*hafel*). The court magicians would be able to tell (חוא [*pael*] in vv. 4, 11; [*hafel*] in vv. 7, 10) the interpretation of the dream only if the king is willing to reveal (אמר vv. 4, 7) his dream. The king, however, insists that they should tell him both the dream and its interpretation (חוא [*pael*] vv. 6 [bis], 9; ידע [*hafel*] vv. 5 and 9). The magicians continue to protest, saying that no king will ever ask a similar thing from them because, as they affirm, only the gods who do not dwell among humankind were in a position to make these two things known (חוא [*hafel*] in v. 10; [*pael*] in v.11). The two parties fail to communicate with each other despite their intention to affirm their respective position. Worse, the dialogue, and for that matter, Act One, ends in the king's decision to put the Babylonian sages to death (v. 12) because of their failure to satisfy his wish. It will be observed that this end is in stark contrast with the final scene in Act Two despite their similarity.

In fact, the conflict and tension in Act One comes from the magicians themselves. The king's first initial wish is, as he himself states

[3] Commentators usually take v. 12 as the end of the previous unit; thus v. 13 starts a new unit. O. Plöger, *Das Buch Daniel* (KAT; Gütersloh, 1965), 50, recognizes v. 14 as a new beginning.

in v. 3, is לדעת את־החלום "to know the dream". Again, the narrator mentions in v. 2 that the purpose of convoking the magicians is להגיד למלך חלמתיו "to tell the king of his dreams".[4] In any case, the king is interested to know what he dreamt the previous night. However, in their response in v. 4 the magicians ask the king to tell them his dream first so that they can interpret it. In fact they introduce a split between the dream and the interpretation (פשרא). Henceforth the two things, the dream on the one hand and its interpretation on the other, become distinct. This split opens the way to the affirmation that they can give the interpretation but they need to have something to interpret first, that is, the dream, which they do not know. Once this conflict emerges, the drama moves on to a crisis in Act Two, Scene 3 (vv. 19–23) and its resolution in Act Three, Scene 2 (vv. 29–36a).

Act Two, vv. 14–24: Crisis and Climax: the Revelation of the Mystery to Daniel

This act has several smaller units or scenes, even if not every scene is presented in the form of dialogue. The beginning of this act (Scene 1, vv. 14–16) and its end (Scene 4, v. 24) contain elements of dialogue and function as a frame for the events described in narration (Scene 2, vv. 17–18 and Scene 3, vv. 19–23). In general, in Act Two the question whether one can tell what the dream is and give its interpretation is no longer the concern as in the previous act. What is highlighted here is how Daniel managed to spare his own life and the life of his companions, including the Babylonian sages. Precisely in v. 18 there occurs for the first time the verb גלא 'to reveal' with its object, that is, רז 'mystery'. The idea of revealing the mystery is also expressed by the use of the verb ידע (*hafel*) in v. 23. Here Daniel, pronouncing a thanksgiving to God, says, וכען

[4] The difference between the plural in v. 2 here and the singular in the king's own words need not be overemphasized. The plural in v. 2, reflected in G, Theodotion, V, and S, does not necessarily mean there was more than one dream. The plural here is a way of expressing indeterminateness, see Gesenius-Kautsch §124o. As far as the king is concerned, all that he wants is to hear his dream revealed. In v. 1 the plural also appears חלם נבכדנצר חלמות ותתפעם רוחו ... G renders it in the plural, so does S, but Theodotion and V give the singular. Ehrlich's idea that ות- may represent a dittography of the following ותתפעם is not likely given the plural in v. 2.

הודעתני די־בעינא מנך די־מלת מלכא הודעתנא ". . . thou hast now made known to me what we asked of thee for thou hast made known to us the king's matter".[5] Then in v. 24 Daniel presents himself to the official whom the king appointed to execute the wise men and tells him that he is ready to show the interpretation of the dream, thus preventing the execution from being carried out.

The use of the verb חוא followed by the word denoting the interpretation (פשרא) here makes it clear that in fact Daniel is no different from the court experts.[6] They had said repeatedly in Act One that they would be able to give the interpretation – but not to relate the dream the king had had. This detail, full of irony, puts emphasis on the idea that revealing a dream can only be done by a divine being. This is actually what the sages themselves had affirmed in vv. 10–11 in Act One. Note also that the verb ידע (*hafel*) in vv. 15 and 17 does not have the dream or its interpretation as its object and therefore these occurrences do not have a bearing on the matter. For the same reason the verb חוא in v. 16 does not have a special significance either.

The dialogue between Daniel and Arioch in Scene 1, vv. 14–16, ends in v. 15b and is followed by the remark that Daniel "went in and besought the king to appoint him a time so that he might show the king the interpretation". In view of v. 25, this information, as mentioned at the beginning of this essay, has often been taken by commentators as evidence that vv. 13–23 are not part of the original composition.[7] If Daniel was introduced by Arioch to the king only in v. 25, the remark in v. 16 that Daniel went in to implore the king looks out of place. But the difficulty can be resolved if one takes v. 16 as an aside whose function is to anticipate what was about to happen in the next act. Once the incongruence of time and action between v. 16 and v. 25 disappears, the ground for arguing that vv. 13–23 is a later addition disappears too.[8]

[5] The recipient of the revelation is Daniel alone, even though his companions are said in vv. 17–18 to join in the prayer. (This and subsequent translations are the author's own.)

[6] See, however, n. 11 on the significance of the diverse renderings of the term חכימין in the G text.

[7] See n. 2.

[8] M of v. 16 has ודניאל על ובעה מן־מלכא די זמן יתן־לה ופשרא להחויה למלכא "And Daniel (G adds ταχεως "quickly" here) went in and implored the king that he give him (Daniel) time in order to tell the king the interpretation". If read in a linear, chronological way – rather than the reading offered above – one will naturally ask why Daniel was not arrested. After all, he was asking for more time, and that is precisely

The sentential adverb אדין in v. 17 marks the beginning of a new scene, that is, Scene 2, which takes up two verses. Here one needs to understand the adverb אדין, not as marking the continuation of time with the previous verse, but as ushering in some new situation in the drama. Even if there is no speech in vv. 17–18, one can still take these as dramatic scenes. Dramatic compositions often include comments about the situation, sometimes said by the choir, sometimes by the narrator, which is the case here. This technique is known as *diegesis* in the analysis of dramatic texts. Here Daniel went into his house to inform his companions about the king's decree and asked them to seek the mercy of the God of heaven concerning this mystery[9] in order to be saved from the death sentence already decreed by the king.

Scene 3, vv. 19–23, starts by announcing that the mystery was revealed to Daniel in a vision of the night. Here again the scene is given in summary form. The reader is invited to use his or her imagination about what is going on. This scene also functions as an anticipation or prolepsis to Act Three, Scene 2 (vv. 29–36a) where Daniel tells the king his dream. This also suggests that the knowledge of the dream itself does not come from Daniel's own wisdom. Thus he is no better than the court magicians. All of them are experts in interpreting the dream rather than saying what the dream is. What makes the difference is that Daniel receives help from his God in knowing the dream. It is implied here that the dream comes from the same source, that is, this God. The content of this dream is called mystery. The monologue in vv. 20–23 is Daniel's response in

---

what makes the king lose his patience and condemn the wise men. Theodotion, followed by S, smoothes this out by omitting ו על so that the sentence reads, "Daniel implored that the king . . .", suggesting that Arioch should intervene for Daniel before the king. Read this way, the incongruence with v. 25 disappears simply because Daniel is not said to have gone to see the king himself. J. A. Montgomery, *Daniel* (ICC; Edinburgh, 1927), 154, even suggests that Theodotion's omission probably represents the original text. Porteous, *Daniel*, 42, also proposes to adopt this reading.

[9] Here the word רז is used for the first time in this chapter. Out of the nine occurrences of this word in the Biblical Aramaic lexicon, eight are found in Daniel 2 (vv. 18, 19, 27, 29, 30, 47a, 47b) and in Dan 4:6. The G rendering of this word shows some interpretive activity. In vv. 18, 28, 29, 30, 47b it is translated using the word μυστηριον (so consistently Theodotion in other occurrences), while in v. 47b it is specified as μυστηρια κρυπτα. In v. 19 the clarificatory rendering takes the form of το μυστηριον του βασιλεως. Pap967 even adds a doublet το πραγμα. (The verb גלא is also doubly rendered as εδηλωθη and εξηφανη.) In v. 27 the rendering gives ὁ ἑορακεν βασιλευς "what the king has seen".

the form of praise to the God of wisdom who reveals hidden things, the Lord of the universe and history, he is the one who reveals mysteries. It will be observed that this praise is echoed in Nebuchadnezzar's confession in v. 47.

Scene 4 re-enacts the meeting between Daniel and Arioch which took place in Scene 1. There Arioch was about to carry out the king's decree to kill the wise men.[10] Now Daniel successfully prevents Arioch from executing the sentence. In this scene Daniel's words abrogate the king's decree. This act ends in a situation that is exactly the opposite of what happened in Act One. While in Act One the affirmation on the part of the sages that only divine beings can reveal the dream and its interpretation leads to a death sentence, here in Act Two the same affirmation by Daniel leads to salvation. Let us examine the wording of the ending of these two acts:

> V. 12: כל־קבל דנה מלכא בנס . . . ואמר להובדה לכל חכימי בבל
> Because of this the king was angry . . . and commanded to kill all the wise men of Babylon.
>
> V. 24: כל־קבל דנה דניאל על על אריוך . . . אמר לה לחכימי בבל אל־תהובד
> Because of this Daniel went to[11] Arioch . . . and said, do not kill the wise men of Babylon.

The similarity in construction and wording between the two verses is such that the contrast becomes even stronger. The contrast between

[10] In Act Two the word for 'wise men', חכימין is consistently rendered by Theodotion as σοφοι. The G rendering varies. It has σοφοι in v. 21 (in Daniel's praise), but σοφισται in vv. 14, 18, 24 (bis). In this version this second word is used when the referents are the Babylonian wise men without Daniel and his friends. G uses σοφος when the reference is generic, as in v. 2. This seems to be a deliberate effort to separate Daniel and his friends from the Babylonian wise men. This does not apply to the use of the word in Act One; see v. 12 where to the σοφοι Daniel and his friends also belong. (In v. 13 וחכימיא, reproduced faithfully in Theodotion, appears as παντας 'all' in G, probably to avoid repeating the word for 'wise men' already used in v. 12 παντας τους σοφους.) In Act Three, v. 27, the generic sense reappears in the use of σοφοι. In v. 25 M's השכחת גבר, spoken by Arioch, is rendered by Theodotion as ἑυρηκα ανθρωπον, but in G it appears as ἑυρηκα ανθρωπον σοφον. Obviously the adjective here is a clarificatory gloss. In Act Four, v. 48, the king set Daniel as chief prefect over the σοφισται of Babylon. Thus by the end of the chapter, as shown in v. 48, G clearly characterizes Daniel as different from the other wise men, in contrast to the generic description of wise men at the beginning and in v. 12, to which Daniel belonged.

[11] M has על על, also witnessed in G, Theodotion, V, and S over against על in 4QDan[a] and some Hebrew manuscripts. The use the verb עלל followed by the preposition על and a personal name is actually known also in the Aramaic of the same period, see 1QapGen 2 3 על על בתאנוש "I went to Bitenosh".

the death sentence in v. 12 and Daniel's aborting the execution in v. 24 is thereby placed in the forefront. At this point the drama reaches its climax and what follows is the sorting out of the issues involved in the form of a denouement.

Act Three, vv. 25–45:
Daniel Tells the King the Dream and Its Interpretation

This act consists of three scenes, the first, vv. 25–28, contains the dialogue between the king and Daniel and the second, vv. 29–36a, presents Daniel's vision of the dream followed by the third scene vv. 36b–45 where he gives the interpretation.

As in Act One, the frequent occurrence of the special expressions of 'making known' is noticeable. Yet, unlike the dialogue between the king and the magicians in Act One, the dialogue in Act Three, Scene 1 ends in mutual understanding and thus communication is established. The verb חוא, however, is no longer used in a significant way as in Act One. The text now uses the verb ידע (*hafel*) and גלא followed by רז 'mystery'. It will be observed that in v. 27 the root חוא does occur, but it only acts to stress the failure of the experts of the divinatory art to satisfy the king's wish: לא ... יכלין להחויה למלכא "they were not able to tell the king". Thus this is a kind of device to return to the situation developed in Act One. The effect is to give more emphasis to Daniel's superiority over the Babylonian experts. In v. 25 Daniel assures the king that he will give the interpretation. The king insists in v. 26, as in Act One, that the wise man should reveal – ידע (*hafel*) – the content of the dream together with its interpretation.

Daniel's reply in vv. 27–28 affirms that only God, the one who reveals mysteries, can inform the king – ידע (*hafel*) – about what will happen in the future. Here Daniel calls the object of king's curiosity רזא "the mystery".[12] His words basically say the same thing the magicians said in Act One (v. 11). The difference lies precisely in Daniel's calling the God who reveals mysteries (including the mystery the king desires to know) upon the scene. One remembers that

[12] In M the *status emphaticus* of the masculine singular רזא is written רזה except in v. 30 where it appears as רזא. This spelling variation is common in the Aramaic of Daniel.

the magicians in Act One (v. 11) mentioned the king's inquiries simply as מלתא "the thing" or "the word". This cannot be answered להן אלהין די מדרהון עם בשרא לא איתוהי "except by the gods who do not dwell among humankind". For Daniel the divine being is the one who reveals mysteries, not simply one of those who do not live among humankind. Thus, despite the similarity in the affirmations, there is a striking difference in two essential matters: the perception about the king's wish (thing vs. mystery) and about the divine being ('gods who do not dwell among humankind' vs. 'the one who reveals mysteries'). These contrasts resolve the tensions that start in Act One and reach their climax in Act Two. The desire to know the dream and its interpretation move from being a mere מלתא to רזא. Also the nature of the true divine beings believed by the magicians ('not living among humankind') is now clarified. It is the God who reveals mysteries. Gradually the king is led to encounter the mystery he was seeking, and even he is brought very close to the God who reveals mysteries.

Scene 2 (vv. 29–36a) recounts the dream and corresponds to what is proleptically said in v. 19 (which belongs to Act Two scene 3). The dream itself is a theological reading of universal history starting from the exilic era to the time of the Maccabees in the form of the king's dream in vv. 31–36a, using the four schemes rendered more explicit in the interpretation of the dream in vv. 36b–45, Act Three, scene 3. The correspondence between this scene and v. 19 (Scene 3 Act Two) is noteworthy. Both are about God's revealing the mystery in a vision of the night and the account of the dream given by Daniel to the king is significant. The dream comes from the God of Daniel, the Lord of history. Daniel's unfolding the meaning of the dream is a consequence of the contact with this divine sphere.

The interpretation of the dream, given in Scene 3, makes it clear that the golden head is Nebuchadnezzar's own time, then after it came the period of the Medes represented by the silver chest and arms. The third period is the Persian era, symbolized by the bronze middle part of the body, and finally, the Hellenistic time, here marked as iron legs and feet half in iron, half in clay. History is read as being under the control of the true sovereign of the universe. He gives power and dominion to those he chooses. The statue is brought down by the small stone that fell from the mountain "without any human agency". This means that the secular power, however imposing it may be, cannot stand the small stone that comes from the divine sphere. This is a wisdom reading on Daniel's part.

Act Four, vv. 46–49: Nebuchadnezzar's Confession

This act concludes the drama. After hearing the account of his dream and its interpretation given by Daniel, in v. 47 the king pays obeisance to Daniel (v. 46) while admitting the superiority of Daniel's God.[13] This profession is an echo of Daniel's own praise in vv. 20–23, in Scene 3 in Act Two. The theme is that of the God who reveals mysteries, sovereign over the universe, worldly power and the sources of wisdom.

In his words the king mentions three epithets of God, namely: (1) אלה אלהין "God of gods", i.e., the supreme Deity; (2) מרא מלכין "the lord of kings", i.e., sovereign over worldly power; (3) גלה רזין "the one who reveals mysteries". The reason for this profession is given in v. 47, די יכלת למגלא רזה דנה "because you have been able to reveal this mystery". Who is this 'you' addressed by Nebuchadnezzar? The context suggests that it is Daniel. Thus what the text says is not quite the same thing as Daniel himself claims, namely that not he, but God, has revealed all this. There is an ironical touch about Nebuchadnezzar's poor understanding of what is going on. Even before, in v. 46, by simply prostrating himself in front of Daniel, he shows himself unable to see that it is Daniel's God whom he should thank and worship, rather than Daniel.

The king who, in the words of his magicians, puts himself on a par with the divine beings by asking the impossible now admits his true position. This theme will be echoed in the stories in Daniel 3 (statue to be revered) and 4 (Nebuchadnezzar's illness and healing). This simplistic understanding on the part of king is itself a message. The worldly king like him is unable to grasp what is really going on. He can only see the surface.

[13] The second person plural suffix in אלהיכון in v. 47 requires some discussion. One is tempted to think that the king had Daniel and his companions in mind, as if they were also present at that moment. The problem is similar to that of v. 36 where the first person plural in נאמר is used by Daniel to refer to himself and his companions even if they were not physically present at this scene. This is also the case with the two occurrences of the first person plural at the end of v. 23.

LE TEXTE MASSORÉTIQUE DE QOHÉLET, TÉMOIN D'UN COMPROMIS THÉOLOGIQUE ENTRE LES 'DISCIPLES DES SAGES' (QOH 7,23–24; 8,1; 7,19)

Yohanan A. P. Goldman

Dans le livre du Qohélet, comme dans le reste de la Bible hébraïque, le texte massorétique se révèle souvent un témoin assez fiable lorsqu'il s'agit de préserver des formes linguistiques difficiles. Cependant, j'aimerais montrer qu'il porte les traces, discrètes mais cohérentes, d'un projet d'édition de la Bible selon la théologie du Judaïsme rabbanite. Il semble en effet que, pour trouver sa place parmi les Écritures Saintes, le livre a souffert quelques corrections dans les passages où il heurtait les principes les plus fondamentaux de la théologie du Judaïsme pharisien.[1] Ces corrections, quoique minimes en quantité, touchent à des points essentiels de la pensée du Qohélet et les versions anciennes du livre permettent en partie de restaurer un texte plus ancien dans ces passages qui ont été modifiés.

Ces retouches ne font pas du texte massorétique un témoin de moindre valeur, loin de là, mais elles dessinent une "ligne rouge" que le milieu de la canonisation du livre a imposée au texte. Pour retracer cette "ligne rouge", je propose deux groupes d'observations. Le premier concerne les réactions négatives d'une partie des maîtres du Judaïsme pharisien envers l'œuvre du Qohélet, le second relève quelques corrections propres au texte massorétique. Le but de la présente étude est de montrer que ces corrections du texte répondaient au malaise de certains grands maîtres du Judaïsme devant les critiques radicales que Qohélet adresse à ceux qui prétendent acquérir la sagesse. Les deux premières sections (1. et 2.) mettent en perspective leur difficulté à admettre cette œuvre de sagesse si particulière que représente le livre du Qohélet, et les deux dernières (3. et 4.) tentent de pointer du doigt les quelques corrections qui ouvraient la possibilité d'une lecture orthodoxe du livre dans le milieu du Judaïsme pharisien.

---

[1] L'adjectif 'pharisien' sert ici la cause exclusive d'une description historique.

1. Une forte opposition à la canonisation du livre

C'est un fait bien connu que le livre du Qohélet a dû surmonter quelques solides réticences avant d'être accepté dans le canon de la Bible hébraïque.[2] Qohélet fait partie de ces livres sur lesquels les rabbins ont posé la question: "Rend-il les mains impures?" C'est-à-dire: les rouleaux sur lesquels il est écrit font-il partie des choses saintes?[3]

L'opposition à la reconnaissance du Qohélet apparaît clairement dans un texte de la Mishna, d'où il ressort que de grands noms du Judaïsme pharisien, à la fin du 1er siècle et au début du 2ème siècle de l'ère chrétienne, soit lui niaient la qualité d'Écriture Sainte, soit reconnaissaient qu'il y avait eu difficulté à admettre ce livre parmi les Écritures Saintes.[4]

---

[2] Voir D. Barthélemy, "L'état de la Bible juive depuis le début de notre ère jusqu'à la deuxième révolte contre Rome (131–135)," in J.-D. Kaestli, O. Wermelinger (éds.), *Le Canon de l'Ancien Testament: Sa formation et son histoire* (Genève, 1984), 9–45; repris et complété en D. Barthélemy, *Découvrir les Écritures* (Lectio Divina; Paris, 2000), 29–65.

[3] Voir à ce sujet M. Haran, "Les problèmes de la canonisation de l'Écriture," *Tarbiz* 26 (1955–6), 245–271; et, sur ce point particulier de l'impureté des mains au contact d'un rouleau: S. Zeitlin, "An Historical Study of the Canonization of the Hebrew Scripture," in *Solomon Zeitlin's Studies in the Early History of Judaism II* (New York, 1974), 1–42. Le principe est dérivé des lois du sanctuaire, comme l'écrit Barthélemy: "L'expression 'souiller les mains' à propos d'un livre signifie que le fait d'avoir touché ce livre oblige ensuite à se laver les mains. De même en effet que le passage du domaine profane au domaine sacré impose une purification, le passage en sens inverse en impose une autre. (. . .) Dire d'un livre qu'il "souille les mains" est donc, pour la *Mishna* et la *Tosefta*, affirmer de façon très précise qu'il fait partie de la catégorie des Écritures Saintes." ("L'état de la Bible juive," 26). L'histoire et les motivations exactes des décrets rabbiniques imposant une impureté des mains est assez complexe et discutée. Un motif profond pourrait être que les maîtres du Judaïsme ont voulu déplacer la notion de sainteté et de contact avec le divin, depuis les activités rituelles du sanctuaire vers les Écritures et la nourriture des laïcs. Zeitlin, par exemple (ibid. 18–19), a montré les liens entre ce décret rabbinique sur l'impureté des mains et les lois réglant la consommation des nourritures du sanctuaire (la Terumah).

[4] L'authentification et la datation des traditions rabbiniques est le lieu de vifs débats, en particulier depuis les études de Jacob Neusner dans les années soixante-dix. Le but n'est pas ici de retracer l'histoire exacte de l'opposition à la canonisation du Qohélet. Il suffit de noter a) que cette opposition nous est présentée dans le corpus rabbinique comme largement répandue à l'époque de la clôture du canon; et b) qu'il n'y a pas de raisons sérieuses de douter du noyau de ces traditions. Je crois en effet que nous pouvons écarter l'idée d'une fiction historique ultérieure, créée *après* que le livre a reçu l'aval des plus hautes autorités du Judaïsme pharisien. Il est peu vraisemblable en effet qu'on ait pu jeter *en leur nom* le discrédit sur un livre déjà reçu comme Écriture Sainte. Le seul intérêt d'une telle fiction aurait

texte a. *m.Yadayim* III, 5[5]
Toutes les Écritures Saintes rendent les mains impures. Le(s rouleaux de)[6] Cantique des Cantiques et Qohélet rendent les mains impures. Rabbi Yehudah dit: le (rouleau de) Cantique des Cantiques rend les mains impures, mais sur Qohélet il y a discussion. Rabbi Yosé dit:[7] (le rouleau de) Qohélet ne rend pas les mains impures, quant au Cantique il y a discussion. Rabbi Shimeon dit: Qohélet fait partie des 'légers' de l'école de Shammay et des 'graves' de l'école de Hillel.[8]
Rabbi Shimeon Ben Azzay a dit: J'ai reçu la tradition de la bouche même des 72 anciens, le jour où ils ont établi Rabbi Eléazar Ben Azaryah sur l'Académie, que (les rouleaux de) Cantique des Cantiques et Qohélet rendent les mains impures.[9]
Rabbi Aqiba a dit: A Dieu ne plaise! jamais personne en Israël n'a été partagé sur le Cantique des Cantiques (pensant) qu'il pourrait ne

été de devancer des objections au livre ou de dissiper des soupçons au sujet de son contenu. Or, les oppositions anciennes au livre sont expressément attribuées à des personnalités ou à des cercles importants de la tradition pharisienne, *sans aucune légitimation de la pensée du Qohélet* (cf. Rabbi Yehuda et Rabbi Yosé ben Ḥalafta, texte a.; Rabbi Shimeon ben Menasyah, texte b.; Bet Hillel et Bet Shammay selon Rabbi Yishmael, cité plus loin à la note 8, Rabbi Méir cité note 12). On peut donc écarter l'idée d'une fiction "légitimante" et considérer, avec un bon degré de probabilité, que les diverses oppositions à la canonisation du livre, citées dans la littérature rabbinique ancienne, remontent effectivement aux personnalités citées, qui ont vécu à l'époque précédant et suivant la clôture du canon. Ce n'est que vers la fin du 3ème siècle, lorsque les dernières oppositions au livre qui s'étaient exprimées tout au long du 2ème siècle s'étaient tues, et que l'autorité du livre ne pouvait plus être contestée, que l'on a ouvertement exprimé les objections des maîtres anciens devant le Qohélet et les réponses qu'ils avaient trouvées dans le livre lui-même (voir textes c. et d.). Ces réponses peuvent être considérées comme des fictions historiques, mais elles ont une part de réalité . . . si, comme j'essaierai de le montrer plus loin, elles ont d'abord eu la forme de corrections textuelles.

[5] H. Albeck, ששה סדרי משנה : סדר טהרות (Jérusalem Tel Aviv, 1959), 481.

[6] Le féminin du verbe (מטמאות) se rapporte au sujet implicite: les *meguillot*, les rouleaux.

[7] Il s'agit de rabbi Yosé ben Ḥalafta, le précédent est Rabbi Yehudah bar Ilay et le suivant Rabbi Shimeon bar Yoḥay. Tous trois sont des disciples de Rabbi Aqiba; de la troisième génération des Tannaim (130–160); H. L. Strack et G. Stemberger, *Einleitung in Talmud und Midrasch.* Siebente, völlig neu bearbeitete Auflage (München, 1982), 82/83.

[8] Les 'lourds' se distinguent des 'légers' par le fait qu'ils rendent impur, dans le cas de l'Écriture il s'agit de l'impureté des mains; cf. *m.'Eduyot* V, 3: "Rabbi Yishmael dit: il y a trois choses qui font partie des 'légers' de l'école de Shammay et des 'graves' de l'école de Hillel: Qohélet ne rend pas les mains impures, c'est l'avis de l'école de Shammay, mais dans l'école de Hillel ont dit qu'il rend les mains impures"; Albeck, סדר נזיקין, 305.

[9] Rabbi Eléazar ben Azaryah a été nommé à Yavneh en remplacement de Rabban Gamaliel II. On a donc discuté de l'inspiration de ces deux livres lors de cette assemblée importante qui eut lieu entre 90 et 105; cf. Barthélemy, "L'état de la Bible juive," 25. Rabbi Shimeon ben Azzay, qui témoigne de l'événement, fait partie avec Aqiba de la deuxième génération des Tannaim (env. 90 à 130); Strack/Stemberger, *Einleitung*, 81.

> pas rendre les mains impures, car le monde en son entier ne vaut pas le jour où le Cantique des Cantiques a été donné à Israël! car tous les écrits sont saints, mais le Cantique des Cantiques est "Saint des Saints".[10] Et s'ils ont été divisés (les sages) ils ne l'ont été qu'au sujet de Qohélet.

La règle générale, celle qui a le consensus de la majorité, est donnée en tête de la Mishna, puis les avis divergents sont ajoutés selon une progression qui montre que le Qohélet est nettement plus contesté que le Cantique des Cantiques. Ainsi, lorsqu'on affirme que le Cantique est saint, on rappelle que le Qohélet ne fait pas l'unanimité (R. Yehuda Bar Ilay); et lorsqu'on estime que le Cantique lui-même ne fait pas l'unanimité, alors on affirme que le Qohélet est en dehors des livres saints (R. Yosé).

L'avis majoritaire et décisionnaire de Yavneh, rapporté par Rabbi Shimeon Ben Azzay, met les deux livres sur le même niveau de sainteté, ce qui aurait dû satisfaire Rabbi Aqiba, pour qui l'inspiration du Cantique n'était pas sujet à discussion. Mais cette présentation des choses est loin de le satisfaire. La réaction d'Aqiba se décrypte aisément: il est tellement évident que le Qohélet est discuté, et même refusé par certains, qu'il ne tient pas du tout à ce qu'on le mette sur un même plan que son cher Cantique, qu'il considère comme inspiré au même titre que les plus saintes des Écritures, dont le Cantique serait le "Saint des Saints".[11]

Il est bien possible qu'au-delà de son amour du Cantique, Aqiba ait partagé les doutes de ceux qui refusaient l'inspiration du Qohélet. Il est remarquable en effet que la résistance au livre se soit prolongée au milieu du deuxième siècle parmi les plus célèbres disciples d'Aqiba: Rabbi Yehuda bar Ilay, Rabbi Yosé ben Ḥalafta et Rabbi Méir, qui avaient suffisamment d'autorité pour ne pas avaliser la décision des 'sages' décrétant l'inspiration du Qohélet.[12] Le statut du

[10] Rabbi Aqiba joue sur l'appellation כִּתְבֵי הַקֹּדֶשׁ "écrits de sainteté/du sanctuaire" pour inviter ses collègues à entrer dans le "Saint des Saints" qu'est le Cantique des Cantiques . . . Voir note 15 plus loin.

[11] Voir les motifs suggérés par Barthélemy (*Découvrir les Écritures*, 47–55) d'une décision à Yavneh concernant le Cantique et Qohélet. A la différence de Qohélet, le Cantique semble avoir eu à cette époque une tradition imposante en sa faveur; cf. Barthélemy, ibid., 239–251.

[12] Pour Rabbi Yehudah l'inspiration du Qohélet est sujette à discussion, et Yosé ben Ḥalafta, lui, ne le considère pas comme Écriture sainte (texte a.). L'opinion de Rabbi Méir, disciple très influent de R. Aqiba, est rapportée dans le Talmud de Babylone à l'occasion d'une discussion sur le statut du livre d'Esther: "Rabbi Méir dit que Qohélet ne rend pas les mains impures et qu'il y a discussion sur le Cantique des Cantiques" (*b.Meguilla* 7a).

Qohélet opposait déjà, semble-t-il, les écoles de Hillel et de Shammay de la génération précédente.

Ce courant de résistance au livre fut assez durable puisqu'un texte de la *Tosefta* nous rapporte qu'un tanna de la quatrième génération, à la fin du 2ème siècle, affirmait encore que le Qohélet n'est pas inspiré.

> **texte b.** *t.Yadayim* II, 14[13]
> R. Shimeon ben Menasyah dit: Le Cantique des Cantiques rend les mains impures car il a été dit dans l'Esprit Saint, Qohélet ne rend pas les mains impures car il est de la sagesse de Salomon . . .

A l'opposé du Cantique, "dit dans l'Esprit Saint", Qohélet ne serait que de la seule "sagesse de Salomon". Autrement dit, pour Rabbi Shimeon ben Menasyah (ou pour le rédacteur/transmetteur de cette boraïta) la sagesse du livre du Qohélet n'est pas une sagesse inspirée, mais une sagesse du même ordre que celle des livres profanes, dans laquelle l'Esprit Saint ne se communique pas et, par conséquent, ne pose pas de problème rituel. Si les maîtres du Judaïsme pharisien posent la question de l'inspiration en termes de pureté rituelle, c'est que, pour eux, une sagesse 'dite dans l'Esprit Saint' est porteuse de sanctification, bien plus que d'une instruction sur les complexités de l'existence. Et c'est précisément ce qui fait entrer un livre dans un statut de sainteté semblable à celui de la Torah. Car la Torah est indissociable de la Théophanie du Sinaï, où elle fut communiquée dans une présence très particulière de Dieu. Au cœur même de la Torah, 'les Dix Paroles' ne sont pas qu'une charte éthique fondamentale mais aussi un objet saint, gravé du doigt de Dieu (Ex 31,18), les 'Tables de l'Alliance', transmises dans le cadre de l'acte liturgique fondateur du peuple d'Israël en tant que nation (Ex 19–20), qui portent témoignage de l'alliance (לחות העדות Ex 31,18)[14] et qui trouvent naturellement leur place dans "l'Arche du Témoignage" (Ex 25,21).[15] Toute Écriture Sainte devrait donc, par nature, être dans une continuité "ontologique" avec la Torah et, bien entendu, s'accorder avec elle. Ce qui nous conduit à la section suivante.

[13] M. S. Zuckermandel, *Tosephta Based on the Erfurt and Vienna Codices with parallels and variants. With "Supplement to the Tosephta" by Rabbi Saul Liebermann*, M.A. (Reprint Jerusalem, 1970), 683.

[14] Pour le sens de עדות, cf. C. L. Seow, "Ark of the Covenant," *ABD* I (1992), 387–388.

[15] Le désir d'associer à tout livre saint une pureté rituelle montre que la croissance du canon des Écritures relève aussi, dans la conscience du Judaïsme antique, de l'extension de la sainteté toute particulière de la Torah à d'autre écrits (Barthélemy,

2. *La nature des objections au livre du Qohélet*

Si les 'contradictions' du livre sont parfois mentionnées comme un handicap à sa canonisation, il semble que le rejet du Qohélet par certaines autorités du Judaïsme pharisien ait eu pour motif des contradictions plus profondes entre la perception de la voie de la sagesse selon Qohélet et leur propre perception de la voie de la Torah. Ceci est illustré dans le passage suivant attesté a plusieurs reprises dans la tradition rabbinique.

> **texte c.** *Pesikta de-Rav Kahana* ח[16]
> Rabbi Binyamin ben Levy a dit: les sages (חכמים) ont voulu mettre en geniza[17] le livre de Qohélet parce qu'ils y trouvaient des paroles qui penchent du côté de l'hérésie.

"L'état de la Bible juive," 9–11). Le Dieu qui parle est nécessairement le Dieu qui se rend présent et communique sa présence (sanctifie) à ceux qui l'écoutent. On assiste dans le Judaïsme ancien à une transposition dans les Écritures de la notion de sanctuaire. Extension du 'lieu saint', les Écritures émergent peu à peu comme nouveau 'lieu saint', dont les maîtres du Judaïsme pharisien sont, en quelque sorte, le nouveau sacerdoce. (La remarque de Rabbi Aqiba, qui fait du Cantique le "Saint des Saints" [texte a.], serait à verser au dossier, en ce qu'il semble user de la comparaison des Écritures au sanctuaire comme d'un *topos* aisément accessible à ses confrères; voir note 10, ci-dessus.) Il ne s'agit sans doute pas aux yeux des rabbanim d'un déplacement purement symbolique, mais bel et bien d'un remodelage de la perception de la réalité socio-religieuse. Les sociologues auraient sans doute beaucoup à dire sur la reconstruction de l'espace social qui conditionne un tel remodelage de l'espace religieux. Il me semble que les études sur la genèse du canon biblique auraient profit à envisager ce saut important dans la psychologie religieuse d'Israël, qui permit, par à-coups, de passer des écritures du Temple au "temple des Écritures" et de dépasser ainsi la notion de territorialité dans le domaine du 'saint' (tout en déplaçant l'autorité de référence! voir plus haut la fin de la note 3). Quelques études ébauchant une réflexion sur le phénomène du canon se trouvent dans: van der Kooij A. et van der Toorn K. (eds.), *Canonization and Decanonization* (StHR 82; Leiden 2002). Pour le reste, on trouvera de nombreuses références bibliographiques sur l'histoire du canon en: E. Schürer, *The History of the Jewish People in the Age of Jesus Christ (175 B.C.–A.D. 135). A New English Version Revised and Edited by G. Vermès, F. Millar, M. Black* (Edinburgh, 1979), II, 314–321; et en L. M. McDonald and J. A. Sanders (eds.), *The Canon Debate* (Peabody MA, 2002).

[16] B. Mandelbaum (ed.), *Pesikta de Rav Kahana According to an Oxford Manuscript* (New York, 1987), Piska ח, 135. Principaux parallèles en Midrash Qohélet Rabbah, cf. C. Motos López, *La vanidades del mundo: Comentario rabínico al Eclesiastés* (Estella, 2001), 53, *QohR* I, §3.1.1.; et en *Lev.R.* XXVIII, ספר מדרש רבות, (Varsovie, 1876), 43a, dans ce dernier recueil la tradition est rapportée par Samuel bar Naḥmani et non Binyamin ben Levy.

[17] On le sait, la *genizah* est ce lieu isolé, le plus souvent muré, où les écrits saints devenus inutilisables sont laissés à leur décomposition naturelle (rouleaux, phylactères, mezuzôt, etc.). L'expression signifie donc que les 'sages' étaient tentés de mettre le Qohélet – qui porte le nom divin et qui est de Salomon – parmi les écrits inutilisables en tant qu'Écriture Sainte.

Ils ont dit: Salomon avait-il besoin de s'exprimer ainsi: *Quel profit pour l'homme de tout son effort qu'il produit sous le soleil?* (Qoh 1,3), peut-être cela inclut-il l'effort de Torah?
Ils sont revenus (après réflexion) et ils ont dit: s'il avait dit *"de tout l'effort"* et s'était tu, nous en aurions déduit qu'il incluait aussi l'effort de Torah. Mais puisqu'il dit *"de tout* son *effort"*, de *son* effort il ne tire pas de profit, mais de l'effort de Torah il tire profit.

Qoh 1,3 dénonce simplement l'illusion qu'entretiennent les humains lorsqu'ils se donnent de la peine en ce monde, mais l'avis des sages est qu'il y a là un problème théologique quant à la pratique de la Torah; ces paroles du Qohélet seraient même *presque* hérétiques ("des paroles qui penchent du côté de l'hérésie"). On peut s'étonner de l'intrusion d'une telle problématique dans l'interprétation de ce verset, mais c'est ici l'ouverture d'un livre de sagesse qui, par son histoire et par le soutien de l'école de Hillel, "postule" à une place parmi les livres saints de la bibliothèque des rabbins. Or la voie de la sagesse a pris des contours bien particuliers dans le Judaïsme pharisien du tournant de l'ère chrétienne. La sagesse concentre tous les efforts du disciple sur une vie dans la Torah. Dans le chemin de vie que dessine la sagesse rabbanite, les difficultés de la vie du disciple sont avant tout les obstacles à la pratique des commandements. Quant aux problèmes que doit résoudre la sagesse, pour indiquer au disciple une ligne de conduite, ce sont principalement ceux d'une juste interprétation de la Torah. En sorte que s'impose progressivement parmi eux le titre de 'sages' pour les interprètes de la Torah, puis de 'disciples des sages'.[18] Quant aux éloges bibliques de la sagesse ils sont *ipso facto* entendus comme des éloges de la Torah.

On sait que l'identification entre la sagesse et la Torah a commencé bien avant le tournant de l'ère chrétienne. Des textes bibliques tels que Jr 8,8; Dt 4,6–8; Ps 1 offraient une base à ce rapprochement.

[18] Probablement au cours du premier siècle de l'ère chrétienne; cf. Ulrich Wilckens, σοφία in G. Friedrich (ed.), *Theological Dictionary of the New Testament* (Grand Rapids, 1971) VII, spéc. 505–507; E. Schürer, *The History of the Jewish People*, 322–325. Moïse lui-même, de prophète sans égal qu'il est selon la Torah (Dt 34,10), deviendra "le sage des sages, le père des prophètes" (H. S. Horovitz, *Sifre Bamidbar* (Leipzig, 1917), קלד, 180, ligne 5; L. Finkelstein, *Siphre ad Deuteronomium* (Berlin, 1939), כט, 46, lignes 2–3 et שו, 341, ligne 13, etc. Les prophètes deviennent ainsi un chaînon dans cette transmission de la Torah entre Moïse "le sage des sages" et les "sages" de la fermeture du canon. Même s'il ne peut être établi que cette idée ait trouvé son expression achevée à l'époque de la canonisation de Qohélet, elle apparaît comme l'aboutissement inéluctable d'une évolution dans la perception de la Torah.

> Déjà Ben Sira, témoin de la piété juive au début du 2ème siècle avant Jésus Christ, identifie clairement la sagesse de Proverbes 8 qui guide la création du monde avec "le livre de l'alliance du Dieu Très Haut, la Torah que Moïse nous a prescrite" (Sir 24,23–24). La tradition juive attestée dans le livre de Ben Sira trouve un écho très net dans la première péricope du Midrash Rabbah sur la Genèse. Là, le midrash cite les versets de Pr 8 sur la sagesse qui était à l'œuvre avec le créateur à l'origine du monde, pour montrer que la Torah est bien ce principe de tout l'ouvrage, ce *Reshît* dans lequel (au moyen duquel) Dieu crée le monde selon Gn 1,1.[19]

Dans cette perspective, qui identifie entièrement le chemin de la sagesse et la vie dans la Torah, on comprend qu'un livre de sagesse qui commence en relativisant d'emblée "tous les efforts" de l'être humain (Qoh 1,3) ait fait l'objet d'une attention circonspecte. Comment une sagesse inspirée pouvait-elle commencer par ces mots qui mettent en doute l'intérêt de tous les efforts humains, alors même que les efforts de l'être humain ont pour objet premier de connaître et pratiquer la sagesse qu'est la Torah? Les avertissements de Qohélet sur l'illusion qui guette les apprentis de la sagesse, ne pouvaient que mettre mal à l'aise les rabbins du tournant de l'ère chrétienne, lesquels, en tant que 'disciples des sages', étaient assurés de la sagesse véritable qu'ils trouvaient dans la Torah. Recevoir le Qohélet comme livre inspiré signifiait donc, pour certains d'entre eux, recevoir parmi les Écriture Saintes un discours relativiste et désabusé au sujet du chemin de la sagesse, chemin de l'étude de la Torah et de la pratique des commandements.

Dans le même sens, comment pouvait-on mettre en doute le profit qu'un homme peut espérer de ses efforts et de sa discipline dans la voie de la sagesse (Qoh 1,3)[20] sans mettre en doute, par là même, l'idée de rétribution divine? La suite du Midrash Qohélet, qui oppose les exigences de Moïse et les conseils de Qohélet, touche précisément à cette question de la rétribution.

[19] Voir aussi le Targum palestinien qui lisait probablement ainsi Gn 1,1: "Dès le commencement *la Parole du Seigneur avec sagesse* créa *et acheva* les cieux et la terre. Cf. Roger Le Déaut, *Targum du Pentateuque I. Genèse* (Sources Chrétiennes 245; Paris 1978), 74, note 1. Pour ces identifications entre sagesse et Torah, voir M. Küchler, *Frühjüdische Weisheitstraditionen* (OBO 26; Göttingen Fribourg, 1979), 33–45.

[20] L'ouverture du livre est capitale, au propre comme au figuré, car la conclusion actuelle de ce livre de sagesse affirme que son auteur a enseigné la connaissance au peuple (Qoh 12,9–11).

texte d. *Pesikta de Rav Kahana* ה[21]
Rabbi Samuel bar Isaac a dit: les sages voulaient mettre en geniza le livre de Qohélet parce qu'ils y trouvaient des paroles qui penchent du côté de l'hérésie.
Ils ont dit: Salomon était-il obligé de s'exprimer ainsi: *Réjouis-toi, jeune homme dans ta jeunesse! Et que ton cœur soit heureux aux jours de ta tendre jeunesse et suis les chemins de ton cœur et la vue de tes yeux* (11,9a)?
Moïse a dit: *Vous ne chercherez pas à suivre votre cœur et vos yeux* (Nb 15,39) et Salomon dit: *suis les chemins de ton cœur et la vision de tes yeux.* La courroie est-elle déliée? n'y a-t-il ni jugement ni juge? mais puisqu'il a dit: *Et sache qu'en toutes ces choses Dieu te conduira au jugement* (11,9b), alors ils ont dit: Salomon a bien parlé!

Qohélet "se sauve" en rappelant qu'il y a sur tous les actes humains un jugement de Dieu. En somme, si l'on en croit ces traditions, l'opposition des rabbins au livre du Qohélet avait un contour assez clairement défini. Son œuvre leur semblait remettre en cause premièrement l'utilité de l'effort de Torah/Sagesse et, par conséquent, le jugement divin et la rétribution de tous les actes humains, y compris des actes non directement visés par la Torah. Et finalement, cette double remise en cause signifiait aussi mettre en doute l'inspiration divine de la Torah, laquelle demande explicitement de la part de Dieu une soumission à la Loi et assure qu'il y a un jugement divin pour tous les actes humains. Il me semble que c'est en ce sens que les 'disciples des sages', associant Torah et Sagesse, ont pu parler, à propos du Qohélet, d'une "tendance à l'hérésie", et c'est probablement là le fond de l'opposition au livre.

Les trois principaux motifs d'exclusion d'un livre hors de la sphère de la sainteté sont: l'hérésie, la dimension profane du contenu et la date tardive (Ben Sira et au delà; cf. *t.Yadayim* II, 13). La dimension de sagesse profane ("non dite dans l'Esprit Saint") du contenu ne fut affirmée que par Rabbi Shimeon ben Menasyah vers la fin du 2ème siècle (texte b.) et l'argument de la date tardive n'entre pas en ligne de compte pour un livre attribué à Salomon. La tradition selon laquelle les sages ont voulu rejeter le livre du Qohélet parce qu'ils y voyaient une tendance à l'hérésie, si elle n'est pas inventée, ne peut que viser l'époque des dernières hésitations sur le statut de Qohélet. C'est la tradition la plus largement attestée dans les textes et elle est transmise par plusieurs Amoras palestiniens de la fin du 3ème siècle,[22] ce qui

[21] Mandelbaum, *PKR* ה, 135; parallèle: Motos López, *La vanidades del mundo, QohR* I, §3.1.1.1; *Lev.R.* XXVIII place ce rapport dans la bouche de Binyamin ben Levy.
[22] Aux textes de la Pesikta de-Rav Kahana cités plus haut (textes c. et d.), il faut

semble indiquer une tradition orale assez répandue. Trois éléments me semblent militer en faveur de l'ancienneté de cette tradition: a) la large attestation de cette tradition; b) l'audace d'un soupçon d'hérésie sur un livre déjà classé parmi les Écritures Saintes (voir note 4); c) le fait que les trois points suspectés d'hérésie, non seulement sont très cohérents entre eux (valeur des efforts de Torah, jugement de Dieu sur nos actes et rétribution), mais touchent au cœur du message du livre aussi bien que du principe pharisien qui veut que toute Écriture Sainte soit en accord avec les exigences de la Torah. Nous verrons plus loin que les passages qui ont fait difficulté au point d'être corrigés touchent justement à la possibilité pour l'être humain de fructifier dans le chemin de la sagesse, alors que tout le livre de Qohélet reflète un doute à ce sujet.

Un texte de la Mishna résume bien ce qu'est un hérétique pour les 'disciples des sages'.

texte e. *m.Sanhedrin* X, 1[23]
Pour tout Israël il y a une part dans le monde qui vient, car il est dit: *Et ton peuple ce sont tous des justes, à tout jamais ils hériteront la terre; rejeton de mes plantations, œuvre de mes mains pour être glorifié* (Is 60,21).
Et voici ceux qui n'ont pas de part au monde qui vient:

Celui qui dit: "il n'y a pas de résurrection des morts [dans la Torah]",[24]

et (celui qui dit): "la Torah n'est pas du ciel",

et l'épicurien.

Ce texte anonyme, à la suite duquel on mentionne les ajouts de maîtres comme Aqiba, reflète probablement un consensus assez large. Les trois catégories de ceux qui n'ont pas de part "au monde qui vient" sont intimement liées entre elles et présentent, dans une grande cohérence de vue, les vérités fondamentales de la théologie du Judaïsme pharisien:

1. La vie du 'monde qui vient' garantit la rétribution ultime de nos actes par Dieu.
2. L'inspiration divine de la Torah garantit un guide sûr de nos actes.

---

ajouter dans le même recueil la Piska כד (שובה, 370–371), Levitique Rabbah et Qohelet Rabba déjà indiqués plus haut, à la note 16, dans lesquels on a plusieurs exemples de ces traditions; puis: Pesikta Rabbati 18a; Yalkut Shimoni תתקסו; Midrash Mishle כה; Midrash Ha-Gadol sur Gn 47,28.

[23] Albeck, סדר נזיקין, 202.

[24] Albeck signale en note que certains manuscrits n'ont pas ces derniers mots: מן התורה.

3. L'idée de providence unit les deux principes précédents; Dieu prenant intérêt à la vie des humains et à leur agir. Une idée refusée énergiquement par Épicure, qui, justement, voulait libérer l'être humain de son inquiétude d'une existence personnelle après la mort et niait que les dieux exercent le moindre contrôle sur les affaires humaines.[25]

Ce n'est évidemment pas un hasard si l'épicurien (אפיקורוס) est devenu, dans le Judaïsme pharisien, la désignation par excellence de l'hérétique.[26] Quant au Qohélet, lorsqu'il semble relativiser les fruits qu'un humain peut tirer de ses efforts de sagesse, il n'est pas étonnant qu'il ait été senti comme prononçant "des paroles qui tendent du côté de l'hérésie".[27] Car une fois établie l'identification entre Sagesse et Torah, entre disciple de la sagesse (תלמיד חכם) et homme de la Torah, l'idée même que la découverte de la sagesse ne soit pas une chose sûre et certaine (cf. Qoh 7,23), aussi bien que la suggestion que nos efforts pour rejoindre cette sagesse ne sont pas vraiment récompensés (texte c.), cela revenait à "délier la courroie" (texte d.), c'est-à-dire à dénouer la nécessaire relation entre l'autorité divine de la révélation et la rétribution de nos actes. Il y a donc une grande homogénéité entre les diverses raisons d'opposition au livre que nous venons de lire.

[25] A. A. Long, *Hellenistic Philosophy: Stoics, Epicureans, Sceptics* (London, 1986), 41–45. L'étroite connexion entre les idées de providence, de jugement et de rétribution de nos actes est illustrée par le fameux dialogue entre Caïn et Abel dans le Targum de Gn 4,8. Là-bas Caïn affirme d'abord que "le monde n'est pas régi selon le fruit des bonnes œuvres" et, devant l'opposition résolue de son frère sur ce sujet, finit par déclarer: "il n'y a ni jugement, ni juge, ni même un autre monde! Point de remise de récompense pour les justes ni de châtiment pour les méchants!"; traduction Roger Le Déaut, *Targum du Pentateuque*, 102–104.

[26] Même si M. Jastrow (*A Dictionary of the Targumim*, New York, 1950, 104), peu fiable en général dans les questions historiques, affirme que la relation de ce mot au philosophe grec serait une coïncidence. Cette coïncidence aurait été si heureuse qu'elle aurait encouragé l'élargissement de la racine פקר au point qu'on y puisse retrouver le nom d'Épicure . . . Mais il est bien plus probable que le Judaïsme pharisien, qui se trouvait si proche des idées du stoïcisme et de la corrélation étroite entre le Logos divin et la conduite humaine ait rapidement vu dans l'épicurisme son exact opposé; voir par ex. M. Hengel, *Judaism and Hellenism* (London, 1974), I, 173s.

[27] Voici ce que Kaufman Kohler pouvait encore écrire au tout début du 20ème siècle dans l'article "Wisdom" de la *Jewish Encyclopedia*, (537b): "The Book of Ecclesiastes, written by some Sadducean pessimist under the influence of Greek Epicureanism and skepticism, reflects the impressions made by a worldly wisdom no longer permeated by the spirit of the Torah, so that the Solomonic wisdom, which had lost sight of the ethical ideal, was mocked and shown to be a failure".

Malgré la forte opposition qu'il rencontra, le livre fut finalement accepté comme faisant partie des ouvrages de Salomon qui, avec les Proverbes et le Cantique des Cantiques, ont été dits dans l'Esprit Saint;[28] cela sans doute en grande partie grâce à l'autorité de l'école de Hillel. Cependant, le texte transmis dans le milieu des 'disciples des sages' accommode, au moyen de quelques corrections, les doutes les plus graves que Qohélet avait jetés sur l'effort de sagesse. Le livre est entré dans le canon des Écritures Saintes, mais au prix de quelques coups de canif qui ont laissé des cicatrices sur le texte protomassorétique. Je vais essayer d'en montrer quelques exemples.

3. *L'inaccessible sagesse: Qoh 7,23b–24*

G	M
εἶπα Σοφισθήσομαι,	אָמַרְתִּי אֶחְכָּמָה
καὶ αὐτὴ ἐμακρύνθη ἀπ' ἐμοῦ	וְהִיא רְחוֹקָה מִמֶּנִּי
μακρὰν ὑπὲρ ὃ ἦν	רָחוֹק מַה־שֶּׁהָיָה
καὶ βαθὺ βάθος,	וְעָמוֹק עָמוֹק
τίς εὑρήσει αὐτό;	מִי יִמְצָאֶנּוּ

De substantielles différences entre le texte grec (G) et le texte massorétique (M) apparaissent dans la synopse qui précède. La différence la plus nette est dans le découpage du texte. En M la première phrase ne recouvre que les deux premières lignes: "J'ai dit: Je vais acquérir la sagesse et elle était loin de moi." En G cette première phrase se continue jusqu'à la troisième ligne: "J'ai dit je vais acquérir la sagesse mais elle s'est éloignée de moi au delà de toute réalité." Ce découpage en G, qui fait de la troisième ligne un complément de la phrase, est lié à la lecture en verbe fini du deuxième mot de la deuxième ligne. En M ce mot est un adjectif féminin: רְחוֹקָה, mais dans *la très littérale* version grecque du livre,[29] on trouve un verbe

[28] *t.Yadayim* II, 14 rappelle la tradition juive selon laquelle Salomon a écrit de nombreux autres textes de sagesse et de nombreux cantiques (3000 proverbes et plus de 1000 cantiques!); ce qui justifiait, somme toute, qu'on ait à discerner parmi ses œuvres celles qui étaient inspirées et celles qui relevaient de son seul talent. Au-delà de l'autorité de l'école de Hillel, on a peine à imaginer que les maîtres du Judaïsme pharisien aient été insensibles à la manière si particulière du Qohélet de dévoiler l'essentiel par le biais du paradoxe et de l'apparente contradiction. Forme de dévoilement du vrai qui convient si bien au Judaïsme et par laquelle ce livre du Qohélet est, malgré sa voix si particulière, en consonance avec le reste de la révélation biblique et avec la réception juive de la révélation.

[29] On a souvent parlé à propos du Qohélet en grec d'une première tentative

conjugué: ἐμακρύνθη dont l'équivalent hébraïque probable est: רָחֲקָה "elle s'est éloignée" ou: "elle s'est tenue loin". En effet G Qoh, qui se tient au plus près de son texte source, aurait probablement présenté un adjectif s'il avait lu comme M ici, car il présente très régulièrement un adjectif pour les adjectifs qu'on trouve en M. De plus, en Qoh 3,5 il traduit l'infinitif du même verbe (לִרְחֹק) par la même voix passive du même verbe (μακρύνω). La lecture de ce verbe (רָחֲקָה) est complétée par la lecture du premier mot de la troisième ligne (רָחוֹק) comme un adverbe (μακρὰν) déterminant ce verbe.

En G, l'ensemble de cette phrase, qui couvre les trois premières lignes de notre synopse, présente des nuances significatives par rapport à M:

> εἶπα Σοφισθήσομαι, καὶ αὐτὴ ἐμακρύνθη ἀπ' ἐμοῦ μακρὰν ὑπὲρ ὃ ἦν
>
> *Je me suis dit: "Je vais acquérir la sagesse" mais elle s'est éloignée de moi plus que toute réalité.*

Dans l'hébreu, tel que nous le lisons en M, le cohortatif אחכמה "je vais devenir (un) sage", laisse clairement entendre le mot de חכמה "sagesse", qui a été mentionné juste avant dans l'introduction du v. 23a, il n'a donc pas besoin de reprendre le mot pour dire qu'elle est loin. Le traducteur l'a bien compris et, lui aussi, a laissé implicite le sujet du verbe, dans le but de suivre au plus près son texte source qui, sur ce point, ne semble pas différer de M.

Ainsi donc, dans le modèle hébreu que traduit G, la sagesse est sujet d'un verbe d'éloignement, elle se dérobe à celui qui la cherche! L'affirmation est plus que gênante pour la canonisation du livre!

---

d'Aquila. Une étude fouillée cherchant à établir la validité de cette idée se trouve dans le remarquable ouvrage de A. H. McNeile, *An Introduction to Ecclesiastes with notes and appendices* (Cambridge, 1904), 115–134. Cette hypothèse d'un premier Aquila a été soutenue par un certain nombre d'auteurs, notamment Barthélemy (*Les Devanciers d'Aquila*, 32–33). Mais l'objection détaillée de K. Hyvärinen (*Die Uebersetzung von Aquila*, Uppsala, 1977, 88–107) obligera certainement à réévaluer les relations de G Qoh avec les traductions littéralistes et révisions de la Bible grecque. Pour une discussion récente, voir F. Vinel, *L'Ecclésiaste* (La Bible d'Alexandrie 18; Paris, 2002), 26–29 et sa bibliographie: 11, § 8. Voir aussi, d'une manière plus générale, la discussion sur les rapports entre Aquila et cette forme de traduction apparentée à καιγε en Lester L. Grabbe, "Aquila's Translation and Rabbinic Exegesis," *JJS* 34 (1982), 527–536; Olivier Munnich, "Contribution à l'étude de la première révision de la Septante," *ANRW* 20 (1987), 190–220; André Paul, "La Bible grecque d'Aquila et l'idéologie du judaïsme ancien," *ANWR* 20 (1987), 221–245. Un résumé sur ce point en Leonard J. Greenspoon, "Recensions, Revisions, Rabbinics: Dominique Barthélemy and Early Developments in the Greek Traditions," *Textus* 15 (1990), 153–167.

En effet, si la tradition juive a naturellement vu dans Salomon le "fils de David" qui a écrit ce livre de sagesse (Qoh 1,1), c'est parce que Salomon est connu pour son activité de sagesse; cette sagesse, Salomon l'a demandée à Dieu (1 R 3,9–12), et Dieu la lui a donnée (1 R 5,9ss.). Quelle serait donc cette sagesse qui a éludé les recherches les plus assidues du Qohélet si ce n'est une sagesse toute humaine, "la seule sagesse de Salomon" et non une sagesse "dite dans l'Esprit Saint" (texte b.)?

Le texte reflété en G est d'autant plus difficile qu'il affirme que la sagesse a fui le Qohélet, s'évanouissant *au-delà même de la réalité*. En effet G, avec μακρὰν ὑπὲρ ὃ ἦν, suppose un comparatif de supériorité et suggère donc, à la 3ème ligne: רָחוֹק מִשֶּׁהָיָה ou encore: רָחוֹק מִמַּה־שֶּׁהָיָה "plus loin que la réalité".[30] Une expression renvoyant à l'ensemble des réalités existantes du monde, ici plus encore qu'en 1,9 ou 3,15.[31]

[30] Cf. Peshitta: ܝܬܝܪ ܡܢ ܟܠ ܕܗܘܐ "plus que tout ce qui existait". C'est aussi l'option de Tomás Frydrych, *Living Under the Sun: Examination of Proverbs and Qoheleth* (SVTSup 90; Leiden, 2002), 158; Frydrych voit juste lorsqu'il estime que la comparaison introduite par la préposition est de nature spatiale; par contre son explication de l'altération textuelle par métathèse du *mem* de la préposition avec un précédent *he* final n'est pas réaliste, puisqu'il n'y a pas de *he* final attesté dans l'adverbe qui précède, ni en M ni en G.

[31] Qoh 1,9 conclut les vv. 4–8, où מַה־שֶּׁהָיָה désigne tout ce qui est dans la nature à côté de tout ce qui se fait dans le monde de l'histoire (וּמַה־שֶּׁנַּעֲשָׂה); cf. T. Krüger, *Kohelet (Prediger)* (BKAT XIX; Neukirchen-Vluyn, 2000), 116. Dans cette perspective, ce qui est, c'est aussi ce qui sera (1,9), ce qui, selon R. Gordis (*Koheleth – The Man and His World* [New York, 1955], 197), signifie que "ce qui a été c'est ce qui est". Le passage du ch. 1 semble indiquer que pour Qohélet ces réalités du monde ne sont pas un ensemble statique, mais une série de réalités qui adviennent (comparer les vv. 5–7). Ici en 7,24 Gordis, à la suite de Rashi (הדברים הרחוקים שהיו ביצירת בראשית), lui donne toutefois une nuance plus statique: "all that has come into being, i.e. all that exists"; voir dans le même sens l'excellente étude de A. Schoors, "Words typical of Qohelet," in A. Schoors (ed.), *Qohelet in context of Wisdom* (BETL 136; Leuven, 1998), 23–24. Du fait "du caractère hautement philosophique du verset", Schoors considère que, sans quitter le sens dynamique qu'elle a ailleurs, l'expression doit être comprise ici, avec Barton, au sens de ce qui existe de manière stable sous toutes les réalités changeantes: "According to G. A. Barton, " 'that which exists' seems here to refer to the true inwardness of things, the reality below all changing phenomena". Françoise Vinel (*L'Ecclésisate*, 146) a choisi de lire le verbe de G à la 1ère personne sg et traduit μακρὰν ὑπὲρ ὃ ἦν par "loin de ce que j'étais". Pourtant, il me semble qu'ici, comme partout ailleurs en G Qoh, ὑπὲρ traduit la comparaison de supériorité exprimée dans l'hébreu par la préposition מן (2,7.13; 4,2.3.6.9.13; 6,3.5.8.9, etc.). Or la comparaison ne se prête pas à la traduction du verbe à la première personne. D'autre part, la traduction en 1ère personne suppose une variante dans le modèle Hébreu de G, or une telle variante ne ferait pas facilement sens. (Le fait qu'en maint passage le traducteur a choisi de

A plusieurs reprises dans son ouvrage, Qohélet montre son désespoir de pouvoir saisir un jour les fondements du réel, tout ce qui a été c'est tout ce qui sera (1,9; 3,15, passim), mais l'être humain, dans son éphémère existence au milieu du fleuve des choses qui vont et viennent, demeure dans l'incertitude (8,17; 10,14) et jamais un humain ne peut *saisir* (מצא) ni exprimer la réalité de ce que Dieu a fait (לא יוכל איש לדבר 1,8). Ici la sagesse se dérobe justement à lui par-delà la réalité changeante. Il me semble que pour le Qohélet la réalité du monde, parce qu'elle ne peut jamais être fixée dans la représentation, interdit l'accès à la sagesse (ou, du moins, toute prétention à l'avoir trouvée . . .). Si la réalité elle-même est insaisissable et demeure incompréhensible, si personne ne peut atteindre et saisir le réel (מצא), comment peut-on jamais affirmer avoir trouvé la sagesse?

Une correction du texte s'imposait à qui voulait garder le livre dans les Écritures Saintes en milieu rabbanite. Il fallait rassurer les 'disciples des sages' sur le chemin ferme de la sagesse. Le texte protomassorétique a subi deux changements importants qu'il est facile d'expliquer selon cette contrainte de la théologie rabbanite qui voit en l'activité du sage l'activité de Torah:

1. La sagesse ne fuit plus celui qui la cherche (G = וְהִיא רָחְקָה), mais au moment où le Qohélet s'est décidé à acquérir la sagesse, il a constaté qu'elle était loin de lui (M וְהִיא רְחוֹקָה). C'est du moins une nouvelle lecture qui est ouverte par la forme de M, car il ne s'agit pas pour le correcteur de réformer le livre (qu'il désire préserver parmi les choses saintes en Israël!), mais d'y introduire la possibilité d'une lecture orthodoxe, comme le montre bien le *Midr.Qoh.* cité plus haut (texte c.) où un suffixe est suffisant pour rendre possible une lecture orthodoxe.

2. Second changement dans le texte protomassorétique: la réalité profonde qui ne se peut saisir est placée dans une seconde phrase (M v. 24), séparée de la première qui parlait de la difficile quête de la sagesse. Cette seconde phrase évoque, comme en écho, le mystère insondable de l'univers, et ne se trouve plus dans une relation logique nécessaire avec la première.

traduire מה־שהיה par un aoriste ou un parfait, est purement contextuel. Ici, le contraste entre une tentative subjective dans le passé [εἶπα σοφισθήσομαι – καὶ αὐτὴ ἐμακρύνθη] et la réalité qui demeure imposait naturellement l'imparfait.)

En effet, au lieu d'un complément circonstanciel de la première phrase (G), M lit à la troisième ligne de la synopse une nouvelle phrase:

רָחוֹק מַה־שֶּׁהָיָה וְעָמֹק עָמֹק מִי יִמְצָאֶנּוּ

Ce qui existe est loin et profond, profond, qui le trouvera ?

Ainsi, M présente deux affirmations séparées, même si elles demeurent côte à côte: (a) "la sagesse était bien loin lorsque je me suis mis à sa recherche"; et (b) "la réalité du monde est d'une profondeur insaisissable?".[32] On pourrait donc parfaitement comprendre que la sagesse, elle, était bien loin au commencement du chemin de Qohélet et quant aux fondements de la création, ils sont, eux, inaccessibles.

Nous avons vu que les 'disciples des sages' ne pouvaient envisager que la recherche de la sagesse soit illusoire, car c'eût été reconnaître qu'une vie toujours plus poussée dans la connaissance de la Torah serait illusoire. Ils ne pouvaient certes pas non plus admettre que la sagesse se refuse d'elle-même à l'être humain qui la recherche alors que toute leur vie était fondée sur une sagesse, la Torah, qui s'adresse à l'être humain et demande d'être reçue par lui.[33] Il est donc significatif que le texte du Qohélet, dans le seul passage où il met en scène la sagesse comme se faisant totalement inaccessible à celui qui la cherche, ait été corrigé.

Il est également éclairant qu'un texte comme Qoh 8,17 n'ait suscité aucune correction de ce genre. En effet, du strict point de vue que nous avons dégagé pour ces corrections, 8,17 ne fait pas difficulté. Non seulement l'impossibilité de trouver concerne là-bas, spécifiquement les mystères de ce que Dieu a fait, les réalités du monde, et non la sagesse dans les affaires humaines, mais le sage existe bel et bien. Et, même s'il ne peut affirmer connaître tous ces mystères, Qohélet le met en scène, acceptant implicitement le sage dans la réalité

[32] G ne commence une seconde phrase qu'à la quatrième ligne: καὶ βαθὺ βάθος, τίς εὑρήσει αὐτό "Et profond est l'abîme, qui le comprendra?" Ce qui signifie que le traducteur a lu les quatre derniers mots ainsi: וְעָמוֹק עֹמֶק מִי יִמְצָאֶנּוּ. (Pour rendre le dernier suffixe, la tradition manuscrite grecque est divisée entre pronom neutre et féminin voir *BHQ, Megilloth*, 95*.) Pour le sens de מצא—εὑρίσκω, cf. A. R. Ceresko, "The Function of Antanaclasis *ms'* "to find" // *ms'* "to reach, to grasp" in Hebrew Poetry, Especially in the Book of Qoheleth," *CBQ* 44 (1982), 551–569, spécialement 565–567.

[33] S'il ne fallait citer qu'un exemple: Dt 4,6 "Vous la garderez et la mettrez en pratique car *elle est votre sagesse* et votre intelligence aux yeux des peuples . . . qui diront *c'est un peuple sage* . . .".

humaine : "et si le sage affirme savoir . . ." (וְאִם־יֹאמַר הֶחָכָם לָדַעַת). C'est aussi à cette distinction entre la connaissance des mystères du monde d'une part, et la sagesse d'autre part, qu'a travaillé le correcteur du texte tel que nous le trouvons en M Qoh 7,23–24.

4. *Sagesse ou présomption du "sage" ? Qoh 8,1 et 7,19*

a) Qoh 8,1

G	M
Σοφία ἀνθρώπου	חָכְמַת אָדָם
φωτιεῖ πρόσωπον αὐτοῦ,	תָּאִיר פָּנָיו
καὶ ἀναιδὴς προσώπῳ αὐτοῦ μισηθήσεται	וְעֹז פָּנָיו יְשֻׁנֶּא

Les différences entre M et G portent, à la troisième ligne, sur la vocalisation et l'interprétation de ועז ainsi que sur le verbe final du verset: ישנא.

M peut se comprendre plus ou moins ainsi: *la sagesse d'un homme illumine son visage et la dureté de son visage est changée.* Je dis "plus ou moins", car c'est le seul passage de la Bible où le mot עֹז, qui signifie 'force', 'puissance', aurait un sens négatif et, surtout, serait doté d'une autre valeur sémantique. Les traducteurs sont d'ailleurs bien en peine pour traduire l'expression: עֹז פָּנָיו, hésitant entre différentes conjectures sémantiques: 'dureté', 'sévérité', 'austérité'.[34] Et ce n'est pas un hasard si Qoh 8,1 est la seule référence biblique mentionnée par les dictionnaires pour ce sens particulier du mot. (Le sens proposé étant plus une conjecture pour accommoder la lecture du verset qu'une véritable information lexicale.) Dans tous les cas, M met ici en évidence l'effet positif de la sagesse qui illumine le visage d'un homme et "transforme" la "dureté"/la "sévérité" de son visage.

Au lieu du substantif עֹז de M, G, appuyé ici par toutes les versions,[35] a lu un adjectif substantivé, probablement: עַז.[36] S'il est original ce mot est à lui seul, sans פָּנָיו, le sujet probable du verbe final. Certes,

---

[34] *BDB* 739a, *HALAT* 761b. La Bible de la Pléïade traduit: "la sévérité de son visage"; la Bible de Jérusalem: "son air austère"; TOB "la dureté de son visage"; Colombe: "la sévérité de sa face"; King James "the boldness of his face"; Revidierte Luther Bibel: "ein freches Gesicht".

[35] G: ἀναιδὴς *impudent, insolent*; Peshitta et Targum: חציף, même sens; Vulgate atteste un adjectif substantivé . . . mais sur la base du mot force: *potentissimus*.

[36] Comme en Ps 59,4.

il existe une expression עַז פָּנִים (Dt 28,50 et Dan 8,23) signifiant 'arrogant', 'impudent', dont s'est inspiré le traducteur grec pour interpréter le passage qui lui était obscur. Mais ce sont les deux mots עַז פָּנִים qui, *ensemble*, signifient 'impudent' ce qui rend superflu et même incongru le suffixe 3 m. sg. de פניו. De plus, dans cette lecture qu'en fait G, le parallélisme est légèrement tronqué, dans la mesure où le visage n'est plus au centre du parallélisme. G sort d'ailleurs du parallélisme et lit ici le *pual* du verbe שׂנא (μισηθήσεται): "et l'impudent de visage sera haï".[37] Le traducteur a été aidé en cela par la présence d'un *alef* au lieu d'un *he* à la fin du verbe, selon la confusion fréquente en hébreu tardif entre les verbes *lamed-he* et *lamed-alef*.

Si l'on veut garder l'adjectif substantivé des versions (עַז), nettement supérieur à la lecture de M, et préserver le jeu du parallélisme, il faut lire avec Jérôme cet adjectif substantivé comme le sujet du verbe final et פָּנָיו "son visage" comme le complément du verbe:[38]

וְעַז פָּנָיו יְשַׁנֵּא

et l'arrogant changera son visage

Le sens de cette expression 'changer son visage' est bien illustré par deux passages de Ben Sira en hébreu où 'changer son visage' signifie 'se trahir', 'laisser paraître involontairement ce que l'on est réellement' (Sir 12,18; 13,25):

אם לטוב ואם לרע לב אנוש ישנא פניו

Que ce soit pour le bien ou pour le mal, le cœur de l'homme changera son visage.

Ce qu'est vraiment un être humain (son cœur) "change son visage", se fraye un chemin jusqu'aux apparences du visage. Le Qohélet nous rappelle que si un homme est arrogant, impudent, même s'il siège au conseil, il le donnera à voir sur son visage; sa présomption le fera se trahir, "il changera son visage".

Dans le cadre du parallélisme antithétique de Qoh 8,1b, cela donne: "La sagesse d'un homme illumine son visage, mais le présomptueux se trahira." Certes, l'adjectif est fort, puisqu'il dit plutôt 'l'impudent' que 'le présomptueux', mais c'est que, se trouvant au

[37] Vinel, *L'Ecclésiaste*, 148.

[38] Mais Jérôme applique le pronom suffixe au sage nommé dans le premier membre du parallélisme: *et potentissimus faciem illius commutabit.*

milieu d'un conseil, celui qui usurpe le rôle du sage exerce une forme d'hubris. On aurait donc ici un avertissement sérieux devant toute présomption à jouer le rôle du sage. "La sagesse illumine le visage d'un homme" signifie dans ce contexte (vv. 2–4), comme l'a bien vu Gordis,[39] 'trouver grâce', 'être en faveur' au conseil. Certes, dit le Qohélet, la sagesse d'un homme le fait apprécier et le rend gracieux et capable d'obtenir l'attention favorable de ses pairs et du roi, mais toute présomption de sagesse se verra bien vite. Un excellent avertissement pour introduire le travail du conseiller à la cour (vv. 2–4). Mais le transmetteur de M ne comprend pas qu'on puisse mettre sur un même niveau le sage illuminé par sa sagesse et l'arrogant qui se trahit. Il ne voit pas, ou ne veut pas voir, qu'il puisse y avoir un rapport entre celui qui est plein de sagesse et la présomption de celui qui est plein de son rôle de "sage".

Cette forme du verset trouve une confirmation dans le contexte immédiat. En effet, cette nouvelle perspective sur le texte de 8,1b laisse entrevoir une autre correction du texte tel que nous le trouvons en M Qoh 8,1a.

M Qoh 8,1a offre: מִי כְּהֶחָכָם וּמִי יוֹדֵעַ פֵּשֶׁר דָּבָר "Qui est comme le sage et qui connaît la solution d'une affaire?" De nombreux témoins offrent une forme différente pour le second mot du verset. Une leçon attribuée à Aquila offre: τίς ὧδε σοφός, laquelle semble corriger un texte grec corrompu par assimilation au prochain verbe du parallélisme (τίς οἶδεν).[40] Symmaque lit τίς οὕτως σοφός suivi par la Vulgate *quis talis ut sapiens*. Norbert Lohfink suggère en conséquence de corriger M et de lire la question suivante: מִי כֹּה חָכָם "Wer ist hier weise?".[41] On peut aussi lire à la suite de Symmaque: "Qui est à ce

---

[39] *Koheleth – The Man*, 276 : " 'To light up, make the face shine', means "to show oneself gracious toward"; cf. Num 6:25b and Dan 9:17. Here the stress is not upon the gracious act, but upon *appearing* gracious toward one's associates in court . . ."

[40] Sur une suggestion de G. Bickell, Sebastian Euringer (*Der Masorahtext des Koheleth kritisch untersucht* [Leipzig 1890], 93–94) a montré de manière assez convaincante que le grec ancien devait être semblable à la leçon attribuée à Aquila ici; c'est aussi l'avis argumenté de McNeile, *An Introduction to Ecclesiastes*, 164.

[41] N. Lohfink, "War Kohelet ein Frauenfeind? Ein Versuch, die Logik und den Gegenstand von Koh. 7,23–8,1a herauszufinden," in M. Gilbert (éd.), *La sagesse de l'Ancien Testament* (BETL 51; Leuven, 1979), 261, n. 10 (= *Studien zu Kohelet* [SBAB 26; 1998], 33. Je ne pense pas qu'on puisse dire que M est ici la *lectio difficilior* (Krüger, *Kohelet*, 272) pour le seul motif que son Hébreu est rendu moins élégant. J'ai moi-même fait cette erreur en *BHQ*, *Megilloth*, 97*, car on a encore trop tendance à confondre la difficulté formelle du côté de M avec la difficulté réelle du

point sage? et qui connaît la solution d'une affaire?". Symmaque, suivi ici encore par Jérôme, peut avoir lu un texte correctement divisé ou avoir restauré spontanément la division originelle de ces premiers mots du verset.

Cette correction, jointe à celle que j'ai proposée pour la seconde partie du verset, rend une grande homogénéité à un verset dont les commentateurs se demandent souvent s'il forme un tout cohérent:

Qui est à ce point sage ? et qui connaît la solution d'une affaire ?
La sagesse illumine le visage d'un homme, mais le présomptueux se trahira !

Qohélet avertit contre toute présomption de sagesse dans le cadre des affaires officielles (vv. 2–4). Mais, dira-t-on, pour quelle raison le milieu rabbanite, tel que nous l'avons évoqué plus haut dans ses rapports à la Torah comme sagesse, aurait-il éprouvé le besoin de corriger ainsi Qoh 8,1? Si on se rappelle que la raison d'être des 'disciples des sages', c'est justement de donner l'interprétation juste de l'Écriture, alors le פשר דבר, pour eux, devait représenter non pas d'abord la solution d'une affaire inextricable, mais plutôt l'interprétation de la parole.[42] S'il en était bien ainsi, on peut comprendre qu'ils aient voulu effacer la possibilité de lire le passage de la façon suivante: "Qui est à ce point sage qu'il puisse donner l'interprétation de la parole?".

Crenshaw a montré que la question rhétorique: "(Qui est assez sage) et qui connaît la solution d'une chose?" implique, au regard des questions parallèles dans le livre (2,19; 3,21; 6,12), que personne ne sait.[43] Il était donc d'autant plus urgent pour les correcteurs du

---

texte; pour la simple raison qu'on a passé des années à résoudre les difficultés formelles du texte massorétique de la Bible pour s'assurer qu'on connaît bien l'hébreu biblique . . . (voir note 52, plus loin). D'un point de vue littéraire, M représente évidemment ici la *lectio facilior*.

[42] Cf. Motos López, *La vanidades del mundo*, 375 et 377, *QohR* VIII, §§1.1.1. et 1.3.1.

[43] J. L. Crenshaw, "The expression *mî yôdeaʿ* in the Hebrew Bible," *VT* 16 (1986), 274–288. Contrairement à P. Beentjes, " 'Who is Like the Wise?' Some Notes on Qohelet 8,1–15," in A. Schoors (ed.), *Qohelet in the Context of Wisdom* (BETL 136; Leuven, 1998), 304–315. Beentjes estime qu'on n'est pas ici en présence d'une question rhétorique, mais une question qui attend sa réponse positive. De façon ingénieuse, il suggère de lire le mot אֲנִי au début du v. 2 comme la réponse à cette question ("Who is like the wise ? . . . I (Qohelet) do"). Une solution qui, dit-il, "a l'avantage de préserver le texte hébreu tel que nous l'avons" ("Who is Like the Wise?," 306). En fait ce mot est absent de la très littérale version grecque et de la Peshitta et je ne suis pas sûr que ce soit un "avantage" pour la connaissance du texte de la Bible hébraïque de choisir toujours autant que possible "le texte hébreu tel que nous l'avons", c'est-à-dire M. En fait, cette réponse intéressante se heurte

texte attesté par M de rétablir que le sage connaît effectivement le פשר דבר, le sens véritable de la parole. Par un simple redécoupage des mots, ils le font réapparaître: "Qui est comme le sage et connaît l'interprétation de la parole?".

On aurait donc un verset originel bien dans la teneur du Qohélet qui avertit vigoureusement de ne pas trop se prendre pour un sage, ici sous l'effet stimulant d'un siège dans le conseil des affaires politiques. Et on retrouve, ici aussi, ces corrections minimes qui veillent, comme en Qoh 7,23–24 à la possibilité pour les 'sages' de connaître la juste interprétation à donner en face de la Parole.

b) Qoh 7,19

J'aimerais citer un dernier texte à l'appui de cette lecture du verset 8,1 et à la possibilité qu'il ait été corrigé selon les explications données ci-dessus. Il s'agit de Qoh 7,19. Ce dernier texte est intéressant aussi en ce qu'il montre qu'on ne peut pas traiter les témoins textuels en les classant trop systématiquement. Tout témoin est susceptible de transmettre des leçons anciennes et même originales à côté de leçons d'époques diverses. M Qoh 7,19 offre la phrase suivante:

הַחָכְמָה תָּעֹז לֶחָכָם מֵעֲשָׂרָה שַׁלִּיטִים אֲשֶׁר הָיוּ בָּעִיר

Le cas est traité en *BHQ* et je ne donne ici que les éléments les plus importants pour notre propos.[44] M lit le *qal* de עזז qu'on traduit généralement par 'rendre fort'; par ex. Pléïade: "La sagesse rend le sage plus fort que dix gouverneurs dans la ville" (= TOB, BJ, KJ, NIV, Revidierte Luther Bibel). On peut se demander si ce sens transitif, qui facilite la logique du verset, est approprié à ce verbe intransitif.[45] Une lecture intransitive de M a été proposée par un certain

à la difficulté majeure que représente l'incise de 8,1b. En effet, entre la question de 8,1a ("Qui est comme le sage? et qui connaît la solution d'une affaire") et la "réponse" אני ("moi") au début du v. 2, se trouve tout le v. 8,1b. Quelle que soit la forme qu'on choisit pour 8,1b, cette phrase en parallélisme crée une rupture qui rend bien difficile de lire אֲנִי comme la réponse à la question de 8,1a; d'autant plus que la question rhétorique est habituelle en Qohélet. Un auteur qui aurait voulu rompre avec ses habitudes n'aurait pas pris le risque qu'on lise de nouveau ici une question rhétorique si telle n'était pas son intention. Au contraire, il aurait placé la réponse à la suite de la question et, surtout, ne l'aurait pas isolée dans un mot unique aussi curieusement placé.

[44] *BHQ*, *Megilloth*, 93*–94*.

[45] Les références de Gordis (*Koheleth – The Man*, 269) sont trop réduites et trop fragiles pour établir le sens transitif du verbe; en Ps 68,29 le complément direct du

nombre de commentateurs: "la sagesse est forte pour le sage plus que dix gouverneurs". Mais, comme le dit Gordis, le sens du passage est ainsi un peu forcé.[46]

De fait, si on ne peut lire le verbe au *qal,* il ne restait qu'à le lire au *hifil,* une lecture intolérable pour la piété de la sagesse. En effet le *hifil* signifie 'se rendre dur', 'se fermer' (Pr 21,29), 'prendre un air de défi, d'insolence' (Pr 7,13) – avec le complément פנים qu'on peut mettre en relation avec l'expression עז פנים de Dt 28,50 et Dan 8,23. On trouve le *hofal* pour un homme en Ben Sira hébreu 10,12, ce qui nous autorise peut-être à lire לחכם comme le complément direct de ce *hifil* ici. Qohélet irait-il jusqu'à dire que la sagesse est source d'arrogance et de fermeture pour le sage? C'est une possibilité qu'il faut envisager sérieusement, à condition de bien comprendre qu'il met en garde le disciple de la sagesse auquel il s'adresse (vv. 16–18) contre les dangers de présomption sur le chemin de l'apprenti de la sagesse.[47]

Je propose donc de lire comme original de 7,19: "La sagesse rend plus présomptueux le sage que dix gouverneurs dans la ville", une phrase qui convient bien au contexte. Qohélet recommande de ne se faire ni trop juste, *ni trop sage* (וְאַל־תִּתְחַכַּם יוֹתֵר), ni trop méchant (7,16–18). Puis il avertit des risques d'arrogance que la sagesse fait courir au disciple (7,19), "car", dit-il, "d'homme juste il n'en est pas sur la terre, qui fasse le bien et ne pèche pas" (7,20). La logique qui va du v. 19, tel que nous le lisons, au v. 20 développe, dans une critique du 'sage' qui s'égare dans sa présomption, la logique des vv. 16–18, qui est introduite au v. 16a par l'apposition de la prétention à la justice et de la prétention à la sagesse. Le retour à un original plus mordant à l'égard des 'sages'; plus adapté aussi, me semble-t-il, à la perspective de Qohélet et à la syntaxe du verset, permet de retrouver une forte homogénéité littéraire du contexte immédiat.[48]

---

verbe n'est pas du tout assuré (M. E. Tate, *Psalms 51–100* [WBC 20; Dallas, 1990], 161, 168) et Pr 8,28 est souvent corrigé en Piel par les chercheurs.

[46] *Koheleth – The Man,* 269. Voir les tentatives de clarification de cette phrase ambivalente chez Krüger, *Kohelet,* 256.

[47] Voir en particulier le v. 16: וְאַל־תִּתְחַכַּם יוֹתֵר "et ne te fais pas trop sage"! . . . Cela semble être l'attitude idéale du sage aux yeux de Qohélet: demeurer un apprenti, conscient de la relativité de la sagesse qu'un humain peut acquérir le temps d'une existence éphémère dans un monde toujours en mouvement.

[48] Le parallélisme entre trop 'juste' (צַדִּיק) et trop 'sage' (חָכָם) du v. 16 qu'on retrouve aux vv. 19–20 est encore confirmé par le parallélisme opposé du v. 17 entre 'l'impie' et 'l'insensé'. La restauration du texte au v. 19, si elle est juste, fait apparaître Qoh 7,15–20 comme une unité nettement délimitée et très homogène.

Ici, les témoins qui s'écartent de M attestent d'une correction plus importante encore pour protéger le sage dans sa relation à la sagesse, puisque 4QQoh[a] présente un texte corrigé par le simple ajout d'un *resh* (תעזר): "la sagesse aidera le sage plus que dix gouverneurs dans la ville". Un texte reflété par G (βοηθήσει). Probablement que le scribe ne voulait pas laisser aux hasards de la prononciation, l'image de la sagesse dans le livre du Qohélet.

Conclusions

Un des arguments des 'disciples des sages' contre l'inspiration du Qohélet est celui des contradictions qu'il contiendrait. Mais il apparaît que les contradictions qui pouvaient réellement les embarrasser sont de nature théologique et touchaient à ce qui pouvait mettre le livre en porte-à-faux avec les exigences de la Torah véritable sagesse de Dieu.[49] De ce point de vue, la forme massorétique du livre semble être l'aboutissement d'une série de retouches que le livre ne pouvait manquer de subir dans le Judaïsme Torah-centrique du tournant de l'ère chrétienne.

Comme on peut s'y attendre, tous les témoins anciens du livre sont porteurs d'éléments originaux aussi bien que de corrections ou d'erreurs scribales. Parmi ces témoins, M, du fait du conservatisme intelligent et de la relative érudition du milieu qui l'a transmis, reste le témoin privilégié du livre. Mais M est aussi porteur d'une série de retouches qui, à la différence des autres témoins, répondent à un projet global d'édition du Tanakh.

La préparation d'un apparat critique pour la *Biblia Hebraica Quinta* m'a semblé confirmer ce que d'autres expériences dans la critique du texte de l'Ancien Testament (entre autres dans le cadre plus global du projet de la *BHQ*) me laissait entrevoir, à savoir:

1. Le milieu de sa canonisation a exercé une réelle influence sur le livre du Qohélet, et probablement sur les autres livres bibliques.

2. On ne peut jamais préjuger de la qualité d'une variante, même lorsque celle-ci apparaît dans une forme de texte attestant une révision systématique ou une certaine liberté du traducteur ou du transmetteur par rapport à son original. Tout témoin ancien peut

[49] La question des contradictions est elle-même de nature théologique d'ailleurs; voir par ex. l'article du présent auteur: "Crispations théologiques et accidents textuels dans le TM de Jérémie 2," *Biblica* 76 (1995), 25–52.

transmettre, même à son insu, des leçons originales.[50] Inversement, même un témoin très conservateur, comme M ou G Qohélet, peut transmettre des interventions tardives sur le texte (7,19!). La recherche du texte original du Tanakh exige de se garder soigneusement des idées scolaires et simplificatrices qui résultent des caractérisations globales des divers témoins. Ces caractérisations sont une aide utile mais elles constituent un danger permanent pour l'objectivité scientifique en critique textuelle. Même si l'on classe inévitablement les versions anciennes de la Bible hébraïque dans un schéma chronologique et un réseau d'influences relativement bien établies (bien du travail reste à faire en ce domaine!), la possibilité de trouver *dans chacune d'entre elles* des leçons anciennes et même originales devrait toujours rester à l'esprit du chercheur dans le domaine de la critique textuelle.

3. Du fait de sa très grande qualité, les crispations sur le texte massorétique restent aujourd'hui encore très fortes parmi les chercheurs; les commentaires et les éditions de la Bible s'en ressentent. J'ai déjà évoqué ailleurs quelques uns des motifs de ces crispations,[51] en particulier la confusion plus ou moins inconsciente entre langue originale et texte original de la Bible;[52] le fait aussi que M reste la

[50] Ainsi, il me paraît intéressant de noter que la réponse des 'sages', différenciant les efforts de sagesse et les efforts en général (texte c.), s'appuie sur un suffixe ("*son* effort") qui a de fortes chances d'être une leçon secondaire; la Peshitta ne l'atteste pas; cf. *Biblia Hebraica Quinta, Megilloth* (Stuttgart, 2004), 65*. On notera d'ailleurs que l'autre explication orthodoxe de ce verset s'appuie sur une forme textuelle qui pourrait bien être tardive elle aussi par rapport à la forme attestée par la Peshitta. On trouve cette explication dans le Talmud de Babylone (*b.Shabbat* 30b): "Rav Yehudah, le fils de Rav Shemouel bar Shilat, a dit au nom de Rav: Les Sages ont voulu mettre le livre de Qohélet en geniza parce que ses paroles se contredisent entre elles. Et pourquoi ne l'ont-il pas mis en geniza ? Parce que son commencement sont des paroles de Torah et sa fin des paroles de Torah. Son commencement des paroles de Torah puisqu'il est écrit: *Quel profit pour l'homme de tout son effort qu'il fait sous le soleil ?* (Qoh 1,3). Ce que l'école de Rabbi Yannay a commenté: c'est sous le soleil qu'il n'en a pas (de profit), avant le soleil il en a." Cette interprétation fait allusion à l'existence de la Torah *avant* la création du soleil (*b.Pesahim* 54a; *b.Nedarim* 39b). Une forme variante (et facilitante à mon avis) dit "sous le soleil il n'en a pas (de profit), mais au-dessus du soleil il en a" (Mandelbaum, *PRK* ח, 136. lignes 1–3). Dans tous les cas, il se trouve que le texte de la Peshitta ancienne n'avait probablement pas ici l'expression usuelle "sous le soleil" (= édition de Leiden), mais "sous le ciel"; voir *BHQ, Megilloth*, 65*.

[51] Goldman, "Crispations théologiques et accidents textuels," 27–31.

[52] Nous avons tous appris la langue du Tanakh dans le texte massorétique et celui-ci reste notre principale référence, mais c'est le travail de la critique textuelle que de libérer cette référence d'un préjugé de prééminence absolue. J'ajouterais aujourd'hui que, non seulement nous avons appris la langue, mais "pire encore", si j'ose dire, beaucoup de chercheurs enseignent la langue hébraïque, apprenant

base première de toute traduction et édition de la Bible. Il me semble qu'il faut y ajouter une confusion qui règne au sujet de la qualité de la transmission du texte massorétique. On a en effet tendance à étendre à la période pré- et protomassorétique la remarquable fidélité de transmission du texte massorétique proprement dit. Or, même pour le Pentateuque, la comparaison des textes de Qumran avec le Grec, le Samaritain et les Targums palestiniens montrent à l'évidence la fluidité de la transmission du texte jusqu'au premier siècle de l'ère chrétienne aussi bien que l'existence de types textuels.

Il relève sans aucun doute des tâches de la critique textuelle de rouvrir le dossier de la Bible hébraïque à partir des versions anciennes et des témoins hébreux non massorétiques. Ceci, en les confrontant au texte massorétique *en tant que témoin particulier* de la Bible hébraïque au milieu d'autres témoins anciens. La chose peut sembler évidente en son principe, mais la pratique des exégètes et des critiques est loin de respecter ce statut de M. Il est certain que M étant le plus souvent la base hébraïque du travail du chercheur, la démarche qui consiste à l'évaluer au regard des versions anciennes exige, outre de la rigueur et de la prudence, une certaine somme d'audace et d'intuition – ce ressort de toutes les sciences! – afin de sortir la critique textuelle de la Bible hébraïque d'un "conformisme massorétique", confortable mais improductif. Cette même audace et cette intuition des chercheurs des sciences naturelles, qui ne se contentent pas de la partie visible et manifeste de leur objet. Aussi est-ce pour moi une joie réelle que de dédier cette modeste étude au Père Adrian Schenker dont les recherches sur la Septante, *en tant que témoin du texte de la Bible hébraïque*, manifestent, outre une érudition magistrale, les grandes qualités du savant authentique.

depuis des années aux débutants à résoudre les difficultés que le texte massorétique peut présenter. En sorte que la familiarité avec la langue du texte massorétique, qui est l'une des grandes qualités de l'exégète, peut devenir un vrai problème en critique textuelle en ce qu'elle fige la capacité d'intuition en direction d'autres formes du texte.

TEXTUAL WITNESSES AND SACRIFICIAL TERMINOLOGY IN LEVITICUS 1–7

Innocent Himbaza

I began to work on the Book of Leviticus within the *BHQ* project only in April 2003, and for this reason I cannot provide a general view of its text as a whole. The sacrificial terminology in Leviticus 1–7 is one of the first problems I encountered when I was comparing the textual witnesses with M.

Sacrificial terminology is not only a problem for the versions, but also for the Hebrew witnesses. However, there is a difference, since it is not possible to have confusion between the terms in the Hebrew witnesses. The question is whether the differences between M and the other Hebrew textual witnesses are only a textual matter, or whether they represent a development of the sacrificial conception in Leviticus 1–7.[1]

1. *Hebrew Witnesses*

The Masoretic Text (M)

The text of M is that of the Leningrad Codex (EBP. I B 19a in the Russian National Library, St. Petersburg), which I have consulted in microfilm. As far as the first seven chapters of Leviticus are concerned, the microfilms are clear and legible. The *BHS* edition follows this text. The other manuscripts used in the *BHQ* project for Leviticus (British Library Oriental Ms. 4445, EBP. II B 17 in the Russian National Library, St. Petersburg, and Sassoon 507)[2] contain some minor differences in the Masorah, but their text is the same.

[1] For the historical and literary context of Leviticus 1–7 see U. Dahm, *Opferkult und Priestertum in Alt-Israel: Ein kultur- und religionswissenschaftlicher Beitrag* (BZAW 327; Berlin, 2003), 184–229.

[2] At times I also use manuscript EBP. II B 10 in microfilm copy.

The Samaritan Pentateuch (Smr)

Many studies of Smr have shown its reworking, in different ways, of a Hebrew text which was somehow different from the proto-Masoretic text.[3] In Leviticus 1–7 we observe some of the well known characteristics of Smr. It shows harmonizations of the text and corrections of the style of M. In some cases, however, the textual differences can be explained by a different *Vorlage*.[4] As regards the sacrificial terminology in Smr, there are some significant differences.

In 1:15 and 5:9 Smr reads אל קיר המזבח as compared with על קיר המזבח in M. This expression occurs only here in the Bible. Elsewhere in M, the preposition על with the word קיר is used in the meaning of 'against' (1 Kgs 6:5; Ezek 5:10; 23:14; Amos 5:19). It is also well known with the word מזבח in the same sense (Exod 24:6; 29:16, 20, 36). Smr may have changed this preposition under the influence of the expression אל יסוד מזבח which occurs more frequently in Leviticus (Lev 4:30, 34; 5:9; 8:15; 9:9). Thus there may be a harmonization of 5:9 with 1:15. However, we know that G uses the same preposition as Smr in 1:15. Can we say that Smr avoids sprinkling the blood "on" the altar as some scholars think G does?[5]

In 2:11 Smr reads the verb תקריבו (= G) as compared with תקטירו in M. Each reading has been interpreted as preferable. What is interesting is that the reasons given to prefer one reading over another are either textual or dogmatic.[6]

In 5:5 Smr reads יחטא as compared with יאשם in M. The use of the term אשם in Lev 5:1–13 is problematic since this kind of offering is explained only from 5:15.[7] According to Adrian Schenker, in the following verse (5:6) the sacrifice אשם is in the form of the sacrifice חטאת.[8] Alternatively, according to Jacob Milgrom the word אשם of

---

[3] For a recent synthesis see: A. Tal, "Le Pentateuque Samaritain," in A. Schenker and P. Hugo (eds.), *L'enfance de la Bible hébraïque: L'histoire du texte de l'Ancien Testament à la lumiere des recherches récentes* (*MdB* 52; Geneva, 2005), 77–104; and J. Margain, "Samaritain (Pentateuque)," *DBSup* XI, col. 762–73.

[4] We often have plural readings in Smr (in accordance with G) against the singular readings in M. We also have a different place for the word עלה in 1:10, some pluses: מנחה היא in 2:1 (= G), על המזבח in 3:5, אשר מלא את ידו in 4:5 (= G), etc.

[5] G = Smr in 1:15 and G = M in 5:9. See the study of G, which has more textual differences.

[6] J. E. Hartley, *Leviticus* (WBC 4; Nashville, 1992), 27.

[7] Hartley, *Leviticus*, 69.

[8] A. Schenker, "Welche Verfehlungen und welche Opfer in Lev 5,1–6?," in H.-J. Fabry and H.-W. Jüngling (ed.), *Leviticus als Buch* (BBB 119; Berlin und Bodenheim b. Mainz, 1999), 249–261.

Lev 5:6 is equivalent to קרבנו of v. 11, denoting punishment or penalty.[9]

I observe that in Smr the problem is not the sacrificial terminology itself, but probably some details in the manner of performing the sacrifice.

The Dead Sea Scrolls

For chs. 1–7 of Leviticus we have seven manuscripts from Qumran: 4QExod-Lev[f] (4Q17), 4QLev[b] (4Q24), 4QLev[c] (4Q25), 4QLev[e] (4Q26a), 4QLev[g] (4Q26b), 11QpaleoLev[a] (11Q1), 11QLev[b] (11Q2); and one from Masada: MasLev[a] (Mas1a).[10] These manuscripts are dated between the middle of the third century B.C.E. and the middle of the first century C.E.

The manuscripts from Qumran contain some minor textual differences compared to M. Sometimes they have single readings[11] or their readings agree with Smr[12] or with G[13] or both together

[9] J. Milgrom, *Leviticus 1–16: A New Translation with Introduction and Commentary* (AB 3; New York, 1991), 303.

[10] D. N. Freedman and K. A. Mathews, *The Paleo-Hebrew Leviticus Scroll (11QpaleoLev)* (Winona Lake, Ind., 1985), 26; F. García Martínez, A. S. van der Woude, and E. J. C. Tigchelaar, *Qumran Cave 11, II: 11Q2–18, 11Q20–31* (DJD XXIII; Oxford, 1992), 3; E. Ulrich, et. al., *Qumran Cave 4, VII, Genesis to Numbers* (DJD XII; Oxford, 1994), 143–144, 177–181, 189–192, 197–198, 203–204; S. Talmon, *Hebrew Fragments from Masada* (Masada VI, Yigael Yadin Excavations 1963–1965, Final Reports; Jerusalem, 1999), 36–39; H.-J. Fabry, "Das Buch Levitikus in den Qumrantexten," in Fabry and Jüngling, *Leviticus als Buch*, 309–341; P. W. Flint, "The Book of Leviticus in the Dead Sea Scrolls," in R. Rendtorff and R. A. Kugler (eds.), *The Book of Leviticus: Composition and Reception* (VTSup 93; Leiden, 2003), 323–341.

[11] In 1:17 4QLev[b] reads היא against הוא אשה of M, Smr and G. In 2:1, 4QExod-Lev[f] reads ק[רבנו against קרבן of M, Smr and G. Cross (Ulrich, et al., DJD XII, 144) thinks the Qumran manuscript anticipates the same reading later in the verse.

[12] In 3:6 4QLev[e] reads לזבח השלמ]ים with Smr against לזבח שלמים of M. In 5:12 4QLev[c] reads היא with Smr against הוא of M. In 7:20, 21 4QLev[g] reads ההיא with Smr against ההוא of M. The Temple Scroll (11QTemple), which is not a biblical manuscript, shares some readings with G against M. In 7:2 the expression of M על־המזבח סביב is rendered with ἐπὶ τὴν βάσιν τοῦ θυσιαστηρίου κύκλῳ in G. We have the same reading in 11QTemple 34:8: על יסוד המזבח סביב. This expression does not occur elsewhere in M. Some differences between M on the one hand, and G and some Qumran readings on the other hand can reflect a late development in performing sacrifices, especially in the sprinkling of the blood against the altar. See *m.Mid.* 3:1; *t.Zebaḥ* 6:11. P. E. Dion, "Early Evidence for the Ritual Significance of the "Base of the Altar": [Around Deut 12:27 LXX]," *JBL* 106 (1987), 487–492.

[13] In 2:8, 4QLev[b] reads והביא with G against והבאת of M and Smr. In 3:1 it reads the plus ליהוה again with G alone.

against the readings of M.[14] The manuscript from Masada (MasLev[a]), which contains Lev 4:3–9, agrees with M.[15] Aside from these kinds of differences, the sacrificial terminology in the Dead Sea Scrolls is the same as that of M.

The only case I am interested in is the reading of 4QLev[g] in 7:25, where it reads קָרְבָּן against אשה of M, Smr, and G. The reading of these three witnesses is understood as a prohibition of eating the fat from any offering by fire (אשה). This may concern the sacrifices of Leviticus 1–3 that are not to be eaten (perhaps without the sacrifice of well-being because of Lev 7:11–18). 4QLev[g] would prohibit eating the fat from any offering at all. I consider this reading to be secondary.

2. *Greek Witnesses*

The Qumran Scrolls

There is only one Qumran scroll in Greek which contains Leviticus 1–7: pap4QLXXLev[b] (4Q120).[16] The other Qumran scroll, 4QLXX Lev[a] (4Q119), contains ch. 26. The manuscript pap4QLXXLev[b] contains some textual differences compared with G, or M and Smr.[17] The textual differences that deal with the sacrificial terminology are found in 4:7 and 5:9.

In 4:7 pap4QLXXLev[b] reads καρ]/π[ωσ]εως against ολοκαυτωματων of G (especially MSS A and B) to translate העלה of M and Smr. The reading of 4QpapLXXLev[b] is also known from some Greek manuscripts.[18]

---

[14] In 1:17 4QLev[b] reads ולא with Smr and G against לא of M. In 3:11 it reads והקטיר with Smr and G against והקטרו of M. In Lev 2:1 4QExod-Lev reads the plus מנחה היא as in Smr and G. However, Cross says that it is an secondary addition to anticipate the same expression in 2:15 (Ulrich, et al., DJD XII, 144).

[15] The only difference is the plene spelling ישפוך against M ישפך in 4:7.

[16] P. W. Skehan, E. Ulrich, and J. Sanderson, *Qumran Cave 4, IV: Paleo-Hebrew and Greek Biblical Manuscripts* (DJD IX; Oxford, 1992), 167–177.

[17] In 2:5 pap4QLXXLev[b] reads πεφυραμ]ενης[instead of the nominative form of G. In 3:4 it reads απο against επι of G (M, Smr). In 3:12 and 4:27 it reads ιαω against κυριος of G. The reconstruction in DJD IX uses Ιαω since κυριος never occurs in the extant text of this manuscript.

[18] See Skehan, Ulrich and Sanderson, DJD IX, 173, and the apparatus of the Göttingen edition by J. W. Wevers (ed.), *Leviticus* (*Septuaginta: Vetus Testamentum Graecum* II/2; Göttingen, 1986), 62–63.

In 5:9 pap4QLXXLev[b] reads αμαρτιας γαρ εστιν against αμαρτια γαρ εστιν of G to translate חטאת הוא of M. By using the genitive form in this verse, the Greek manuscript from Qumran does not identify the sin and the sacrifice for the sin as the actual Septuagint does. These two cases raise the question of whether the Qumran scroll represents an earlier translation or a revision of the vocabulary.[19]

The readings of this Qumran manuscript (ca. 50 C.E.) teach us first that the so-called "Old Greek" is difficult to attain since there are different ancient readings.[20] Second, the sacrificial terminology is not always the same as in the rest of the Greek manuscript tradition.

The Septuagint (G)

G is the main witness among the versions. Its sacrificial terminology brings us back to the consideration of its readings as one of the ancient textual witnesses.[21] The situation of G is different from that of the Hebrew witnesses and the way its resolves the question posed by different technical terms in Hebrew is very interesting. For some scholars, the misunderstanding of the Hebrew text by the translator occasionally resulted in a confused text.[22] For others, G is a literal translation from one of the available textual traditions in circulation in the Second Temple period.[23]

In Leviticus 1–7 the Hebrew text uses various technical terms. Some of them are used only in one chapter while others are present through the whole text. The translator has progressively resolved the problem of sacrificial terminology.

---

[19] Comparing 4QLXXLev[a] with G, Metso and Ulrich argue that the G tradition has revised according to later vocabulary usage. See S. Metso and E. Ulrich, "The Old Greek Translation of Leviticus," in Rendtorff and Kugler, *The Book of Leviticus*, 266–267.

[20] Some readings of the Qumran scrolls antedate the other Greek manuscripts we know. See Metso and Ulrich, "Old Greek Translation of Leviticus," 264.

[21] S. Daniel, *Recherches sur le vocabulaire du culte dans la Septante* (Etudes et commentaires 61; Paris, 1966); U. Rapallo, *Calchi ebraici nelle antiche versioni del "Levitico"* (Studi Semitici 39; Roma, 1971); Metso and Ulrich, "Old Greek Translation of Leviticus," 247–268.

[22] J. W. Wevers, *Notes on the Greek Text of Leviticus* (SBLSCS 44; Atlanta, 1997), xvii.

[23] P. Harlé and D. Pralon, *Le Lévitique: Traduction du texte grec de la Septante, Introduction et Notes* (La Bible d'Alexandrie 3; Paris, 1988), 24, 49. However, the authors accept that "cependant, un vocabulaire technique plus diversifié, parfois mystérieux, dans le Lévitique hébreu oblige les traducteurs à des adaptations, à des innovations, parfois à des hésitations" (ibid., 25). Metso and Ulrich, "Old Greek Translation of Leviticus," 251, 261, 267. On the last page the authors argue that "the OG of Leviticus is the most literal of the Pentateuchal translations".

In chapter 1 the rendering of קרבן does not raise any problem, because it is always translated by δῶρον(-α).[24] In vv. 9, 13, 17, where the words אשה and עלה are together, אשה is θυσία and עלה is κάρπωμα. However, in vv. 3, 6, 10, where the word עלה is used alone, G reads ὁλοκαύτωμα although κάρπωμα is used in vv. 4, 14.

In chapter 2 the word עלה is not used, but we have a new word, מנחה, which is rendered by θυσία. Yet the word אשה is also used in this chapter, and G continues to render it with θυσία. The interesting case is in v. 3, where the two words מנחה and אשה are used, and both are rendered by the same word θυσία. Afterwards the word מנחה is used several times in vv. 4–9 alone, and it is rendered with θυσία. This is probably why the word אשה, which is used in the end of v. 9, is rendered with κάρπωμα. This word was used in ch. 1 to translate עלה. Since then (2:9) the word אשה is κάρπωμα, whereas מנחה is θυσία.

The verb קטר was rendered with ἐπιτίθημι in 1:9, 17 and 2:9. However, in 2:11 the same verb is rendered with προσεγγίζω. One cannot say that G has a different *Vorlage*, as is the case for Smr, which reads תקריבו two times. If that were the case, the translator would have used the same verb twice. The fact that he uses two different verbs (προσφέρω for הקריב)[25] may reflect the same *Vorlage* as M. From 2:16 through ch. 3, the same Hebrew verb הקטיר is rendered with ἀναφέρω.

In ch. 3 the word מנחה is not used, but we have a new word זבח which is rendered again by θυσία (vv. 1, 6, 9).[26] However, the word עלה recurs, and it is rendered with ὁλοκαυτώματα (v. 5) while אשה continues to be rendered with κάρπωμα (vv. 3, 5, 9, 11, 14, 16; 6:10, 11).[27]

One has the impression that the difficulties of the sacrificial terminology have been resolved by the end of ch. 3, but in ch. 4 the same

---

[24] This is so even outside Leviticus. See also Daniel, *Recherches sur le vocabulaire*, 120. For this author the lack of a translation of קרבן in 3:14 and 4:28 would be interpreted as an intentional omission (ibid., 122–125).

[25] See Rapallo, *Calchi ebraici*, 146.

[26] The word מזבח is normally translated by θυσιαστήριον, thus the word זבח is well translated by θυσία.

[27] In the same chapter, the words ואת שתי הכלית are translated differently in 3:4, 10, 15. In v. 4 the Greek manuscript tradition agrees on καὶ τοὺς δύο νεφρούς while in vv. 10, 15, we have two different readings: καὶ ἀμφοτέρους τοῦς νεφροὺς (Origen and some MSS) and καὶ τοὺς δύο νεφροὺς (Aquila, Theodotion, Symmachus and some MSS).

The translators of Leviticus in *La Bible d'Alexandrie* explain the reason why אשה is not always rendered by κάρπωμα: "on ne saurait «apporter» ou «amener» un *kárpōma*; le *kárpōma*, «apanage du Seigneur», ne se détermine comme tel que sur problem recurs. Here, a new word, חטאת, is used. I observe that in vv. 4, 10, 18, the word עלה is translated one more time by κάρπωσις instead of ὁλοκαυτώματα, which we have in vv. 7, 24, 25, 29, 30, 33, 34. And in 4:35 the word אשי (in this spelling) is rendered by ὁλοκαύτωμα as well. One can think either of different translators, or of the same translator who took a long time between the translation of Leviticus 1–3 and the following chapters, so that he forgot how he had resolved the problem of sacrificial terminology earlier on.

In 4:3 the nouns and the verbs of the roots אשם and חטא are rendered with the same root in G: ἁμαρτάνειν – ἁμαρτία. This root continues to be used in this manner in G until 4:27.

In 4:21, 24 the Hebrew חטאת הוא is rendered by ἁμαρτία ἐστίν. One would think that the Greek word changes its meaning as in Hebrew: 'sin' or 'sin offering', according to the context. We have the same situation in 6:18a.[28] However, in 4:29 ראש החטאת is rendered with κεφαλὴν τοῦ ἁμαρτήματος, את־החטאת with τὴν τῆς ἁμαρτίας, and in v. 33 ראש החטאת is rendered with κεφαλὴν τοῦ τῆς ἁμαρτίας. In vv. 25, 34, דם החטאת is rendered with αἵματος τοῦ τῆς ἁμαρτίας. In these cases the translator does not want to identify the animal sacrificed for the sin with the sin itself.[29]

The cases of 4:21, 24, on the one hand, and of 4:29, 33, on the other hand, show that there was not a systematic harmonizing revision of G. Indeed, seeing that the word ἁμαρτία does not mean the sin and the sin offering (as חטאת does in Hebrew), a revision would correct the reading of 4:21, 24.

In 5:3 ואשם is rendered with καὶ πλημμελήσῃ, as in 4:27. However, in 5:4 we again have καὶ ἁμάρτῃ. The same root is used in v. 5 for two different Hebrew roots, as in 4:3.

In 5:6 the two Hebrew roots (אשם and חטא) are translated by two different roots in Greek. However, in v. 7 G uses again one root to translate them.[30]

l'autel; il ne se manipule pas comme une offrande ou un holocauste." (Harlé and Pralon, *Le Lévitique*, 40). However, in 3:3, 9 the word אשה is κάρπωμα although it is "brought". See the comment of Harlé and Pralon on 3:3 (*Le Lévitique*, 92). In 3:14 the Hebrew and the Greek do not agree on the action performed: to present (Hebrew); to incense (Greek).

[28] Daniel, *Recherches sur le vocabulaire*, 303, sees the same confusion in 6:19, 20 where the feminine pronoun is used.

[29] Rapallo, *Calchi ebraici*, 124.

[30] Here the apparatus of *BHS* wonders if the *Vorlage* of G did not contain the root חטא. However, my point is that the translator had not yet resolved the problem of rendering the sacrificial terminology.

In 5:9 the expression דם החטאת is αἵματος τοῦ περὶ τῆς ἁμαρτίας. The translator avoids identifying the sacrificed animal and the sin. We have the same case in 6:23 where כל־חטאת is πάντα τὰ περὶ τῆς ἁμαρτίας. However, in the same verse (5:9) and in vv. 11, 12 G reads ἁμαρτία γάρ ἐστιν for (הי״א) חטאת הוא (cp. 7:5, where אשם הוא is περὶ πλημμελείας ἐστίν).

From 5:15 on, the sacrificial terminology is almost completely stabilized. The word חטאת is ἁμαρτία and אשם is πλημμελεία. However, in 5:17, where three different roots are used, the third one, עון, is also translated by ἁμαρτία in G. Moreover, in 6:19 the participle המחטא is ὁ ἀναφέρων. For the first time, the translator avoids using the root of the word 'sin' (ἁμαρτάνω).

In 7:37, 38, where all kinds of offerings are used together,[31] G has all the sacrificial terminology in place and the translations do not raise any problems. I notice that G, like M, alludes by anticipation to the sacrifice of investiture, which is explained only in chapter 8.[32]

To summarize, I observe that the translator had difficulties finding his way. Sometimes he uses the same root to translate two different Hebrew roots. A Hebrew term is not always rendered with the same word in Greek, even when it is used in the same context. When a new sacrificial word in Hebrew is used, I observe a confusion of the translator, and this confusion is resolved after some hesitation. The sacrificial terminology of the three first chapters seems to be established from Lev 2:9 onwards, and that of chapters 4–7 is resolved after 6:20. I have remarked on a double confusion in the utilization of two words חטאת and אשם. First, the words used to render one of them are also used for the other. Second, the manner of explaining the meaning of sin and/or sin offering is neither well established nor harmonized in G. This analyis is valid, of course, only if the translator read the same text as that which we have in M. What is astonishing is that when a problem is resolved, the translator does not come back to control and to harmonize his translation. It is also to be noted that the supposed late corrections of G did not affect this situation.[33] It seems likely that the Greek text of Leviticus has not been

[31] All the known sacrifices are not described in Leviticus 1–7. See A. Marx, "The Theology of the Sacrifice According to Leviticus 1–7," in Rendtorff and Kugler, *The Book of Leviticus*, 103–120, esp. 103.

[32] On this point, there is no intention of the translator of G to correct M as we see in the Targum.

[33] These kinds of observation show that G of Leviticus is well preserved. I have observed a similar phenomenon nowadays, when the revisers of an edition of the

deeply reworked. However, we should recall that, as pap4QLXXLev[b] has shown, the manuscript tradition of G is not unified.

I think that the translation of the Hebrew sacrificial terminology in Greek is to be understood with respect to internal considerations of the Book of Leviticus.[34] For my present opinion, I do not need to consider that the choice of the words in Exod (29:25, 41) has influenced the choice of the words in Leviticus.[35] The translator seems to have no previous work on the same problem to help him. He progressively tries to resolve the problem of the sacrificial terminology. Thus, we should not study the terminology of G of Leviticus in reference to that of Exodus. We have also observed that in some cases, G is in accordance with Smr against M. This can reflect a different *Vorlage* used by the translator of G.

3. *Aramaic Witnesses: The Targumim (T)*

Targum Onqelos (T°) is the principal text employed in this study, and a reading without further attribution can be assumed to be taken from T°. However, I have also used Neophiti (T[N]), Pseudo-Jonathan (T[J]) and fragmentary manuscripts 110, 264 and 440.[36]

Bible correct one aspect or another (orthography, division of the text) without alluding to the conformity of the text base. See I. Himbaza, *Transmettre la Bible. Critique exégétique de la traduction de l'AT: le cas du Rwanda* (Rome, 2001), 242–245.

[34] According to Daniel, *Recherches sur le vocabulaire*, 155, in relation to the word אשה it is possible to identify a "doctrine d'exégèse et de traduction" in Leviticus while "aucun principe directeur n'apparaît . . . dans le livre de l'Exode, quant à la traduction de ce mot." For the other differences between Exodus and Leviticus see Daniel, *Recherches sur le vocabulaire*, 242–244 on עלה, 278 on שלמים, and 302–303 on חטאת.

[35] *Contra* Harlé and Pralon, *Le Lévitique*, 39. Indeed, the terms used in Genesis and Exodus are not always the same as in Leviticus. In Genesis 10 G translates זבחים ועלות by ὁλοκαυτώματα καὶ θυσίας. To reverse those two words in Greek (as some MSS do) would have been to assimilate to what we read here in Leviticus. In Exod 29:18, G translates עלה by ὁλοκαύτωμα and אשה by θυσίασμα. In Exod 29:25, 41 אשה is rendered with κάρπωμα. In Exod 29:28 מזבח is θῦμα (see Gen 43:16 where that word renders טבח). In Exod 29:41 (מנחה) and 42 (עלה) G uses the same word θυσία to render the two different Hebrew words. The word אשה, which is between them in v. 41, is rendered with κάρπωμα.

[36] A. Díez Macho (ed.), *Leviticus* (Biblia Polyglotta Matritensia, Series IV: Targum Palestinense in Pentateuchum, L. 3; Madrid, 1980). The Targum of Leviticus from Qumran (pap4QtgLev) need not concern us since it contains only ch. 16. See R. de Vaux and J. T. Milik, *Qumran Grotte 4, II, I. Archéologie, II. Tefillin, Mezuzot et Targums (4Q128–4Q157)* (DJD VI; Oxford, 1977), 86–89. For the Targum of Smr, Abraham Tal does not mention any problem of rendering the sacrificial terminology. See A. Tal, *The Samaritan Targum of the Pentateuch. A Critical Edition, Part III: Introduction* (Texts and Studies in the Hebrew Language and Related Subjects VI; Tel Aviv, 1983).

As we have already observed in G, the Targumim identify the two Hebrew words קרבן and אשה, both being translated by קורבן (or the plene spelling קורבנא). A typical example is found in 3:14 where they are used together, the Targumim repeating the same word. I cannot imagine a different Hebrew *Vorlage* that would have read קרבן instead of the אשה of M. The other technical words are rendered differently, as in Hebrew.[37]

In 2:8 the two Hebrew verbs והקריבה and והגישה are rendered by the same verb in Aramaic ויקרבינה, even though the vocalization is not exactly the same.[38]

In ch. 4 the sin offering חטאת is usually rendered with חטתא. However, the verb of the same Hebrew root (חטא vv. 2, 3) is rendered in a different way (חוב). This is also the case in T^{J}, but T^{N} uses the root חטא for the same verb, as in M (4:2; 5:1, 15). In 4:3 of T^{N}, however, the word is יתחייב. This shows us that T^{N} is also not consistent in its terminology. I observe that the Targumim avoid confusing the sin and the sin offering by rendering those words by חובתא and חטתא. This is the case in 4:14. The Hebrew הכהן המשיח of 4:3, 5, 16 is כהנא רבא in T° and T^{J} or כהנא דמתרבי (דמתרבה) in T^{N}.[39] This rendering reflects an evolution of terminology in the Targumim. In 4:22 T^{N} uses the same expression (כהנא דמתרבי) for the Hebrew נשיא, while we have רבא בעמיה in T^{J} and רבא in T°.

In 5:1, 2 the three different roots חטא, עון, and אשם are rendered by the same root חוב in T° and T^{J}, while T^{N} reads תחטא for the Hebrew חטא in 5:1. In 5:5 T° reads יחוב for יאשם of M even though this was how it rendered יחטא (תחטא) of M in ch. 4. Did the translator of T° read the Hebrew יחטא as in Smr? If it is the case, then we are facing a textual case, not a translational problem.

In 5:6 the text of M אשמו ליהוה על חטאתו is rendered חובתיה לקדם יוי על חובתיה in T°. I observe that the two different Hebrew roots are identified. Note the same case in v. 7 where אשמו אשר חטא of

[37] It should be noted that there is an omission in the translation of Grossfeld in 2:2, if it is based on the same text as that of Leiden edition. At the end of the verse we read "which is received with acceptance before the Lord" for קורבן דמיתקבל ברעוא קדם יוי omitting the word "sacrifice" (קורבן). Therefore, the translation would have been "(It is) a sacrifice received with acceptance before the Lord". See 2:9; 3:5.

[38] S uses two different verbs as in M.

[39] In 4:3 G also renders the same expression by ἀρχιερεύς, but with ὁ ἱερεὺς ὁ χριστὸς in 4:5, 16.

M is rendered חובתיה דחב in T°,[40] presupposing the Hebrew חטאתו אשר חטא as in 5:10, 14. The other Targumim diverge from the reading of T°. In 5:6 T^N reads אשמיה קדם ייי על חובתיה and T^J reads אשמיה לקדם ייי מטול חובתיה. In 5:7 the two Targumim read respectively אשמיה דאתחייב and אשמיה דחב.

From 5:15 on, the Hebrew אשם is rendered with אשמה in T°, but the verb אשם continues to be rendered by חב (v. 17). An interesting mixture is visible in 5:19, where the verb and the substantive are used together. The root אשם in T° is limited to the substantive to designate the reparation offering. Thus, the Targumim correct M, which uses the root אשם before 5:15.[41]

According to T°, the substantive אשמה is used only from 5:15. We may then understand that until 5:13 we are dealing with the sin offering (חטאת), not the reparation offering (אשם). However, the other Targumim, T^N and T^J, do not correct M since they use the word אשמיה before 5:15. We should conclude that in this case, then, that T° contains targumisms that the other Targumim do not have. In 5:23 the two Hebrew verbs יחטא ואשם are יחטי ויחוב in T° and the distinction is made in the following verses (6:10, 7:7). Thus I posit that the choice of T° is intentional until 5:13.

In 7:37, the word מלואים is קורבניא in the Targumim.[42] In T° the plural form seems to be specific to that kind of offering (Exod 29:22, 26, 31, 34; Lev 8:22, 26, 28, 29, 31, 33).

We may conclude that, in the Targumim, there are also some difficulties in rendering the sacrificial terminology. Aside from the identification of the two nouns אשה and קרבן, on the one hand, and the verbs הקריב and הגיש, on the other hand, we have noticed also the identification of the three verbs חטא, עון, and אשם in 5:1, 2.

I have argued that T° corrected the Hebrew text intentionally, since it uses the substantive אשמיה only from 5:15, while M uses it

[40] G reads ἁμαρτίας αὐτοῦ, supposing חטאתו.

[41] This interpretation is shared with V. M. McNamara observes other shared interpretations in the Palestinian Targumim (Neofiti I and Fragmentary Targumim) and the Greek versions. See M. McNamara, "Reception of the Hebrew Text of Leviticus in the Targums," in Rendtorff and Kugler, *The Book of Leviticus*, 269–298, esp. 278–279.

[42] For the targumist, to fill the hand of a priest means to offer a sacrifice. In Exod 28:41 the expression ומלאת את־ידם (you will ordain them, lit. "you will fill their hand") is ותקריב ית קורבנהון (and offer their sacrifices) in T°. See the discussion in B. Grossfeld, *The Targum Onqelos to Exodus: Translated with Apparatus and Notes* (ArBib 7; Wilmington, Del., 1988), 81.

already in 5:6. In some cases, the Targumim reflect an interpretation or a misunderstanding of the Hebrew text. The targumic tradition is not unified since all the Targumim do not have the same readings. Sometimes, T° contains targumisms while other Targumim are in accordance with M. Thus, when the Targumim have a different reading from that of M, it is not easy to decide in favor of a textual case or a translational/exegetical one.

4. *Syriac Witness: The Peshitta (S)*

For the Syriac witness, I use the Leiden edition of S.[43] The Peshitta text of Leviticus is considered as follows by the editor: "Thus it must be admitted at the outset that Leviticus does not provide a significant or interesting range of variant readings which would suggest the reconstruction of a Hebrew text different from the MT."[44] Elsewhere he argues: "The source for Leviticus is clearly the pre-Masoretic Hebrew Bible text tradition: no manuscript variants suggest otherwise".[45]

Scholars have already pointed out the problem of the sacrificial terminology of S in Leviticus.[46] Hebrew technical terms are not consistently translated by the same words in S. However, even though the changes in S are described as intentional,[47] it seems to me that

---

[43] For my own interest I compare it with the English translation of George Lamsa which contains some minor textual differences. G. M. Lamsa, trans., *Holy Bible, From the Ancient Eastern Text* (San Francisco, 1975). In 2:2 Lamsa's translation has the plural "Aaron's sons the priests" as does M, instead of the singular reading in the Leiden edition. In 2:14 the word "pure" to qualify the ears is a plus peculiar to the translation. In 4:10 the translation maintains the differences according to the Hebrew השלמים and העלה while S reads twice ܕܒܚܬܐ.

[44] D. J. Lane (ed.), "Leviticus," in *Leviticus, Numbers, Deuteronomy, Joshua* (*The Old Testament in Syriac, According to the Peshitta Version* I/2 and II/1b; Leiden, 1991), XI.

[45] D. J. Lane, "The Reception of Leviticus: Peshitta Version," in Rendtorff and Kugler, *The Book of Leviticus*, 299–322, esp. 309.

[46] D. W. Gooding, *The Account of the Tabernacle* (Cambridge, 1959); D. J. Lane, " 'The Best Words in the Best Order': Some Comments on the 'Syriacing' of Leviticus," *VT* 39 (1989), 468–479. Some other problematic passages are known, such as 11:14–19, where twenty different kinds of birds become only fifteen in S. See J. A. Emerton, "Unclean Birds and the Origins of the Peshiṭta," *JSS* 7 (1962), 203–211. For the other examples see, D. J. Lane, *The Peshiṭta of Leviticus* (Monographs of the Leiden Peshitta Institute 6; Leiden, 1994), 116–126.

[47] Lane, *The Peshiṭta of Leviticus*, 85, explains the differences between M and S by "the translation process rather than the basic text." Having studied only Leviticus 1–7, I have the impression that the translator of S was influenced by neither G nor T in the choice of sacrificial terminology. For further discussions see A. Vööbus, *Peschitta und Targumim des Pentateuchs. Neues Licht zur Frage der Herkunft der Peschitta aus*

the way of rendering the sacrificial terminology creates a confusion which was not entirely controlled by the translator.

In Leviticus 1–7 the word עלה usually is rendered with ܥܠܬܐ while ܩܘܪܒܢܐ is used for the Hebrew קרבן. However, in 1:4 the Hebrew עלה from the expression ראש העלה is rendered by ܩܘܪܒܢܗ.[48] In v. 6 it becomes ܢܟܣܐ, in 7:2, 8 (second occurrence) it is rendered with ܢܟܣܐ ܫܠܡܐ, and in 7:37 with ܢܟܣܐ ܕܥܠܬܐ. Even ܣܠܩ ܚܛܗܗ is used for the first occurrence of 7:8. In this verse it seems that the translator avoids the Syriac term ܥܠܬܐ that he uses especially for השלמים in 7:11, 13, 14, 15, 18, 21, 33. The expression זבח שלמים is rendered with ܕܒܚܐ ܫܠܡܐ in 3:1, 3 (cf. 6:5; 7:20, 29, 32, 34) and with ܕܒܚܐ ܕܥܠܬܐ in 3:6, 9 and 4:10 (cf. 7:13, 14).[49]

The word אשה is also rendered with ܩܘܪܒܢܐ. Thus those two Hebrew words, אשה and קרבן, are identified in S.[50] In the typical verse 3:14, where they are used together, S twice reads the same word: ܩܘܪܒܢܗ ܩܘܪܒܢܐ for קרבנו אשה of M.

The new word מנחה of ch. 2 is rendered many times with ܣܡܝܕܐ. However, in 2:14, 15 it is three times rendered with ܩܘܪܒܢܐ. Thus the word ܩܘܪܒܢܐ is used in S to render the Hebrew קרבן, אשה, מנחה and אשם.[51]

In chs. 5–7 all the occurrences of the substantive אשם are rendered by ܩܘܪܒܢܐ, except in 7:5 where we have ܚܛܗܐ. This translation can be explained by the presence of the word אשה, which is

dem Altpalästinischen Targum (Stockholm, 1958); Lane, *The Peshitta of Leviticus*, 89–98; P. B. Dirksen, "The Old Testament Peshitta," in M. J. Mulder (ed.), *Mikra* (Assen/Maastricht & Philadelphia, 1988), 225–297; C. E. Morrison, *The Character of the Syriac Version of the First Book of Samuel* (Monographs of the Leiden Peshitta Institute 11; Leiden, 2001), 98–134; P. B. Dirksen and A. van der Kooij (eds.), *The Peshitta as a Translation* (Monographs of the Leiden Peshitta Institute 8; Leiden, 1995), note especially in the same volume Y. Maori, "Methodological Criteria for Distinguishing between Variant Vorlage and Exegesis in the Peshitta Pentateuch," 103–120, R. P. Gordon, "Variant Vorlage and the Exegetical Factor: Response to Y. Maori," 121–125, Y. Maori, "Remarks on R. P. Gordon's Response," 126–128.

[48] As in 3:2, 8 where we have ראש קרבנו in M.

[49] In Exod 29:28 the expression is ܘܕܒܚ ܫܠܡܝܗܘܢ.

[50] It is the case in the Targumim.

[51] Lane has described the technique of translation in S as follows ("'The Best Words in the Best Order'," 476): "Again, if the statement about sacrifices is general, then ܩܘܪܒܢܐ is used, regardless of the Hebrew אָשָׁם, קָרְבָּן, אִשֶּׁה or חַטָּאת . . . The translator reserves distinctive technical terms for those plain instances where a specific purpose or a specific method takes the offering from the general to the particular. The principle is entirely logical: no technical term can be used until enough information has been given for the correct term to be identified."

rendered with ܩܘܪܒܢܐ in the same verse. In this case, the translator avoids identifying two different Hebrew words used side by side, even though he did it in 3:14 for קרבנו אשה of M. Indeed, in 7:7 אשם again becomes ܩܘܪܒܢܐ in S. The verb אשם is rendered with ܚܘܒ in ch. 4, while it is rendered with ܚܛܐ in ch. 5, except in 5:23 where it is rendered by ܚܘܒ. This rendering can also be explained by the presence of the Hebrew חטא rendered by ܚܛܐ in the same verse. Here again the translator avoids identifying two different Hebrew terms. The Hebrew והביא את־אשמו in 5:6, 7, 15 and והביא את־קרבנו in 5:11 are likewise rendered by ܠܚܛܐ ܩܘܪܒܢܗ.[52] Thus there is no specific term for the substantive אשם in S! Accordingly, S does not allow the reader to know that there is a special reparation offering described from 5:15.

In 7:37–38 almost all the sacrificial technical terms are used. I observe that the words אשם and קרבניהם are rendered in the same way by ܩܘܪܒܢܐ and ܩܘܪܒܢܝܗܘܢ, and the words עלה and השלמים are likewise rendered by ܥܠܬܐ. Thus in S there is a confusion until the end of the text we are studying. These two verses are the synthesis of sacrificial terminology in Leviticus 1–7. All the terms are used here except אשה. We have seven terms including a new one, מלואים, which appears in chapter 8. Altogether we have eight different sacrificial terms in M and only six in S.[53]

I am not sure that the translator wanted to create such great confusion. I really think that the logical principle described by David Lane for the translation of S is either not correct or not sufficient to explain how the sacrificial terminology is used in Leviticus 1–7 of S. It is possible that the translator wanted to resolve some problem, but as against this, he created a greater one.

5. Latin witness: The Vulgate (V)

Jerome, the translator of V, explained his translation technique in his *Epistula LVII ad Pammachium: De optimo genere interpretandi*.[54] Even

---

[52] Then the problem is to know whether one would consider Lev 5:7, where G reads τῆς ἁμαρτίας αὐτοῦ, and S ܩܘܪܒܢܐ ܕܚܛܗܗ instead of M אשמו, as a textual case or not.

[53] Lamsa's English translation has no confusion since it has eight different terms like M!

[54] See PL 22, col. 568–579. In a letter he addressed to St. Augustine, Jerome

though he did not write a commentary on the book of Leviticus itself,[55] it is possible to know about his use of sacrificial terminology in V. As scholars have already remarked, Jerome used intentionally different terms for one Hebrew term.[56] Thus, different readings in V would not necessarily suggest another *Vorlage* than M.

In general, V translates the word קרבן by *oblatio* (1:3, 10, 14, etc.), but sometimes we have *hostia* (1:2) or *victima* (3:2). This last translation, in the expression ראש קרבנו, is intentional in order to designate the animal to be sacrificed. In 1:4, 6 we have the same word *hostia*, as if the translator had קרבן, while M has עלה.[57] In 2:4 קרבן is not translated.

The word אשה, which is usually rendered by *oblatio* (1:17; 2:3, 10; 3:3, 5, 11; 7:30), is not translated in 1:9, 13; 2:2, 9. Even the expression אשה ליהוה of 2:16 is not translated. In 3:14, 16 it is rendered with *ignis* and in 3:9 with *sacrificio*. In 3:11 ליהוה לחם אשה is rendered as *in pabulum ignis et oblationis Domini*. In 7:25 אשה ליהוה is rendered by *incensum Domini* although in 7:30 אשי יהוה is rendered *oblatio Domini*.[58]

The word עלה is rendered with *holocaustum*; זבח, which is new in ch. 3, is rendered with *hostia* and עונו (5:1, 17) is rendered with *iniquitatem suam*. The translation of these words is consistently well harmonized.[59]

The word מנחה is rendered with *sacrificio* (2:1, 3, 4), but in 2:5, 11, 13 it is rendered with *oblatio*. The expressions מנחה הוא of 2:6 and מנחה in 2:8, 10 are not translated. However, מנחה הוא is rendered

alludes probably to the same writing. See PL 33, col. 261–262; Augustine, *Lettre 75,5–6*, vol. 4 of H. Barreau (trans.), *Œuvres complètes* (Paris, 1873), 539–541.

[55] P. Jay, "Jérôme et la pratique de l'exégèse," in J. Fontaine and L. Pietri (eds.), *Le monde latin antique et la Bible* (La Bible de tous les temps 2; Paris, 1985), 523–542; R. Kieffer, "Jerome: His Exegesis and Hermeneutics." in M. Saebø (ed.), *Hebrew Bible/Old Testament: The History of Its Interpretation*, vol. 1, *From the Beginning to the Middle Ages (Until 1300), Part I: Antiquity* (Göttingen, 1996), 663–681.

[56] A. Condamin, "Les caractères de la translation de la Bible par Saint Jérôme," *RSR* 2 (1911), 425–440; Rapallo, *Calchi ebraici*; G. J. M. Bartelink, *Hieronymus, Liber de optimo genere interpretandi (Epistula 57): Ein Kommentar* (Leiden, 1980), 45. For the comment on Jerome's famous principle *"non verbum e verbo, sed sensum exprimere de sensu"* (Ep. 57,V,2, see ibid., 46–47). However, this was not the only principle of Jerome. See E. Schulz-Flügel, "The Latin Old Testament Tradition," in Saebø, *Hebrew Bible/Old Testament: The History of Its Interpretation*, 642–662, esp. 654–656.

[57] See Rapallo, *Calchi ebraici*, 76–77. S supposes the same reading. Maybe this reading is a result of an interpretation to make clear that here the עלה is a still living animal, not yet a "holocaust".

[58] In 5:12 אשי יהוה חטאת הוא is changed in *in monumentum eius qui abtulit.*

[59] If we consider the case of 1:4, 6 as a result of an interpretation.

with *oblatio Domini est* in 2:15. In 6:7 (V 6:14) תורת המנחה is rendered with *lex sacrificii et libamentorum*, providing an addition.

In 4:2 the verb חטא is rendered with *peccavere*, and in 4:3 אשם is rendered with *delinquere*. The substantives, in the meaning of offerings, are rendered respectively with *pro peccato* and *pro delicto*. However, in 5:25 (V 6:6) the substantive אשמו is rendered with *pro peccato*, and the substantive ואשמו in 4:13 and the verb אשם in 4:22 are not translated. This must be judged as an omission.[60] I observe many other omissions like that of אשר חטא in 4:14, 23, probably to avoid a repetition.[61] One may judge the omission of אשמו ליהוה על חטאתו אשר חטא in 5:6 in the same way. However, this omission and that of the same word את אשמו in 5:7 allow the translator to introduce this kind of reparation offering only from 5:15, as is the case in T°. The word אשם of 5:18, rendered by *peccatus*, is not taken as an offering.

In 7:37–38 the sacrificial terminology seems clear; the text of V does not provide an identification of two different kinds of offerings as we saw in S. However, the translation of מנחה (v. 37) seems lacking in V. Its text is as follows: *37 ista est lex holocausti et sacrificii pro peccato atque delicto et pro consecratione et pacificorum victimis 38 +quam+ constituit Dominus Mosi in monte Sinai quando mandavit filiis Israhel ut offerrent oblationes suas Domino in deserto Sinai.*

On the one hand, we have noticed that the word מנחה is rendered with either *sacrificio* or *oblatio*. On the other hand, those terms also are used for other kinds of offerings: *oblatio* for קרבן and *sacrificio* for אשה. In this text *pro peccato atque delicto* seems to be the determinative complement of the word *sacrificii*.[62] However, this situation never occurs elsewhere in Leviticus 1–7. Thus I would suggest understanding *sacrificii pro peccato atque delicto* in the meaning of *sacrificii et pro peccato atque pro delicto*.[63] In that case the translation of the word מנחה in this verse is restored.

To summarize, I would say that in V the translation of some technical terms is well harmonized while confusion remains for others.[64] Some terms seem to be out of control (אשה and מנחה) since they are

[60] So Rapallo, *Calchi ebraici*, 194.

[61] We observe also that in 4:5, 6 the words הכהן המשיח and הכהן are rendered by pronouns.

[62] The English translation of V in the Douay version has "the sacrifice for sin, and for trespass".

[63] This is the reading of two manuscripts from Paris (Lat. 7) and Florence (Laur.).

[64] Similar observations have been made by P. Jay concerning Jerome's com-

rendered by different words, or some of their occurrences are not translated. However, I noticed also that the translator intentionally avoids rendering the substantive אשם in 5:6, 7 since the reparation offering is described only from 5:15 onwards in M.

6. Final Observations

For all the versions we have studied, scholars point out, on the one hand, the accuracy of the translation, and, on the other hand, the intentional changes in rendering of the Hebrew. No version renders the sacrificial terminology of M without difficulties. Can we say that the sacrificial terminology in Hebrew is richer than that of the versions? Scholars have described Leviticus 1–7 as a handbook for priests or as case-law written to systematize ritual performance.[65] However, I observe that the ritual performance is not always well systematized in the versions since some technical terms are confused.

Some witnesses share the same interpretations against M. An interesting example among others is that of T° and V, which avoid rendering the substantive אשם before Lev 5:15. Thus, the text of Leviticus seems to be well established according to M, except that doubt remains for some minor cases.

The study of the following chapters of Leviticus within the progress of the *BHQ* project shall surely allow me to have more precise and pertinent observations on the textual state of Leviticus. It is a pleasure to offer this contribution to Adrian Schenker, president of the editorial committee of the project.

mentary on Zechariah; see P. Jay, "Remarques sur le vocabulaire exégétique de Saint Jérôme," *Studia Patristica* 10 (1970), 187–189.

[65] J. W. Watts, "The Rhetoric of Ritual Instruction in Leviticus 1–7," in Rendtorff and Kugler, *The Book of Leviticus*, 79–100, esp. 94–95.

LE GREC ANCIEN DES LIVRES DES RÈGNES UNE HISTOIRE ET UN BILAN DE LA RECHERCHE

Philippe Hugo

Dans ses multiples recherches sur l'histoire du texte des livres des Rois, Adrian Schenker – éditeur de ces livres pour la *Biblia Hebraica Quinta* – émet l'hypothèse que la *Vorlage* de la Septante ancienne représente un état littéraire antérieur à celui attesté par le texte massorétique (M).[1] Dans sa dernière monographie sur le sujet, *Älteste Textgeschichte der Königsbücher*, il énonce la conclusion suivante:[2]

> An fast allen untersuchten Stellen entspricht die Textgestalt der ursprünglichen LXX einem älteren hebräischen Text als jenem, der im MT greifbar ist. Der MT als Fortsetzung des prae- und protomassoretischen Textes stellt dementsprechend eine jüngere Textgestalt dar.

La thèse de Schenker apporte une contribution déterminante au débat actuel sur l'histoire du texte hébreu du livre des Rois[3] et ouvre

[1] A. Schenker, *Älteste Textgeschichte der Königsbücher: Die hebräische Vorlage der ursprünglichen Septuaginta als älteste Textform der Königsbücher* (OBO 199; Fribourg-Suisse/Göttingen, 2004); id., *Septante et Texte massorétique dans l'histoire la plus ancienne du texte de 1 Rois 2–14* (Cahiers de la Revue Biblique 48; Paris, 2000); id., "Junge Garden oder akrobatische Tänzer? Das Verhältnis zwischen 1 Kön 20 MT und 3 Regn 21 LXX," in A. Schenker (ed.), *The Earliest Text of the Hebrew Bible: The Relationship between the Masoretic Text and the Hebrew Base of the Septuagint Reconsidered* (SCS 62; Atlanta, 2003), 17–34; id., "Jéroboam et la division du royaume dans la Septante ancienne. LXX 1 R 12,24a–z, TM 11–12; 14 et l'histoire deutéronomiste," in A. de Pury, T. Römer, J.-D. Macchi (éds.), *Israël construit son histoire: L'historiographie deutéronomiste à la lumière des recherches récentes* (Le monde de la Bible 34; Genève, 1996), 193–236; id., "The Relationship Between the Earliest Septuagint and the Masoretic Text in the Book of Kings in Light of 2 Kings 21:2–9," in R. David, M. Jinbachian (éds.), *Traduire la Bible hébraïque.* De la Septante à la Nouvelle Bible Segond (Sciences bibliques; Montréal, 2005), 127–149.

[2] Schenker, *Älteste Textgeschichte*, 173.

[3] On peut mentionner ici en particulier les travaux de quatre auteurs: Julio Trebolle Barrera pense également que la *Vorlage* hébraïque du G présente un état littéraire distinct et parfois antérieur au M: cf. J. Trebolle Barrera, *Jehú y Joás. Texto y composición literaria de 2 Reyes 9–11* (Institución San Jerónimo 17; Valencia, 1984); id., *Salomon y Jeroboán*: *Historia de la recensión y redacción de I Reyes 2–12; 14* (Bibliotheca Salmanticensis. Dissertationes 3; Salamanca/Jerusalem, 1980); id., "Redaction, Recension, and Midrash in the Books of Kings," *BIOSCS* 15 (1982) 12–35. Dans son étude toute récente, Percy S. F. van Keulen soutient la position exactement inverse, estimant que le G est presque systématiquement secondaire et qu'il faut situer l'origine de la révision dans le travail d'un éditeur grec: P. S. F. van Keulen,

la voie à de nouvelles études.[4] Les implications de cette recherche dépassent les seuls livres des Rois et sont en mesure de renouveler notre connaissance de l'histoire de la Bible hébraïque, de la nature du M et des circonstances historiques et théologiques qui l'ont vu naître. Au récent congrès de l'IOSOT à Leiden (août 2004), Schenker pouvait émettre l'hypothèse suivante:[5]

> Die Königsbücher präsentieren nicht allein die Situation von zwei literarisch verschiedenen Textrezensionen. Exodus, Jeremia, Ezechiel, Daniel, Esra-Nehemia, 1–2 Samuel, aber auch Teile des Pentateuchs bieten solche Doppelrezensionen bei denen die Hebräische Vorlage der LXX (erhalten bisweilen nur in der VL) die andere Rezension oder Fassung widerspiegelt, auf der jene des MT fusst. Die Frage ist damit gestellt, ob es sich nicht um eine einzige, grosse Rezension oder Neuausgabe handelt, die grosse Teile der hebräischen Bible umfasst hat. Sie hätte mehr oder weniger tief in die überlieferten biblischen Texte eingegriffen, um sie in einer neuen Ausgabe herauszugeben.

Pourtant, cette approche du témoignage textuel du Grec (G) comme attestation d'une forme hébraïque antérieure au texte proto-massorétique suscite parfois des résistances[6] et souvent un étonnement perplexe. L'une des difficultés réside précisément dans la complexité de la Bible grecque et de son histoire, ainsi que dans la connaissance

Two Versions of the Salomon Narrative: An Inquiry into the Relationship between MT 1 Kgs. 2–11 and LXX 3 Reg. 2–11 (VTSup 104; Leiden, 2005). Zipora Talshir pense également que le G représente un état littéraire secondaire; elle estime, quant à elle, que la *Vorlage* du G représente un midrash: p. ex. Z. Talshir, *The Alternative Story. 3 Kingdoms 12:24 A–Z* (Jerusalem Biblical Studies 6; Jerusalem, 1993). Hermann-Josef Stipp estime pour sa part que le G et le M ont connu des développements littéraires parallèles: H.-J. Stipp, *Elischa – Propheten – Gottesmänner. Die Kompositionsgeschichte des Elischazyklus und verwandter Texte, rekonstruiert auf der Basis von Text- und Literarkritik zu 1 Kön 20.22 und 2 Kön 2–7* (Arbeiten zu Text und Sprache im Alten Testamen 24; St. Ottilien, 1987).

[4] J'ai soutenu ma thèse sur cette question: P. Hugo, *Les deux visages d'Élie: TM et LXX en 1R 17–18. Une contribution à l'histoire la plus ancienne du texte des livres des Rois*, (OBO; Fribourg/Göttingen, 2006).

[5] A. Schenker, "Die Textgeschichte der Königsbücher und ihre Konsequenzen für die Textgeschichte der hebräischen Bibel, illustriert am Beispiel von 2 Kön 23:1–3," in *Congress Volume IOSOT, Leiden 2004* (VTSup; Leiden) à paraître, (sous le §8.).

[6] Cf. W. Thiel, "Beobachtungen am Text von 1 Könige 18," in J. F. Diehl, R. Heitzenröder, M. Witte (Hrsg.), *"Einen Altar von Erde mache mir . . ." Festschrift für Diethelm Conrad* (Kleine Arbeiten zum Alten und Neuen Testament 4/5; Waltrop, 2003), 283–291; Z. Talshir, "Literary Design – A Criterion for Originality? A Case Study: 3 Kgdms 12:24a–z; 1 K 11–14," in Y. Goldman, Ch. Uehlinger (éds.), *La double transmission du texte biblique: Études d'histoire du texte offertes en hommage à Adrian Schenker* (OBO 179; Fribourg-Suisse/Göttingen, 2001), 41–57.

partielle qu'en ont beaucoup d'exégètes. En effet, la grande diversité du G provoque l'embarras du lecteur non averti, car il n'est effectivement pas possible de parler "du" texte de la Septante comme s'il s'agissait d'un témoin unifié. Il suffit de consulter l'apparat critique de l'édition de Cambridge pour s'en convaincre.[7] Or, l'absence d'édition critique pour les Règnes dans la *Septuaginta* de Göttingen et l'usage encore largement répandu chez les biblistes de l'édition manuelle de Rahlfs (1935) ajoutent au malaise.[8] En effet, cette dernière donne précisément l'image erronée d'un texte grec unifié souvent proche du M.[9] Mais puisque ce n'est précisément pas le cas, la question se pose de savoir quel texte grec doit servir de base à la comparaison textuelle et littéraire avec le M. En d'autres termes, que faut-il entendre par le Grec ancien (ou Septante ancienne)? Adrian Schenker donne de manière schématique la réponse à cette question complexe:[10]

> Die älteste LXX der Königsbücher ist meistens im Vaticanus (3 Regn 2–21 = 1 Kön 2–21) und in den antiochenischen oder – wie früher meistens gesagt wurde – lukianischen Handschriften (3 Regn 22–4 Regn 25) erhalten geblieben. Doch sind insbesondere die lukianischen Zeugen nicht einfach mit der ältesten LXX gleichzusetzen. Dies erweist sich namentlich am Vergleich mit den *Vetus latina* Fragmenten des *Vindobonensis* L 115 und anderer Zeugen, die stellenweise eine ursprünglichere Textgestalt der LXX bezeugen. Diese Zeugen der ursprünglichsten Form der LXX sind leider nur sehr bruchstückhaft erhalten und überdies in lateinischer Sprache. Daher ist die älteste Textform der LXX heute überhaupt nicht mehr überall bezeugt.

[7] A. E. Brooke, N. McLean, (H. St. J. Thackeray), *The Old Testament in Greek*, 3 vol. (Cambridge, 1906–1940). Rappelons que cette édition inachevée reproduit le texte du codex *Vaticanus* (G^B) assorti d'un apparat donnant les variantes des principaux mss en onciales et en minuscules.

[8] A. Rahlfs, *Septuaginta id est Vetus Testamentum graece iuxta LXX interpretes* (Stuttgart, 1935, 1979²).

[9] Les choix méthodologiques de Rahlfs dépendent largement des connaissances de son époque et ne se justifient plus aujourd'hui. L'édition – qui n'avait pas la prétention d'être une édition critique complète – repose en effet principalement sur les grands onciaux, *Vaticanus, Alexandrinus, Sinaiticus* (cf. A. Rahlfs, *Septuaginta*, L–LIII) et ignore dans une large mesure les mss en minuscules. Cela prive le chercheur des variantes parfois les plus intéressantes, en particulier pour les Règnes. Son apparat n'est donc plus en mesure d'illustrer l'histoire du texte de la Bible grecque telle que l'envisage la recherche récente. En outre, Rahlfs procède à un choix sélectif des variantes souvent en harmonie avec le M (cf. p. ex. la critique récente de Y. Goldman, *Megilloth* [*BHQ* 18; Stuttgart, 2004], 15*).

[10] Schenker, *Älteste Textgeschichte*, 172.

Dans le cadre de cet article en hommage à mon maître Adrian Schenker, je voudrais précisément définir ce que l'on entend par le Grec ancien des livres des Rois. Mon propos consistera donc à montrer comment la recherche a progressivement identifié les témoins – mentionnés dans cette citation de Schenker – qui représentent le mieux le Grec ancien et quelles sont les difficultés qui subsistent. En me situant délibérément en amont des conclusions sur l'histoire du texte hébreu des livres des Rois, évoquées ci-dessus, j'entends apporter un éclairage théorique sur la méthode qui permet à la critique de rejoindre le texte le plus proche possible de la version grecque originaire des Rois.[11]

1. À la recherche du Grec ancien, perspective générale

La grande diversité textuelle des témoins du G est le fruit de l'histoire complexe de ses révisions et recensions successives. Ces retouches du texte poursuivaient trois buts principaux:[12] d'abord la correction des erreurs inévitables à toute transmission manuscrite; ensuite l'actualisation du style et de la qualité de la langue grecque; enfin la conformation au texte hébreu proto-massorétique (ou rabbinique). Le travail des réviseurs juifs – selon l'ordre aujourd'hui reçu: Théodotion auquel on associe la recension καίγε, Aquila et Symmaque – et des recenseurs chrétiens – essentiellement la recension mise sous le nom de Lucien et l'œuvre d'Origène – eurent pour effet d'éloigner progressivement leurs textes des traductions originales. La perspective générale de la recherche consiste donc à tenter de retrouver la forme la plus proche possible de la traduction originaire d'un livre biblique en identifiant les recensions dont elle a été l'objet et en repérant les éventuelles corrections et/ou abâtardissements internes au grec pour reconstituer le texte le plus ancien.

Cette perspective, largement admise par la recherche récente,[13] est

[11] Cf. les bilans de la recherche en B. Botte, P.-M. Bogaert, "Septante et versions grecques," in *DBS* XII (Paris, 1993), 590–601; S. Jellicoe, *The Septuagint and Modern Study* (Oxford, 1968), 283–290. Voir encore E. Ulrich, *The Qumran Text of Samuel and Josephus* (Harvard Semitic Monograph 19; Missoula, 1978), 15–37.

[12] J. Trebolle Barrera, *The Jewish Bible and the Christian Bible: An Introduction to the History of the Bible* (Leiden-Grand Rapids, 1998), 309.

[13] Cf. Botte, Bogaert, "Septante et versions grecques," 552–555; G. Dorival, M. Harl, O. Munnich, *La Bible grecque des Septante. Du judaïsme hellénistique au christianisme*

l'héritière de Paul de Lagarde. En 1863, dans ses *Anmerkungen zur griechischen Übersetzung der Proverbien*,[14] il énonçait les trois principes qui guidaient ses recherches. 1° Tous les mss du G sont, de manière directe ou indirecte, le résultat d'un processus éclectique; pour restaurer le texte, il faut donc adopter une méthode éclectique. 2° Quand un verset se trouve en deux formes, la première en traduction libre et la seconde littérale, la première doit être la plus ancienne. 3° Quand deux leçons sont concurrentes et que l'une suit le TM et l'autre ne peut s'expliquer que par un original différent, il faut préférer la seconde. Dans les grandes lignes, c'est encore la perspective de l'édition en cours à Göttingen,[15] qui vise à retrouver le G le plus ancien possible en recherchant les témoins antérieurs aux activités recensionnelles ou en en reconstituant le texte.

Dans le cadre des livres des Règnes, la recherche a progressivement mis en évidence l'importance de deux témoins principaux qui offrent l'accès le plus sûr au G le plus ancien. Il s'agit de la "recension lucianique" ou édition antiochienne (G^{L})[16] – attribuée à Lucien d'Antioche (~ 250–311/312) – et du codex Vaticanus (G^{B}). Tel sera le fil rouge de notre parcours.

2. Recherches sur le G des Règnes avant les découvertes de la Mer Morte

L'histoire de la recherche sur le G des Règnes se divise en deux grandes étapes, dont les découvertes des mss du désert de Juda et de la Mer Morte marquent le tournant. Avant de disposer de ces "nouveaux" témoins, plusieurs grands savants ont exploré la tradition manuscrite de la Bible grecque ainsi que ses citations dans la littérature antique juive et chrétienne. Cette enquête livra l'image d'une

ancien (Initiations au christianisme ancien; Paris, 1994²), 182–184; Jellicoe, *The Septuagint*, 5–9; Trebolle Barrera, *The Jewish Bible and the Christian Bible*, 306–307.

[14] P. de Lagarde, *Anmerkungen zur griechischen Übersetzung der Proverbien* (Leipzig, 1863), 2–3.

[15] Cf. Jellicoe, *The Septuagint*, 9–21.

[16] Pour une histoire de la recherche et la nature du texte antiochien, cf. B. M. Metzger, "The Lucianic Recension of the Greek Bible," in *Chapters in the History of New Testament Textual Criticism* (NTTS 4; Leiden, 1963), 1–41; N. Fernández Marcos, "Some Reflections on the Antiochian Text of the Septuagint," in D. Fraenkel, U. Quast, J. W. Wevers (eds.), *Studien zur Septuaginta. Robert Hanhart zu Ehren* (MSU 20;

Septante très complexe, dont l'entrecroisement des traditions anciennes et plus tardives (jusqu'au 4ème siècle) restait inexpliqué.

2.1. Premières études systématiques du texte du G (fin 19ème)

Les premiers chercheurs à avoir identifié, dans les livres historiques, ce que l'on appellera la "recension lucianique" (G^L) furent Julius Wellhausen,[17] Frederic Field[18] et Antonio Maria Ceriani.[19] Ils observèrent en effet une parenté importante entre certains mss en minuscules et la Polyglotte d'Alcalá (*Complutensis*),[20] les citations des Pères antiochiens – particulièrement Jean Chrysostome et Théodoret de Cyr – et les notes marginales de la Syro-Hexaplaire dont les leçons, marquées d'un *lomad*, étaient attribuées à Lucien.[21] Ce sont les mss 19 82 93 et 108 selon la classification de Göttingen et boe_2 selon l'édition de Cambridge.[22] Travaillant de manière indépendante, Paul de Lagarde aboutit à peu près au même résultat. Dans la perspective qui était la sienne d'identifier les principales recensions qui contaminaient les mss pour restituer le prototype dont elles dérivaient – ou l'*Urtext* du G –, Paul de Lagarde estima qu'il fallait commencer par la recension dite lucianique, dont il tenta de faire l'édition en 1883.[23]

Göttingen, 1990), 219–229; N. Fernández Marcos, "The Lucianic Text in the Books of Kingdoms: From Lagarde to the Textual Pluralism," in A. Pietersma, C. Cox (ed.), *De Septuaginta: Studies in Honour of John William Wevers on his Sixty-fifth Birthday* (Mississauga, 1984), 161–174; J. Trebolle Barrera, *Jehú y Joás*, 44–73.

[17] J. Wellhausen, *Der Text der Bücher Samuelis* (Göttingen, 1871), 223–224.

[18] F. Field, *Origenis Hexaplorum quae supersunt sive veterum interpretum Graecorum in totum Vetus Testamentum Fragmenta*, 2 vol. (Oxford 1875), vol. 1, lxxxiv–xciv; spéc. lxxxv, n. 5 et lxxxvii.

[19] A. M. Ceriani, *Monumenta Sacra et Profana. Tom. II* (Milan, 1864), spéc. xi, et 76, 98, 102; id., *Rendiconti del R. Istituto Lombardo* Ser. 2, 19 (1886), 206.

[20] Sur la Polyglotte d'Alcalá, imprimée en Espagne entre 1514–1517, cf. A. Schenker, "Der alttestamentliche Text in den vier grossen Polyglottenbibeln nach dem heutigen Stand der Forschung," *ThR* 90 (1994), 177–188, spéc. 179–181.

[21] Sur la discussion de l'interprétation des sigles καὶ λ̥, dans les notes marginales des mss hexaplaires, et *lomad* dans la Syro-Hexaplaire, cf. Metzger, "The Lucianic Recension," 162; D. Barthélemy, "Les problèmes textuels de 2 Sm 11,2–1 Rois 2,11 reconsidérés à la lumière de certaines critiques des *Devanciers d'Aquila*," in id., *Études d'histoire du texte de l'Ancien Testament* (OBO 21; Fribourg-Suisse/Göttingen, 1978), 253–254; N. Fernández Marcos, "La sigla *lambda omicron* (λ̥) en I–II Reyes-Septuaginta," *Sef* 38 (1978), 243–262.

[22] Les ms 19 et 108 correspondent tous deux au b; le ms 127 correspondant au c_2 ne fut identifié comme antiochien que plus tard par A. Rahlfs, *Septuaginta-Studien III* (Göttingen, 1965²), 369–378.

[23] P. de Lagarde, *Librorum Veteris Testamentis canonicorum pars prior Graece* (Göttingen, 1883).

Si les conclusions qu'il en tira pour le Pentateuque étaient erronées, ce qui rendit son édition caduque,[24] son travail permit d'identifier le type antiochien de certains mss des livres historiques.[25]

C'est également à la fin du 19ème siècle qu'apparaît clairement pour la première fois l'importance du témoignage de la Vieille Latine (La) pour déterminer la nature du texte de G^L. Alors que Ceriani signalait la présence de leçons de type lucianique dans la *vetus latina* (La) des Lamentations,[26] Carlo Vercellone attirait l'attention sur la nature des notes marginales La des Règnes dans le ms de la Vulgate de León, en Espagne.[27] En effet, quand ces gloses se distinguaient du G majoritaire, elles étaient en accord avec les mss du groupe lucianique. Ces remarques conduisirent Driver, en 1890, à tirer des conclusions pour l'histoire du texte:[28] La étant datée du 2ème siècle de notre ère, elle ne peut pas se baser sur la recension de Lucien lui-même. Un bon siècle avant Lucien, il existait donc déjà des témoins de leçons typiquement lucianiques.

En 1893 et 1894, Siegfried Silberstein consacra deux études au texte grec des Règnes.[29] Constatant la grande différence de caractère de la traduction de 3 Règnes dans le codex *Vaticanus* (G^B) et le codex *Alexandrinus* (G^A) – ce dernier étant plus proche de M – Silberstein entreprit leur comparaison systématique avec la recension origénienne transmise par la Syro-Hexaplaire. Il en conclut que l'état textuel reflété par G^A trouve son origine dans la recension d'Origène mais que G^B n'en dépend pas; ce dernier représente manifestement un texte pré-hexaplaire.[30] Notons que, contrairement à l'option de Paul de Lagarde, Silberstein n'entra pas dans la question du rapport de

---

[24] Cf. les critiques de A. Rahlfs, *Lucians Rezension der Königsbücher* (Göttingen, 1911), 23–30 (= Rahlfs, *Septuaginta-Studien*, 383–390). Sur les apports décisifs et les limites de l'œuvre de P. de Lagarde voir aussi Jellicoe, *The Septuagint*, 5–9.

[25] de Lagarde, *Librorum Veteris Testamentis*, spéc. V, XIII–XIV; il identifie donc comme lucianiques les mss h, f, m et d (= dans l'ordre 19 82 93 108).

[26] A. M. Ceriani, *Monumenta Sacra et Profana. Tom. I* (Milan, 1861), xvi (addenda).

[27] C. Vercellone, *Variae lectiones vulgatae latinae Bibliorum editionis*, vol. 2 (Rome, 1864), spéc. XXI–XXII, et les renvois en pp. 179, 436, 455, 594.

[28] S. R. Driver, *Notes on the Hebrew Text of the Books of Samuel* (Oxford, 1890), lxxvii–lxxix.

[29] S. Silberstein, "Über den Ursprung der im Codex Alexandrinus und Vaticanus des dritten Königsbuches der alexandrinischen Übersetzung überlieferten Textgestalt," *ZAW* 13 (1893), 1–75; 14 (1894), 1–30.

[30] Il partage les conclusions de travaux contemporains sur d'autres livres de la Bible, p.ex. de P. de Lagarde, *Anmerkungen*; C. H. Cornill, *Das Buch des Propheten Ezechiel* (Leipzig, 1886).

la recension dite lucianique (G^L) avec La – dont il souligna la proximité – et les Hexaples.[31]

La recherche sur la nature du texte de G^L franchit une étape supplémentaire avec la contribution de Adam Mez.[32] Il démontra que Flavius Josèphe, dans ses *Antiquités juives* V–VII, témoignait d'un texte grec qui était en accord avec G^L contre G^{A-B} et M. La méthodologie de Mez consistait à comparer le texte de Josèphe à d'autres témoins textuels (M, G^A, G^B, G^L, La, le Targum, la Peshitta, Jérôme et l'*onomastica sacra*) sur deux critères principaux: les noms propres et le compte rendu de faits positifs.[33] Mez aura donc été le premier à démontrer, à son grand étonnement, que des leçons typiquement lucianiques existaient chez Josèphe déjà deux siècles avant Lucien, et que la recension qu'on lui attribuait témoignait pour une grande part de ce texte ancien. Il peut être considéré comme l'un des "inventeurs" du texte proto-lucianique. L'importance de G^L pour l'accès au Grec ancien émergera encore de façon plus déterminante avec les travaux de Rahlfs.

2.2. Rahlfs et le texte de G^L des Règnes

Dans les premières années du siècle dernier, Alfred Rahlfs entreprit la première étude véritablement systématique des livres des Règnes.[34] Dans son premier travail, *Studien zu den Königsbüchern* (1904), il s'attacha en premier lieu à mettre en évidence l'importance des citations de Théodoret pour déterminer le caractère lucianique des témoins textuels. Il dégagea ensuite une méthode pour repérer les mss hexaplaires à partir des citations des Règnes dans l'œuvre d'Origène. De cette enquête, il conclut clairement, comme Silberstein l'avait déjà fait, que G^B représente un texte pré-hexaplaire comme la version éthiopienne. Il montra en outre que G^L était peu influencé par le texte origénien.[35]

Le second travail de Rahlfs sur les livres de Règnes, *Lucians Rezension der Königsbücher* (1911), nous intéresse plus directement encore. Sans

---

[31] Silberstein, "Über den Ursprung," 19–20.

[32] A. Mez, *Die Bibel des Josephus untersucht für Buch V–VII der Archäologie* (Basel, 1895), spéc. 79–84.

[33] Mez, *Die Bibel des Josephus*, 2–4.

[34] A. Rahlfs, *Studien zu den Königsbüchern* (Göttingen, 1904); id., *Lucians Rezension der Königsbücher* (Göttingen, 1911), rassemblées dans A. Rahlfs, *Septuaginta-Studien I–III* (Göttingen, 1965²), 17–104 et 361–658.

[35] Cf. Rahlfs, *Septuaginta-Studien*, 79–80.

contester le caractère proprement antiochien de G^L – montré notamment par Ceriani, Field et de Lagarde – il reprit la question que s'était posée Adam Mez à propos du témoignage de Josèphe: le texte lucianique ne serait-il pas un témoin plus ancien que l'époque de Lucien, martyrisé en 312? Autrement dit, Rahlfs cherchait à étudier l'origine de G^L des Rois pour déterminer si le texte était le fruit d'une activité recensionnelle propre à Lucien – ou au moins du milieu antiochien du début du 4ème siècle de notre ère – ou s'il ne se basait pas plutôt sur un texte contenant déjà des caractéristiques dites lucianiques le distinguant des autres témoins grecs, un texte que l'on appellera proto-lucianique. Son étude se divisait donc en deux étapes.

1° En premier lieu Rahlfs considéra le témoignage des écrivains antiques, juifs et chrétiens, antérieurs à Lucien. Pour le cas de Josèphe d'abord, il conclut que, pour le livre des Rois, il ne cite que peu de leçons de type lucianique mais suit principalement le texte hébreu.[36] Rahlfs prenait ainsi ses distances avec les résultats de Mez.[37] Pour un certain nombre d'auteurs grecs et latins, jusqu'à la fin du 3ème ou le début du 4ème siècle (dont Théophile d'Antioche, Irénée, Clément d'Alexandrie, Hyppolite, Origène, Tertullien, Cyprien, Lucifer de Cagliari, ainsi que La), le résultat fut plus manifeste que pour Josèphe: un certain nombre de leçons offraient des caractéristiques lucianiques, alors que d'autres leçons spécifiquement lucianiques, telles qu'on les trouve dans les mss G^L, ne se retrouvaient pas chez ces auteurs. Bien qu'il restât très prudent, Rahlfs reconnaissait l'existence de caractéristiques propres à G^L plus anciennes que Lucien.

2° Dans une seconde étape, Rahlfs entreprit une comparaison de G^L avec les autres témoins grecs et hébreu des Rois. Il en tira plusieurs conclusions déterminantes: G^L se base sur un texte pré-hexaplaire apparenté à G^{A-B} et à la version éthiopienne mais parfois mieux conservé dans le texte lucianique que dans les autres témoins; malgré leur parenté, G^L et G^{A-B} ne sont pas identiques, et certaines de leurs différences ne peuvent s'expliquer que par l'existence d'un texte antérieur au travail de Lucien. Enfin, il faut mentionner le fait

[36] Cf. Rahlfs, *Septuaginta-Studien*, 471.

[37] Dans son analyse (Rahlfs, *Septuaginta-Studien*, 443–452), il critique la position de Mez qui, selon lui, a surévalué les accords de Josèphe avec G^L. Ce jugement sera contesté et révisé par Ulrich, *The Qumran Text of Samuel and Josephus*, 22–27 et 250–252 (cf. ci-dessous).

que, pour Rahlfs, G^L ne témoigne pas d'un texte unifié dans ses principes ni cohérent dans ses options de traduction, même si dans l'ensemble son grec est meilleur que dans les autres témoins et souvent plus proche de M.

Les travaux de Rahlfs manifestèrent clairement, bien qu'avec prudence, l'importance et l'antiquité du témoignage de G^L. Il montra que la recension attribuée à Lucien se basait elle-même sur un texte pré-hexaplaire dont elle était occasionnellement le seul témoin. Le travail de Thackeray lui permettra de pousser encore plus loin ses conclusions.

2.3. Les cinq sections des Règnes délimitées par Thackeray

La première hypothèse globale sur l'origine des livres des Règnes fut proposée, en 1907, par Henry St. J. Thackeray.[38] Contrairement à une partie de la recherche avant lui, il basa son étude sur le codex *Vaticanus* (G^B). Il n'ignorait cependant pas la valeur des autres témoins textuels, en particulier de G^L, mais relevait en ce dernier trop de traces de recension pour le juger fiable.[39] Pourtant, en 1929, il affinera son jugement sur la nature de G^L en reconsidérant le témoignage de Flavius Josèphe. Il rejoignait alors les conclusions de Rahlfs et surtout de Mez, soulignant l'importance du témoignage de Josèphe "qui prouve que le texte lucianique non seulement est antérieur à Lucien, mais qu'il existait déjà, avec des différences mineures, un siècle et demi avant Origène." Mais il alla encore plus loin qu'eux en affirmant que "la Bible de Josèphe est uniformément de type lucianique de 1 Samuel à 1 Maccabées."[40] Or si, dans ses premiers travaux, il se basait encore exclusivement sur le texte plus largement

[38] H. St. J. Thackeray, *The Septuagint and Jewish Worship: A Study in Origins* (London, 1923²), 16–28, 114–115, 123–124, étude parue d'abord sous le titre: "The Greek Translation of the Four Books of Kings," *JTS* 8 (1907), 262–278.

[39] Thackeray, *The Septuagint and Jewish Worship*, 16: "The only serious rival to B is the Lucianic text. This too, as will appear, has its contribution to yield; but, while it undoubtedly contains an ancient element, it also bears clear marks of editorial revision, and the more homogeneous and less eclectic B text, notwithstanding many shortcomings, forms a safer basis for our inquiry."

[40] H. St. J. Thackeray, *Flavius Josèphe. L'homme et l'historien*. Adapté de l'anglais par Étienne Nodet (Josèphe et son temps; Paris, 2000), 55 (= H. St. J. Thackeray, *Josephus: The Man and the Historian* [New York, 1929], 85). Voir encore sa "Note on the Evidence of Josephus" dans la préface de l'édition de Cambridge: A. E. Brooke, N. McLean, H. St. J. Thackeray, *The Old Testament in Greek*, vol. 2, *The Later Historical Books* (Cambridge, 1927), ix.

attesté, son étude marqua cependant une étape décisive pour l'histoire du texte grec des Règnes.

Thackeray observa des différences de caractéristiques dans la traduction qui le conduisirent à postuler plusieurs traductions successives. Avec ces critères, il divisa le livre en cinq sections: α = 1 Rg; ββ = 2 Rg 1,1–11,1; βγ = 2 Rg 11,2–3 Rg 2,11; γγ = 3 Rg 2,12–21,43; γδ = 3 Rg 22–4 Rg. Selon Thackeray, ces sections reflétaient deux étapes de traduction. Une traduction primitive partielle, faite à Alexandrie par un ou plusieurs traducteurs, se composait des sections α, ββ, γγ. Elle produisait une version expurgée de l'histoire de la monarchie[41] qui passait sous silence le péché de David, la révolte de son fils Absalom et la mort de David, ainsi que la décadence de la monarchie. Une seconde étape de traduction, probablement de la main d'un seul traducteur d'Asie Mineure, complétait les lacunes: sections βγ et γδ. Thackeray, reconnaissant l'absence de preuve externe pour soutenir son hypothèse, fonda son analyse sur les procédés internes de la langue et du style. La principale caractéristique des parties dites anciennes α, ββ, γγ, est le présent historique qui n'apparaît presque pas dans les sections βγ et γδ, et uniquement dans des cas suspects.[42] Thackeray nota ensuite que la caractéristique des sections dites ultérieures résidait dans leur plus grande proximité avec l'hébreu: la traduction y semble en effet plus littérale. Parmi les indices qu'il mit en évidence, dans le vocabulaire ou dans des solécismes, on peut mentionner l'usage de ἐγώ εἰμι devant un verbe fini pour traduire אנכי, ou l'emploi de la conjonction καίγε pour l'hébreu גם.[43] Cette dernière remarque fera fortune dans la suite de la recherche, avec les travaux de Barthélemy.

La théorie de Thackeray sur les étapes de traduction et les raisons qui auraient guidé le (ou les) premier(s) traducteur(s) est abandonnée aujourd'hui. Mais son mérite est d'avoir repéré, dans la langue et la syntaxe, des éléments de distinction dont la nature exacte lui a échappé.

[41] Cf. Thackeray, *The Septuagint and Jewish Worship*, 16: "Here, moreover, we can account for the reserve of the earlier translators; patriotic concern for their nation's honour led them to produce an expurgated version of the history of the monarchy."

[42] Il relevait 227 cas, dont 151 en α, 28 en ββ, 48 en γγ, soit près de deux tiers des cas de l'ensemble de G; les deux autres sections ne comptent que 9 cas dont certains sont discutables (cf. 20).

[43] Voir son développement en 23–24 et son tableau récapitulatif en 114–115.

Ce fut Rahlfs qui, le premier, tira la conclusion la plus significative de l'étude de Thackeray. Dans *Lucians Rezension der Königsbücher* il avait montré que la différence entre G^{L} et G^{A-B} était plus significative en 2 Rois qu'en 1 Rois. Il eut donc l'intuition qu'en 2 R G^{L} pouvait reposer sur un texte grec témoignant d'une étape textuelle plus ancienne que G^{A-B}.[44] Il faudra les découvertes du désert de Juda et l'étude minutieuse de Barthélemy pour apporter une confirmation à cette hypothèse et faire avancer le dossier de manière décisive.

Dans la ligne directe de l'étude de Thackeray, un certain nombre de travaux se sont attachés à étudier de plus près les caractéristiques et les méthodes de traduction dans les différentes sections des Règnes. Les études de H. S. Gehman[45] et de J. W. Wevers[46] en particulier ont affiné et perfectionné certains aspects de la théorie de Thackeray. Si elles n'envisagent pas l'hypothèse que Rahlfs avait déjà énoncée, leur intérêt réside aujourd'hui encore dans l'analyse minutieuse du texte grec de G majoritaire et, lues à la lumière des découvertes ultérieures, elles sont riches de renseignements.

3. Les découvertes du désert de Juda, tournant des études sur le texte du G

Les découvertes du désert de Juda jetèrent une lumière nouvelle sur l'histoire de la Bible grecque et permirent de relancer la question de la recherche du Grec ancien, en particulier pour les Règnes. Deux événements principaux, simultanés et étroitement liés l'un à l'autre, contribuèrent à ce renouveau. Ce furent d'une part, en 1953 puis en 1963, les études de Barthélemy sur les membres du groupe καίγε identifiés à la suite de la découverte du Dodécaprophéton de Naḥal

---

[44] Rahlfs, *Septuaginta-Studien*, 653–654: "Vielmehr möchte man glauben, daß schon Lucians Vorlage im zweiten Buche stärker von 𝔊 (= G) abgewichen sei, als im ersten. Da nun die Übersetzung des zweiten Buches, wie Thackeray gezeigt hat, nicht die ursprüngliche Fortsetzung derjenigen des ersten, sondern später angehängt ist, könnte man auf den Gedanken kommen, daß L (= G^{L}) noch die ursprüngliche Fortsetzung vorgefunden und zugrunde gelegt hatte" (654).

[45] H. S. Gehman, "Exegetical Methods Employed by the Greek Translator of I Samuel," *JAOS* 70 (1950), 292–296.

[46] Cf. J. W. Wevers, "Exegetical Principles Underlying the Septuagint Text of 1 Kings ii 12–xxi 43," *OTS* 8 (1950), 300–322; id., "Principles of Interpretation Guiding the Fourth Translator of the Books of the Kingdoms (3 K. 22:1–4 K. 25:30)," *CBQ* 14 (1952), 40–56; id., "A Study in the Exegetical principles Underlying the Greek Text of 2 Sm 11:2–1 Kings 2:11," *CBQ* 15 (1953), 30–45.

Ḥever (8ḤevXIIgr), dont les sections βγ et γδ des livres des Règnes.[47] Ce fut d'autre part, en 1953 et 1955, la publication par Cross des fragments hébreux du livre de Samuel de la 4ème grotte de Qumran (4QSam a-b-c)[48] qui relançait le débat sur la nature de la traduction grecque des Septante et sur le statut de G^L.

3.1. La recènsion καίγε des Règnes et le Grec ancien

L'étude du 8ḤevXIIgr permit à Barthélemy d'identifier une recension juive antérieure à Aquila et proche des caractéristiques de Théodotion qu'il nomma "groupe καίγε".[49] Il montra que certaines sections des Règnes appartenaient à ce groupe.[50] Alors que Thackeray pensait que le texte majoritaire représenté par G^B des sections βγ et γδ était l'œuvre d'un traducteur plus tardif, Barthélemy démontra qu'il s'agissait en fait d'une révision hébraïsante. Il compara, par de nombreux sondages dans la section βγ, le texte G^L, nommé "antiochien",[51] au texte majoritaire (dont G^B) qui comportait les caractéristiques propres au groupe καίγε (qu'il nommait le groupe "palestinien").[52] Nous pouvons résumer ses résultats en quatre points:

[47] D. Barthélemy, "Redécouverte d'un chaînon manquant de l'histoire de la Septante," *RB* 60 (1953), 18–29 (= id., *Études d'histoire du texte*, 38–50); D. Barthélemy, *Les devanciers d'Aquila. Première publication intégrale du texte des fragments du Dodécaprophéton* (VTSup 10; Leiden, 1963). Voir l'édition diplomatique de E. Tov, R. A. Kraft, *The Seiyâl Collection, I. The Greek Minor Prophets Scroll from Naḥal Ḥever (8ḤevXIIgr)* (DJD VIII; Oxford, 1990).

[48] Cf. F. M. Cross, "A New Qumrân Biblical Fragment Related to the Original Hebrew Underlying the Septuagint," *BASOR* 132 (1953), 15–26; id., "The Oldest Manuscripts from Qumran," *JBL* 74 (1955), 147–172.

[49] Barthélemy, *Les devanciers*, 47: "Nous classerions dans cette catégorie: la traduction des Lamentations et vraisemblablement celles du Cantique des Cantiques et de Ruth, la recension majoritaire des sections βγ et γδ Règnes, la recension des Juges dont témoignent plus spécialement les mss i r u a_2 et B e f s z, la recension Théodotion de Daniel, les ajoutes Théodotion à la Septante de Job et celles souvent anonymes à la Septante de Jérémie, la colonne Théodotion des hexaples et la Quinta des Psaumes. La nouvelle recension anonyme du Dodécaprophéton trouverait naturellement place dans cet ensemble."

[50] Barthélemy, *Les devanciers*, spéc. 91–143; et les compléments dans: id., "Les problèmes textuels," 218–254.

[51] Barthélemy affirme que la recension lucianique est un mythe, et que l'on a plutôt affaire à une édition antiochienne placée, au 4ème siècle, sous l'autorité de Lucien martyr (~250–311/312): Barthélemy, *Les devanciers*, 126–127; id., "Les problèmes textuels," 243–254, spéc. 247.

[52] Pour l'étude des caractéristiques propres du groupe καίγε dans les Règnes cf. Barthélemy, *Les devanciers*, spéc. 34–41 pour la traduction de גם par καίγε, 48–80 pour les autres caractéristiques.

1° il existe une identité fondamentale entre la forme antiochienne et palestinienne du texte qui n'est pas due au hasard, il s'agit donc de la même traduction originelle; 2° la forme palestinienne diffère essentiellement par un souci de plus grande fidélité au M; 3° les divergences de la forme καίγε, supposée recensée, ne peuvent être le fruit d'un abâtardissement du texte; 4° il ressort donc que le texte antiochien "témoigne ici d'une traduction grecque ancienne faite sur un texte hébraïque antérieur à l'unification du texte consonantique massorétique et divergeant assez fortement de celui-ci [il fait alors explicitement référence aux fragments de Samuel trouvés à Qumran], tandis que pal. [texte palestinien] est essentiellement le produit d'une recension postérieure faite après cette étape décisive pour l'histoire du texte hébraïque de la Bible."[53] Les caractéristiques "proto-lucianiques" de Josèphe – comme l'ont montré les études précédentes – soutiennent ces conclusions.

En clair, Barthélemy soutient l'hypothèse selon laquelle nous avons accès au Grec ancien des Règnes par deux sources principales pré-hexaplaires et non soumises à la recension καίγε: 1° G^B pour les sections α, ββ et γγ; 2° G^L pour les deux sections restantes, βγ et γδ. Pourtant il ne faut pas réduire et simplifier cette thèse. Barthélemy lui-même, en considérant en particulier le problème soulevé par les doublets, reconnaît la complexité de la tradition textuelle et nuance ses résultats: "le ms. B (= G^B) représente une tradition textuelle qui a subi des contaminations (. . .). On peut se demander si un certain nombre de ces doublets ne juxtaposent pas la vieille Septante à une *révision hébraïsante* que l'on devrait qualifier à la fois de *pré-hexaplaire* et de *non-καίγε.*"[54] De même pour G^L: "il faut ajouter vraisemblablement à cela une recension grécisante assez étendue subie par le texte de boc$_2$e$_2$."[55] Ces deux témoins privilégiés ne représentent donc pas purement et simplement "le" Grec ancien des Règnes,[56] mais le plus sûr accès à la strate la plus ancienne qu'il nous soit possible d'atteindre. Ces constatations ont pour conséquence qu'il faut, outre le choix de la forme textuelle certainement la plus ancienne, une

[53] Barthélemy, *Les devanciers*, 113.
[54] Barthélemy, "Les problèmes textuels," 221.
[55] Barthélemy, "Les problèmes textuels," 224.
[56] Barthélemy, *Les devanciers*, 125: "On ne peut donc identifier purement et simplement le texte des mss B h a$_2$ à celui de la recension palestinienne, quoiqu'ils en soient les meilleurs représentants, de même qu'on ne peut identifier purement et simplement celui des mss b o c$_2$ e$_2$ à la Septante ancienne."

analyse détaillée des leçons propres de ces textes pour s'assurer, autant que possible, qu'il ne s'agit pas de recensions hébraïsantes ou grécisantes plus tardives.[57]

3.2. 4QSam^{a-b-c} et ses conséquences pour l'histoire de G

La découverte des fragments hébreux de Samuel à Qumran, dont l'édition complète vient de paraître,[58] relancèrent quant à eux la recherche dans deux directions. 1° On trouvait dans ces fragments un texte très proche de la probable *Vorlage* de G des Règnes, sans y être totalement identique. Il apparaissait alors que les traducteurs grecs n'avaient pas interprété librement leur texte de base, comme on le pensait jusque là,[59] mais qu'ils avaient lu un texte hébreu différent du M.[60] Cela redonnait à G une place importante dans la critique textuelle de la Bible hébraïque. 2° La seconde ouverture qu'offrait cette découverte concernait l'histoire de la Bible grecque elle-même. Cross nota immédiatement que ces fragments soulignaient l'importance de G^B dans la reconstruction de Grec ancien.[61] Cela confirmait une partie de la recherche qui le précédait. Par ailleurs, il apparut assez vite que ces fragments hébreux contenaient également des leçons typiques du G lucianique,[62] souvent partagées par Josèphe et le Chroniste. En bref, dans les sections α et ββ (1 S 1–2 S 11,1) 4QSam^a, Chroniques, Josèphe et G^{B-L} s'accordent contre M; au contraire dans la section βγ (1 S 11,2–24.25), 4QSam^a s'accorde normalement avec G^L contre G^B et M. Jusqu'ici, les données confirment totalement la thèse de Barthélemy sur la recension καίγε et G^L. Pourtant les conclusions de Cross pour l'histoire du texte grec ne

[57] Notons ici que le travail approfondi de Barthélemy pour la section βγ du livre des Règnes n'a pas été fait de même pour la section γδ, "ce qui pourrait faire l'objet d'un autre travail", comme le reconnaît l'auteur lui-même: cf. Barthélemy, *Les devanciers*, 127 et 140.

[58] F. M. Cross, D. W. Parry, R. J. Saley, E. Ulrich (eds.), *Qumran Cave 4–XII. 1–2 Samuel* (DJD XVII; Oxford, 2005).

[59] Cf. P. A. H. De Boer, *Research into the Text of I Samuel I–XVI* (Amsterdam, 1938), 44–69.

[60] Cf. les réflexions "à chaud" de Cross, "A New Qumrân Biblical Fragment," spéc. 23–25; et id., "The Oldest Manuscripts," spéc. 171–172.

[61] Cross, "A New Qumrân Biblical Fragment," 24: "Our fragments underline the importance of the family of Codex Vaticanus in reconstructing the old Greek version of Samuel, commonly the Septuagint."

[62] Cross, "The History of the Biblical Text," 292–297: "4QSam^a stands with LXX^L against MT and LXX^B" (292).

sont pas identiques à celles de Barthélemy, puisqu'il ne considère pas G^L comme le Grec ancien (ou ce qu'il appelle le type textuel égyptien). Il y voit plutôt une première étape de recension du Grec ancien aujourd'hui totalement perdu: une recension hébraïsante sur un texte palestinien du type des fragments de Samuel de Qumran.[63]

Les travaux de Cross ont été poursuivis par Eugene Ulrich dans sa thèse sur le rapport entre le premier fragment de Samuel de Qumran et le texte utilisé par Josèphe.[64] Reprenant le dossier tel que l'avaient laissé Mez et Rahlfs, il le confronta à la perspective ouverte par Cross. Il entreprit donc la comparaison de 4QSam^a avec G majoritaire, G^L, M, Chroniques et Josèphe. Il arriva à la conclusion que, d'une part, Josèphe utilisait une base grecque proche de l'état textuel dont témoigne 4QSam^a et que, d'autre part, G^L étant parfois seul à s'accorder à certaines leçons de 4QSam^a, le texte proto-lucianique était une recension du Grec ancien sur un document hébreu du type du fragment de Qurman.[65] Il soutenait ainsi l'hypothèse de Cross contre celle de Barthélemy. Pourtant Ulrich reconnaissait lui-même qu'il était prématuré de tirer une conclusion définitive,[66] car les indices sont trop peu nombreux étant donné la petite dimension du fragment.[67]

[63] "The Old Greek is lost in this section as in 2 Kgs (Thackeray's γδ). The first stage, then, in the history of the Greek recensions was the Proto-Lucian recension of the second or first century B.C., revised to conform to a Palestinian Hebrew text." Cf. Cross, "The History of the Biblical Text," 295–296.

[64] Ulrich, *The Qumran Text of Samuel and Josephus*.

[65] "Thus, one must definitely reckon with a proto-Lucianic text tradition, based on OG, but even in its early stratus (before the turn of the era) revised. It did not simply suffer corruption, as Barthélemy alleges, but it was revised, with corrections and additions provided to make it conform to the 4QSam text tradition in contemporary Palestine." Cf. Ulrich, *The Qumran Text of Samuel and Josephus*, 258.

[66] "Since we do not have the precise exemplar from that tradition, but only a close affiliate in 4QSam^a, since that affiliate is less than 10% extant, and since it itself is close to the original Hebrew Vorlage of OG, clear, solid evidence for proto-lucianic revisional activity does not come in quantity. More precisely, the *possibility* for evidence is severely limited quantitatively." Cf. Ulrich, *The Qumran Text of Samuel and Josephus*, 258.

[67] Tov, dans sa recension de la thèse de Ulrich, émet quelques critiques méthodologiques: la difficulté de ne pas pouvoir vérifier les reconstructions et les options paléographiques de l'auteur, l'édition ni les photos n'étant disponibles (274); le manque de méthode dans les rétroversions de G qui sont proposées (274–275); enfin l'organisation des résultats qui oriente leur interprétation (283). Cf. E. Tov, "The Textual Affiliations of 4QSam^a," in id., *The Greek and Hebrew Bible. Collected Essays on the Septuagint* (VTSup 72; Leiden, 1999), 271–283 (version retravaillée d'un article paru en *JSOT* 14 (1979), 37–53).

4. Le Grec ancien des Règnes, un chantier ouvert: vers des conclusions provisoires

Les perspectives ouvertes par Barthélemy et Cross ont renouvelé notre connaissance du G. Les découvertes de Qumran semblent avoir, en effet, largement contribué à soutenir l'hypothèse, déjà énoncée par Paul de Lagarde, selon laquelle la Bible grecque ancienne a été soumise à plusieurs recensions hébraïsantes. Cette dimension recensionnelle du G a été résumée de manière très claire dans la thèse de James D. Shenkel.[68] Ces études montrent de toute évidence que l'on ne peut rechercher le Grec ancien sans confronter le(s) texte(s) grec(s) au(x) texte(s) hébreu(x), que ce soit celui de Qumran – si on en dispose – ou celui de M. L'histoire du G est donc indissociable de celle de la Bible hébraïque. Pourtant, comme nous l'avons déjà observé, toutes les questions ne sont pas résolues, tant s'en faut. Dans le sillage des deux pionniers que furent Barthélemy et Cross, un grand nombre de chercheurs se sont engagés dans des débats qui restent ouverts aujourd'hui encore. Il faut à présent évoquer certaines de ces questions encore en chantier – les étapes de l'activité recensionnelle, la nature de G^L et l'apport de La – et en tirer les conclusions provisoires pour la reconstitution du Grec ancien des Règnes.

4.1. Les étapes de recensions: quatre ou trois strates? Où est le Grec ancien?

La première question que nous héritons du débat entre Barthélemy et Cross est celle du nombre de strates recensionnelles du Grec ancien. La recherche se divise en deux opinions majoritaires. La première – soutenue par Cross, Ulrich, Shenkel – considère quatre étapes textuelles principales: 1° le Grec ancien qui nous est perdu; 2° le texte proto-lucianique – dont témoigne G^L, les mss boc_2e_2 – qui serait une révision du Grec ancien sur un texte hébreu palestinien du type de 4QSam^a au 2ème ou 1er siècle av. J.-C.;[69] 3° la recension

[68] J. D. Shenkel, *Chronology and Recensional Development in the Greek Text of Kings* (HSM 1; Cambridge, Massachusetts, 1968), spéc. 5–21. L'étude de Shenkel perfectionne également les observations de Barthélemy. Il découvre en effet quelques caractéristiques supplémentaires de la recension καίγε (13–18 et "Appendix A," 113–116) et montre que 2 Sm 10,1–11,1 appartient déjà à la section βγ marquée par la recension καίγε ("Appendix B," 117–120). Il montre surtout la cohérence et l'antiquité des indications chronologiques des rois selon G.

[69] Notons qu'en faisant du texte proto-lucianique une recension palestinienne, Cross préserve sa théorie des textes locaux et particulièrement l'existence d'un type

καίγε – identifiée en particulier en G^B pour les sections βγ et γδ – qui est une recension hébraïsante du Grec ancien ou de G^L (la question est ouverte) sur un texte de type babylonien ou proto-massorétique durant le 1er siècle de notre ère; 4° enfin la recension hexaplaire d'Origène, que l'on retrouve en G^A, dans quelques mss en minuscules et dans la Syro-Hexaplaire. Origène, au milieu du 3ème siècle, révisa en effet sa base grecque en fonction du texte proto-massorétique stabilisé et des versions juives anciennes, Théodotion et Aquila (héritiers du proto-lucianique) et Symmaque. La seconde opinion – Barthélemy, Tov[70] – ne distingue que trois étapes: le texte proto-lucianique n'est pas une première révision du Grec ancien mais son témoin le plus proche, soutenu par les témoins de Qumran.[71] Pour les autres étapes, les deux courants de recherche sont en accord.

Au stade de nos connaissances, on ne peut tirer de conclusion certaine sur cette première étape de l'histoire du G. Cependant, si la question reste ouverte, une perspective pragmatique nous conduit à résoudre provisoirement le problème. En effet, nous avons souligné que, selon l'option des quatre étapes, Cross et Ulrich doivent reconnaître que le Grec ancien – le texte grec qui servit de base à la supposée recension proto-lucianique – est perdu. Nous n'y avons donc accès qu'au travers des témoins qui subsistent, donc précisément le groupe antiochien, reflet du texte proto-lucianique. Il ressort donc qu'en l'état G^L est bien le texte qui présente les éléments les plus anciens qui nous soient accessibles. C'est précisément le raisonne-

égyptien, source de la traduction grecque originale. Voir p. ex. F. M Cross, *The Ancient Library of Qumran* (The Biblical Seminar 30; Sheffield, 1995[3], première édition 1958), spéc. 121–142.

[70] Pour Tov, la diversité de la Septante n'est pas à chercher d'abord dans des types de textes correspondant à une évolution du texte hébreu – autrement dit dans un processus de recension vers l'hébreu – mais dans une évolution interne au grec. Le cas de la recension καίγε est une exception et non une règle. Ainsi, il n'est pas prouvé que G^L soit, comme le suggère Cross, une recension hébraïsante: "In conclusion, I propose that the existence of a proto-Lucianic revision of the LXX has not been established. I further suggest that the substratum of boc_2e_2 contains either *the* Old Greek or any single Old Greek translation." E. Tov, "Lucian and Proto-Lucian. Toward a New Solution of the Problem," *RB* 79 (1972), 101–113, spéc. 110 (cet article a été retravaillé, notamment en ce qui concerne la bibliographie, en E. Tov, *The Greek and Hebrew Bible*, 477–488).

[71] "Mieux vaut commencer l'histoire textuelle de Samuel par la vieille forme palestinienne que nous ont fait redécouvrir les fragments de la 4e grotte de Qumrân et qui constitue plus ou moins la Vorlage de la Septante ancienne pour laquelle un processus de recension de type "proto-lucianique" a dû commencer presque dès que le traducteur a fini son travail." Barthélemy, "Les problèmes textuels," 240.

ment que fait Shenkel quand, admettant l'hypothèse de Cross comme probable, il considère G^{L}, en accord avec Barthélemy, comme un substitut du Grec ancien, "the Lucianic as a surrogate for the Old Greek."[72] Il note que, même si l'on distingue entre Grec ancien et proto-lucien, ces deux types de textes sont très proches en comparaison avec les recensions plus récentes. Quoiqu'il en soit, le Grec ancien n'est donc pas très différent du proto-lucien, respectivement de G^{B}, et sa *Vorlage* ne devait pas être très différente du type que nous retrouvons dans les fragements de Samuel de Qumran.

Nous pouvons donc en tirer une première conclusion provisoire. La recherche pragmatique et concrète dans le domaine de la Bible grecque la plus ancienne des Règnes conduit à accepter la thèse du P. Barthélemy selon laquelle G^{B}, pour les sections α, ββ et γγ, et G^{L}, en βγ et γδ, sont les témoins les plus sûrs et les plus proches de la strate la plus ancienne de G. Ces textes ne sont pourtant pas purement et simplement "le" Grec ancien, écrit sous la plume des premiers traducteurs. Cette considération doit s'accompagner d'une attention particulière à la nature textuelle de G^{L} et à sa complexité textuelle.

4.2. La nature de G^{L}

Le deuxième champ du débat actuel sur le texte grec est celui de la nature du texte antiochien. Il faut mentionner ici encore plusieurs travaux qui ont permis de progresser dans notre connaissance de ce groupe de textes.

La thèse de Sebastian Brock en 1966, publiée en 1996 à l'initiative de Bruno Chiesa, est la première étude systématique du texte "lucianique".[73] Alors qu'il apparaissait encore à Rahlfs que G^{L} n'avait pas de principe clair,[74] Brock montra que cette tradition textuelle contenait bel et bien certaines caractéristiques propres qui l'apparentaient plus à une recension effective qu'au résultat d'un processus évolutif de dégénérescence, comme le pensait Barthélemy dans un premier temps.[75] Mis à part les nombreuses leçons clairement

---

[72] Shenkel, *Chronology*, 10.

[73] S. Brock, *The Recensions of the Septuagint Version of I Samuel* (Quaderni di Henoch 9; Turin, 1996), spéc. 13*–17*, 297–299, 303–307.

[74] Rahlfs, *Seputaginta Studien*, 653.

[75] "(G^{L}) est essentiellement la Septante ancienne plus ou moins abâtardie et corrompue. Seulement en certains livres cette forme de la Septante a subi une recension

hexaplaires, Brock montra effectivement que certaines formules linguistiques ne peuvent s'expliquer que par une activité de révision du texte, qu'il nomme "recension".[76] Il s'agit principalement de deux caractéristiques spécifiques: 1° les corrections grammaticales et lexicographiques visant à convertir les expressions hellénistiques en attiques; 2° l'adaptation du texte à une lecture publique, en particulier en introduisant les noms propres à la place des pronoms. Or, l'examen de ces deux caractéristiques montre qu'elles datent de la période même de Lucien. Que ce soit lui-même ou l'un de ses contemporains qui en fut l'auteur a finalement peu d'importance, mais cela prouve pour le moins qu'une révision atticisante est effectuée sur un texte grec ancien dans les milieux antiochiens à la fin du 3ème ou début du 4ème siècle. Il montra par ailleurs que les nombreuses leçons attestées par le seul G^L doivent s'interpréter de manières diverses: si beaucoup d'entre elles témoignent incontestablement du Grec ancien, certaines doivent être considérées comme secondaires quoique très anciennes. Barthélemy a admis en partie ce dernier point en concédant qu'"un processus de recension de type 'proto-luciani-que' a dû commencer presque dès que le traducteur a fini son travail."[77] En définitive, Brock décrit G^L comme un témoin textuel à l'histoire unique et complexe à la fois: unique, car il a montré que G^L des Règnes représente un courant distinct qui s'est séparé du tronc de G dès le 1er siècle ap. J.-C. sans qu'il y ait eu de relations réciproques depuis lors;[78] complexe, car il contient des éléments nombreux du Grec ancien, des traces de recensions anciennes proto-lucianiques,[79] et une recension – ou un travail d'édition – à l'époque de Lucien, ce à quoi il faut ajouter de nombreuses contaminations hexaplaires tar-

systématique mais éclectique à partir de Symmaque, et parfois d'Aquila ou Théodotion. Jamais, à ma connaissance, il ne s'agit d'une recension de première main faite directement sur l'hébreu." Barthélemy, *Les devanciers*, 127. Nous avons vu qu'il révisa partiellement son jugement dans "Les problèmes textuels," 224 (cf. ci-dessus §3.1.).

[76] Brock, *The Recensions*, spéc. 297–299. Voir encore S. Brock, "*Lucian redivivus*. Some Reflections on Barthélemy's *Les Devanciers d'Aquila*," in F. L. Cross (éd.), *Studia Evangelica*, vol. 5 (TU 103; Berlin, 1968), 176–181.

[77] Barthélemy, "Les problèmes textuels," 240. Il n'admet pourtant pas purement et simplement l'existence d'une recension proto-lucianique au sens où l'entend Cross, comme le manifeste le début de cette citation citée plus haut.

[78] Brock, *The Recensions*, 304.

[79] S'il s'approche ici de la théorie de Cross, il ne l'adopte pourtant pas comme telle. Mais il n'accepte pas plus la thèse d'une large recension hébraïsante ancienne de G, comme καίγε de Barthélemy. Pour lui, l'activité recensionnelle ancienne est plus diffuse dans l'ensemble des témoins, l'effort plus systématique commençant autour du 2ème ou 3ème siècle. Brock, *The Recensions*, 303.

dives. Brock entend surtout éviter l'écueil qui consisterait à préjuger de la valeur d'une leçon parce qu'elle est attestée uniquement en G^L.[80] Des leçons secondaires de différentes natures – hexaplaires ou non – côtoient en effet les nombreux éléments du Grec ancien.

Natalio Fernández Marcos s'inscrit dans la même perspective générale que Brock.[81] Il souligne le fait que le texte antiochien des Règnes est une édition du 4ème siècle de notre ère dont la principale caractéristique est de réarranger son matériel en introduisant ou en supprimant des éléments et en apportant certaines corrections de clarification et d'harmonisation.[82] Pour Fernández Marcos, ces caractéristiques sont suffisamment nombreuses au regard du reste de la tradition grecque pour qu'on puisse y voir l'activité éditoriale d'un rédacteur antiochien. Dans certains cas pourtant, il n'est pas impossible que ces leçons représentent le Grec ancien ou même qu'elles attestent d'une *Vorlage* concurrente à M.[83] Mais Fernández Marcos se refuse à toute conclusion définitive en la matière.[84] Grâce à son travail, nous disposons d'une édition critique très précieuse de G^L pour les livres historiques.

---

80 Brock, *The Recensions*, 299.

81 N. Fernández Marcos, "Literary and Editorial Features of the Antiochian Text in Kings," in C. E. Cox (ed.), *VI Congress of the IOSCS, Jerusalem 1986* (SCS 23; Atlanta, 1987), 287–304; N. Fernández Marcos, "The Septuagint and the History of the Biblical Text," in id., *Scribes and Translators. Septuagint and Old Latin in the Books of Kings* (VTSup 54; Leiden, 1994), 3–37, spéc. 27–37. Voir également les introductions des éditions des Règnes, N. Fernández Marcos, J. R. Busto Saiz, *El Texto Antioqueno de la Biblia Griega*, vol. 1, *1–2 Samuel*, vol. 2, *1–2 Reyes* (Textos y Estudios "Cardenal Cisneros" de la Biblia Políglota Matritense 50, 53; Madrid, 1989–1992).

82 Fernández Marcos, "Literary and Editorial Features," fait l'étude de ces caractéristiques: a) des compléments apportés aux non-dits dans les schéma prédictions / accomplissements (292–294), b) des ajouts de petites phrases pour clarifier la narration (293–294), c) la réécriture stylistique de certains textes en éliminant les hébraïsmes et en introduisant des formes atticisantes (295–297), d) des corrections d'ordre théologique et de caractère midrashique, ou simplement des corrections savantes (297), e) enfin l'usage des doublets, juxtaposant traduction et translitération ou des leçons concurrentes de l'hébreu consonantique, M et/ou autre *Vorlage* (297–298).

83 Fernández Marcos, "Literary and Editorial Features," spéc. 291–292, 293–294 et 295.

84 Avec prudence, il ne pense pas que le texte antiochien, malgré la qualité de son témoignage ancien, représente le Grec ancien comme tel, voir p.ex. Fernández Marcos, *Scribes and Translators*, 36: "I realize that with our edition the Old Greek of the Septuagint is far from restored. (. . .) Text criticism has its own, strict rules. Each reading must be examined according to these rules, taking into account the development of the Greek language and everything we know of the whole text transmission before labeling it as the Old Greek."

Plus récemment encore, Bernard A. Taylor a fait une étude de G^L du premier livre des Règnes.[85] Au moyen d'analyses statistiques fournies par une recherche informatique, il poursuit un double objectif:[86] 1° établir les relations qu'entretiennent G^L, G^B et G^A en 1 Règnes, et 2° mettre en lumière les caractéristiques propres de G^L sur la base d'une analyse informatique synoptique des témoins. Il arrive à des conclusions proches des études précédentes.[87] Il établit d'abord que G^L ne partage pas les caractéristiques de G^B, qui est lui-même proche des leçons non hexaplaires de G^A. Cette conclusion soutient l'hypothèse communément admise selon laquelle G^B représente le Grec ancien en 1 Règnes. Pour ce qui est des caractéristiques propres à G^L, Taylor établit que le texte lucianique contient des caractéristiques cohérentes propres à une recension et d'autres qui ne sont pas appliquées systématiquement. Il en conclut que le texte majoritaire reconstitué dans son premier volume – représenté spécialement par les cinq témoins principaux déjà reconnus, b*b*oc_2e_2 – est une recension ou rédaction partielle qu'il faut dater du 4ème siècle, époque même de Lucien. L'étude de Taylor confirme donc, dans l'ensemble, les études qui l'ont précédé. Dans la ligne de Brock il met en évidence l'aspect recensionnel tardif de ce texte dans son état final, mais souligne également le caractère partiel de cette entreprise.[88]

Nous pouvons conclure que, si Barthélemy a prouvé la valeur indéniable de G^L pour notre accès au Grec ancien des Règnes – spécialement pour les sections où G majoritaire est marqué par la recension καίγε – la recherche actuelle souligne la nature complexe de ce témoin. Outre les interpolations hexaplaires évidentes, les études mentionnées manifestent clairement que le texte a été retravaillé plus ou moins largement dans une période ancienne d'abord, puis au 4ème siècle ensuite, époque de Lucien lui-même. Si, comme le notait déjà

[85] B. A. Taylor, *The Lucianic Manuscripts of 1 Reigns. Volume 1 Majority Text. Volume 2 Analysis* (Harvard Semitic Monographs 50–51; Atlanta, 1992–1993). Voir spécialement l'étude dans le vol. 2.

[86] Taylor, *The Lucianic Manuscripts*, vol. 1, 2.

[87] Taylor, *The Lucianic Manuscripts*, vol. 1, spéc. 127–128.

[88] Notons que si la méthode statistique fournit ici des résultats intéressants, on peut se demander si elle permet de juger efficacement de la valeur qualitative des variantes. À cet égard, il serait intéressant de comparer l'édition de 1 Règnes G^L que Taylor donne dans son premier volume avec celle de Fernández Marcos et Busto Saiz, parue en 1989, dont il ne s'est manifestement pas servi. Ni la bibliographie ni le chapitre I décrivant l'élaboration de la base de données ne mentionnent cette édition.

Barthélemy,[89] l'on ne peut véritablement donner le nom de "recension" à cette dernière intervention, il s'agit pour le moins d'une édition renouvelée de son texte grec de base. Nous pouvons en tirer une conclusion pratique supplémentaire: en considérant les sections où G^L représente vraisemblablement la strate la plus ancienne de la version grecque, il faut une vigilance particulière et un examen attentif de ses leçons spécifiques, pour s'assurer qu'il ne s'agit pas de variantes secondaires. Dans cette perspective, le témoignage de la *vetus latina* (La) revêt une importance déterminante.

4.3. Le témoignage de La

L'apport de La pour notre accès au Grec ancien est un champ de recherche qui s'est beaucoup développé dans les dernières décennies.[90] Il faut commencer par rappeler les travaux de Bonifatius Fischer qui, dès 1951, attirait l'attention sur la présence de leçons lucianiques dans la plus ancienne version latine.[91] Il soulignait en particulier l'importance de trois témoins: les citations de Cyprien et les mss de La 91 – gloses marginales de la Vulgate de León, *Legionensis*, 10ème siècle, déjà signalées par Vercellone – et La 115, *Vindobonensis*, palimpseste du 5ème siècle de la Bibliothèque de Naples.[92] En

[89] Barthélemy, admettant une révision antiochienne du texte, préférait pourtant parler d'une "édition" pour le cas de G^L. En effet elle ne répond pas, selon lui, aux caractéristiques propres d'une "recension" comme le font les recensions καίγε et hexaplaire: une recension "est l'intervention d'un individu ou d'une école pour améliorer cette traduction, ou bien en corrigeant la langue, ou surtout en conformant plus fidèlement le texte grec dont on a hérité au texte hébraïque auquel on a accès, et cela quelle que soit la façon plus ou moins étrange dont le recenseur entend cette fidélité." (Barthélemy, "Les problèmes textuels," 247, voir 243–250).

[90] Pour les Rois spécialement, cf. J. Trebolle Barrera, *Jehú y Joás*, 17–43; pour une vue d'ensemble J. Gribomont, "Latin Versions. 1. The Old Latin Bible," in K. Crim (ed.), *The Interpreter's Dictionary of the Bible. Supplement Volume* (Nashville, 1976), 528–530; J. Gribomont, "Les plus anciennes traductions latines," in J. Fontaine, C. Pietri (éds.), *Le monde latin antique et la Bible* (Bible de tous les temps 2; Paris, 1985), 43–65; P.-M. Bogaert, "La Bible latine des origines au moyen âge. Aperçu historique, état de la question," *RTL* 19 (1988), 137–159 et 276–314, spéc. 143–156; B. Kedar, "The Latin Translations," in M. J. Mulder (ed.), *Mikra. Text, Translation, Reading and Interpretation of the Hebrew Bible in Ancient Judaism and Early Christianity* (Compendia rerum iudaicarum ad Novum Testamentum 2.1; Assen/Maastricht, Philadelphia, 1988), 299–338.

[91] B. Fischer, "Lukian-Lesarten in der Vetus Latina der vier Königsbücher," in A. Metzinger (ed.), *Miscellanea Biblica et Orientalia A. Miller oblata* (Studia Anselmiana 27–28; Rome, 1951), 169–177.

[92] B. Fischer, *Verzeichnis der Sigel für Handschriften und Kirchenschrifsteller* (Vetus Latina 1; Freiburg, 1949), 17–18.

comparant ces témoins avec G^L et G majoritaire, il conclut que les leçons partagées par La et G^L attestent d'un type textuel grec ancien dont ils sont parfois les seuls témoins.[93] Fischer publia une nouvelle édition du palimpseste *Vindobonensis* en 1983 qui reste l'un des principaux témoins de La dont nous disposions pour les Règnes.[94]

Pour la recherche contemporaine, le témoignage de La n'est pas uniquement une contribution à la reconstitution du Grec ancien. Comme témoin de la version grecque la plus ancienne, elle apparaît comme un moyen privilégié de rejoindre sa *Vorlage* hébraïque, comme l'affirme Bogaert: "les exemples ne sont pas exceptionnels où la *vetus latina* atteste un "Old Greek" perdu ou moins bien conservé, lui-même témoin d'un texte hébreu différent du texte reçu; c'est le cas dans les Règnes (1–2 S; 1–2 R)."[95] C'est dans cette ligne qu'il faut situer les principaux résultats de la recherche récente sur La des Règnes. Nous pouvons mentionner quatre auteurs qui ont développé cette perspective pour les Règnes.

Ulrich a fait une étude comparative des différents témoins de 2 Sm 11–24 – section βγ des Règnes –: G^L, La (dont en particulier le 115, *Vindobonensis*) et 4QSam[a,c].[96] S'il lui semble difficile de tirer une conclusion définitive pour l'ensemble des Règnes, il ressort de son analyse que La s'accorde fréquemment avec les fragments de Qumran et le texte de G^L contre G majoritaire – marqué dans cette section par la recension καίγε – et M.[97] En clair, il montre que La permet non

[93] "All diesen Gegebenheiten werden wir nur dadurch gerecht, dass wir einen besonderen griechischen Texttyp annehmen, der nicht in den erhaltenen griechischen Hss überliefert wird. Vieles aus diesem verlorenen Texttyp hat Lukian in seine Rezension übernommen. Weithin folgte die VL diesem Texttyp. Ungewiss bleibt, ob die Vorlage der VL (= La) diesen Texttyp rein dartellte, oder ob sie wenigstens stellenweise von *G* beeinflusst war", Fischer, "Lukian-Lesarten," 177.

[94] B. Fischer, "Palimpsestus Vindobonensis," in id., *Beiträge zur Geschichte der lateinischen Bibeltexte* (Aus der Geschichte der Lateinischen Bibel 12; Freiburg, 1986), 308–438 (reprise d'une publication avec la collaboration de E. Ulrich et J. E. Sanderson, *BIOSCS* 16 [1983], 13–87). Il existait déjà une édition de ce texte par J. Belsheim, *Palimpsestus Vindobonensis* (Christiania, 1885).

[95] Bogaert, "La Bible latine," 155.

[96] E. Ulrich, "The Old Latin Translation of the LXX and the Hebrew Scrolls from Qumran," in id., *The Dead Sea Scrolls and the Origins of the Bible* (Studies in the Dead Sea Scrolls and Related Literature; Grand Rapids, 1999), 233–274 (paru pour la première fois en E. Tov [ed.], *The Hebrew and Greek Texts of Samuel. 1980 Proceedings IOSCS – Vienna* [Jérusalem, 1980], 121–165).

[97] "The frequency of the pattern L = 4QSam[a,c] $G^L \neq$ M G and the infrequency of the pattern L = M G $\neq$ 4QSam[a,c] G^L again confirm the general hypothesis according to which this study has been structured and conducted, namely, the theory of the textual history of Samuel conceived by Barthélemy, developed by Cross, and

seulement de reconstituer le Grec ancien, mais encore de restituer, selon toute vraisemblance, une *Vorlage* hébraïque différente de M qui témoigne d'un type textuel parfois plus ancien.[98]

Dans le même sens, Julio Trebolle démontre que, dans plusieurs passages des Règnes, La témoigne effectivement de la version grecque ancienne qui remonte elle-même à un texte hébreu ancien différent du M.[99] Très récemment, Adrian Schenker est arrivé à des conclusions analogues.[100] Ces contributions sont de toute première importance pour l'histoire du texte biblique de Samuel-Rois.

Fernández Marcos[101] a également manifesté l'importance du témoignage de La en soulignant spécialement la place particulière qu'occupent, selon lui, les gloses marginales des Vulgates espagnoles. L'étude des leçons propres de ces gloses – non attestées par d'autres témoins textuels – montre qu'à côté des nombreuses activités de type éditorial internes à La,[102] la plus ancienne version latine témoigne, dans des cas assez rares, de leçons qui remontent certainement à sa *Vorlage*

tested in *QTSJ* [*The Qumran Text of Samuel and Josephus*] and elsewhere: the Old Greek and some of its early developments, including conscious revisions, are based predominantly on the text tradition shared by 4QSam^{a,c} as opposed to the Masoretic text, whereas the majority Greek text for 2 Samuel 11–24 displays a text that in its basic stratum was the same but that underwent subsequent recension toward conformity with the ascendant Masoretic text." Ulrich, "The Old Latin Translation," 270.

[98] "L proves to be a reasonably faithful and controllable witness to the Old Greek, which in turn is not infrequently a witness superior to the Masoretic text for the ancient text of Samuel." Ulrich, "The Old Latin Translation," 270.

[99] J. Trebolle, "From the *Old Latin*, through the *Old Greek* to the *Old Hebrew* (2 Kings 10:23–25)," *Textus* 11 (1984), 17–36; J. Trebolle, "Old Latin, Old Greek and Old Hebrew in the Books of Kings (1 Ki. 18:27 and 2 Ki. 20:11)," *Textus* 13 (1986), 85–94.

[100] P. ex. dans sa conférence au congrès de l'IOSOT de Leiden pour le cas de 2 R 23,1–3 où il a souligné spécialement le témoignage de Lucifer de Cagliari: Schenker, "Die Textgeschichte der Königsbücher"; voir encore id., "The Origin of the Masoretic Text of the Books of Kings", à paraître; id., *Älteste Textgeschichte*, 134–167.

[101] N. Fernández Marcos, "Aberrant Texts in the Books of Kings," in id., *Scribes and Translators*, 39–91; id., "The *Vetus Latina* of 1–2 Kings and the Hebrew," in L. Greenspoon, O. Munnich (ed.), *VIII Congress of the IOSCS Paris 1992* (SCS 41; Atlanta, 1995), 153–163.

[102] Il souligne particulièrement trois caractéristiques de ce type de leçons: 1° la présence de nombreux doublets qui suivent et parfois développent même les caractéristiques propres de leur *Vorlage* grecque, G^L; 2° des accidents de transmission du texte et des erreurs paléographiques qui peuvent avoir eu lieu dans le travail de traduction en latin, dans la *Vorlage* grecque de La ou même dans le texte source hébreu; 3° des corrections de type midrashique ou exégétique dans des passages difficiles ou corrompus. Fernández Marcos pense que les traducteurs latins faisaient preuve d'une grande créativité littéraire (cf. Fernández Marcos, "Aberrant Texts," 53–70).

grecque perdue et, par elle, probablement à une source hébraïque différente de TM.[103] Fernández Marcos reste donc très prudent dans ses conclusions, invitant les chercheurs à soumettre La à un examen critique avant de considérer ses leçons comme témoins d'un pluralisme textuel hébreu.[104]

La présence de nombreux hébraïsmes en La et sa proximité avec un modèle hébreu a conduit certains chercheurs, comme Umberto Cassuto, à se demander si la plus ancienne version latine ne trouverait pas son origine dans des traductions juives faites directement à partir de l'hébreu.[105] Mais ce type de considération est encore loin d'offrir des preuves satisfaisantes.[106] De son côté, Benjamin Kedar estime plutôt que La aurait été révisée par des "demi-savants" ("half-learned") qui auraient introduit des corrections juives hébraïsantes.[107] Fernández Marcos, pour sa part, pense au contraire que les hébraïsmes de La dans les Règnes ne trouvent pas leur source directement dans l'hébreu. Ils traduisent littéralement une *Vorlage* grecque qui elle-même traduit littéralement son modèle hébreu ou qui a pu subir

[103] Fernández Marcos, "Aberrant Texts," 71–82.

[104] "In brief, these considerations preclude any use of the Old Latin for the restoration of the Biblical text and for the discussion of textual pluralism until it has been first critically examined according to the proper criteria of inner textual criticism" (Fernández Marcos, "Aberrant Texts," 87).

[105] U. Cassuto, "The Jewish Translation of the Bible into Latin and its Importance for the Study of the Greek and Aramaic Versions," in id., *Biblical and Oriental Studies*, vol. 1 (Jérusalem, 1973), 285–298. En 1949, Umberto Cassuto émit en effet l'hypothèse que les communautés juives de la diaspora en milieu latin auraient progressivement utilisé cette langue dans la traduction orale des lectures à la synagogue et dans l'enseignement biblique des enfants. Pour des modalités pratiques, ces traductions auraient probablement été consignées par écrit. Sans le dire ici explicitement, Cassuto adopte de fait la position de Kahle – multiplicité des traductions originelles – en ce qui concerne l'origine de La comme celle de G (298). Pour le cas du latin, il conclut: "Although all the translations and glossaries were private efforts, which had no official character and were not intended to provide a definitive edition, and hence differed in details, yet basically they all represented a single, uniform tradition, which but continued the ancient Latin tradition" (297). Voir également d'autres auteurs mentionnés par Fernández Marcos, "Aberrant Texts," 86 n. 33.

[106] Gribomont, "Les plus anciennes traductions latines," 46.

[107] Cf. Kedar, "The Latin Translations," 308–311. Il relève quatre types d'interventions hébraïsantes pour lesquelles il donne des exemples: les erreurs de traduction, l'érudition hébraïque, les ajouts et les translittérations. Il en tire la conclusion suivante: "This leads us to believe that most of these points of contact with Hebrew text, or with Jewish exegesis, are not remnants of an old Jewish Latin version – some, of course, may be such – but rather the result of later corrections and insertions at the hand of persons who had sufficient knowledge of the respective languages to notice the many imperfections of the version, yet did not possess sufficient skill nor authority to perform a thorough job" (310–311).

une correction hébraïsante.[108] Une étude récente de Matthew Kraus reprend les conclusions de Fernández Marcos et analyse à nouveau frais les cas textuels étudiés par Kedar.[109] Pour notre propos, nous pouvons résumer ses conclusions en trois points principaux: 1° il n'y a aucune preuve que La dérive directement d'une *Vorlage* hébraïque ni qu'elle soit l'objet d'une recension directement à partir de l'hébreu. Les hébraïsmes de La ont alors deux origines possibles. 2° Ils peuvent en premier lieu provenir de leur source grecque qui parfois représente une *Vorlage* hébraïque différente de M, et parfois semblent être le fruit d'une recension hébraïsante vers M. 3° Les hébraïsmes peuvent avoir une seconde origine qui serait l'influence plus tardive de Jérôme et du mouvement qui cherche à conformer le texte latin à l'hébreu. Ce mouvement n'est pas originaire mais date du 4ème siècle, époque où les communautés juives latinophones empruntaient des traductions chrétiennes en les corrigeant peut-être.

L'étude de Kraus appelle pourtant quelques observations. D'abord il manifeste clairement l'importance de la *Vorlage* grecque de La. Je pense en effet avec lui que c'est principalement en se fondant littéralement sur sa source grecque que La reflète des hébraïsmes. Quant à la considération de l'hébraïsation de cette *Vorlage* grecque, Kraus considère implicitement que G^L représente une recension hébraïsante,[110] ce que les acquis de la recherche ne permettent pas d'affirmer si simplement, nous l'avons vu. Nous pouvons conclure provisoirement que, quand La témoigne d'hébraïsmes qui se distinguent du substrat hébreu reflété par M, elle représente le plus ancien G que nous puissions atteindre et non une correction du 4ème siècle.

Nous pouvons enfin tirer trois conclusions sur l'apport du témoignage textuel de La. 1° Les études mentionnées montrent que, pour les Règnes, il y a trois témoins principaux de la plus ancienne version latine: le *Vindobonensis* édité par Fischer (La 115 selon la nomenclature de la *Vetus Latina* de Beuron), les gloses marginales des Vulgates espagnoles (La 91–96)[111] et les citations de Lucifer de Cagliari (mort

[108] Cf. Fernández Marcos, "Aberrant Texts," 87 n. 36, et id., "The *Vetus Latina* of 1–2 Kings and the Hebrew," 154–155.

[109] M. Kraus, "Hebraisms in the Old Latin Version of the Bible," *VT* 53 (2003), 487–513.

[110] M. Kraus, "Hebraisms," 492 et 512. Il dépend ici de l'opinion qui procède des conclusions de Cross sur une recension proto-lucianique. Je me suis expliqué plus haut (§4.1.) sur la perspective pragmatique que l'on peut adopter dans la considération de la couche la plus ancienne de G.

[111] C. Morano Rodríguez, *Glosas marginales de* Vetus Latina *en las Biblias Vulgatas*

en 370/371) qui est l'un des principaux témoins patristiques de La par l'abondance de ses extraits.[112] 2° La est un témoin privilégié du Grec ancien. À ce titre, elle est en général très fidèle à G^L, particulièrement dans les sections où le G majoritaire est marqué par la recension καίγε.[113] Elle permettra de vérifier certaines leçons du Grec ancien et de prouver, le cas échéant, qu'elles ne sont pas le fruit d'une évolution interne au grec. 3° Dans certains cas, La permettra même de reconstituer la version la plus ancienne de la Bible grecque disparue des témoins dont nous disposons. Elle pourra alors remonter à une source hébraïque éventuellement différente de M. Dans ces cas, il faudra cependant observer la prudence préconisée par Fernández Marcos.

5. *Conclusion: G^B et G^L témoins privilégiés du Grec ancien des Règnes*

À la fin de ce parcours de l'histoire de la recherche critique du Grec ancien des livres des Règnes, il est possible de résumer les acquis de cette investigation en trois points.

1° Grâce à l'étude de Dominique Barthélemy – fondée sur les recherches de ses prédécesseurs Mez, Rahlfs et Thackeray, nuancée et complétée par les travaux ultérieurs de Cross, Brock, Ulrich, Shenkel et d'autres – nous pouvons affirmer que le codex *Vaticanus* et le texte antiochien sont les meilleurs témoins directs de la strate la plus ancienne des Règnes accessible aujourd'hui. Dans les sections α, ββ et γγ, G^B témoigne d'un texte pré-hexaplaire et non soumis à la recension καίγε. Dans les sections βγ et γδ où le G majoritaire a subi la recension καίγε, G^L témoigne d'un texte à la fois épargné par cette recension et à l'abri de la recension origénienne, mis à part quelques interpolations tardives; elle y représente donc fondamentalement la couche la plus ancienne à laquelle nous ayons accès.

2° G^B et G^L ne reflètent pourtant pas directement la traduction initiale du livre. Plusieurs études ont en effet attiré l'attention sur le

españolas. 1–2 Samuel (Textos y Estudios "Cardenal Cisneros" de la Biblia Políglota Matritense 48; Madrid, 1989), et A. Moreno Hernández, *Las Glosas marginales de* Vetus Latina *en las Biblias Vulgatas españolas. 1–2 Reyes* (Textos y Estudios "Cardenal Cisneros" de la Biblia Políglota Matritense 49; Madrid 1992).

[112] Cf. G. R. Diercks, *Luciferi Calaritani opera quae supersunt* (Corpus Christianorum Series Latina 8; Tourhout, 1978), une première approche de la nature de sa Bible CV-CXVIII. Il faut souligner que la tradition manuscrite de Lucifer est très réduite puisqu'elle ne compte que deux mss (description XXXVIII–LI).

[113] Cf. le tableau de statistiques chez Fernández Marcos, "Aberrant Texts," 51–52.

fait que ces deux témoins n'étaient pas toujours exempts de traces de recensions ou de révisions anciennes – déjà au 2ème ou 1er siècles avant notre ère, selon Cross et Ulrich – ou plus tardives – 4ème siècle, d'après Brock et Fernández Marcos. C'est pourquoi il faudra également soumettre les leçons propres de ces témoins textuels à un examen approfondi pour s'assurer, autant que possible, qu'elles ne sont pas le fruit de modifications internes au grec. À cet égard, plusieurs études – dont celles de Ulrich, Trebolle et du prudent Fernández Marcos – ont montré que le témoignage de La offrait un accès à une couche très ancienne de G dont elle est parfois le seul témoin.[114]

3° Une des grandes leçons de cette histoire de la recherche réside dans la constatation qu'il ne faut pas isoler les témoins grecs du reste de la tradition textuelle. Déjà le troisième principe de Paul de Lagarde pour la recherche du Grec original affirmait que si deux leçons étaient concurrentes et que l'une suivait M et que l'autre ne pouvait s'expliquer que par un original hébreu différent, il fallait préférer la seconde. Dans le cas des Règnes, la découverte des fragments de Samuel à Qumran a souligné l'importance de ce principe. L'analyse comparative entre la tradition grecque et les témoins hébreux – M et les découvertes du désert de Juda – contribue à éclairer l'histoire de la Bible sur deux niveaux. Premièrement cette comparaison permet d'expliquer l'histoire de la transmission du G, puisque Barthélemy et Cross ont montré que les traditions grecques initiales ont été soumises à des recensions successives vers un texte hébreu de type proto-massorétique. Deuxièmement, si le Grec ancien – parfois attesté par La – témoigne d'une *Vorlage* hébraïque différente de M et de sa source proto-massorétique, il jette une lumière nouvelle sur l'histoire même de la Bible hébraïque. C'est à ce point de la recherche que l'œuvre d'Adrian Schenker apporte une contribution de premier plan.

[114] L'importance de La dans l'accès au Grec ancien pose des questions méthodologiques pour l'élaboration d'une édition critique des livres des Règnes. Comment en effet introduire les leçons latines jugées originales dans une édition grecque; faut-il reconstituer le texte grec perdu et introduire cette leçon conjecturale dans l'édition, ou faut-il se résoudre à choisir une leçon grecque secondaire? *A fortiori* des questions analogues se posent sur l'usage de G et de La, dans une édition critique de la Bible hébraïque, cf. A. Schenker, P. Hugo, "Histoire du texte et critique textuelle de l'Ancien Testament dans la recherche récente," in A. Schenker, P. Hugo (éds.), *L'enfance de la Bible hébraïque. L'histoire du texte de l'Ancien Testament à la lumière des recherches récentes* (Le monde de la Bible 52; Genève, 2005), 11–33, spéc. 22–27 ("Les raisons qui empêchent l'établissement d'un texte critique").

THE TEXT OF ISAIAH AND ITS EARLY WITNESSES IN HEBREW

Arie van der Kooij

I

A main characteristic of the new edition, the *Biblica Hebraica Quinta* (*BHQ*), is the use of the textual evidence from manuscripts discovered in Qumran and other places in the Dead Sea region. From the point of textual criticism these texts are of great significance. In the period before Qumran the critical assessment of the Masoretic text (M) was mainly done on the basis of the early versions – translations, which by their nature do not provide direct evidence of the Hebrew text. Instead, the underlying parent text has to be reconstructed first, a procedure which in many instances creates a great deal of uncertainty. Most biblical texts of Qumran, however, are written in the language of the Hebrew Bible, Hebrew or Aramaic, thus representing direct evidence of the text. Moreover, they date from the earliest period in which the biblical text is attested, viz., the third century B.C.E. up to the second century C.E. In comparison to the other witnesses of the early period – the Septuagint (G) and the Samaritan Pentateuch (Smr) – the Qumran texts have an additional value in that they constitute manuscript evidence that goes back to this early period directly, and not indirectly, i.e., via a reconstruction of the text of a witness on the basis of manuscripts of a later date, as is the case with the G and Smr.

Given the great significance of the biblical texts from the Dead Sea region it is, on the other hand, frustrating that in general the evidence is so fragmentary. Fortunately, the book of Isaiah – my part in the Quinta project – is attested by a large number of mostly fragmentary manuscripts from Qumran (22), but also by one complete scroll (1QIsa[a]), and another one that has been preserved for a fifth of the book (1QIsa[b]).[1] As a whole the Qumran evidence now avail-

[1] For a listing of the evidence see, for example, M. G. Abegg, Jr., "1QIsa[a] and

able is very important, the more so since G-Isaiah – a version also going back to the early period – represents an indirect witness which, due to its nature as a 'free' translation, causes much uncertainty as far as the underlying Hebrew text is concerned. Consequently, the evidence of the Dead Sea region will play a leading role in the selection of cases for the critical apparatus of Isaiah in *BHQ*.

In this contribution in honour of Adrian Schenker, I like to discuss a number of variant readings in Isaiah which are attested by two or more Qumran MSS.

II

In some cases the available evidence provides us with an interesting variety of readings. Here are some examples.

5:19 M תקרב ותבואה; 1QIsa[a] ותקרבה ותבואה; 4QIsa[b] ותקרבה ותבא

The lengthened form of the third person sing., תבואה (cohortative), is rare in M (cf. יחישה in the same verse).[2] The reading תקרבה may be due to influence of תבואה.[3] It is difficult to say which text tradition is to be preferred here.

22:17 M ועטך; 1QIsa[a] יעוטך; 1QIsa[b] ויע]טך; 4QIsa[a] ויעטך

The Qumran witnesses reflect a tendency related to later Hebrew.[4]

26:1 M השיר הזה; 1QIsa[a] השיר הזואת; 1QIsa[b] השירה הזאת; 4QIsa[c] השיר ה]זה

The reading of M is a *hapax*, whereas that of 1QIsa[b] is the usual one in M (e.g., Exod 15:1; Num 21:17). 1QIsa[a] offers a mixed reading. The reading of M (= 4QIsa[c], with some uncertainty) is the more difficult one and hence the preferable one.[5]

1QIsa[b]: a Rematch," in E. D. Herbert and E. Tov (eds.), *The Bible as Book: The Hebrew Bible and the Judaean Desert Discoveries* (London, 2002), 222f. In addition, there are a number of citations from Isaiah in Q-documents such as the pesharim.

[2] See H. Bauer and P. Leander, *Historische Grammatik der hebräischen Sprache des Alten Testamentes* (Halle, 1918; repr. Hildesheim, 1965), §56u", 59p.

[3] E. Y. Kutscher, *The Language and Linguistic Background of the Isaiah Scroll (1QIsa[a])* (*STDJ* 6; Leiden, 1974), 328.

[4] See Kutscher, *Language*, 357f.

[5] Cf. D. Barthélemy, *Critique Textuelle de l'Ancien Testament*, vol. 3, *Ézéchiel, Daniel et les 12 Prophètes* (OBO 50/3; Fribourg & Göttingen, 1992), cviii. (= *CTAT* 3).

46:10 M אחרית; 1QIsa[b] = M; 1QIsa[a] אחרות; 4QIsa[a] אח]רונות
46:13 M קרבתי; 1QIsa[b] = M; 1QIsa[a] קרובה; 4QIsa[c] הקרבתי

In both cases M = 1QIsa[b] represents the better reading. The reading אחרות (1QIsa[a]) may be an error,[6] or a plural form conveying the same meaning as the reading of 4QIsa[a], אח]רונות.[7] (This latter reading, which is not attested in M, is also found in 1QIsa[a] 41:22. Compare the plural form ראשנות in 41:22; 42:9.)

As to קרבתי, the reading of 1QIsa[a] may be due to influence of 56:1, whereas the reading in 4QIsa[c] is an adaptation to the more common usage in biblical Hebrew (the *hifil* of קרב occurs many times in M; the *piel*, however, is rare).

III

Of particular interest are those cases where more than one biblical Qumran MS of Isaiah attests the same variant reading against M. The shared evidence may enhance the possibility that the Qumran MSS attest a reading which is earlier and better than the Masoretic one. On the other hand, it is one of the principles of textual criticism that MSS should not be counted, but weighed, a rule which also applies to the date of MSS. Each case therefore should be evaluated individually. First, we will deal with some cases of 1QIsa[a] = 1QIsa[b] against M, secondly, with cases of 1QIsa[a] = 4Q MS, and thirdly, with cases of 1QIsa[a] = two Qumran MSS.

A. 1QIsa[a] = 1QIsa[b] ≠ M

45:2 M הדורים; 1QIsa[a] הררים; 1QIsa[b] הרורים

Hebrew הדורים presents a difficulty since its meaning is uncertain and disputed ('spiral roads', 'uneven places'?).[8] Scholars, therefore, have argued that the variant reading attested by 1QIsa[a] (1QIsa[b]?) and G, "mountains", is to be preferred, as it makes good sense in the context.[9] However, the difficulty with this solution is that the

[6] Kutscher, *Language*, 366.

[7] A. van der Kooij, *Die alten Textzeugen des Jesajabuches* (OBO 35; Freiburg & Göttingen, 1981), 95.

[8] For a detailed discussion, see J. L. Koole, *Isaiah, Part 3*, vol. 1, *Isaiah 40–48* (HCOT; Kampen, 1997), 434–435.

[9] See, e.g., D. Barthélemy, *CTAT* 3, cviii.

reduplicated plural (הררים; see also 1QIsa[a] 42:11) does not occur in biblical Hebrew in the absolute state.[10] As has been argued by other scholars, M-Kethib may well represent the original reading if taken in the sense of 'the walls', in line with Akkadian *duru*.[11] Contextually, this would fit even better because of the 'doors of bronze' and 'bars of iron' in the rest of the verse.

49:7 M יהוה; 1QIsa[a] = 1QIsa[b] אדני יהוה

According to Barthélemy[12] the short reading of M is the better one. The long expression occurs at some places (thirteen) in M Isaiah where it is also attested by 1QIsa[a] (except in a few instances [49:22; 50:5; 52:4; 61:11]). It is difficult to say which reading in 49:7 is the primary one, but it may well be that the long reading of 1QIsa[a] = 1QIsa[b] is due to influence of 48:16.

51:7 M ומגדפתם; 1QIsa[a] וממגדפותם; 1QIsa[b] וממגדפתם

The second *mem* in 1QIsa[a] has been added, in superscript, by a second hand. The feminine plural in M is a *hapax*. Instead of the *qittul*-form in M both Qumran witnesses offer a *miqtal*-form, which seems to be an adaptation to a more usual form.

53:1 M על; 1QIsa[a] = 1QIsa[b] אל

The *nifal* of גלה with על occurs here and in Exod 20:26. The variant reading in both 1QIsa[a] (the *ʾalep* was corrected here from *ʿayin*) and 1QIsa[b] is in line with the usage at other places (e.g., Gen 35:17; 1 Sam 3:7, 21). The same is true for Smr Exod 20:26 (אליו). M seems to be the better reading.

54:3 M יירשׁ; 1QIsa[a] = 1QIsa[b] יירשו

The plural form may be an assimilation to יושׁיבו,[13] but it is also possible that this form was introduced because of the subject זרע, 'seed' (M reads זרעך גוים יירשׁ). For a similar case see 57:3.

55:11 M אשׁר; 1QIsa[a] = 1QIsa[b] את אשר

The plus in both Qumran MSS is probably due to harmonization with the first half of v. 11b (את אשר חפצתי).

[10] Koole, *Isaiah*, 435.

[11] See C. H. Southwood, "The problematic *hadurim* of Isaiah xlv 2," *VT* 25 (1975), 801f.

[12] Barthélemy, *CTAT* 3, cix.

[13] Barthélemy, Ibid.

58:3 M נפשנו; 1QIsa[a] נפשותינו = 1QIsa[b] נפשתינו

The plural form in both Qumran MSS is an adaptation to the idiom as found in texts such as Lev 16:29, 31 and Num 29:7.[14]

62:6 M תמיד; 1QIsa[a] = 1QIsa[b] >

The Hebrew תמיד, which in M follows the expression 'all the day and all the night', may well have been regarded as superfluous.

B. 1QIsa[a] = 4Q ≠ M

10:32 M בית; 1QIsa[a] = 4QIsa[c] בת

The reading of the Qumran MSS agrees with M Qere. The latter, "(the mountain) of the daughter (of Zion)", is the original one (cf. Isa 16:1). For this reading, see also 4QpIsa[a] 5–6, l. 4.

11:8 M צפעוני; 1QIsa[a] = 4QIsa[c] צפעונים

The plural reading of the Qumran MSS is the secondary one.[15] For a similar case see 1QIsa[a] Isa 59:5.

12:4 M ואמרתם; 1QIsa[a] ואמרתה; 4QIsa[e] ואמרת

The singular in the Qumran MSS seems to be an assimilation to v. 1.

19:9 M חורי; 1QIsa[a] = 4QIsa[b] חורו

M is difficult here.[16] The reading of the Qumran MSS seems to be the preferable one – "(and weavers) shall wax pale" (of the root חור)[17] – because this verb makes good sense parallel with בוש in the same verse (cf. 29:22).

19:18 M ההרס; 1QIsa[a] = 4QIsa[b] החרס

As has been argued by scholars, the Qumran MSS offer the better reading here: "(the city) of the sun" (instead "the city of destruction" in M).[18]

---

[14] Cf. Kutscher, *Language*, 398; Barthélemy, *CTAT* 3, cx.

[15] See Kutscher, *Language*, 399.

[16] *DCH* suggests: חורי, 'white stuff'. The reference to 4QpIsa[c] (4Q163), however, is misleading since the reading involved is not attested by the MS, but has been reconstructed to fill in a lacuna.

[17] See, e.g., Kutscher, *Language*, 235; D. Barthélemy, *Critique textuelle de l'Ancien Testament*, vol. 2, *Isaïe, Jérémie, Lamentations* (Fribourg & Göttingen, 1986), 139. (= *CTAT* 2)

[18] See, e.g., D. Barthélemy, *CTAT* 2, 143–150; van der Kooij, *Textzeugen*, 216.

24:4 M אמללו; 1QIsa[a] = 4QIsa[c] אמלל

The M reading may represent the primary one,[19] but in this instance the evaluation of the evidence depends on the interpretation of the word that follows, מרום. (M reads אמללו מרום עם הארץ.) If one takes this word, together with עם, in the sense of people that are in a high position (cf. Job 5:11), then the plural reading is fitting, but if מרום is understood in the sense of a high place, the singular reading is more plausible.

24:6 M חרו; 1QIsa[a] = 4QIsa[c] חורו

The Qumran MSS offer a reading here which is the same as in 19:9 (see above). The M reading is best explained as a form of חרה[II], 'to diminish in number' (cf. the parallel, נשׁאר). It fits the context better than the verb חור.[20]

26:12 M תשׁפת; 1QIsa[a] תשפוט; 4QIsa[b] תשׁפט

As is often the case, particularly in 1QIsa[a], a common word – in this case שׁפט – has been substituted for a rarer one, שׁפת.[21] The verb שׁפת occurs at a few other places (2 Kgs 4:38; Ezek 24:3; Ps 22:16) and carries the meaning 'to set'.

42:11 M ישׂאו; 1QIsa[a] = 4QIsa[h] ישא

The verbal form is followed by מדבר, 'the desert', and it therefore seems appropriate to have a singular form here. However, it may well be that the M reading is the better one since contextually speaking (see v. 11b) the inhabitants of the desert are meant.

49:7 M לבזה; 1QIsa[a] = 4QIsa[d] לבזוי

The M reading לבזה is a difficult one since its vocalization (infinitive construct) does not seem to make sense. Rather, one expects an adjective, or participle (cf. מתעב) as continuation of "Thus says the Lord to . . .". One therefore could read the Kethib בזה as an active participle, as some scholars prefer (cf. G), but most scholars agree that a passive sense is the more plausible understanding of the verse.[22] Consequently, the variant reading בזוי is likely to be the primary

[19] So Barthélemy, *CTAT* 2, 174.

[20] Cf., for example, H. Wildberger, *Jesaja* (BKAT 10; Neukirchen-Vluyn, 1972–1982), 915.

[21] See Kutscher, *Language*, 293.

[22] See Koole, *Isaiah*, 31f.

reading, as many scholars believe.[23] Alternatively, since this reading may have been due to a harmonization to מחעב, and since the collocation לבזוי נפש suggests the meaning, 'despised *by* someone'[24] rather than 'despised as far as (his) נפש is concerned', it is more likely to regard the Kethib בזה as the primary reading and to vocalize it as בְּזֹה.[25]

C. 1QIsa[a] = Two Qumran mss ≠ M

46:11 M Kethib עצתו / Qere עצתי; 1QIsa[a] = 1QIsa[b] = 4QIsa[d] עצתו

The Qumran MSS support M Kethib which is the primary reading.

48:11 M יחל; 1QIsa[a] = 4QIsa[c] = 4QIsa[d] איחל
(4QIsa[d] with a second *ʾalep* in superscript)

McCarthy has argued that the variant of the Qumran MSS testifies to the primary reading since M represents here an example of a *tiqqûn*, a theological correction. The phrase "How should I be profaned" (איך אחל / איחל) was changed into "How should it be profaned", in order to avoid blasphemy.[26] Other scholars, however, consider M to be the better reading. The verbal form (יחל) should be understood as referring to "my name" in v. 9 ("How should my name be profaned"). Furthermore, according to this view, the first person singular in the Qumran MSS is easily understood as a change due to the context.[27] The plene spelling of the reading in the Qumran MSS seems to be in favour of this opinion because, if the first person singular were the original reading, one would expect the form אחל as it is found in Ezek 22:26 (where it is used with God as subject!). So there is reason to believe that the M reading is the primary one.

The form איחל in the Qumran MSS may be regarded as plene of אחל (so McCarthy), or as a *piel* form of the verb יחל, 'to wait'.[28] The

---

[23] Koole, *Isaiah*, 32.

[24] Compare בזוי עם in Ps 22:7.

[25] Cf., for example, Barthélemy, *CTAT* 2, 358–360; M. C. A. Korpel and J. C. de Moor, *The Structure of Classical Hebrew Poetry: Isaiah 40–55* (OTS 41; Leiden, 1998), 401.

[26] C. McCarthy, *The Tiqqune Sopherim and Other Theological Corrections in the Masoretic Text of the Old Testament* (OBO 36; Freiburg & Göttingen, 1981), 207–209. See also Barthélemy, *CTAT* 2, 354f.; Korpel and De Moor, *Isaiah 40–55*, 364.

[27] See, e.g., Kutscher, *Language*, 242; J. Koenig, *L'herméneutique analogique du Judaïsme antique d'après les témoins textuels d'Isaïe* (VTSup 33; Leiden, 1982), 373 ("une retouche par petite mutation"); Koole, *Isaiah*, 575.

[28] See Kutscher, *Language*, 242; P. Pulikottil, *Transmission of Biblical Texts in Qumran: The Case of the Large Isaiah Scroll 1QIsa[a]* (JSPSup 34; Sheffield, 2001), 102.

latter interpretation makes sense if understood as "How shall I wait" (i.e., I will not wait to act for my name's sake), and not as "How shall I hope for".[29]

53:11–12
(1) M יראה; 1QIsa[a] = 1QIsa[b] = 4QIsa[d] יראה אור
(2) M חטא; 1QIsa[a] = 1QIsa[b] = 4QIsa[d] חטאי (1QIsa[b] י[ )
(3) M ולפשעים; 1QIsa[a] = 1QIsa[b] = 4QIsa[d] ולפשעיהם (1QIsa[a] -המה)

This is a most interesting situation since in three instances three Qumran MSS offer in each case the same variant reading against M. In view of the fact that not only the three available Qumran MSS agree in each case, but also because 1QIsa[b] as 'pre-Masoretic' witness is part of the picture, Barthélemy is of the opinion that the Qumran readings are to be regarded as the primary ones.[30] The evidence is impressive indeed, but one has also to consider and evaluate each case on its own.

(1) M "he will see"; Qumran "he will see light"
This is the most intriguing case of the three. It is disputed, however, whether the plus אור, 'light', was part of the original text, or not. The expression, 'to see light', is well known in the Hebrew Bible in the sense of 'to enjoy life' (e.g., Ps 36:10). However, in our text there seems to be a relationship between 'light' and 'knowledge, insight' (דעת) since the text continues as ישׂבע בדעתו (M).[31] Hence the expression "to see light" would then convey the meaning of 'gaining insight'. Seeligmann has argued rightly that since the expression 'to see light' in this sense has no parallel in the Hebrew Bible, the plus 'light' should be regarded a secondary reading.[32] In addition, one could say that the verb ראה itself carries here the connotation of gaining insight comparable to Isa 5:19; 6:9; 41:20; 44:9 (ראה // ידע).[33] However, the difficulty with this latter argument is that in 53:11 the verb 'to see' is followed by the verb 'to be satisfied' (שׂבע), and not by 'to know'. Of course, the verb שׂבע is followed by בדעתו, "with his knowledge", but here the question arises whether this word

[29] For this latter meaning, see the *hifil* in 1QIsa[a] 51:11 (M *piel*).
[30] Barthélemy, *CTAT* 2, 403–407; idem, *CTAT* 3, cix.
[31] Cf. G.
[32] I. L. Seeligmann, "Δεῖξαι αὐτῷ φῶς," *Tarbiz* 27 (1956), 127–141. Most recently, this article has been published in a German translation in: I. L. Seeligmann, *Gesammelte Studien zur Hebräischen Bibel* (ed. by E. Blum; FAT 41; Tübingen, 2004), 401–419.
[33] See, e.g., W. A. M. Beuken, *Jesaja: deel II* (Nijkerk, 1979); Koole, *Isaiah*; and De Moor and Korpel, *Isaiah 40–55*.

belongs to ישׂבע, or rather should be taken as the first word of the next clause ("with his knowledge he will justify . . ." [בדעתו יצדיק]).[34] The latter option seems the more plausible one because of the suffix, for it is strange to say that the servant will be satisfied with *his* (own) knowledge.[35]

On balance then it seems that the original text read (in translation) "he will see and be satisfied".[36] As has been suggested by Bonnard, both verbs are to be understood in the light of the preceding verse (v. 10) where it reads, "he will see offspring, prolong his days" (יראה זרע יאריך ימים).[37] As to the verb 'to be satisfied' as denoting a long life he points to texts such as Gen 25:8 (שׂבע), and Gen 35:29 and Job 42:17 (both שׂבע ימים).[38] Compare also the expression ארך ימים אשׂביעהו in Ps 91:16.

(2) M "sin" (sg.); Qumran "sins" (pl.)

The singular חטא in M (והוא חטא רבים נשׂא) occurs only here in Deutero-Isaiah. According to Barthélemy, the singular represents an adaptation to the singular in v. 6 (עון) and in v. 8 (פשׁע).[39] Koole, on the other hand, argues that the plural "is better explained as a harmonization with the plural forms in the context" (see vv. 4–5, 11b).[40] So the context does not help us any further. As has been observed by Kutscher, the reading of Qumran (חטאי רבים) is a double plural which is typical of later Hebrew (e.g., Chronicles).[41] It therefore seems to be a secondary reading.[42]

(3) M "sinners"; Qumran "their sins"

Some consider the reading of the Qumran witnesses as the original one (e.g., Barthélemy), but it is also possible that, as Kutscher argues, this reading is due to harmonization with the first half of the line

[34] So 1QIsa[a], T, and V.

[35] This may have been the reason why G, followed by S, does not offer an equivalent of the suffix.

[36] For suggestions of what may have been the reason of the plus "light", see Seeligmann (due to the notion of 'light' in the sense of knowledge in texts of the Qumran community [1QSb IV 25–27; 1QH IV 27–28]); Koenig, *L'herméneutique analogique*, 275f. (influence of 9:1 and 50:11); Koole, *Isaiah*, 329 (influence of 50:10 and 9:1); and Korpel and De Moor, *Isaiah 40–55*, 549 (influence of 42:16).

[37] P. E. Bonnard, *Le Second Isaïe son disciple et leurs éditeurs, Isaïe 40–66* (Paris, 1972), 278.

[38] Bonnard, *Second Isaie*, 278 note.

[39] Barthélemy, *CTAT* 2, 406.

[40] Koole, *Isaiah*, 341.

[41] Kutscher, *Language*, 399.

[42] For the expression נשׂא חטא see, e.g., Lev 19:17; 20:20; 22:9; 24:15.

(cf. the Qumran reading under [2]).[43] It may well be that the original reading was spelled defectively (פשעם) because this would explain both interpretations – "sinners" as well as "their sin" (sg.),[44] the latter of which was changed into the plural, "their sins" (cf. [2]). For a similar case of a shift from singular to plural see 58:1: M פשעם (= 1QIsa[b]) vs. 1QIsa[a] פשעיהמה.

IV

From the above analysis the picture emerges that while in a few cases shared readings in Qumran MSS testify to a better text, in many cases the combined evidence turns out to be of a secondary nature in comparison to M. This may not be surprising as far as concerns 1QIsa[a], but it is interesting to note that 1QIsa[b], a MS that is considered to be archaic, or 'pre-Masoretic' (Barthélemy), also contains readings – albeit to a much lesser extent, which testify to tendencies such as linguistic adaptation to later Hebrew or to a more common usage in the Hebrew Bible. The same is true of Isaiah MSS from Cave 4.

Thus, as far the above evidence goes, M attests a textual tradition which was transmitted in the early days – third century B.C.E. up to second century C.E. – in a more strict and accurate way. This is in line with the view that there has been a situation of textual fluidity *alongside* textual stability, or uniformity, in the early period.[45]

The Qumran MSS of Isaiah referred to above reflect a practice of copying texts which was marked by linguistic adaptation and changes due to context. This mode of copying texts testifies to a scholarly interest in the language and the content of the text,[46] and may have been characteristic of the production of MSS for study purposes.[47]

[43] Kutscher, *Language*, 383.

[44] For this view see K. Elliger, "Nochmals Textkritisches zu Jes 53," in J. Schreiner (ed.), *Wort, Lied und Gottesspruch: Festschrift für J. Ziegler* (FB 2; Würzburg, 1972), 2:143f.

[45] See in particular A. S. van der Woude, "Pluriformity and Uniformity: Reflections on the Transmission of the Text of the Old Testament," in J. N. Bremmer and F. García Martínez (eds.), *Sacred History and Sacred Texts in Early Judaism* (CBET 5; Kampen, 1992), 151–169.

[46] A very interesting case is the plus "light" in Isa 53:11. The question whether this plus reflects a specific or sectarian interpretation, as has been suggested by Seeligmann, needs further investigation.

[47] For this phenomenon, see M. H. Goshen-Gottstein, "Biblical Manuscripts in the United States," *Textus* 2 (1962), 36–39.

THE EZEKIEL TEXT

Johan Lust

The following pages offer a survey of some major introductory matters concerning the Hebrew text of Ezekiel.[1]

Sources

For the Hebrew text of Ezekiel, as for the other Prophets, the most important complete witnesses are three medieval Tiberian manuscripts: the Codex Leningradensis or EBP. I B 19a of the Russian National Library in St. Petersburg, and the Aleppo and Cairo Codices. A relatively small number of Ezekiel passages are preserved in some six scroll fragments found at Qumran and in a series of fragments of a manuscript excavated at Masada, all of which can be dated to the pre-Christian era. Generally speaking these texts are in agreement with the non-vocalised text of M as preserved in the medieval manuscripts. The texts preserved in the smaller fragments can be listed as follows: Ezek 1:10–13, 16–17, 20–24 (4QEzek[b]); 4:3–6 (11QEzek); 4:16–5:1 (1QEzek); 5:11–17; 7:9–12 (11QEzek); 10:5–15; 10:17–11:11 (4QEzek[a]); 16:31–33 (3QEzek); 23:14–18, 44–47; 41:3–5.[2]

[1] After the final composition of the present essay, I received a copy of the beautiful edition of M. H. Goshen-Gottstein and S. Talmon, eds., and G. Marquis, assoc. ed., *The Book of Ezekiel* (The Hebrew Bible Project; Jerusalem, 2004).

[2] The sixth manuscript survives in only one fragment (4QEzek[c]) containing three words and a couple of letters from six other words from Ezek 24:2–3. For a survey of the other five fragments and of the Ezekiel quotations in the Qumran scrolls see J. Lust, "Ezekiel Manuscripts in Qumran: Preliminary Edition of 4QEzek[a] and 4QEzek[b]," in J. Lust (ed.), *Ezekiel and His Book* (BETL 74; Leuven, 1986), 90–100. See also L. A. Sinclair, "A Qumran Biblical Fragment: 4QEzek[a]," *RQ* 14 (1989), 99–105; E. Puech, "4QEzek[a], note additionnelle," *RQ* 14 (1989), 107–108; G. J. Brooke, "Ezekiel in Some Qumran and New Testament Texts," in J. Trebolle Barrera and L. Vegas Montaner (eds.), *The Madrid Qumran Congress: Proceedings of the International Congress on the Dead Sea Scrolls, Madrid 1991* (*STDJ* 11/1; Leiden, 1992), 317–337. The fragments are published in DJD: 1QEzek in DJD I, 68–69 (D. Barthélemy); 3QEzek in DJD III, 94 (M. Baillet); 4QEzek[a,b,c] in DJD XV, 209–220 (J. E. Sanderson); 11QEzek in DJD XXIII, 15–28 (E. D. Herbert).

The Masada fragments contain portions of 35:11–15; 36:1–10, 13–14, 17–35; 37:1–16, 23, 28; 38:1–4, 7–8 (MasEzek).[3]

An excellent critical edition of the Greek text has been provided by J. Ziegler.[4] When he published his work in the Göttingen series in 1952, however, he did not yet have the Ezekiel fragments of the Antinoopolis papyri, containing parts of 33:27–31 and 34:1–5, 18–24, 26–30, at his disposal. In addition, only the sections belonging to the Chester Beatty and the John H. Scheide Papyri of papyrus 967[5] had been available to him. Ziegler himself collated the evidence of the Antinoopolis fragments with his Ezekiel edition and published the data in his edition of *Susanna, Daniel, Bel et Draco*.[6] The more recently discovered and more substantial sections of p967 were collated by D. Fraenkel and incorporated, together with Ziegler's collation of the Antinoopolis fragments, as a *Nachtrag* in the second edition of Ziegler's Ezekiel.[7] The preserved parts of p967 cover most of Ezek 11:25–48:35. Papyrus 967 is, together with *Codex Vaticanus*, the main witness to the pre-Hexaplaric Old Greek text. One of the special features of p967 is its ordering of the materials which differs notably from that in M and in the mainstream Greek manuscripts: chs. 12–36; 38–39; 37; 40–48.

The Old Latin sources cover large parts of chs. 7–48.[8] The *Codex Wirceburgensis* translates a Greek text of the type preserved in p967 with its typical arrangement of final chapters.[9] The *Codex Constantiensis* and the *Fragmenta Sangallensia* stand closer to the B-type text.

---

[3] S. Talmon, "Fragments of an Ezekiel Scroll from Massada (Ezek 35,11–38,14) 1043–2220 MAS ID," *Orientalia Lovaniensia Periodica* 27 (1996), 29–49.

[4] J. Ziegler (ed.), *Ezechiel* (*Septuaginta: Vetus Testamentum Graecum* XVI/1; Göttingen, 1952; 2nd ed. 1977).

[5] The edition of p967 is spread over several books and periods: F. G. Kenyon, *The Chester Beatty Biblical Papyri: Ezekiel* (London, 1937); A. C. Johnson, H. S. Gehman and E. H. Kase, *The John H. Scheide Biblical Papyri: Ezekiel* (Princeton, 1938); L. G. Jahn, *Der griechische Text des Buches Ezechiel, nach dem Kölner Teil des Papyrus 967* (Bonn, 1972); M. Fernández-Galiano, "Nuevas Paginas del codice 967 del A.T. griego," *SPap* 10 (1971), 7–76.

[6] J. Ziegler (ed.), *Susanna, Daniel, Bel et Draco* (*Septuaginta: Vetus Testamentum Graecum* XVI/2; Göttingen, 1954), 77–88.

[7] Ziegler, *Ezechiel*, 331–332, 332–352.

[8] For a detailed list see the 1952 and 1977 editions of Ziegler, *Ezechiel*, 13–14.

[9] See P.-M. Bogaert, "Le témoignage de la Vetus Latina dans l'étude de la tradition des Septante: Ézéchiel et Daniel dans le Papyrus 967," *Bib* 59 (1978), 384–395.

Commentaries

Introductions of recent major commentaries do not extensively discuss the state of the text.[10] Most of them are of the opinion that "MT deserves far more credit than modern critics have tended to give it".[11] According to earlier important commentators M-Ezekiel was in a rather deplorable state.[12] At the beginning of his lengthy section on *Text and Versions* G. A. Cooke states that "In the Hebrew Bible perhaps no book, except 1 and 2 Samuel, has suffered more injury to its text than Ezekiel."[13] Cooke's appreciation largely depends on C. H. Cornill's detailed study of the text.[14] He opens his commentary with the observation that it is common knowledge that the text of Ezekiel is in an extremely bad condition: "Der Satz, dass der Text Ezechiels in besonders schlechtem und verderbten Zustand auf uns gekommen sei, geht durch alle Einleitungen ins Alte Testament und durch alle Schriften, welche sich mit dem alttestamentlichen Texte beschäftigen." In his well-known monograph on Ezekiel, as well as in his commentary, G. Fohrer likewise acknowledges the corrupt state of the text.[15] He singles the following passages out as particularly corrupt: ch. 7; 21:13–22; 28:11–19. W. Zimmerli's work, considered standard for many years, holds a middle position.[16] In his view some parts of the text of M-Ezekiel are perfectly well preserved, but other parts are badly damaged. Among the former he includes chs. 3, 6, and 18, as well as 20:1–31 and 28:1–10. Among the latter he lists the sections referred to by Fohrer: chs. 7 and 21; 28:11–19.[17]

---

[10] Without trying to be exhaustive we include the following works among the recent major critical commentaries: L. C. Allen, *Ezekiel* (WBC 28, 29; Waco, Tex., 1990, 1994); M. Greenberg, *Ezekiel 1–20* (AB 22; Garden City, NY, 1983); idem, *Ezekiel 21–37* (AB 22A; Garden City, NY, 1997); D. I. Block, *The Book of Ezekiel* (NICOT; Grand Rapids, 1997, 1998); K.-F. Pohlmann, *Das Buch des Propheten Hesekiel (Ezechiel),* (ATD; Göttingen, 1996, 2001); see also D. Barthélemy, *Critique textuelle de l'Ancien Testament,* vol. 3, *Ézéchiel, Daniel et les 12 Prophètes* (OBO 50/3; Fribourg & Göttingen, 1992) (*CTAT* 3).

[11] Greenberg, *Ezekiel 1–20,* 24.

[12] C. H. Cornill, *Das Buch des Propheten Ezechiel* (Leipzig, 1886); G. A. Cooke, *The Book of Ezechiel* (ICC; Edinburgh, 1936); G. Fohrer *Die Hauptprobleme des Buches Ezechiel* (BZAW 72; Berlin, 1952), 53–60; G. Fohrer and K. Galling, *Ezechiel* (HAT[2] 13; Tübingen, 1955); W. Eichrodt, *Der Prophet Hesekiel* (ATD; Göttingen, 1959, 1966); W. Zimmerli, *Ezechiel* (BKAT 13; Neukirchen, 1969).

[13] Cooke, *Book of Ezechiel,* xl.

[14] Cornill, *Das Buch des Propheten Ezechiel,* 4.

[15] Fohrer *Hauptprobleme,* 53–60; Fohrer and Galling, *Ezechiel,* vii.

[16] Zimmerli, *Ezechiel,* 116*.

[17] K.-F. Pohlmann (*Das Buch des Propheten Hesekiel,* 41) obviously agrees with

The Septuagint and Textual Criticism of M

The value of the Septuagint and the Old Latin versions has often been acknowledged in scholarly endeavours to reconstruct the Hebrew text of Ezekiel. Textual critics and commentators tend to retranslate the Greek text into Hebrew and treat the resulting hypothetical *Vorlage* of G as if it were a variant Hebrew manuscript reading. Indeed, they sometimes argue that it represents an older and superior witness to the original M than the preserved Hebrew manuscripts, and they emend the Hebrew text accordingly.[18]

An early protagonist of this view is A. Merx[19] who offers a review of Smend's commentary on Ezekiel. According to Merx, Smend's use of textual criticism is absolutely uncritical and lacks basic principles. He is convinced that, as a basic principle, the "corrected" Septuagint should be taken to be a third-century pre-Christian witness to the Hebrew text, which did not yet include the corruptions found in M.

More recently, M. Greenberg has warned against a haphazard use of G in attempts to correct M.[20] He addresses the treatment of Ezekiel 2–3 in the commentaries of Fohrer, Eichrodt, and especially Zimmerli, and qualifies their use of G as a means for restoring the "original text" as completely arbitrary.

In a similar way, Halperin[21] observes that most textual critics (such as Merx, Lind) treat the hypothetical *Vorlage* of G as if it were a variant Hebrew manuscript reading, often arguing that it is superior to M and emending the Hebrew text accordingly. His main point

Zimmerli when he also distinguishes between well preserved chs. such as 3, 6, 15 and 18, as well as badly corrupted chs. such as 7 and 21.

[18] The first chapters of Ezekiel have repeatedly been selected as a test case. See, for instance: A. Merx, "Der Werth der Septuaginta für die Textkritik des Alten Testamentes am Ezechiel aufgezeigt," *Jahrbücher für protestantische Theologie* 9 (1883), 65–77; M. Greenberg, "The Use of the Ancient Versions for Interpreting the Hebrew Text: A Sampling from Ezekiel ii,1–iii,11," *VT* (1978), 134–148; W. A. Lind, "A Textcritical Note to Ezekiel 1: Are shorter readings really preferable to longer?" *JETS* 27 (1984), 135–139; see also D. J. Halperin, "Merkabah Midrash in the Septuagint," *JBL* 101 (1982), 351–363; idem, "The Exegetical Character of Ezek. 10,9–17," *VT* 26 (1976), 129–141; W. B. Barrick, "The Straight-legged Cherubim of Ezekiel's Inaugural Vision (Ezekiel 1:7a)," *CBQ* 44 (1982), 543–550; J. Lust, "Notes to the Septuagint: Ezekiel 1–2," *ETL* 75 (1999), 5–31, esp. 6–8 and 28–31.

[19] See above, n. 18.

[20] See above, n. 18.

[21] See above, n. 18.

is that it is not a Hebrew manuscript, but rather a translation, that reflects the religious needs and exegetical perceptions of Alexandrian Jews in the third and second centuries B.C.E.

Of course, the simple lack of an equivalent in G for a word, a group of words, or a complete sentence in M, is not a sufficient reason to eliminate this word, group of words, or verse, from the restored original Hebrew text. It is slightly unfair, however, to suggest that commentators such as Zimmerli arbitrarily deleted these expressions and sentences in some cases, whereas they did not do so in other instances, without any rules.[22] Zimmerli never suggests that an element in M should be considered an addition or a gloss exclusively on the basis of the shorter character of the version preserved in G. He always adduces parallel reasons taken from the Hebrew text itself and, when available, from the other versions. The main problems are to be found elsewhere and are connected with the following questions: which Hebrew text does one try to reconstruct, and what is the role of the so-called glosses?

Glosses and Stages of Development

Several stages can be discerned in the development of the Hebrew text.[23] The first stage is that of the oral and written production of literary texts or *Urtext(s)* and is the object of historical-literary or source criticism. The following stages are those of the transmission of the written text(s) and are the object of textual criticism. The first of these is that of the earliest textual form or forms partly preserved in the earliest manuscripts we now have at our disposal. It can be referred to as the pre-Masoretic stage and is marked by a considerable degree of textual fluidity. The second is that of the proto-Masoretic or unvocalized text accepted as normative by the Jews in the first century C.E. The final stage is that of the "Masoretic text",

[22] See Greenberg, "Use of the Ancient Versions," 134.

[23] See, for example, D. Barthélemy, *Critique textuelle de l'Ancien Testament*, vol. 1, *Josué, Juges, Ruth, Samuel, Rois, Chroniques, Esdras, Néhémie, Esther* (OBO 50/1; Fribourg & Göttingen, 1982), *68–*69 (*CTAT* 1), referring to D. Barthélemy, et al., *A Preliminary and Interim Report of the Hebrew Old Testament Text Project* (London, 1973) 1:xx (same page also in volumes 2–5 [Stuttgart, 1976–1977; New York, 1979–1980]); J. A. Sanders, "Stability and Fluidity in Text and Canon," in G. J. Norton and S. Pisano (eds.), *Tradition of the Text* (OBO 109; Freiburg & Göttingen, 1991), 203–217, esp. 204–205; E. Tov, *Textual Criticism of the Hebrew Bible* (Minneapolis & Assen, 1992), 164–197.

or textual form defined by the Masoretes in the ninth and tenth centuries. Greenberg aims at a reconstruction of the final stage. He wishes to correct M when it proves to be corrupt or indistinct, and admits that in these instances the value of *Vorlage* variants of versions such as G should not be underestimated.[24] When M proves to be sound in Greenberg's eyes, however, the only role of the versions is to draw attention to literary devices and meanings in M that otherwise run the risk of going unnoticed. Zimmerli's approach is different. He seeks to trace an earlier form of the text, going beyond the Masoretic and proto-Masoretic stages. With the help of the earliest textual witnesses and inner textual arguments he aims at a reconstruction of the *Urtext*, at the risk of confusing the domains of literary and textual criticism.

Greenberg's aims are on the safer side. He reduces the textual criticism of the Old Testament to an attempt towards a correct edition of the Masoretic text. It is true that textual criticism in the stricter sense should not lightly go beyond the written evidence preserved in the manuscripts. The only stages of which a good written evidence is available are those of the Masoretic and proto-Masoretic texts. As soon as one tries to reach the earlier stage of the pre-Masoretic text major problems occur. The scrolls found in the neighbourhood of Qumran are an important help in this endeavour, but they are plagued with lacunae. The earliest translations of the Bible are also important tools. They are, however, to be handled with circumspection. When using a translation such as G, the textual critic has first to evaluate its literalness, and then to determine whether its *Vorlage* is identical to that of the proto-Masoretic text. If the evidence proves or suggests that its *Vorlage* was largely different from that of M, then its value for the reconstruction of M and of the proto-Masoretic text is significantly reduced. It may, however, have an important role to play in an attempt towards the reconstruction of the so-called hypothetical *Urtext* or the main stem from which the *Vorlagen* of M and G are off-shoots. This may be the case in the study the Ezekiel text. M and G of Ezekiel appear to reflect two different redactional stages of the book.[25] M is longer and many of

[24] Greenberg, "Use of the Ancient Versions," 147.

[25] See, for example, J. Lust, "The Use of Textual Witnesses for the Establishment of the Text: The Shorter and Longer Texts of Ezekiel," in Lust, *Ezekiel and His Book*, 7–20; E. Tov, "Recensional Differences between the M and G of Ezekiel," *ETL* 62 (1986), 89–101.

its "pluses" are probably due to the hand of an editor. This implies, however, that most of the important deviations from M detected in G do not pertain to the domain of textual criticism, but rather to that of literary criticism.

The pluses in the Hebrew text of the Bible are often qualified as glosses. This is especially so in Ezekiel.[26] These glosses are said to be marginal or interlinear notes that were erroneously incorporated in the main text. To a certain extent, the evaluation of these cases is based on textual evidence. There is evidence of a shorter text, mainly preserved in G, and a longer text, mainly evidenced by M. This kind of textual evidence is the starting point for claims that longer readings are secondary and that this can be objectively demonstrated in the written accounts.[27] These claims are obviously based on the hypothesis that the literal character of the G translation allows us to reconstruct its Hebrew *Vorlage*, and that this *Vorlage* was identical to that of M. The pluses in M are said to be scribal additions and are considered to be out of place. They belong in the margin or in between the lines, as interlinear remarks or glosses. According to Allen, a further complication of the data arose due to the fact that some of these glosses where inserted in the wrong verse through inter-columnar confusion.[28]

The "glosses"-theory is tempting. In several instances it offers a plausible interpretation of the differences between G and M. One should not forget, however, that its basis is very hypothetical. Direct evidence for the existence of glosses is lacking in Hebrew biblical manuscripts,[29] and *a fortiori* for their insertion in the wrong column. The argumentation in favour of the existence of these glosses is often

---

[26] See P. Rost, "Miscellen. I. Ein Schreibgebrauch bei den Sopherim und seine Bedeutung für die alttestamentliche Textkritik," *OLZ* 7 (1904), 390–393; J. Herrmann, "Stichwortglossen im Buche Ezechiel," *OLZ* 11 (1908), 280–282; G. Fohrer, "Die Glossen im Buche Ezechiel," *ZAW* 63 (1951), 33–53 = BZAW 99, 204–221; K. S. Freedy, "The Glosses in Ezekiel i–xxiv," *VT* 20 (1970), 129–152; M. Dijkstra, "The Glosses in Ezekiel Reconsidered: Aspects of Textual Transmission in Ezekiel 10," in Lust, *Ezekiel and His Book*, 55–77; E. Tov, "Glosses, Interpolations, and Other Types of Scribal Additions in the Text of the Hebrew Bible," in S. Balentine and J. Barton (eds.), *Language, Theology, and the Bible: Essays in Honour of James Barr* (Oxford, 1994), 40–66; L. C. Allen, "Some Types of Textual Adaptation in Ezekiel," *ETL* 71 (1995), 5–29.

[27] Lind, "Textcritical Note on Ezekiel 1," 136; Allen, "Types of Textual Adaptation," 5.

[28] See, for example, Allen, *Ezekiel*, 2:8, n. 23a (ישרות).

[29] Tov, "Glosses, Interpolations," 49.

based on the indirect evidence found in G, or supported by it. It is implicitly assumed that G is translated literally, and that its Hebrew *Vorlage* was more or less identical to that of M. Our analysis of the first chapters of this prophetic book confirmed that the translation of G-Ezekiel displays indeed a high degree of literalness.[30] This does not allow us to conclude, however, that major differences, such as the pluses in M, are misplaced glosses. They may have originated at an earlier editorial level. Several of them may have been intended as interpolations and should not be labelled as errors.[31]

In fact, Greenberg's position is not necessarily in sharp contradiction with that of Zimmerli, read through the glasses of Tov. The main difference is that Zimmerli's textual criticism is a textual criticism in the broader sense of the term. We already noted that Zimmerli seeks to reconstruct the hypothetical original text, whereas Greenberg limits his efforts to a reconstruction of the uncorrupted Masoretic text. Greenberg admits that the version preserved in G may be a valuable text in its own right and with its own message. He refuses, nevertheless, to accept that G should be preferred over M. Zimmerli is less concerned with M, or for that matter, with G. He tries to find the original text, and in his view, G is an important tool helping him in his efforts to reach his goal. In his endeavour to go back beyond the evidence of the Hebrew manuscripts, he may at times seem to fail to take M seriously. On the other hand, Greenberg seems to accuse Zimmerli too easily of arbitrariness in his appeal to G. Indeed, where Zimmerli prefers G over M, he most often clearly notes that the evidence of G is supported by other factors.

Shorter and Longer Texts: The Longer Pluses in M

The Greek translation of Ezekiel is notably shorter than M. When one considers the critical editions, however, the phenomenon is not as obvious as in Jeremiah. In Ezekiel the combined minuses of G do not amount to more than 4–5% of the text.[32] This picture changes

[30] J. Lust, "Notes to the Septuagint: Ezekiel 1–2," *ETL* 75 (1999), 5–31. See also Tov, "Recensional Differences," 92, n. 11, with references to Marquis and Sollamo.

[31] Tov, "Glosses, Interpolations," 56.

[32] Tov, "Recensional Differences," 89–101; Lust, "Use of Textual Witnesses," 7–20.

when one takes into account the minuses in p967.[33] H. S. Gehman, one of its editors, concluded that of all our Greek MSS, this papyrus preserved a text of Ezekiel closest to the original G. In his view, the authority of the Codex Vaticanus as our best source for the original text must yield to this new evidence. Gehman's high esteem of p967 has been corroborated by Ziegler[34] and Payne,[35] and has received general adherence. This does not apply to the "minuses" in the papyrus, which have frequently been labelled as omissions or corruptions due to parablepsis. Elsewhere, I have refuted this view and defended the thesis that the three longer minuses, Ezek 12:26–28, 32:25–26, 36:23b–38, are not due to errors of scribes or translators.[36] They are witnesses to an earlier Hebrew text in which these sections were not yet added. A fourth set of omissions, in ch. 7, witnessed by all major MSS of G, confirms this. The longest plus (36:23b–38) is combined with a reorganisation of the materials. In G 36:23a is followed by chs. 38–39, and then by chs. 37 and 40–48. In changing this order, M had to insert 36:23b–38 to prepare for the transposed ch. 37. The longer text of M and the reordering of chs. 36–40 display their own theological accents, somehow connected with the editor's opinions concerning eschatology and apocalypticism.[37]

The Language of Ezekiel: Late Biblical Hebrew?

According to most scholars the history of biblical Hebrew is characterised by two successive language states: pre-exilic or Early Biblical

[33] Fernández-Galiano ("Nuevas Paginas," 15) mentions three major omissions: 12:26–28; 36:23b–38; 38–39. He overlooked that, although chs. 38–39 are missing in the leaves published by him, they were not missing in the manuscript as a whole. Their transposition is to be studied together with the absence of 36:23b–38. Two of the longer omissions received full attention from F. V. Filson, "The Omission of Ezek 12:26–28 and 36:23b–38 in Codex 967," *JBL* 62 (1943), 27–32. The third one, 32:24–26, is most often overlooked. The text of p967 is supported by the *Vetus Latina Codex Wirceburgensis*, see P.-M. Bogaert, "Le témoignage de la Vetus Latina dans l'étude de la Septante: Ézéchiel et Daniel dans le p967," *Bib* 59 (1978), 384–395.

[34] Ziegler, *Ezechiel* (1952), 28; J. Ziegler, "Die Bedeutung der Chester Beatty-Scheide Papyrus 967 für die Textüberlieferung der Ezechiel-Septuaginta," *ZAW* 61 (1945/48), 76–94.

[35] J. B. Payne, "The Relationship of the Chester Beatty Papyri of Ezekiel to Codex Vaticanus," *JBL* 68 (1949), 251–265.

[36] J. Lust, "Ezekiel 36–40 in the Oldest Greek Manuscript," *CBQ* 43 (1981), 517–533.

[37] See J. Lust, "Major Divergences Between LXX and MT in Ezekiel," in A. Schenker (ed.), *The Earliest Text of the Hebrew Bible* (SBLSCS 52; Atlanta, 2003), 83–92.

Hebrew (EBH) and post-exilic or Late Biblical Hebrew (LBH). It cannot be our intention here to discuss all the complex issues connected with this and similar distinctions.[38] Our main interest is to explore some of the characteristics of the Hebrew language used in Ezekiel. Special mention should be made of the studies of A. Hurvitz and M. F. Rooker at this juncture.[39] Inspired by Hurvitz's pioneering work, Rooker developed the thesis that Ezekiel displays a considerable number of grammatical and lexical features typical of LBH. Under grammatical features Rooker lists matters regarding orthography (e.g. דויד / דוד "David"),[40] morphology (e.g., אנכי / אני "I")[41] and syntax (e.g., the use of את before the nominative).[42] Under lexical features he includes matters such as the interchangeable use of על / אל.[43]

The presence of these features cannot be denied. They clearly show that M-Ezekiel exhibits some of the characteristics of LBH.

---

[38] For a fuller discussion and bibliography see I. Young, *Biblical Hebrew: Studies in Chronology and Typology* (JSOTSup 365; London, 2003). A. Hurvitz is the main protagonist of the view that language variations between the books of Samuel-Kings and Chronicles provide a solid base for establishing linguistic oppositions between EBH and LBH. He has also shown that there are correspondences between the biblical evidence and other extra-biblical written documents regarding the characteristics of both First Temple and Second Temple Hebrew; cf. A. Hurvitz, "The Historical Quest for 'Ancient Israel' and the Linguistic Evidence of the Hebrew Bible: Some Methodological Observations," *VT* 47 (1997), 310–315.

[39] See especially A. Hurvitz, *A Linguistic Study of the Relationship between the Priestly Source and the Book of Ezekiel: A New Approach to an Old Problem* (CahRB 20; Paris, 1982); M. F. Rooker, "The Diachronic Study of Biblical Hebrew," *JNSL* 14 (1988), 199–214; idem, *Biblical Hebrew in Transition: The Language of the Book of Ezekiel* (JSOTSup 90; Sheffield, 1990); Young, *Biblical Hebrew*, 314–316.

[40] Cf. ibid., 68–71.

[41] Cf. ibid., 72–74; see also E. Y. Kutscher, *A History of the Hebrew Language* (Jerusalem, 1982), 81 §119. Other features listed by Rooker under the header "Morphology" are: the pluralizing tendency, the use of the lengthened היה; the increased use of the *piel* stem; the plural verb with masculine suffix.

[42] Cf. Rooker, 1990, 88–90. Other syntactic features listed by Rooker are: the proleptic pronominal suffix; collective nouns construed as plurals; the tendency to use ל to introduce the direct object; the diminished employment of the *waw* consecutive tense; the tendency to omit ויהי or והיה before the infinitive construct with ב; the infinitive as indicative; the use of היה with the participle; the use of אשר with a subordinate clause; the placement of the measurement dimension before the measurement; the avoidance of repetition; the use of בין ל instead of בין ובין; the use of the asyndetic imperfect apodosis.

[43] Cf. Rooker, "Diachronic Study," 127–131. Other lexical matters listed by Rooker are: מקטרת; the preference of זעק; the noun כתב; the *piel* of נתץ; the term קהל; the verbs כעס and עמד; the *piel* of הלך; the verb כנס; the term רשפה; the *hiphil* of הדיח; the nominal form מהליך; the term עזרה; the phrase למען לא.

The interpretation of this observation, however, remains open to debate. It is too often taken for granted that the language of the text under consideration has a direct relationship with the language used by the (alleged original) author of that text. I. Young rightly observed that "the linguistic profiles of the attested copies of biblical books cannot simply be assumed to represent the form and language used by the 'original author'. Instead, language . . . was subject to constant revision at the hands of the scribes who passed the material down through the generations."[44] Furthermore, most, if not all, biblical texts were subject to editorial revision. For an example of scribal interference we may refer to the plene spelling דויד in Ezek 34:23, contrasting to the defective spelling דוד in Ezek 34:24; 37:24.25. The plene spelling is typical of LBH, the defective of EBH. Using the plene spelling, albeit only once, Ezekiel is said to occupy an intermediate or transitional status.[45] Rooker does not seem to be aware that he undermines his own thesis when he looks at occurrences of דויד in 1QIsa[a], which is always plene, against the corresponding passages from M that are always defective. These data clearly demonstrate that the use of plene or defective forms is dependent on the scribe, not on the alleged original author.

Similar remarks are in order in as far as the אני/אנכי shift is concerned. Rooker notes that, in the use of the short form אני, Ezekiel is aligned unequivocally with LBH. Here again Rooker draws attention to the preference of the shorter form in the DSS biblical scrolls when the M-text has the longer form. Once more, however, he fails to note that this underlines the role of the scribes in these matters, rather than the role of the original authors. He also overlooks the fact that Ezekiel's use of אני is typical of his Priestly style. Indeed, the prophet shares the preference of the shorter form with the Priestly layers of the Pentateuch. Remarkably, the only occurrence of the long form אנכי in Ezekiel is to be found in 36:28, in a section added by a later redactor leaning heavily on Jeremiah.[46]

Some of the special features have an impact on textual criticism of Ezekiel. A case in point is the confusion in the use of the prepositions

---

[44] Young, *Biblical Hebrew*, 312, quoting his earlier work "Notes on the Language of 4QCant[b]," *JSS* 52 (2001), 130.

[45] Rooker, "Diachronic Study," 69.

[46] Zimmerli, *Ezechiel*, 873; Lust, "Ezekiel 36–40 in the Oldest Greek Manuscript," 517–533, esp. 522; compare Rooker, "Diachronic Study," 73, n. 24.

על and אל. In LBH the preposition על became more prominent at the expense of אל. This state has probably arisen due to Aramaic influence.[47] It has long been observed that there is a great confusion in the use of these prepositions in Ezekiel. According to Rooker it is readily apparent that this inconsistency reflects a period of transition.[48] This may be true, but then again, some questions remain. Let us have a look at the facts. There are about hundred and ten instances where the said confusion can be detected.[49] Running against expectations, however, אל is used instead of על in about a hundred of these cases.[50] Only in about ten cases one finds על where אל might have been expected.[51]

BHK[3] commands the reader to correct these "errors" and to read על in the first series, and אל in the second. *BHS* is less directive and simply notes each time אל = על, or על = אל, suggesting that there is a confusion between the two prepositions. This suggestion is probably correct. However, the question is: when and how did this confusion arise? Most likely it was due to Aramaic influence obscuring the difference between על and אל. This probably did not happen in the times of the original author, but rather in a much later period when scribes used to writing Aramaic transmitted the text.

Once more, Rooker seeks support from the Qumran scrolls. No relevant cases are preserved in so far as the Ezekiel MSS are concerned. Passages taken from other biblical books are adduced in which the scrolls appear to replace M אל by על.[52] This phenomenon is evidently to be ascribed to Aramaic influence exerted on the

[47] Rooker, "Diachronic Study," 131.

[48] Rooker, "Diachronic Study," 131.

[49] Most of the instances are signalled in the critical notes provided by Zimmerli in his excellent commentary, and in *BH* and *BHQ*.

[50] See 2:6, 10; 3:15; 6:2, 9, 11, 13; 7:6, 12, 18, 26; 9:5; 10:1; 11:11; 12:12, 19; 13:2, 8, 9, 17, 20; 14:4, 7, 19, 21; 16:5; 17:8; 18:6; 19:1, 4, 9; 21:2, 7, 8, 9, 17, 19, 22, 26, 33, 34; 22:9; 23:5, 12, 42; 24:2; 25:2, 3, 6; 26:7; 27:31, 32; 29:10, 18; 30:22, 25; 31:7, 12, 13; 32:9; 33:22; 34:10, 13, 14; 35:3; 36:1, 15; 38:3, 12; 39:1; 40:2, 17, 26, 39, 42, 49; 41:4, 6, 7, 12, 15, 17, 19, 25, 26; 42:7, 10; 43:3, 16, 20; 44:4, 7, 11, 30; 45:7, 19; 47:16; 48:1, 12, 20, 21, 28.

[51] See 1:17, 20; 9:5; 10:4; 16:36; 17:7; 19:11; (29:2; 35:2;) 38:7; 44:11; 47:18. The figures in between brackets refer to passages that perhaps should not be listed among the cases in which על and אל are confused. Thus the expression שׂים פניך על (29:2 and 35:2) is exclusively used by Ezekiel, and does not seem to be less correct than שׂים פניך אל which also occurs exclusively in Ezekiel (6:2; 13:7; 21:7; 25:2; 28:21; 38:2).

[52] Rooker, "Diachronic Study," 130.

Qumran scribes. Again, Rooker fails to note the possibility, or probability, that the confusion in M-Ezekiel may also be due to a similar influence, or to a scribal effort to correct that influence by an attempt towards archaising.

Rooker's remarks on the use of the particle את before a noun in the nominative are interesting. Although all his examples are not equally convincing, they help to explain grammatically difficult passages such as Ezek 44:3 את הנשׂיא נשׂיא הוא ישב. Nevertheless, questions still remain concerning the interpretation of the phenomenon in Ezekiel. Is it characteristic of the alleged "original" author, living and working in the Babylonian exile, or is it typical of a late scribe transmitting the text somewhere in the second century B.C.E.? In addition, the data given by Rooker do not clearly demonstrate that Ezekiel has significantly more cases of this type than the writings of the EBH period. A comparison with J. Hoftijzer's detailed analysis of the phenomenon might be useful.[53]

The Double Name

In the M-text of the Bible the double name אדני יהוה occurs 301 times. It is typical for the book of Ezekiel where it is attested 217 times.[54] In these instances, the critical editions of the Hebrew text, *BHK*[3] and *BHS*, characterise אדני as a secondary intrusion, either by commanding the reader to delete it (dl), or by saying that it is an addition (add). The main reasons for this correction are the Greek texts, and the suggestion that אדני was inserted into the text as a help for the reader, to remind him of the fact that the Tetragram could not be pronounced and was to be replaced by Adonai.

We already mentioned that the excavation of Masada by the late Y. Yadin yielded about fifty fragments of an Ezekiel MS dated to the second half of the first century B.C.E. Generally speaking, the text

[53] J. Hoftijzer, "Remarks concerning the Use of the Particle *'t* in Classical Hebrew," *OTS* 14 (1965), 1–99.

[54] Talmon, "Fragments of an Ezekiel Scroll," 29–48; P. W. Skehan, "The Divine Name at Qumran, in the Massada Scroll, and in the Septuagint," *BIOSCS* 13 (1980), 14–44; A. Pietersma, "Kyrios or Tetragram: A Renewed Quest for the Original G," in A. Pietersma and C. Cox (eds.), *De Septuaginta: Studies in Honour of John William Wevers on his sixty-fifth birthday* (Mississauga, Ont., 1984); J. Lust, "אדני יהוה in Ezekiel and Its Counterpart in the Old Greek," *ETL* 72 (1996), 138–145; idem, "'Mon Seigneur Jahweh' dans le texte hébreu d'Ézéchiel," *ETL* 44 (1968), 482–488.

accords with M and in several instances, the double name or traces thereof, are preserved (Ezek 35:12, 15; 36:2, 3, 4, 7, 22, 23; 37:3, 5, 9, 12). All these instances exhibit full agreement with M. This offers support to the view that אדני was already in the proto-Masoretic text of Ezekiel.

Supplementary reasons for the authenticity of the double name can be found in the contexts in which it is used. In Ezekiel, the name יהוה occurs 434 times. In exactly half of these instances (217), it figures in the expanded form אדני יהוה. This double name occurs almost exclusively in the "framing-formulae" at the beginning and at the end of the oracles (כה אמר אדני יהוה "thus says my Lord YHWH", 122 times; נאם אדני יהוה "word of my Lord YHWH", 81 times). Four of the remaining fourteen occurrences are attested in the prophetic formulaic prayer אהה אדני יהוה "Ahah, my Lord YHWH".

In all these cases, אדני was most likely originally vocalised אֲדֹנִי "my Lord". When the double name is used, it is never placed on the lips of the Lord, or of the enemy, nor even of the Israelites, but only on the lips of the prophet, when he speaks in the name of *his* Lord. The double name is not used in the word-event formula. The reason for this may be that the prophet uses the double name only when he is speaking about *his* Lord to the third party, in a direct address.

The same vocalisation explains why the title was not put in the mouth of the Lord. Put in a more positive way, one may state that the double name expresses the privileged relation between the prophet and *his* Lord.

The five exceptions (13:9; 23:49; 24:24; 28:24; 29:16), in which the Lord says, "they/you shall know that I am אדני יהוה", contrast with the fifty occurences of this formula in which the double name is not attested. We can assume that these exceptions are due to the work of late glossators or copyists who no longer understood the system.

The only seemingly strong argument in favour of the spurious character of אדני in the double name in the book of Ezekiel has been the witness of the Greek text. The pre-Hexaplaric MS B and especially the ancient papyrus 967 of Ezekiel as a rule render the double name by a single κύριος and support the view that the G text of Ezekiel originally had a single κύριος.[55] The exceptions may be due to occasional recensional activity. The *Vorlage* of G probably

[55] See L. J. McGregor, *The Greek Text of Ezekiel: An Examination of Its Homogeneity* (SBLSCS 18; Atlanta, 1985), 75–83, 227–257; J. Lust, "Notes to the Greek Text of Ezekiel 6, and the Double Name," *ETL* 76 (2000), 396–403.

read the double name where M has it. The translator most likely took אדני to be an interpretation of יהוה.

G appears to indirectly support the double name in M. There are three special cases in which M unexpectedly uses יהוה without a preceding אדני in the messenger formula. In two of them (21:8; 30:6) the pre-Hexaplaric MSS B and p967 do not have the formula. The third instance (11:5) occurs in a section of the papyrus that is still missing. In B the passage is influenced by recensional activities.[56] This evidence shows that the slightly anomalous single name in the messenger formula in M 11:5; 21:8; 30:6 was not yet found in the pre-Masoretic *Vorlage* of G.

Data from Ezekiel may be compared with that found in other biblical books. As far as I can see, the earliest and only pre-Christian MS offering evidence of the rendition of אדני is to be found in the Greek Minor Prophet's Scroll from Naḥal Ḥever.[57] In Zech 9:4, where M reads אדני, the scroll writes the Tetragrammaton in paleo-Hebrew characters. The absence of other instances in which the earliest rendition of אדני can be checked is perhaps not all that important. Indeed, it is clear that in the days of the Qumran scribes אדני and יהוה could be used indiscriminately, at least in the biblical texts. The large Isaiah scroll gives ample proof of this phenomenon. The origin of this practice most likely is to be sought in the pronunciation of יהוה as אדני.

The earliest Greek MSS preserving a full translation of the double name outside of Ezekiel are to be dated to the third century of the Christian era. They do not offer a uniform picture. The Oxyrhynchus fragment of Genesis 15 seems to have opted in favour of δέσποτης as a rendition of אדני and of a blank for the Tetragrammaton.

None of these call for a deletion of אדני in the double name in the Masoretic text of Ezekiel.

It is not without some hesitation that I present these tentative introductory notes to colleague A. Schenker at the occasion of his retirement, hoping that time and good health will be granted him and me to see the more finished version of these notes in a completed *BHQ* edition.

---

[56] It must be admitted that in 11:5 B follows M, but influence of recensional activities is clearly to be detected in the insertion of λέγε in a context in which the original translator always uses εἶπον: see the 1952 and 1977 editions of Ziegler, *Ezechiel*, 41.

[57] E. Tov, *The Greek Minor Prophets Scroll from Naḥal Ḥever (8ḤevXIIgr)* (DJD VIII; Oxford, 1990).

HOW *BHQ* DIFFERS FROM *BHS* IN THE BOOK OF EZRA-NEHEMIAH

David Marcus

The major differences between *BHQ* and previous editions of *Biblia Hebraica* (and in particular *BHS*) have been described in detail in the General Introduction to *BHQ* in the recently published *Megilloth* volume.[1] These include format changes such as the layout of the text, the principles for inclusion of collated witnesses, explanation of the critical apparatus, and the rationale for including cases in the commentary volume. This article will illustrate more specific points of differences between *BHQ* and *BHS* as far as the book of Ezra-Nehemiah[2] is concerned. These points are to be seen in the following five areas: (1) availability of new resources; (2) comparison with other Tiberian MSS; (3) representation of the Masorah; (4) inclusion of 1 Esdras as a constant witness; and (5) the circumscribed use of suggestions for textual emendation.

1. Availability of New Resources

The first major improvement of *BHQ* over *BHS* is to be seen in the availability of new resources such as the color transparencies and new facsimile edition of M^L, the publication of the Qumran fragments of Ezra, and of new editions of G and S.

a. The Color Transparencies and New Facsimile Edition of M^L

The color transparencies of the text of M^L were made available by the Ancient Biblical Manuscript Center in Claremont, California, who also produced the new facsimile edition in 1998.[3] Although the

[1] A. Schenker, et al. (eds.), *General Introduction and Megilloth* (*Biblia Hebraica Quinta* 18; Stuttgart, 2004), VII–XXVI. It is a pleasure to present this essay in honor of our colleague Adrian Schenker whose energetic leadership has helped bring our *BHQ* project from dream to reality.

[2] The Masoretic tradition regarded the books of Ezra and Nehemiah as one book, and in this article we shall refer to the book as Ezra-Nehemiah.

[3] D. N. Freedman, et al., *The Leningrad Codex* (Grand Rapids, Mich., 1998).

actual text of Ezra-Nehemiah has not suffered any damage, the availability of both the color transparencies and the new facsimile edition has enabled some clearer readings to be seen. Here are three examples. One is at Ezra 4:11, where *BHS* identified a Kethib and Qere on עַבְדָיךְ. But closer scrutiny of the transparencies and facsimile shows that there is no Kethib and Qere here. Another is at Ezra 7:14 in the form יָעֲטֹהִי, where an attempt was made by a second hand to erase an original *wāw*. The attempt was not entirely successful since the upper part of the *wāw* is clearly visible on the color transparencies. A final example is at Ezra 10:44 where the Kethib and Qere appear to have exactly the same form (נשׂאו/נָשְׂאוּ). Closer investigation shows that a second hand has changed the *yôd* of an original Kethib form נשׂאי into a *wāw*.

b. Qumran Fragments of Ezra

Entirely new in *BHQ* is the inclusion of the Qumran fragments from the book of Ezra (4QEzra) which were published by E. Ulrich in 1992 and again in 2000.[4] The fragments contain parts of Ezra 4:2–6, 9–11; 5:17–6:5, and exhibit two orthographic and two grammatical variants with M[L]. The two orthographic variants, involving interchanges of א and ה, are at 4:10 where 4QEzra reads נַהֲרָא for נַהֲרָה, and at 6:2 where 4QEzra reads מְדִינְתָּא for מְדִינְתָּה. The two grammatical variants concerning singular and plural forms of verbs are at 6:1 where 4QEzra reads a singular ובקר "he searched" for וּבַקַּרוּ "they searched", and at 6:5 where 4QEzra reads a plural והיבלו "they brought" for וְהֵיבֵל "he brought." Apart from these minor variations 4QEzra generally reflects M[L] and, where extant, agrees with it in those cases where the other witnesses have different readings. For example, at 5:17, 4QEzra agrees with M[L] against 1 Esdras and V in reading דֵּךְ; at 6:3, 4QEzra agrees with M[L] against 1 Esdras, V and S in reading בַּיְתָא; and at 6:5, 4QEzra agrees with M[L] against 1 Esdras in reading בְּבֵית אֱלָהָא. As a pre-Tiberian witness, 4QEzra is constantly cited in the critical apparatus whenever it offers relevant testimony.

---

[4] E. Ulrich, "Ezra and Qoheleth Manuscripts from Qumran (4Q[Ezra], 4Q[Qoh a, b])," in E. Ulrich, et al. (eds.), *Priests, Prophets and Scribes* (JSOTSup 149; Sheffield, 1992), 139–157. See also E. Ulrich, et al., *Qumran Cave 4, XI, Psalms to Chronicles* (DJD XVI; Oxford, 2000), 291–293.

c. New Edition of the Septuagint

The text for the Septuagint or Old Greek (G) is based on the Göttingen edition published in 1993,[5] which was not available to *BHS*. G is a very literal translation of Ezra-Nehemiah. Differences with M are for the most part translational, and concern minor grammatical matters such as variations in use of the *wāw* conjunction, singular and plural, and different suffixes. G follows M very closely except in Nehemiah 11 where, in vv. 16–35, it has a very much abbreviated text. A characteristic of G is its tendency to transliterate classes of people or place names that are otherwise capable of translation. For example, G transliterates עַבְדֵי שְׁלֹמֹה "servants of Solomon" as Ἀβδησελμά (Ezra 2:55), אַדִּירֵיהֶם "their nobles" as ἀδωρηέμ (Neh 3:5), תַּנּוּרִים "ovens" as θαννουρίμ (Neh 3:11) and בִּירָה "fortress" as βιρά (Neh 7:2). When the word בֵּית "house" is combined with a name, G will also include it in its transliteration as in בֵּית הַגִּבֹּרִים "House of the Warriors" which G renders Βηθαγγαβαρίμ (Neh 3:16) or בֵּית אֶלְיָשִׁיב "House of Eliashib" which is rendered as Βηθελισούβ (Neh 3:20). On one occasion G even transliterates an adjoining word next to a name when it renders שַׁעַר־הַגַּיא לַיְלָה "Valley Gate at night" as πύλη τοῦ γωληλά "Gate of Golela" (Neh 2:13).

d. New Edition of the Peshitta

Another constantly cited witness for Ezra-Nehemiah in *BHQ* is the Peshitta (S). The text used is based on a pre-publication MS of the edition prepared for the Leiden Peshitta Project by M. Albert.[6] S is essentially a literal translation with occasional paraphrases and expansions. S has a tendency to amplify names and places such as adding "the king" to Nebuchadnezzar, "the scribe" to Ezra, and "the city" to Jerusalem. Most of the differences between S and M are minor and involve grammatical matters such as variations in use of the *wāw* conjunction and of the singular and plural. Neither of these two variations are usually recorded in the critical apparatus, the first because of the ubiquity of its occurrences particularly in formation of numbers and lists of names, and the second because of the unreliability

[5] R. Hanhart (ed.), *Esdrae liber II* (*Septuaginta: Vetus Testamentum Graecum* VIII/2; Göttingen, 1993).

[6] Thanks are due to Dr. K. D. Jenner of the Peshitta Institute in Leiden for his kindness in providing the author with a copy of this work prior to publication.

of the *sĕyāmē* dots (an external indicator of the plural) in Codex Ambrosianus,[7] the base text of the Leiden edition.

Some of the more notable text critical variants between S and M include the regular interchange of the verbs of שׁוּב "to return" and יָשַׁב "to dwell" and the use of ܫܒܝܬܐ "captivity" for שָׂבֵי "elders" (Ezra 5:5 and *passim*). Two striking variants in S are its translation of וְהַשֵּׁגַל "concubine" by ܣܟܠܐ "fool" (Neh 2:6) and of קְהִלָּה "assembly" by ܩܠܐ "voice" (Neh 5:7).

2. *Comparison of M^{L} with Other Tiberian* MSS

Another new feature in the *BHQ* is a comparison of the text of M^{L} with two other prominent Tiberian MSS. The two Tiberian MSS which have been chosen for this purpose are Sassoon 1053 (M^{S1}) and Cambridge University Library Ms. Add. 1753 (M^{Y}). Choosing two excellent Tiberian manuscripts for comparison purposes represents a marked change from the procedure in *BHS* which, when comparing the base text of M^{L}, often refers to Hebrew MSS contained in the collections of Kennicott, de Rossi, and Ginsburg (e.g., at Ezra 1:8; 2:25, 27 and *passim*). The actual MSS are not identified, but the approximate number of MSS which preserve the reading are indicated either as a few (three to ten MSS), as several (eleven to twenty MSS), or as many (more than twenty MSS).

M^{S1} has been described in brief by I. Yeivin.[8] It is dated to the tenth century and originally contained the entire Bible. Parts of it are missing and about one-third of the book of Ezra-Nehemiah is lost. Also some of the extant text is damaged and difficult to read. M^{Y} has recently been described anew by S. C. Reif.[9] It is dated to the fifteenth-sixteenth centuries and contains only the Writings.

The differences between the three Tiberian MSS are primarily orthographic. Some examples are: variation of consonants: Ezra 7:21, כָּהֲנָא (M^{S1} and M^{Y})/כָּהֲנָה (M^{L}), plene and defective writing: Neh 7:4, וּגְדֹלָה (M^{S1} and M^{Y})/ וּגְדוֹלָה (M^{L}), variation of vowels: Ezra 6:8, תַּעַבְדוּן

[7] D. Barthélemy, *Critique textuelle de l'Ancien Testament*, vol. 3, *Ézéchiel, Daniel et les 12 Prophètes* (OBO 50/3; Fribourg & Göttingen, 1992), ccv. (*CTAT* 3)

[8] I. Yeivin, *Introduction to the Tiberian Masorah* (E. J. Revell [trans. and ed.]; SBLMasS 5; Missoula, Mont., 1980), §34.

[9] S. C. Reif, *Hebrew Manuscripts at Cambridge University Library* (Cambridge, 1997), 70–71.

(M^Y)/ תַּעַבְדוּן (M^L). At Neh 2:13, both M^{S1} and M^Y read הַגַּיְא for הַגַּיא (M^L), and at Neh 1:6, M^Y reads פְּתוּחוֹת for the anomolous פְּתֻוּחוֹת in M^{S1} and M^L. In accordance with the principles of *BHQ* these phonological and orthographic variants are not included in the critical apparatus. The only significant variant among the three Tiberian MSS is at Ezra 8:12, where M^Y reads וְעֶשְׂרִים "and twenty," and M^L reads וַעֲשָׂרָה "and ten."

3. The Representation of the Masorah

The M^L text of Ezra-Neh. is embellished with a full Masorah parva (Mp), Masorah magna (Mm) and a very brief Masorah finalis. In *BHS*, G. E. Weil, who prepared the Masoretic notes to *BHS*, did not present a diplomatic rendition of the Mp of the Codex. Weil often supplemented the Mp notes in the Codex with pertinent notes based on the spirit of the Codex. By his own admission he intended to provide "a complete, revised, integrated, and intelligible apparatus."[10] But the reader of *BHS* cannot tell what is in the Codex or what are Weil's additions.[11] For its part BHQ reverts back to a diplomatic representation of the Mp as existed in the third edition of *Biblia Hebraica* (*BHK*^{3}). Thus the reader can see at a glance that the contents of the Mp are mostly of the enumerative type, and easily translatable by reference to the abbreviation chart supplied. However, where the Mp is thought to be ambiguous or liable to be misunderstood an explanation has been supplied in the Masorah commentary.

Furthermore, unlike *BHS*, where the text of the Mm was relegated to a separate volume,[12] *BHQ* includes the Mm just below the text on the same page as the lemma to which it relates. By this placement of the Mm the reader can see quite clearly the relationship of the Mm to the Mp. Thus the reader will notice that most Mm notes have associated Mp notes. But there are some which do not (e.g., on וְאֵלֶּה at Ezra 2:1, and on בְּנֵי יוֹרָה at Ezra 2:18). The new *BHQ* arrangement of the Masorah thus allows the reader to peruse the actual contents of the Mm notes to Ezra-Nehemiah as they are

[10] G. E. Weil, "Prolegomena," *BHS*, xv.

[11] See also the remarks of I. Yeivin, "The New Edition of the Biblia Hebraica—Its Text and Massorah," *Textus* 7 (1963), 121; and D. S. Mynatt, *The Sub Loco Notes in the Torah of Biblia Hebraica Stuttgartensia* (N. Richland Hills, Tex., 1994), 12–13.

[12] G. E. Weil, *Masorah Magna* (Rome, 1971).

present on the Codex. In addition, all the Mm notes are fully translated in the commentary volume.

In general, the Mm notes are mostly of the enumerative type where the Mm enlarges on the information given in brief in the Mp by listing the catchwords for the references mentioned. However, there are other notes that deal with other matters such as a superfluous *ʾālep* at the end of a word (וְשֵׁיצִיא, Ezra 6:15), prepositional phrases (וְעַל יָדָם, Neh 3:4) and words or phrases occurring at the beginning (וְלֶחֶם, Neh 9:15), middle (וּבְנֵי יִשְׂרָאֵל, Neh 7:72) and end of a verse (הֵם, Neh 7:61). There are also notes concerning special writing of words such as שֵׂא (Ezra 5:15); לֹא for לוֹ (Ezra 4:2), אֵל used in non-sacred sense (Ezra 5:15), and הוּא used for righteous people (Ezra 7:6).

Some of Mm notes are of the *Okhlah*-type dealing with the entire verse rather than just the lemma. Thus the Mm note on דִּי at Ezra 4:15 discusses verses in which a word occurs three times, the first of which is at the beginning of a verse. The Mm note on עַד at Ezra 7:22 discusses verses which consist of identical combinations of four words, all except the first having a *wāw* conjunction. There are a number of Mm notes in Ezra 2 which compare similar forms which occur in the parallel lists in Nehemiah 7 (at v. 1 וְאֵלֶּה, at v. 16 לִיחִזְקִיָּה, and at v. 18 בְּנֵי יוֹרָה). There are also observations about usages of different groups such as Easterners and Westerners. For example, the Easterners write זַכַּי but the Westerners זַבַּי (Ezra 10:28), or in the East they permit one *wāw* to be written in the word וּמִצְוֹות (Neh 9:14). Of particular interest is the occurrence of three Aramaic mnemonics, on כְּאֶחָד at Ezra 2:64, on שֶׂכֶל, at Ezra 8:18, and on וָחֶסֶד at Neh 1:5.[13]

4. Inclusion of 1 Esdras as a Constant Witness

As with previous editions of *Biblia Hebraica*, *BHS* tended to be very selective in its use of 1 Esdras (Gα). For its part *BHQ* treats Gα as a constant witness on a par with G, V and S, and it is cited for each lemma whenever it offers relevant testimony.[14] The text for

[13] D. Marcus, "Aramaic Mnemonics in Codex Leningradensis," *TC: A Journal of Biblical Textual Criticism* 4 (1999), n.p., on line (http://purl.org/TC/).

[14] On the other hand, one witness which *BHS* cites many times (e.g., at Ezra 2:46, 50 and *passim*), but which *BHQ* does not include at all, is the Arabic version since this witness has been shown (see D. Barthélemy, *CTAT 3*, ccxiv) to be of minimal use for comparison purposes.

1 Esdras is based on the Göttingen edition of 1974.[15] Gα translates the entire book of Ezra and a small section of Neh. with two striking differences in order. The first is that Ezra 4:6–24 in M is placed between chapters 1 and 2, and the second is that the Ezra material from Nehemiah (7:72–8:13) is attached directly to Ezra chapter 10. To assist the reader, all the Gα chapter and verse parallels are indicated on every page of *BHQ*. Gα follows M fairly closely, but there are times when it exhibits pluses and omissions.

Some of the pluses are only of a word or two, particularly where the lemma is amplified by means of adding an epithet, a more complete genealogy, or an extra person in a list. The larger pluses are more extensive and informative. There is one at Ezra 2:64 stating that the list of returnees enumerated in detail consisted only of people twelve years or older and did not include servants. At Ezra 4:1, there is a note that it was from the sound of the trumpets that the antagonists of the Jews discovered that the Jews were building the temple. It is possible that some of these large pluses are the result of homoioteleuton in M. For example, the large plus at Ezra 3:8 after the word "Jerusalem" ends in "Jerusalem." Similarly, at Ezra 6:20 at the word כְּאֶחָד "together," Gα has a large plus which ends with the same word "together."

In a number of places Gα displays a large omission of more than a word or phrase (e.g., at 2:19, 28–29, 31–33). A special case is Ezra 4:6–11 where Gα has an abbreviated text of just two verses (1 Esdras 2:15–16). In this section Gα uses some of the same words and phrases as M but there is not a consistent correspondence between Gα and M at the verse level. Similarly there are a few passages where Gα exhibits a different text than M (at 2:47–48; 10:30, 35–43). In both these type of cases an attempt has been made as far as possible to find identifiable parallels, but where Gα does not have relevant testimony it is marked in the critical apparatus as indeterminate.

One of the most salient features of Gα's translation technique is the use of doublets or double translations.[16] These doublets can consist of one word as at 4:20, where תַּקִּיפִין is rendered ἰσχυροὶ καὶ σκληροί "mighty and cruel", and as at 5:11, where רַב is rendered μεγάλου καὶ ἰσχυροῦ "great and strong", or of a phrase as at 5:10,

[15] R. Hanhart (ed.), *Esdrae liber I* (*Septuaginta: Vetus Testamentum Graecum* VIII/1; Göttingen, 1974).

[16] Z. Talshir, *1 Esdras: From Origin to Translation* (SBLSCS 47; Atlanta, 1999), 238–247.

where שְׁאֵלְנָא לְהֹם is rendered by ἐπηρωτήσαμεν . . . αὐτοὺς . . . ᾐτοῦμεν αὐτούς "we asked . . . them . . . we asked them".

There are scores of differences between Gα and M especially in the onomastic sections where many divergent names and numbers are to be found. There are also minor differences in grammar, the most noticeable being those involving the presence or omission of the *wāw* conjunction, the vast majority of which are not recorded in the critical apparatus.

5. Circumscribed Use of Suggestions for Textual Emendation

Unlike *BHS* (as, for example, at Ezra 2:16, 21, 25 and *passim*) *BHQ* is very circumscribed in its suggestions for textual emendation in the book of Ezra-Nehemiah. These suggestions are limited to cases where the text is manifestly due to scribal error such as at Ezra 2:25, where the suggestion is made to read the familiar town קִרְיַת יְעָרִים instead of an otherwise unknown קִרְיַת עָרִים. Similarly, at Ezra 10:32, the common name בִּנְיָמִן is suggested instead of an abnormal בִּנְיָמִן, and at Neh 3:13, the suggested reading is הָאַשְׁפּוֹת; instead of an anomalous הָשֲׁפּוֹת.

At Neh 9:17, the suggested reading of the familiar phrase וְרַב חֶסֶד instead of M's וְרַב וחֶסֶד is supported by the Mp which observes in its note that the *wāw* is superfluous (יתיר ו). At Ezra 10:16 M's reading לְדַרְיוֹשׁ "to Darius" makes no sense in context, and appears to be a copyist error for לִדְרוֹשׁ, which is the underlying form that all the versions have used in their translations. Lastly, at Neh 7:67, on the basis of a comparison with Ezra 2:65–66 and the partial support of G, a suggestion is made to restore the line beginning and ending with מָאתַיִם. The comparison with Ezra shows that it is most likely that M has suffered a textual dislocation. The scribe's eye wandered from the first מָאתַיִם to the second resulting in a homoioteleuton, thus omitting seven words which include the listing for horses and mules.[17]

[17] See Barthélemy, *CTAT 3*, ccxxxiii–ccxxxiv.

A COMPARATIVE STUDY OF THE MASORAH MAGNA AND PARVA OF THE BOOK OF DEUTERONOMY AS ATTESTED IN THE LENINGRAD AND MADRID M1 MANUSCRIPTS

Carmel McCarthy

"As a body can be said to be naked without its clothes, so the Masoretic text of a given manuscript of the Hebrew Bible is incomplete when presented without its own particular Masorah." This figurative depiction of the unique relationship between a biblical manuscript and its Masorah I once heard on the lips of Professor Adrian Schenker in a seminar many years ago. It is a description that has stayed with me as I became more familiar with the complexities and riddles of the Masorah as a result of participating in the *Biblia Hebraica Quinta* project. It is therefore both an honour and a pleasure for me to dedicate this essay to Adrian in gratitude for his friendship and learning over many years. In this study I propose to explore some of the more striking agreements and differences in the two sets of Masorah magna (Mm) and Masorah parva (Mp) notes which clothe the respective manuscripts of the Leningrad Codex (M^L),[1] and the Madrid Codex M1 (M^{M1})[2] in relation to the book of Deuteronomy, and to explore whether the Masorah of M^{M1} can be of any help in unravelling some of the more complex Masoretic notes of M^L in Deuteronomy.

The pedigree of the Leningrad MS is well known, and its high quality frequently acknowledged: a case in point is its continued choice as the base MS for the successive diplomatic critical editions of *BHK*, *BHS* and most recently, *BHQ*. Originating in Cairo about 1008, it was produced by Shemu'el ben Ya'aqob, who copied and corrected all aspects of the manuscript: consonantal text, pointing, and Masorah.

---

[1] EBP. I B19a in the Russian National Library, St. Petersburg, Russia (Leningradensis), as read from recent photographs (films and colour transparencies) of folios 98r–121r taken by B. and K. Zuckerman for the Ancient Biblical Manuscript Center of Claremont, Calif. (U.S.A.).

[2] As edited by M. G. Seijas de los Ríos-Zarzosa, *Las masoras del libro de Deuteronomio* (Madrid, 2002).

The Madrid MS of the Complutensian University of Madrid witnesses to the Sephardi (Tiberian) Masoretic tradition of the thirteenth century: the colophon of M^{M1} locates its origin in Toledo, 1280 C.E. The book of Deuteronomy is the third volume of the research project "Edición de Textos Bíblicos y Parabíblicos" to be published.[3] Not only is the tradition represented by M^{M1} of value in itself as witnessing to the Sephardi Masoretic tradition, its timely publication by the Madrid research project also makes comparison with the Mm and Mp data of other Tiberian MSS of high quality considerably easier – in particular those of M^{L} and M^{A} (Aleppo Codex). While not without its own peculiarities and errors, M^{M1} can, in certain instances as will be illustrated below, help to unravel with greater confidence some of the complexities, frequency issues and incomplete notes to be found in M^{L}.

I

From a formal point of view the Masoretic information accompanying both M^{L} and M^{M1} with regard to Deuteronomy does not differ very significantly. However, there are some initial general observations that are interesting. The first most obvious difference between the two MSS has to do with quantity: the number of Mp notes featured in M^{L} for Deuteronomy (1,430) exceeds that of M^{M1} (1,062) by 368, whereas by contrast the number of Mm in M^{M1} (310) exceeds that of M^{L} (254) by fifty-six. Translated into percentage figures, M^{L} has an additional 35% over M^{M1} regarding the number of Mp notes, while M^{M1} has an additional 22% over M^{L} regarding the number of Mm notes.

	M^{L}	*M^{M1}*	*excess*	*% excess*
Mp	1,430	1,062	368	35% (= M^{L})
Mm	254	310	56	22% (= M^{M1})

[3] Directed by N. Fernández Marcos in the Philology Institute of the Consejo Superior de Investigaciones Científicas of Madrid, the first two volumes of this project: M. J. Azcárraga Servert (ed.), *Las masoras del libro de Números*, and M. T. Ortega Monasterio (ed.), *Las masoras del libro de Éxodo*, have already appeared in 2001 and 2002 respectively.

A second general observation concerns the Mp and Mm notes that are common to both MSS. Out of the 1,430 Mp notes of M^L and the 1,062 Mp notes of M^{M1}, only 715 (50% of M^L and 67% of M^{M1}) share the same lemma, while in the case of the 310 Mm of M^{M1} and the 254 Mm of M^L, only seventy-four are shared (24% of M^{M1} and 29% of M^L). The term "shared" here is used in a broad sense to include a small number of notes that are present in both with respect to the same lemma, but which vary in content (either in the choice of description of the same phenomenon, or, more rarely, when they each highlight a quite different feature in the lemma in question).[4]

A third observation concerns the level of accuracy in the Masorah of the respective MSS. It is a somewhat risky business to attempt to catalogue with complete confidence the exact level of "inaccuracy" in the respective MSS, since in some cases there are already discrepancies in the traditional lists,[5] due especially to variations in plene and defective spellings, and so one cannot always be sure if a discrepancy is due to error or to the fact that the Masoretic note in question is following a different tradition. Bearing this *caveat* in mind, what follows should be regarded as an attempt to give as close a picture as possible of the two MSS when compared with each other.

In the case of both Mp and Mm notes, three categories of inaccuracies or discrepancies will be isolated as noteworthy for the purposes of this comparative study:

- Frequency issues (where the number of occurrences of a given feature appears inaccurate for varying reasons, such as proximity to a similar number);
- Placement errors (where a note is attached to the incorrect lemma);
- Incomplete or inaccurate information (where a necessary limiting clause such as "in the Torah" is absent in some cases, or incorrect in others, as when "in the Prophets" may be featured instead of "in the Torah", etc.).

A fourth category of mismatch between the main text and its Masoretic annotation consists of the so-called *contra textum* cases, and these too, in the case of M^L, will be referred to in the following

[4] Some examples include Deut 1:38 ינחלנה; 1:39 יירשוה; 2:30 העברנו; 3:9 צידנים; 3:16 ונבל; 3:17 ונבל; 4:41 מזרחה; 8:16 להיטבך and following.

[5] As well documented by C. D. Ginsburg in his monumental work, *The Massorah* (London, 1880–1905).

analysis. These cases are different from the above three in that for these it is the main text, and not the Mm or Mp, which is problematic, giving rise thereby to discrepancies between the biblical text itself and the information given in the Masoretic notes.

In the case of Mm notes the amount of inaccuracy would be further increased if one were to include details relating to the content of the respective references. Thus, in certain Mm notes, even though the general point of a note may be accurate (a certain feature occurs "four" times, for example), the note can still contain minor errors or inaccuracies in the citation of otherwise correct references, or it may be accompanied by an incomplete list of correct references, or indeed other references may have been erroneously substituted for correct ones. For practical purposes these additional "inaccuracies" (considerably more frequent in M^{M1} than in M^{L}) are not included in the analysis which follows.

But before looking at the finer details, it must first be stated that the overall accuracy of detail for both MSS is truly remarkable. How the Masoretes succeeded in recording and holding together so succinctly this huge volume of information with such a high level of exactitude will never cease to amaze. A glance at the figures which follow will illustrate how in general M^{L} is clearly more careful with regard to both its Mp and Mm information than M^{M1}. They will also provide an interesting comparison of two somewhat different traditions, and of how the time difference of almost three hundred years between them nevertheless conveys the impression of a total tradition that has not changed very radically during that span of time.

	Discrepancies in M^{L}	*Discrepancies in M^{M1}*
Mp	41 (2.9%)	73 (6.9%)
Mm	5 (2%)	17 (5.5%)

As the table above shows, M^{L} has forty-one discrepancies in 1,430 Mp notes (2.9%) and only five discrepancies in its 254 Mm notes (just under 2%). By contrast M^{M1} has seventy-three discrepancies in 1,062 Mp notes (6.9%) and seventeen discrepancies in 310 Mm notes (5.5%). Of the seventy-three Mp discrepancies in M^{M1} more than half (forty-seven) are frequency issues, with the remainder being incomplete for lack of specification (such as "in the Torah" or "in the book", and similar). Approximately the same proportion is present in the considerably smaller amount of Mp discrepancies in M^{L} (twenty-seven frequency issues, eleven incomplete notes, and three placement errors).

II

Given the overall more accurate nature of M^{L}, it is nevertheless possible in a certain number of cases to draw on a parallel Mm or Mp in M^{M1} to help clarify the nature of some of the discrepancies or incomplete notes in M^{L}. As already indicated above, in relation to the Mp notes in Deuteronomy, there are forty-one discrepancies in M^{L}, of which twenty-seven are frequency issues, three are placement errors and eleven are incomplete for varying reasons. Of the twenty-seven frequency issues, only a third of them have Mp notes paralleled in M^{M1}. In the case of five[6] of these the "correct" Mp information is given in M^{M1}, thereby confirming that M^{L} is either in error or is following a different tradition, while in the case of the remaining four, M^{M1} also attests frequency issues other than those attested in M^{L}![7]

In the first of the five cases, that of 1:12, M^{L} states "sixteen", but M^{M1} records "seventeen".[8] The variation here is more likely due to varying traditions than to actual error.

The error in 2:31 in M^{L} ("five" instead of "two") probably arises from proximity to the following Mp note in this same verse attached to ואת ארצו, which lists "five". M^{M1} correctly lists "two" and gives the same parallel (1 Sam 22:15) as M^{L}.[9]

With regard to the third case, 22:14, the Mp of M^{L} is inaccurate in reading "twice" (unless it is referring to the book only, in which case it is incomplete); it should read "eight" times.[10] Here the Mp

[6] These five cases are: 1:12; 2:31; 22:14; 28:63; 32:51.

[7] 6:10; 31:11; 32:50; 33:21.

[8] Cf. Ginsburg, *Massorah*, 4, א, §366, who refers to the number "seventeen" found in a MS at Deut 1:12; and Weil, *Massorah Gedolah*, §1095, who likewise lists "seventeen".

[9] Since the Mp in M^{L} includes a reference to the only other occurrence of the form at 1 Sam 22:15, a practice which occurs quite frequently when the Mp is noting a form which occurs only twice, this is additional confirmation of a proximity error. Ginsburg, (*Massorah*, 4, ח, §246) explains the Mp note's function as protecting the two defective forms in question as against the two plene occurrences in Deut 3:24 and Esth 6:13.

[10] Gen 30:41; Deut 22:14; 27:15; 1 Sam 8:11; Isa 28:25; Jer 17:5; Zech 10:3; Ps 50:23.

of M^{M1} gives the correct figure, agreeing with those of the Damascus Pentateuch (M^{S5}) and EBP. II B 17 (M^{L17}) in attesting "eight" times,[11] with the Mp of M^{L} at Deut 27:15 also reading "eight".

In the case of 28:63 the Mp of M^{L} appears to be "incorrect" in noting "five" times for the form שׂשׂ, information which is "corrected" to "four" times in *BHS* to agree with the list given in Weil (Deut 28:63; 30:9; Isa 64:4; Ps 119:162).[12] In actual fact the respective Mp notes at these locations in M^{L} give "four" in the Mp notes of Deut 30:9 and Isa 64:4, and "five" in the remaining two. The variation in this tradition is reflected in M^{M1}. Its Mp at Deut 28:63 gives the four references listed by Weil for M^{L},[13] together with one further case spelled with *sāmek* (Isa 51:8: סס).[14] Interestingly, the Mp in M^{L} for Isa 51:8 notes "once written with ס". Thus, the agreement here in Deuteronomy between M^{L} and M^{M1} in reading "five" for Deut 28:63 can be linked to a tradition that included the case of סס in Isa 51:8 as part of the general information regarding these similar sounding forms, rather than that M^{L} should be deemed to be in error here, even if its corresponding Mm lists "four" instances (attached to an incorrect lemma in the same verse).[15]

Finally, with regard to the fifth instance, 32:51, there is a complex frequency issue, and a possible conflation of information in M^{L}. Both Mp and Mm state that אותי occurs "thirty-three times plene in the Torah" (a confusion or conflation perhaps originating from ל as "unique" and the number "thirty"? – though normally the form כׄ is used for "thirty" in the Masorah, as in M^{M1} for this case). In reality the plene occurrence in the Torah is unique (as corroborated by M^{M1}, M^{A} and M^{L17}) whereas M^{L} erroneously says "thirty-three

---

[11] Cf. Weil, *Massorah Gedolah*, §224 and the emended Mp of both *BHK* and *BHS*.

[12] Weil, *Massorah Gedolah*, §1210. Ginsburg does not list this particular tradition in his *Massorah*.

[13] Weil, *Massorah Gedolah*, §1210.

[14] However, there is some variation in the Mp notes of M^{M1} for Isa 51:8 ("once written with ס and five times with שׂ") and Isa 64:4 ("four times" = Weil, *Massorah Gedolah*, §1210). In the case of Ps 119:162 the Mp notes "four times", but the Mm, also given here, notes "four times (corrected from "five" in the first hand) written with שׂ (this is followed by five *sîmanîm*, including Isa 66:14 (ושׂשׂ), and once with ס (Isa 51:8)". I am indebted to M.T. Ortega Monasterio (both here and further below) for supplying me with M^{M1} details for the Masorah of cross-references outside of Deuteronomy.

[15] The four Mm references linked with שש are incorrectly tagged to the lemma ולהשמיד which occurs further on in this same verse.

times plene in the Torah". The Mm then gives thirty-one references (Jer 32:39 is cited twice, with different words for each citation). Ginsburg also gives the number "thirty-one" (but with differing content), while Frensdorff comments on the many discrepancies he found in his sources for the total number of plene occurrences of this word.[16]

Regarding the remaining four cases (6:10; 31:11; 32:50; 33:21), both M^{L} and M^{M1} attest differing frequency issues as follows:

In the case of 6:10, the Mp of M^{L} states that the form there (וטבת) occurs "three times defective". Forming part of the complex traditions enumerating the defective and plene occurrences of the feminine plural of טוב, disregarding prefixes, this Mp most likely contains a frequency error.[17] Of the sixteen occurrences of this feminine plural adjective in the Hebrew Bible, in M^{L} five are written doubly defectively (Gen 6:2; 41:26a, 26b, 35 and Deut 6:10), nine are defective for the first *wāw* only (טבות: Gen 41:5, 22, 24; 2 Kgs 25:28; Jer 24:2, 3a, 3b, 5; 52:32), and the remaining two are doubly plene (טובות: Jer 12:6; Esth 2:2). Regarding the five doubly defective cases in M^{L}, the Mp at Gen 41:26b indicates: "five times defective", the Mp at Gen 6:2 reads "four times defective", and, as already noted above, the Mp at Deut 6:10 indicates "three times defective". There are no Mp notes for either Gen 41:26a or 41:35. In *BHS* Weil has systematized this conflicting M^{L} information with Mp notes at four of the five occurrences (Gen 6:2; 41:26a, 26b and Deut 6:10), with each of them reading "four times defective". Ginsburg's data is no less complex. He gives two lists, the former with the heading "five times defective in this form" and listing Gen 6:2; 41:26a, 26b, 22[18] and Deut 6:10 as the loci, and the latter with the same four loci as listed by Weil.[19] Thus, the absence of Gen 41:35 in both of Ginsburg's

[16] Ginsburg, *Massorah*, 1, א, §1422; S. Frensdorff, *Die Massora Magna* (Hannover, 1876; repr. New York, 1968), 225.

[17] D. S. Mynatt, *The Sub Loco Notes of the Torah in BHS* (Fort Worth, Tex., 1994), 90, 190.

[18] The reference to Gen 41:22 in Ginsburg's first list is *contra textum* of M^{L} (וטבות), and was considered by Ginsburg to be "the work of a careless Masorete" (*Massorah*, 4, ט, §54a).

[19] Ginsburg's second list (*Massorah*, 4, ט, §54b) then continues with the two plene forms (Jer 12:6; Esth 2:2), and finishes by indicating that "the remainder have the form טבות".

lists, as well as in Weil's option in *BHS*, would indicate that they both reflect a tradition which did not include a doubly defective form for Gen 41:35, and that M^{L} is either following another tradition which did, or that its text has accidentally dropped a *wāw* here. When we turn to M^{M1} the situation is similarly complex and contradictory. The Mp of M^{M1} at Deut 6:10 features "four times defective in this form", and its Mm indicates "four times doubly defective", after which it lists Gen 6:2; 41:2a, Deut 6:10 and Jer 12:6 (which is doubly plene in M^{L}). The Mm and Mp cross-references in M^{M1} for this form are similarly confused and contradictory.[20] Thus, the complexity of these varying lists points to considerable variation in the different traditions regarding these doubly defective occurrences, illustrating yet again the thin line between possible frequency error and varying traditions.

For 31:11 there is a frequency issue in M^{L},[21] since in reading "four" here it is at variance with the Mm list given at 2 Kgs 5:18,[22] and with most of the respective Mp notes in M^{L} for this word (cf. 2 Kgs 12:10; Pss 51:2; 52:2; Prov 18:3, all of which list "nine"). The Mp in M^{A} and M^{S5} for this word likewise record "nine" (M^{L17} is illegible for this verse, while M^{M1} records "eight times plene"!).[23] Ginsburg explains that, out of the twenty occurrences of this infinitive construct, there are eleven defective and nine plene.[24] He further notes that, of the twelve lists which he collated, eleven agree that there are nine plene occurrences, but in enumerating them they differ with regard to the passages in which they occur. He explains

[20] Gen 41:22 and 41:35 have no Masorah; the Mp at Gen 6:2 reads: "five times defective" (= M^{L}); at Gen 41:26 the Mp states: "four times doubly defective with *hê* or with *waw*", while its Mm gives the *sîmanîm* for Gen 6:2; 41:26 (twice in the verse); Deut 6:10; Jer 12:6; Esth 2:2; and, finally, at Jer 12:6 the Mp there reads "twice plene".

[21] Weil corrects this Mp to "nine" in *BHS*.

[22] Gen 42:15; Deut 31:11; 2 Kgs 5:18; 12:10; Ezek 46:8, 9; Pss 51:2; 52:2; Prov 18:3 (cf. Ginsburg, *Massorah*, 1, ב, §84 and Weil, *Massorah Gedolah*, §2069).

[23] Even though M^{M1} records "eight plene" here, it actually annotates all nine instances *in loco* with some degree of inconsistency as follows: Gen 42:15 (Mp: "seven times plene"; Mm: all the *sîmanîm* except those for Ezek 46:8 and 9); 2 Kgs 5:18 (Mp: "eight times plene"); 12:10 (Mp: "eight times plene"); Ezek 46:8, 9 (Mp: "four times, twice plene and twice defective"; Mm: "four": Exod 34:34; Num 7:89; Ezek 46:8; 46:9); Ps 51:2 (Mp: "nine times plene"); Ps 52:2 (Mp: "nine times plene"); Prov 18:3 (Mp: "nine times plene"; Mm gives the nine *sîmanîm* as in Weil, *Massorah Gedolah*, §2069).

[24] Ginsburg, *Massorah*, 4, ב, §84.

this conflict as due to variation between Eastern and Western traditions (in the Western lists Ps 54:2 is plene and Ezek 46:8 is defective, while in the Eastern tradition the reverse situation obtains for these two cases).

In the case of 32:50 the Mp of M^{L} is incorrect ("four times plene in the Torah"); it should read "three times plene in the Torah" (cf. M^{L}'s Mm list at Num 31:2 which gives three references: Num 27:13; 31:2; Deut 32:50). It is also at variance with M^{M1} which reads "five times plene" here (but "four times plene" in the Mp at Num 27:13, and "three times plene" in the Mp at Num 31:2).

Finally, in the fourth case, 33:21 both MSS appear to "agree" in that both give the same reading: however, the Mp in M^{L} is incorrect (four times), and at variance with its own Mm (five times). It is also "incorrectly" recorded as "four" in the Mp of M^{M1} (but as "five" in M^{A}).

With regard to the eleven incomplete notes of M^{L}, in the case of five of them M^{M1} gives the fuller correct information;[25] and in one of the three placement errors there is similar help from the corresponding Mp in M^{M1} (10:2 הלחת 1°).

Turning now to the Masorah magna of M^{L}, in relation to its 254 Mm notes, it is striking that there are only five inaccuracies (four frequency issues and one placement error).[26] In the case of two of the frequency notes (32:51 and 33:14) and the one placement error (28:63), confirmation of the correct forms is found in M^{M1}.

With regard to the six *contra textum* Mp cases in M^{L}, in which it is the main text that has been incorrectly written and is thereby at odds with its Mp, four of these are paralleled in M^{M1},[27] confirming the Mp information and thereby showing the main text of M^{L} to have been indeed mistakenly written. One (30:9) of the two *contra textum* cases in the Mm of M^{L} is likewise confirmed by M^{M1}.

III

There are some other striking agreements and differences between the two MSS that are worthy of note and will be examined briefly

[25] These are: 1:7; 4:6; 7:1, 13; 32:8.

[26] Bearing in mind, of course, that there are also some minor material errors such as inaccurate, incomplete or misplaced citations.

[27] Deut 3:25; 8:12; 20:1; 30:9.

below. Mention need hardly be made, on the one hand, of the occasional instances of Mms with no corresponding Mps, and, on the other, of Mps with no *circelli* – phenomena shared by both MSS.

1. Qere-Kethib Occurrences

The convergence between the two MSS on Qere-Kethib occurrences is impressive. M^{L} lists twenty-four, while M$^{\text{M1}}$ attests twenty-five. The MSS agree on the twenty-four they share, the only difference being that M$^{\text{M1}}$ more logically flags only the first occurrence of the recurring הוא/היא cases at 2:20, also adding that there are "ten in the book", whereas M^{L} records only one of these ten, at 13:16, with no comment other than noting it as Qere. The additional case in M$^{\text{M1}}$ occurs at Deut 34:7, which by contrast receives only a Mp note in M^{L}: "once, and written with *hê*", while for M^{A} it is merely recorded as occurring once.

2. Ben Asher and Ben Naphtali Differences

In the introduction to the edition of M$^{\text{M1}}$ Seijas de los Ríos-Zarzosa observes that "the book contains 29 differences between Ben Asher (BA) and Ben Naftali (BN), all of them without *circellus* except if they also have masorah."[28] She also notes that these "are written by a different hand, with softer ink." According to the text as it appears in this edition, however, there would appear to be in fact forty-three instances in Deuteronomy for which M$^{\text{M1}}$ records differences between BA and BN (eight[29] of these carrying a Mp note in addition). A significant number of these differences (nineteen) are concerned with the presence, absence or location of *meteg*, thirteen of which understandably show agreement between BA and M^{L} as against BN,[30] while the remaining six show agreement between BN and M^{L} as against BA.[31] Another group (nine), also concerned with *meteg*, shows instances where *meteg* is present in BA, and *māqqēp* in BN (or vice versa), but with both *meteg* and *māqqēp* present in each corresponding case in M^{L}.[32] Other variations are concerned with *māqqēp* on its

[28] Seijas de los Ríos-Zarzosa, *Las masoras*, 16.
[29] These eight are: 1:29, 41, 44; 3:24; 6:10; 15:10; 32:6, 41.
[30] 1:29, 41, 44; 3:24, 24; 6:10; 7:9; 9:7; 20:15; 21:8; 32:10; 33:17, 28.
[31] 2:34; 8:2; 11:19; 14:26; 22:25; 29:12.
[32] 1:14; 2:29; 9:2; 10:4; 11:11; 12:20, 22; 22:25; 31:27.

own (five), three of them showing BA in agreement with M^L,[33] and the remaining two showing BN agreeing with M^L;[34] others are concerned with *pāsēq* (1), *rapê* (1), vocalization (1) and certain accents (7). Finally, it is worth noting that in three of the overall total BA, BN and M^L all differ from each other.[35]

3. Aramaic Mnemonics

A striking feature of the Mm of Deuteronomy in M^{M1} is the significant number of Aramaic mnemonics it contains (thirty-one in Deuteronomy alone) in contrast to M^L which only attests three in Deuteronomy: 8:7; 13:3 and 29:4.[36] A further difference between these MSS is that, whereas M^L gives the references in Aramaic only for the so-called Aramaic mnemonics, M^{M1} does this only for Deut 14:7 and 26:2, but features both Aramaic and Hebrew sets of references in all the other instances, beginning with the Aramaic sets in the case of Deut 1:5, 38; 3:4, 8, 22; 4:1, 10, 32,[37] 37; 5:5, 16, 23; 6:18; 7:5, 10, 13; 9:9; 12:31; 19:9; 21:23; 27:6; 30:7; 31:26; 32:29, and with the Hebrew sets first for Deut 1:7; 7:15; 12:23; 26:8; 28:63. In the case of 1:35 the Aramaic mnemonics in question are given in the Mp only (bringing the full total then to thirty-two, if one includes this Mp with the above-listed Mm occurrences).

4. Occurrences of Pāsēq

Scholars such as Wickes and Yeivin estimate that the introduction of *pāsēq* was relatively late, and established after the system of conjunctives and disjunctives, which it completes.[38] As its name implies (פסק, "to cut off"), the function of *pāsēq* was the introduction of a slight pause between two or more words joined by accents, for the

---

[33] 7:1; 15:10; 16:2.

[34] 23:16; 17:20.

[35] 22:10; 27:3; 32:6.

[36] There are thirty-eight Aramaic mnemonics in all in M^L and twenty-five in M^A. See further C. McCarthy, "Moving in from the Margins: Issues of Text and Context in Deuteronomy," in A. Lemaire (ed.), *Congress Volume Basel 2001* (Leiden, 2002), 109–112.

[37] This reference is incomplete in that only one Aramaic mnemonic is given, instead of eight.

[38] W. Wickes, *A Treatise on the Accentuation of the Twenty-One So-Called Prose Books of the Old Testament* (Oxford, 1887), 120–129; I. Yeivin, *Introduction to the Tiberian Masorah* (Missoula, Mont., 1980), 216–218.

sake of effect in the reading of the text. With no proper musical value as such, *pāsēq* was not therefore numbered among the accents. The lateness of its introduction most likely explains the lack of system in its use, and why the cases where it might be expected but does not occur are far more numerous than those where it does occur.[39] A further complication in its use is that one needs to keep in mind that there was one exception to its basic meaning of introducing a slight pause – namely, when associated with *mûnaḥ* to constitute the independent musical accent known as *lĕgarmeh*.[40] Consequently, it is not surprising to find considerable differences in the annotation of *pāsēq* in the two MSS under examination. While M^{L} features instances of *pāsēq* throughout the biblical text in Deuteronomy, at no point does it mark their presence with corresponding Mp notes. However, it does give a list of twenty-two occurrences in the Masorah finalis (Mf) for Deuteronomy as part of its records for the use of *pāsēq* in the Torah, a list which is also given in Ginsburg (and in the Mf of M^{M1}, as will be discussed further below).[41] But, in addition to these occurrences of what Wickes insists are occurrences of true *pāsēq*, an examination of the text of M^{L} shows that it contains a further fifty-nine occurrences of *pāsēq* associated with the accent *lĕgarmeh*,[42] a usage to be distinguished from that contained in the list of twenty-two. As dryly observed by Wickes, "the inventive faculty of the accentuators was certainly at fault here,"[43] and the potential confusion this double usage of *pāsēq* caused comes to fruition when we turn to M^{M1}. In contrast to the Leningrad Codex, M^{M1} contains varied *pāsēq* information in the form of Mp notes at various points in the MS. These

[39] Wickes wryly observes that "the *failure* of the sign is more conspicuous than its presence. It is constantly wanting where it might have marked a necessary *distinction*, or *emphasis* . . . Writers on the accents, from Ben-Asher to Ewald, have not troubled themselves at all about this strange lack of consistency in the use of Paseq, although it stands in such marked contrast to the precision in the employment of the accentual signs. This circumstance seems again to point to a (comparatively) late introduction of the sign" (Wickes, *Treatise*, 127).

[40] Wickes, *Treatise*, 121. He takes pains to illustrate how the use of *pāsēq* has been greatly misunderstood, and sets out "to ascertain *where it is really due* in the text" (italics his).

[41] Ginsburg, *Massorah*, 1, ט, §404. The twenty-two listed occurrences in all three sources are: Deut 3:20; 4:32; 5:8; 5:8; 6:4; 6:22; 7:1; 7:26; 7:26; 9:4; 8:15; 9:21; 16:16; 17:8; 22:6; 25:19; 27:9; 28:12; 28:20; 28:25; 28:68; 29:12.

[42] Wickes, *Treatise*, 119, illustrates the difference between the function of *lĕgarmeh* (usually linked with *rĕbîaʿ*, and subordinate to it) as distinct from that of *pāsēq* (when not linked with *rĕbîaʿ*). See also Yeivin, *Introduction*, 213–14.

[43] Wickes, *Treatise*, 121.

show considerable discrepancies. First of all, the number of Mp notes concerned with *pāsēq* in the M^{M1} edition totals "eighteen",[44] which differs formally from that given in the Mf of M^{L} and Ginsburg and indeed the Mf of M^{M1} itself.[45] Second, all of these occurrences differ from those of the M^{L} list, apart from Deut 4:32 (a true *pāsēq* in Wickes' estimation). The remaining seventeen coincide with some of the fifty-nine occurrences of *pāsēq* featured in the text of M^{L} linked with the accent *lĕgarmeh*, but represent only a fraction of the total occurrences of this particular feature in M^{L}. Third, there is considerable conflicting variation in M^{M1} regarding their number: six Mp notes simply indicate *pāsēq*,[46] one case mentions "ten occurrences of *pāsēq* in the book" (4:32) and eleven indicate "twelve occurrences of *pāsēq* in the book".[47] Thus, it would appear that both M^{L} and M^{M1} are accurate in recording "twenty-two" instances of *pāsēq* (when not linked with *lĕgarmeh*) in their respective Mf notes, whereas M^{M1} is inconsistent, incomplete and confused with regard to its Mp information *in situ*.

5. *Seder and Parashah Notes*

The variations between M^{L} and M^{M1} are minimal in this regard in comparison to the foregoing variations in the use of *pāsēq*. The Mf of Deuteronomy in M^{L} lists thirty-one, all of which are also marked, often enclosed in illuminations, in M^{M1}, with the omission of just two (Deut 4:25 and 9:1).

6. *Three-dotted Gîmel*

In the Mp note at Deut 1:1 ולבן in M^{L} there are three dots over a single *gîmel* in the form of *sĕgôltâ*, a feature also found in M^{L} at Deut 1:3, 5, 7, 22, 31, 37; 3:24; 4:10; 8:20 and the Mm at Deut 3:17 and 4:43. A three-dotted *gîmel* will often interchange freely in M^{L} with one carrying a single dot, and would appear to have no special significance, both forms of the *gîmel* indicating a three-fold occurrence

[44] These eighteen references are: Deut 2:7; 4:5; 4:47; 5:4; 5:14; 5:15; 7:6; 11:2; 12:15; 13:7; 17:3; 17:6; 19:15; 22:6; 26:2; 28:55; 31:16 (that of 4:32 is a true *pāsēq*).

[45] Seijas de los Ríos-Zarzosa, *Las masoras*, 16, simply notes that "Appendix 1 of the manuscript" (presumably its Mf) mentions twenty-two occurrences of *pāsēq* in Deuteronomy.

[46] Deut 2:7; 4:5; 4:7; 5:4; 5:14; 13:7.

[47] Deut 5:15; 7:6; 11:2; 12:15; 17:3; 17:6; 19:15; 22:6; 28:55; 31:16.

of the particular feature being noted. The origins of this peculiarity are unclear, and may have remote links to practices in Judaeo-Arabic texts (where a one-dotted *gîmel* was the equivalent of the Arabic letter *jîm* – as opposed to a dotless *ghayin*). A somewhat parallel feature occurs in M^{M1} in a slightly different format: at Deut 1:41 the Mp note there carries three *gîmel* signs together, the middle of which carries a *sĕgôltâ*, a combination which the editor of M^{M1} notes appears often in the MS.[48] However, its precise function at Deut 1:41 in M^{M1} is unclear as the lemma here (ונלחמנו) is a unique occurrence.

7. Features of M^{M1} Not Found in M^{L}

There are four Mp references containing the word מוגה in M^{M1} (3:16 הגלעד עד; 22:19 כסף; 28:1 שמוע; 32:5 לא). In all four cases the intervention of "another" hand can be seen. As noted by Yeivin the word *mûggâ*, "corrected" (or ספרי מוגהי, "corrected codices") seems to refer not to a specific text, but to any sort of "carefully corrected text".[49] There is also a reference to Hilleli (הלליה) at 32:24 ושן בהמת. Yeivin includes this latter among the names of various other texts given in late MSS, noting that "while they were no doubt well known and renowned in their day for their accuracy and their authoritative Masorah, we know nothing about them today."[50] A religious Masorah is present at 31:1, while striking also in M^{M1} is the considerable length of some of the Mm associated with the Song of Moses (Deut 32:1–43) as compared with those of either M^{L} or M^{A}. Two such Mm notes partially reproduce *Okhlah* lists (32:15 and 32:18). Finally, whereas the Mp notes of M^{L} never give more than the text of one further parallel reference, those of M^{M1} occasionally give a more fulsome text (in 1:35 five references are given).

IV

As illustrated in the foregoing paragraphs, a certain number of the Mm and Mp notes accompanying Deuteronomy in M^{M1} differ in varying ways from those contained in M^{L}. As a final illustration of

[48] See Seijas de los Ríos-Zarzosa, *Las masoras*, 15. She does not offer a view on its purpose or significance.
[49] Yeivin, *Introduction*, 138.
[50] Idem.

just how individual the Masoretic annotation of each MS can be, what follows is a comparison between the Mm and Mp notes for the Leningrad, Aleppo and Madrid M1 MSS in the case of a sample chapter, Deut 33:1–29.

Deuteronomy 33:1–29

Total in M^{M1}	Mm: 9	Mp: 38
Total in M^{L}	Mm: 8	Mp: 48
Total in M^{A}	Mm: 7	Mp: 76
Shared by all three MSS	Mm: 1	Mp: 21
Common to M^{M1} and M^{L}	Mm: 0	Mp: 1
Common to M^{M1} and M^{A}	Mm: 1	Mp: 8
Common to M^{L} and M^{A}	Mm: 3	Mp: 24
Unique to M^{M1}	Mm: 7	Mp: 8
Unique to M^{L}	Mm: 4	Mp: 2
Unique to M^{A}	Mm: 2	Mp: 23

A first striking observation arising out of this comparison for Deuteronomy 33 is the great quantity of Mp notes in M^{A}, exactly double those of M^{M1} and significantly greater than those of M^{L}. A second noteworthy fact, at least for this chapter, is the very low number of notes shared by all three (only one Mm and twenty-one Mps), especially when one takes the profusion of Mp notes in M^{A} into account. Not surprisingly, there is a greater convergence between M^{L} and M^{A} than between M^{A} and M^{M1} or between M^{L} and M^{M1} – more than half the Mp notes in M^{L} are also found in M^{A}. Perhaps the most striking aspect of all, however, is just how different the selections of Mm and Mp notes accompanying each of the three MSS are.

So, to return to the metaphor quoted at the beginning, not only can one reaffirm that any given Masoretic manuscript is incomplete without its own particular Masorah, one should also insist that one must not try to put on one manuscript the clothes that properly belong to another!

A DIPLOMATIC EDITION OF THE PSALTER?

Gerard J. Norton, O.P.

This paper arose from work undertaken in the preparation of the text of the Psalter for the edition of the Hebrew Bible to be known as *Biblia Hebraica Quinta*. It was decided that this edition, like its immediate precursors, should adopt the text of EBP. I B 19a of the Russian National Library in St. Petersburg as its basic text and provide a diplomatic edition of that text in an *editio minor* rather than try to produce an *editio maior* or an eclectic text. The task of the editor is to present the text of the Leningrad Codex as honestly as possible. Some may ask how the text of such an edition differs from the facsimile volume produced by Eerdmans. They may point out that it is by no means difficult to read the photographic reproduction of the manuscript with a little practice. The Masorah takes a little more effort but is not impossible. What then is the role of the editor in presenting the text of the Leningrad codex?

In some ways, that question seems hard to answer. Certainly the printing of the text in typeface (or standard computer font) with clear gaps between the words is a favour to students and other readers. But there is more. In many places the layout of the text on the page of the manuscript needs to be interpreted, so that the text transmitted by M^L can be distinguished from features contingent on the particular codex. Included in this latter group would be decorative features specific to M^L. These can be noted, but need not be considered as a major part of the tradition. On the other hand, traditional features following rules which were observed by the scribe of M^L should be retained. These latter would include paragraph breaks and markers, and cases where a traditional page-layout of poetic texts can be discerned.

For example, because we are not working with pages or print columns of the same size as the scribe of M^L, we do not try to reproduce all page breaks or line breaks in our edition, whether it is of prose or poetry. However in some places these elements are fixed by tradition, such as the canticles in Exodus 15 and Deuteronomy 32. Here we believe the scribe is following tradition rather than improvising and we will follow the format found in the manuscript.

The antiquity of the paragraphing system in prose texts of Biblical manuscripts has been demonstrated by Oesch and others by reference to the Dead Sea Scrolls.[1] It is precisely on the basis of these phenomena in the Pentateuch that we can identify the Aleppo Codex as that praised by Maimonides.[2]

Our concern here is with the Psalms in the manuscript at the basis of our edition to be known as *Biblia Hebraica Quinta*. Like the two other books traditionally considered to be poetry (Proverbs and Job) the Psalter presents particular features of layout that have to be explained. We do not speak here of the full or partial blank lines that are found between the Psalms, and can usually be described as section-marking *petuḥot*, or *setumot* comparable to those found in prose texts. I. Yeivin published a list found in the Cairo Genizah and relating to the division into sections of the Psalter. The list was written before 900 C.E. and is of Babylonian origin. In fact, with the exception of the alphabetic acrostic in Psalm 119, all the notes concern the boundaries between Psalms. Yeivin's study, based on the Cairo Genizah list, was the first modern study of *petuḥot* and *setumot* in the Psalter. Yeivin does not comment on all the gaps of the manuscript M^L, only those which are relevant to his list and which relate to the divisions between psalms and the writing of the headings.[3] Here we are concerned with the gaps in the writing of the Psalter in our manuscript other than those at Psalm beginnings and endings. Our study can best begin with an overall description of the Psalter in the manuscript at hand. Some of this will replicate the standard codicological descriptions of our manuscript,[4] but it seems useful to repeat it here as a basis of the subsequent discussion.

---

[1] J. M. Oesch, *Petucha und Setuma: Untersuchungen zu einer überlieferten Gliederung im hebräischen Text des Alten Testaments* (OBO 27; Fribourg & Göttingen, 1979).

[2] I. Ben Zvi, "The codex of Ben Asher," *Textus* 1 (1960), 7; D. Barthélemy, *Critique Textuelle de l'Ancien Testament*, vol. 3, *Ézéchiel, Daniel et les 12 Prophètes* (OBO 50/3; Fribourg & Göttingen, 1992), x–xi, lxii. (*CTAT* 3)

[3] I. Yeivin, "The Division into Sections in the Book of Psalms," *Textus* 7 (1969), 76–102.

[4] A. Harkavy and H. L. Strack, *Catalog der hebräischen Bibelhandschriften der kaiserlichen öffentlichen Bibliothek* (St. Petersburg & Leipzig, 1875), and more recently, M. Beit-Arié, C. Sirat and M. Glatzer, *Codices Hebraicis Litteris Exarati Quo Tempore Scripti Fuerint Exhibentes*, vol. 1, *Jusqu'à 1020* (Monumenta Palaeographica Medii Aevi, Series Hebraica; Turnhout, 1997), 114–131.

Description of the Psalter of M^L

The Psalter starts at the top right of the recto of a folio, and ends at the bottom left of the verso of a folio. Strikingly, this is not the case with the Job-Proverbs border, nor indeed the Proverbs-Ruth border. The books of Genesis, Joshua and 1 Chronicles all begin on the verso of a folio. Book divisions within Torah, Prophets or Writings do not otherwise coincide with page breaks. At the division between Proverbs and Ruth, where we return from the two columned 'poetical' format to a three-columned prose format, there is simply an interval of three blank lines after the Masorah finalis of Proverbs and the first seventeen verses of Ruth are written in a two-column format matching that of Proverbs, before returning to a three column per page format at the next page. Both at the division between books (Proverbs and Ruth) and between poetic and prose layout within a book (Judges 5–6; Job 2–3), the poetic layout is given priority.

Psalms, Job and Proverbs stand out from the rest of the Hebrew Bible in that they are written in two columns per page. The rest of the Hebrew Bible is written in three columns per page, except the canticles of Exodus 15, Deuteronomy 31–32 and Judges 5. The last verses of Judges 5 are not centred on the page, but aligned to a right hand margin so that it occupies a space equivalent to the first two columns of a three columned page. The following prose text occupies this two-column space, allowing a narrow "third" column to the left of the broad column. Thus the scribe achieved an economy of space while following traditional layout of the song.

The books within the Psalter are separated from one another by three blank lines. This space is comparable to the divisions between other books of the Hebrew Bible, but since there is no Masorah finalis between the books of the Psalter it is hard to make a definite comparison.

Twenty-seven lines of text are found in each column. This layout in twenty-seven lines is similar to most of the rest of the Hebrew Bible in this manuscript. Exodus 15 is written in one twenty-six-line column per page. Deuteronomy 31–32 is written in one twenty-eight-line column per page. Judges 5 is written in one twenty-seven-line column per page. The Psalter of the Aleppo Codex, like the rest of that codex, is written in twenty-eight lines per page.

In M^L gaps are found within the lines. If these were found in prose texts, they would nearly all be described as *setumot*. Although the line gaps in the poetic books are similar in form to the *setumot* of prose, they mostly seem to be quite unrelated. They differ from *setumot* in being quite narrow compared with the *setumot* in prose texts. Further they always occur within a line and do not carry over from one line to the other. Their semantic significance is unclear. We shall simply call them 'gaps' here. These intralinear gaps are to be distinguished from the section breaks between psalms, studied by Yeivin in the article mentioned above.

What factors contributed to this presentation of the Psalter? By what conventions was the scribe working?

Firstly he was following a twenty-seven-line arrangement. The twenty-seven-line convention had already been established for the rest of the manuscript.

Secondly, the text was in two columns per page. The two-column arrangement was either an innovation, or inherited from existing scrolls or codices of the poetical books. The change from scroll to codex (or possibly from one-column partial Hebrew Bible codex to two-column and three-column full Hebrew Bible codex) seems to have involved a change from one poetic column to two per page, in a limited page-space. Each column in the two-column per page format was narrower than the columns in previous formats. The one-verse per line arrangement found in earlier manuscripts found, for example, in Berlin Or. Qu. 680/New York JTS 510[5] was therefore largely impossible. Neither was any particular attempt made to keep one stichos per line as seems to have been the option for 4QPs[d] in columns IV and V for Ps 104:13ff, even if such stichography does not seem to have been the general practice at Qumran.[6]

Thirdly, in transcribing the Psalms, he gave priority to traditions concerning the opening of Psalms, similar but not identical to those now published by Yeivin. So close is the correspondence between the phenomena at the divisions between Psalms in our manuscript and the prescriptions of the Yeivin manuscript that the two are clearly in the same tradition.[7]

Fourthly, the columns are aligned (or 'justified') to the right and left sides. This is to be taken in conjunction with the following feature.

[5] I. Yeivin, *Bible – Hagiographa: Codex Berlin Or.Qu. 680 – Codex New York JTS 510* (Jerusalem, 1972).

[6] E. Ulrich, et al., *Qumran Cave 4, XI, Psalms to Chronicles* (DJD XVI; Oxford, 2000), 63–71.

[7] Yeivin, "The Division into Sections in the Book of Psalms," 97.

Fifthly, the scribe took care to write the top and bottom lines of each column without a break, but to include a single gap in most (about two thirds) of the other lines. These gaps are the principal concern of this article. In line sequences they sometimes appear at patterned intervals, and sometimes appear to follow a pattern, such as a 'zig-zag' down the column. The room for manoeuvre is not great, given the relatively narrow columns and that this gap occurs between two complete words. In general the gaps tend to appear in the central third of the line. Contrary to what one might expect, these gaps do not seem to have a clear relationship to the phenomenon of justifying the lines to the left and right. (For example, in fol. 383v line fillers are used as well as the gaps.) This is somewhat surprising.

We find that in some manuscripts the width of the column is such that lines corresponding to verses can be justified to the left by use of a gap of variable length at the main sense break of the verse. This is the arrangement in Berlin Or. Qu. 680/New York JTS 510, published by Yeivin and already mentioned, MS Ec2, Oxford Bodleian MS Heb. d.37 from the Cairo Geniza and MS Ec22, New York, MS JTS 508, both the latter also published by Yeivin.[8] It seems reasonable that the process of justifying the lines to the left in columns much narrower than these manuscripts just mentioned, such as the columns in M^L, meant that in cases where the verse or half verse did not simply coincide with a line, the gaps which could be placed at different places within the line became more important than the end of the line break which became a mechanical feature. This may in fact have been the case with Qoh 3:2–8; Ezra 2:43–54; Esth 9:7–10. In these places the gap in the course of the line is used rather than the break between lines to mark the different units. This is not the case in the Psalter.

The gap on occasion coincides with the major sense break in the line. However, when we consider the constraints, howsoever imposed, of a single gap per line; that gap occurring in a restricted section of the line (i.e., it cannot occur at the beginning or end of the line); and the occurrence of a gap in only two thirds of the lines, then it becomes clear that a simple correspondence of gap in the line and sense break does not work for texts of long or irregular line length.

[8] I. Yeivin, *Geniza Bible Fragments with Babylonian Massorah and Vocalization*, vol. 3, *Hagiographa* (Jerusalem, 1973).

The placing of the gaps in the text lines has occasionally been described as though they coincided with sense breaks in the poetic text, even stichoi. Yeivin says,

> The spaces between the hemistichs, even though extending more than the width of a CS [Closed Section or Setumah], would not be considered as a division into sections, but merely as the consequence of the licence allowed to poetry.[9]

Yet this is difficult to maintain as an absolute given the regular occurrence of lines without any breaks at all. Are we to suggest that the gaps were only used when they coincided with a sense break outside of those lines that were to be left complete to observe the pattern? But this does not prove to be the pattern of their occurrence. Could we hypothesize that where a gap occurs it is a sense break but not all sense breaks have a gap? On first principles, this might work, but observation soon shows that it is not the case in many of the Psalms, where gaps do not coincide with sense breaks. (Psalm 29 is a fair example). On occasion, where they do seem to coincide with some sort of sense breaks, more significant sense breaks are found in the same line without gap.

Then it could be suggested that the gaps were a luxury to be used in lines where there is space but easily omitted when the line did not allow. However this presumes that end of line breaks are of significance, something that is difficult to maintain, and also makes it difficult to account for the patterns of gapped and whole lines that we are about to note.

The pattern is not straightforward, but it is hard to avoid the conclusion that the gaps in the lines seem to have no semantic force, apart from indicating to the reader that this is poetry. It might be thought to reinforce the two-column presentation that also alerts the reader to the different nature of the text.

Two things are at issue here, and must be distinguished. One is the layout of the psalm in lines on the page and the other is the literary element of verse structure. The verse structure rarely coincides with the line structure in the manuscript, or even with the line structure modified by the gaps as a second point of division.

[9] Yeivin, "The Division into Sections in the Book of Psalms," 79. On this issue, he refers to E. N. Adler, *An Eleventh Century Introduction to the Hebrew Bible* (Oxford, 1897), and others.

(Exceptions, such as Psalm 136, occur.) It is possible that at one stage there was a convention that the verse did indeed coincide with the line as written on the page, and that this line was of variable length. Here, gaps occurring towards the centre of the written line could easily coincide with the sense break. However in the text of the Psalter as presented to us in the Leningrad Codex, the text is not generally presented to us in sense lines. The gaps in the short lines of fixed length do not, indeed cannot, coincide systematically with sense gaps or verse breaks of an earlier presentation. Are the gaps then completely random, with no coherent relationship to the sense breaks? It is tempting to think so. Yet this article suggests that patterns can be discerned in the occurrence of these gaps that can help us to put them in perspective.

Two principal categories of ornamental line gapping can be determined in the Psalter of our manuscript: (1) 'one plus two', (2) zig-zag. Together they account for almost all of the Psalter apart from (3) those few Psalms where other factors prevail. In this third category we include those Psalms for which there is some traditional pattern of transmission, e.g. acrostic (as in Ps 119) or response (as in Ps 136).

Ornamental Line Gapping

The One Plus Two Arrangement

The most common arrangement of the occurrence of the columns in the Psalter shall be described here as the 'one plus two'. Essentially it means that one full line is followed by two gapped lines. The same pattern could also be described as a 'two plus one' or even as a repeated 'ABA', depending on the starting point, largely determined by how other conventions followed by the scribe disturb the 'one plus two'. However, since in this pattern each column begins with a full line, 'one plus two' is the most usual way in which the pattern presents itself to the reader.

The scribe varied the number of gapped lines when another convention required such variation. The impression is given that this pattern, although prevalent, is subsidiary to almost all other factors and conventions. Only the alphabetic acrostic can be secondary to the 'one plus two' pattern. Sometimes there is a single gapped line after a full line; on occasions three. Usually, however, it does not exceed three. In almost all cases where the column is generally written in the pattern 'one plus two' variations in the number of gapped lines occur either (1) at the end of a Psalm where other conventions may take precedence, or (2) towards the bottom of the column where the scribe's wish to have a full line at the end of a column led to variations in the number of preceding gapped lines. The scribe seems to take care to avoid writing two consecutive full lines in any column (but see also below). On rare occasions full lines do follow one another in the same column, but these are usually attributable to some conflict with other conventions being observed.

It is clear that the scribe preferred to have a full line top and bottom of each column. In the case where there are no other conventions to be observed, this is inconsistent with the 'one plus two' convention he has adopted as a dominant pattern in the Psalter. In many columns however a break between two Psalms disrupts the 'one plus two' pattern. In this way it can be considered a peculiar inner-Psalm pattern, although it is related to the layout of the text on the page rather than any particular Psalm. Yet in a folio such as fol. 368v, first column, Ps 18:7–30, where there is no interruption of the 'one plus two' pattern, the pattern is shortened at the end to a 'one plus one' to observe the convention that the last line should be a complete one. It is tempting to muse on the existence of a twenty-eight-line convention such as that of the Aleppo codex somewhere in the background. Other possibilities present themselves, such as a twenty-five-line convention or a twenty-two-line convention. Any of these would allow a 'one plus two' pattern to end and begin with a full line without distortion.

The combination of the convention not to have two full lines following one another immediately in a column and the desire to have columns begin and end in a complete line make us think that the layout on the page that resulted from these conventions was specific to this manuscript, or perhaps copied exactly from another similar manuscript. Yet on the basis of other manuscripts there is no reason to suspect that this represented a stable tradition of transmission.

The Zig-Zag Pattern

Although some patterning will seem to occur inevitably in the 'one plus two' arrangement we have just seen, there are at least two folios where a deliberate pattern seems to occur that toys with and then abandons the 'one plus two' pattern. These are fol. 374v, 375v, and

380v (first column). In each of these columns we see the gaps are so arranged in succeeding lines that they zig-zag from side to side over a series of about five lines per directional thrust of the gaps. This pattern maintains the conventions of having only a single gap per line, that gap occurring between two words, and never extending to the edge of the column. On fol. 374v column one, the 'one plus two' convention is also observed for half of the column. In most of these zig-zag sections the full lines are abandoned, perhaps to make the pattern all the more clear.

What is the function of such a scribal device? The proximity to the beginnings of books Two (Psalm 42) and Three (Psalm 73) are hard to ignore. Could they have been intended to help the reader to find the breaks between books? Yet there is nothing similar at the beginnings of book Four (Psalm 90) or Five (Psalm 107).

Other Factors Affecting Layout

(a) One Verse per Line, and One Verse per Line (modified)

As noted above very few Psalms are written one verse per line (Psalms 119 and 136 are examples), but where they do occur, there is no attempt to have a 'one plus two' arrangement or to pattern the gaps within the line. In other Psalms, or sections of Psalms we see an attempt to give the gaps semantic force. Here either the end of a line, or the gap in the course of a line coincides with an important sense break of the Psalm. We find sections of Psalms written so (Pss 18:3–6; 49:4–7; 115:8–11). In most of these the 'one plus two' pattern is maintained.

(b) Alphabetic Acrostics

These are included in this category because, curiously, at some times the acrostic element seems to dominate, although in most instances the 'one plus two' pattern dominates.

Psalm 25 is laid out in what is now seen to be a conventional 'one plus two' layout, with a distortion to a single gapped line at the bottom of the column. The end of the Psalm at the top of the next column in fol. 370r is written as two full lines. The key words occur after a gap or at the beginning of a line ten times.

Psalm 34 is written in a single column observing the 'one plus two' pattern with the exception of the first and last lines of the column where other rules relating to the intervals between Psalms presumably have precedence. Within the constraints of that pattern, the alphabetic acrostic nature of the text is highlighted, but not mechanically so. The key words occur after a gap or at the beginning of a line nine times, and in two other cases other words with the relevant letters seem to be highlighted. The first words of the verses at the beginning and end of the acrostic are among those found after a gap or at the beginning of a line, and perhaps this was considered sufficient to indicate the acrostic features of the Psalm as a whole.

Psalm 37 is an unusual acrostic in that the key acrostic words occur every second verse. It is laid out in a 'one plus two' form (with the necessary single gapped line before the final full line of the first column). A key acrostic word occurs at the beginning of a line or after a break in only seven instances. In other gaps and line endings, it seems that a decision has been taken to obscure rather than highlight the word by placing it at the end of a line or just before a gap. This is particularly the case in verses 5, 7, 14, 16, 23, and 30. In the remaining instances the key words are buried in the full lines of the 'one plus two' pattern.

Psalm 111 spans two columns and so the exact arrangement is hard to discern. Nonetheless it approximates to a 'one plus two' arrangement. Within those constraints, and recognising that the elements of the acrostic are monostichs, it is surprising that a key acrostic word occurs at the beginning of a line or after a break in only fourteen instances.

Psalm 112 is apparently similar to Psalm 111. It is written in 'one plus two' pattern except for the last line. Within those constraints, and recognising that the elements of the acrostic are short monostichs, it is surprising that a key acrostic word occurs at the beginning of a line or after a break in only eleven instances.

Psalm 119 retains its two columned single-gapped format throughout. The gaps occur at the principal sense break in the verse, and coincide with the Masoretic punctuation. Each verse occupies a complete line, and where necessary this means that there is no gap. These full lines are not part of any overall pattern, and there is no attempt to avoid having more than one of these occur together, or to have full lines at the top and bottom of the twenty-seven-line columns. There are empty lines between each group of eight-line alphabetic elements, corresponding to *petuḥot.* These are noted also in the tradition published by Yeivin noted above.

Psalm 145 largely abandons the 'one plus two' pattern seen in Psalm 144. Even so, a key acrostic word occurs at the beginning of a line or after a break in only twelve instances. A one verse per line strategy is adopted for verses six to eleven.

Summary: It is striking that in all of the acrostic psalms (except 119) on occasion the gap occurs in the line in such a way as to obscure the acrostic element, or the relevant word is squeezed into the end of a line, when the acrostic would be more evident if it began a new line. It can be said then that the alphabetic acrostic, although significant for the scribe, does not dominate the line layout. The 'one plus two' pattern was generally seen to be stronger.

(c) Psalms with refrains (responsories)

These are not always as clear as Psalm 136, where the layout highlights the responsory. The fact that one verse fits per line in this Psalm makes it possible that this layout is older than the manuscript under examination. It is also worth noting that in Ps 115:9–11, where we seem to have a kind of response, the 'one plus two' pattern that has previously been observed in this column is abandoned to make the three-line refrain clearer on the page. The repeated element is also brought out clearly at Ps 118:1–4 and again in 118:10–11. The general layout of this Psalm is one verse per line when possible, and when the verse runs on to a new line, it ends before the gap.

Psalm 135 ends with a four-line litany/refrain. Again, the lines are arranged to highlight this. The arrangement previously in this Psalm has seemed to highlight sense units, with most of the verses ending either at the end of a line or at the beginning of a gapped line. At this late stage of the Psalter the 'one plus two' pattern seems to be used sporadically, and for complete psalms, e.g., Psalm 140. In the earlier sections of the Psalter the 'one plus two' pattern seems to be related to columns rather than to individual Psalms. The shift is of little significance in itself. Perhaps it indicates that the scribe is tiring of his own innovation.

Psalm 136 is laid out on the page as one verse per line. This reinforces its litany character. The gaps coincide with the sense breaks.

Psalm 150 is one of the few instances in the Psalter of M^{L} where we have two gaps per line. This is probably connected with the scribe's concern to get all of the Psalm on to the end of the folio. The final arrangement is slightly peculiar, and one can only imagine how it would have been laid out if space had not been a constraint.

Summary: Refrains and repeated texts are given high priority by the scribe of M^L, and lead him to abandon whatever other conventions he is following in the body of the Psalm to lay out the lines in a way that draws attention to the phenomenon.

Overall Conclusions, and Consequences for an Edition of M^L

Although this study has been limited by the fact that it has been confined to the Psalter of a single manuscript, we can nonetheless identify the graphic conventions followed by the scribe. The dominant pattern described here as 'one plus two' is found throughout the book, with some weakening in the last books when compared to the first books. In general the gaps in texts written in this pattern have no necessary connection with sense breaks between verses or as suggested by the accentuation. There is no reason to try to reproduce them in a modern edition.

This pattern is broken at the intervals between Psalms, where another tradition predominates. We have other evidence of such a tradition, published and discussed by Yeivin. These traditions should be represented in a modern edition.

The pattern is not broken to display acrostic features, although the scribe is sensitive to them. The pattern is broken by Psalm 119, and also by the occurrence of psalms with refrains, and in the psalms written one line per verse. This may indicate an older traditional layout. In the matter of the divisions between psalms, and in the layout of Psalm 119, it seems reasonable for a modern editor to follow the practice of the scribe of M^L. Similarly in the case of psalms with refrains, and in those psalms set out as one-line verse, the clarity of M^L is easily accepted as a model. The two Tiberian manuscripts constantly collated for the edition of *BHQ* (M^A and M^Y) will also be consulted in these matters.

The layout of the acrostics is easily adapted to that of the scribe in Psalm 119 to allow the acrostic structure to be visible. Should it be so? Or should the gentle obscurity of the acrostic be preserved as in the manuscript? The matter is perhaps decided by the decision to abandon the 'one plus two' structure with its full line at top and bottom of the columns, as contingent on this particular manuscript. The editor of Psalms for *BHQ* will begin each verse at a new line, and return to a one verse per line format wherever possible.

The acrostics will thus emerge. This return to a one verse per line format is not simply for pedagogical ends. The psalms that are presented this way in the Psalter of M^L, as well as earlier witnesses to the phenomenon attest the antiquity of this practice. The columns of *BHQ* will be wider than those of the manuscript, and therefore better able to accommodate this convention. Where it is necessary to break lines, this will be an articulation of the Masoretic punctuation system, rather than any reflection of the presentation in short aligned columns in the manuscript.

The spirit of having a different layout for poetry than for prose is observed in *BHQ* as in its precursors. *BHQ* differs from its precursors in having a layout that tries to articulate Masoretic accentuation rather than modern theories of Hebrew poetry. To this end, a gap is left at the major accentual break of the line. In some ways this gap phenomenon can be seen as a descendant of the gapped lines of the manuscript of M^L. However its pedagogic function is far from the still somewhat enigmatic gaps of the manuscript.

This essay is dedicated to Adrian Schenker as a token of fraternal respect, in appreciation of his great academic leadership of the *BHQ* project, and in gratitude for his personal generosity and hospitality over many years in Fribourg.*

* This paper was of long gestation, and was discussed with Dominique Barthélemy, who seemed to accept the point.

DIE TEXTÜBERLIEFERUNG DES BUCHES NUMERI AM BEISPIEL DER BILEAMERZÄHLUNG

Martin Rösel

Wer sich den Herausforderungen stellt, die das Gebiet der alttestamentlichen Textkritik der Forschung zu bieten hat, wird schnell feststellen, daß sich Aufgaben ganz unterschiedlicher Schwierigkeiten finden lassen. Zu den herausforderndsten gehören gewiß die Bücher, die in parallelen Ausgaben überliefert wurden. Am besten bekannt ist der Fall des Jeremiabuches;[1] deutlich diffiziler noch ist der Fall der Königebücher. Hier hat Adrian Schenker unlängst wahrscheinlich gemacht, daß der älteste Text nicht in der Fassung des MT, sondern in der Septuaginta und der Vetus Latina zu finden ist.[2] Demgegenüber stellt sich die Textüberlieferung im Bereich der Tora als vergleichsweise übersichtliche Problematik dar, da die früh erreichte hohe Autorität dieses Grunddokumentes des Judentums zu einer stabilen Textüberlieferung führte.

Doch auch hier sind Differenzierungen nötig. Nach einer Beobachtung von Baruch A. Levine ist die Textüberlieferung im Bereich der gesetzlichen Partien am genauesten gewesen, während die in erzählerischen und besonders in poetischen Abschnitten weniger sorgfältig war.[3] Als weiteres Problemfeld ist die Überlieferung des Samaritanus zu nennen; nur in der Tora steht ja dieser weitere hebräische Textzeuge mit seinen charakteristischen Abweichungen zur Verfügung.[4] Hinzu kommen auch im Falle des hier interessierenden Numeribuches einige Fragmente aus Qumran, von denen besonders 4QNum[b] von hohem Interesse ist.

---

[1] Als Einführung dazu vgl. E. Tov, *Der Text der Hebräischen Bibel* (Stuttgart/Berlin/Köln, 1997), 264–270, mit weiterer Literatur.

[2] A. Schenker, *Älteste Textgeschichte der Königsbücher: Die hebräische Vorlage der ursprünglichen Septuaginta als älteste Textform der Königsbücher* (OBO 199; Fribourg/Göttingen, 2004); vgl. zum grundsätzlichen Problem auch A. Schenker (Hg.), *The Earliest Text of the Hebrew Bible: The Relationship between the Masoretic Text and the Hebrew Base of the Septuagint reconsidered* (SCSS 52; Leiden/Boston, 2003).

[3] B. A. Levine, *Numbers 1–20* (AB 4; Garden City, 1993), 85.

[4] Als sehr gute Einführung s. jetzt St. Schorch, *Die Vokale des Gesetzes. Die samaritanische Lesetradition als Textzeugin der Tora, 1. Das Buch Genesis* (BZAW 339; Berlin/New York, 2004).

Im folgenden soll ein paradigmatischer Einblick in die Probleme der Textüberlieferung des Numeribuches gegeben werden. Dabei beschränke ich mich auf die Kapitel 22–24. Dies geschieht zum einen aus praktischen Gründen der Umfangsbeschränkung, zum anderen wegen der Tatsache, daß diese Perikope zu den bekanntesten und meist rezipierten Texten des Numeribuches gehört;[5] hier also das In- und Nebeneinander von bewahrender und interpretierender Textüberlieferung von narrativen und poetischen Stücken besonders gut zu beobachten ist. Außerdem sind Teile dieses Abschnittes in biblischen wie nichtbiblischen Texten aus Qumran erhalten, so daß sich hier besonders gut die textkritischen Probleme im Umgang mit den Funden vom Toten Meer erkennen lassen.[6]

Eine weitere Beschränkung geschieht insofern, als ich mich auf Erörterungen zum MT, zum Samaritanus, zur Überlieferung aus Qumran und zur Septuaginta beschränke. Diese wichtigsten Textzeugen sollen kurz vorgestellt und ihre Charakteristika an eindeutigen Beispielen charakterisiert werden. Auf Peschitta, Vetus Latina, Vulgata und Targumim wird hier nicht eingegangen, da sie in keinem Fall *alleine* eine abweichende, als ursprünglich gelten könnende Lesart aufweisen.

Der Text des Codex L

Der Zustand des Codex ist im Bereich der Kapitel 22–24 (Folio 89r–90v) relativ gut.[7] Einzig auf Fol 89v ist in der unteren Hälfte ein Verblassen der Tinte zu beobachten, so daß manche Wörter, besonders aber die Listen der Masora magna (Mm) am unteren Rand schlecht zu lesen sind; manche der *Simanim* sind kaum lesbar. Abweichend von der modernen Zählung werden die Grenzen für die Leseabschnitte in 22,2 markiert; hier beginnt die Parasche "Balak", die bis Num 25,9 reicht.[8] Seder 20 beginnt ebenfalls in Num 22,2

[5] Vgl. dazu meinen Überblick in: M. Rösel, "Wie einer vom Propheten zum Verführer wird. Tradition und Rezeption der Bileamgestalt," *Biblica* 80 (1999), 506–524.

[6] S. dazu Dana M. Pike, "The Book of Numbers at Qumran: Texts and Context," in: D. W. Parry, St. D. Ricks (eds.), *Current Research & Technological Developments on the Dead Sea Scrolls* (Leiden, 1996), 166–93.

[7] Vgl. D. N. Freedman, *The Leningrad Codex. A Facsimile Edition* (Grand Rapids u.a., 1998); herangezogen wurden außerdem die den Herausgebern im Rahmen des *BHQ*-Projektes zugänglich gemachten farbigen Großdias des *West Semitic Research Project.*

[8] Dazu J. Milgrom, *Numbers* (The JPS Torah Commentary; Philadelphia/New York, 1990), 185.

und reicht bis 23,9; Seder 21 reicht dann bis 24,25; Seder 22 ist sehr kurz, reicht bis 25,9 und stellt so den Anschluß an die Paraschenzählung wieder her.[9]

Poetische Partien werden nicht durch eine besondere Textanordnung gekennzeichnet; dies ist im gesamten Buch Numeri nur für den Priestersegen Num 6,24–26 zu beobachten. In Übereinstimmungen mit den Richtlinien der *BHQ* werden die Bileam-Orakel dennoch stichographisch gesetzt werden, dies auf der Basis der masoretischen Akzente. Im Unterschied zur *BHS* bedeutet das, daß in 23,7 nach בָּלָ֤ק keine Trennung erfolgen kann, da der Akzent *Mehuppak* eindeutig verbindend ist.[10] Änderungen werden sich auch in 24,18.19 und 24,23.24 ergeben, da das Versende nach den Richtlinien (Nr. I.3) als Ende einer poetischen Zeile gilt; in der *BHS* steht die erste Hälfte der Verse 24,19+24 in einer Zeile mit dem Schluß des vorhergehenden Verses.

Zu den Richtlinien des *BHQ*-Projektes gehört, daß die Textvarianten drei großer tiberischer Handschriften in den Apparat mit aufgenommen werden; Variantensammlungen wie die von B. Kennicott oder J. B. de Rossi finden nur in Ausnahmefällen Berücksichtigung. Für das Buch Numeri werden die Handschriften British Museum Oriental 4445 (Mitte des 9. Jh.?);[11] Firkovich II.17 (um 930)[12] und der Damaskus-Pentateuch (Sassoon 507, etwa 10. Jh.?)[13] kollationiert, die alle durch Mikrofilme zugänglich sind. Im Bereich der Bileam-Perikope weist Firkovich II.17 erhebliche Beschädigungen auf, so daß viele Lesarten unsicher bleiben müssen. Eindeutig erkennbar ist, daß in 22,38 הֲיָכוֹל defektiv gelesen wird. Dies ist ebenfalls in Oriental 4445 der Fall, hier werden außerdem noch אֵילִם in 23,29 defektiv und אֵיבָיו plene geschrieben. Die Vokalisationsvarianten zu 22,38 und 23,29 sind auch in Sassoon 507 zu finden; auch diese Handschrift ist zum Teil

[9] S. als Einführung J. M. Oesch, "Textgliederung im Alten Testament und in den Qumranhandschriften," *Henoch* 5 (1983), 289–321; ders., *Petucha und Setuma* (OBO 27; Fribourg/Göttingen, 1979), 32–34.

[10] Dazu I. Yeivin, *Introduction to the Tiberian Masorah* (Masoretic Studies 5; 1980), 165ff.

[11] Vgl. etwa C. D. Ginsburg, *Introduction to the Massoretico-Critical Edition of the Hebrew Bible*, ed. by H. M. Orlinsky (New York, 1966), 471–474, votierte für eine Entstehung zwischen 820 und 850, ähnlich *BHQ*, "General Introduction," XXI (mit Literatur); Yeivin, *Tiberian Masorah*, 19f. votiert für 925.

[12] P. Kahle, *Masoreten des Westens* (BWAT 8; Stuttgart, 1927), 58f.

[13] Yeivin, *Tiberian Masorah*, 21; andere Datierungen sind das 9. Jh. und ca. 1000; dazu *BHQ*, "General Introduction," XXIII.

nur sehr schlecht lesbar. So läßt sich nicht eindeutig entscheiden, ob in 24,23 מֵי statt מִי steht. In 23,23 steht sicher בִּישְׂרָאֵל statt בְּיִשְׂרָאֵל; in 23,15 liest man תְּבָרְכֶנּוּ statt תְּבָרֲכֶנּוּ und in 24,11 אֵל statt אֶל־. Letztgenannte Handschrift ist demnach am wenigsten genau abgeschrieben.

Die deutlich gemachten Differenzen sind textkritisch insignifikant; für die Masora aber zum Teil von Bedeutung (s.u.). Es ist auffällig, daß sich keine der in *BHK* und *BHS* aus anderen Handschriften mitgeteilten hebräischen Varianten in diesen ältesten Codices findet, was die relative Geschlossenheit der masoretischen Textüberlieferung belegt und die Konzentration auf diese wenigen Handschriften rechtfertigt.

Die Masora

Zu den herausragenden Merkmalen der kommenden *BHQ* gehört die Tatsache, daß erstmals die Masora des Codex L vollständig wiedergegeben und zu großen Teilen übersetzt und – wo nötig – kommentiert wird. Um einen Eindruck von der Vielfalt der Probleme zu geben, die bei dieser Aufgabe begegnen, werden im folgenden einige besonders interessante Phänomene der Masora zu Num 22–24 dargestellt.

Eine besondere Schwierigkeit bereitet etwa die Mp-Anmerkung zu עֲבוֹר in Num 22,26. In der Handschrift wird hier ה̇ notiert (5 Vorkommen), in *BHS* findet sich demgegenüber ד̇ (4x). Konkordanzarbeit führt zu dem Ergebnis, daß die Anmerkung in *BHS* richtig ist; die anderen drei Vorkommen sind Am 7,8; 8,2; 2.Sam 17,16 (Inf. Abs.). Eine Mm-Liste zu dieser Frage findet sich nicht in L. In der *BHS* steht allerdings zusätzlich der Hinweis "Mp sub loco"; doch bekanntermaßen ist G. E. Weil nicht mehr dazu gekommen, diese zusätzlichen Erläuterungen zu Problemfällen der Masora fertigzustellen.

Das Bild verwirrt sich noch dadurch, daß die anderen drei tiberischen Referenzhandschriften in der jeweiligen Mp auf insgesamt 7 Formen dieser Art hinweisen. Die gleiche Zahl findet sich bei Ginsburg, II, ע, Nr. 56;[14] hier werden aber auch Formen mit vorangestellten Partikeln mitgezählt. Von diesen wird wiederum die Form לַעֲבוֹר in

---

[14] Chr. D. Ginsburg, *The Massorah Compiled from Manuscripts*, 4 vols. (London, 1880–1905).

einer weiteren Liste mit drei zusätzlichen Vorkommen der präfigierten Form des Infinitivs aufgeführt (vgl. Mm 1259; Ginsburg, a.a.O., Nr. 54b). In L trägt keine der bei Ginsburg zusätzlich vermerkten Stellen die zu erwartende gleichlautende Mp-Anmerkung. Im Anschluß an Frensdorff,[15] stellt daher D. Mynatt in seiner Untersuchung zu den Sub loco Anmerkungen die Problematik dar,[16] ohne Erklärungen liefern zu können. Die *BHS*-Version wird so erklärt, daß G. E. Weil die Konfusion vermindern wollte, indem er nur die *plene*-Formen des Infinitivs auflistete.

Alle Konkordanzarbeit hat die Suche nach dem Sinn der L-Mp, daß es in dieser Handschrift fünf Vorkommen von עֲבוֹר gebe, ergebnislos gelassen. Offenkundig stammt also diese Anmerkung erneut aus einer anderen Texttradition. Zu folgern ist auch, daß es in der Frage der Kategorisierung von עֲבוֹר erhebliche Unsicherheiten bei den Masoreten gab,[17] anders ist der ungewöhnliche, völlig disparate Befund von Mp und Mm in den verschiedenen Handschriften nicht erklärbar.

Ein interessantes Masora-Problem ergibt sich auch in 22,38, wo in der Mp zu הֲיָכוֹל angemerkt ist, daß diese Form nur zweimal vorkomme, einmal plene, und einmal defektiv geschrieben. Allerdings steht das Wort bei seinem zweiten Vorkommen in 2.Chr 32,13 ebenfalls plene. Die drei anderen tiberischen Referenzhandschriften lesen übereinstimmend das Wort in Num 22,38 defektiv;[18] was wohl die auch hier zu bevorzugende Lesung ist. Dieses Urteil hat auch G. Weil in der *BHS* durch den Hinweis "MP contra textum" signalisiert, das offenbar immer dann steht, wenn er die Angabe der Masora für richtiger als den konkreten Text hielt.[19] Möglicherweise sollte die Mp-Anmerkung den MT gegen die Lesart des Samaritanus verteidigen, der hier (plene geschriebenes) Hofal היוכל liest.[20]

---

[15] S. Frensdorff, *Die Massora Magna nach den ältesten Drucken mit Zuziehung alter Handschriften*, I., Die Massora in alphabetischer Ordnung (Hannover und Leipzig, 1876), 134 (= The Massorah Magna I. Prolegomenon by G. E. Weil, 1968.)

[16] D. S. Mynatt, *The Sub Loco Notes in the Torah of Biblia Hebraica Stuttgartensia* (Bible Dissertation Series 2; N. Richland Hills/Texas, 1994), 170.

[17] So kann man überlegen, ob nicht die in der Tradition recht stabile Angabe "7 Vorkommen" daher rührt, daß es tatsächlich sieben Stellen mit dem *plene* geschriebenen Inf. cstr. gibt, von ihnen drei ohne (Num 22,26; Am 7,8; 8,2) und vier mit dem Präfix ל (Jos 4,1.11; 2.Sam 15,24; Na 2,1). Der in L mitgezählte Inf. abs. aus 2.Sam 17,16 würde dann ursprünglich nicht hierher gehören.

[18] Ebenso Ginsburg, *Massorah*, IV, θ, 314.

[19] Dazu P. H. Kelley, D. S. Mynatt, T. G. Crawford, *Die Masora der BHS* (Stuttgart, 2003), 62–64.

[20] So Ginsburg, ebd.

Ein weiteres schwieriges Masora-Problem findet sich in 22,39: Der zweite Teil des Ortsnamens קִרְיַת חֻצוֹת trägt in L folgende Mp: ב̇ חס וכל ירמ̇ ב̇ מ̇ ד̇. Auch die Mp der *BHS* bestätigt, daß die Form an zwei Stellen so geschrieben werde, daß das Wort (pl. cstr. von חוּץ) überall im Buch Jeremia so geschrieben werde, mit nur einer Ausnahme, in der es plene begegnet (Jer 5,1; vgl Mm 2026).[21] Tatsächlich ist die Sachlage in L so, daß es neben den 10 defektiv geschriebenen Stellen aus dem Jeremiabuch keine weitere Stelle gibt, an der der erste Vokal des Wortes plene geschrieben wäre. Mm 2026[22] weist auf 1.Kön 20,26, das aber in L doppelt plene steht. Da die Rabbinerbibel ausweislich *BHK*[2] an dieser Stelle aber חֻצוֹת hat, wird einmal mehr anzunehmen sein, daß der auch in der Mp des MS Firkovich II.17 gemachte Hinweis auf zwei Vorkommen der Form sich auf diese abweichende Textform bezieht; zumal dort (Folio 200v des Codex L) der entsprechende Eintrag der Mm steht.[23]

Unerklärlich ist mir dagegen der zweite Teil der Mp in L. Es kann keine Rede davon sein, daß es im Jeremiabuch vier plene geschriebene Pluralformen von חוּץ gibt.[24] Folglich muß es sich hier um ein Versehen handeln. Für diese Annahme spricht, daß im folgenden Vers Num 22,40 das Wort וָצֹאן exakt diese Mp-Notiz ד̇ trägt; hinzu kommt, daß das darauf folgende Wort וַיְשַׁלַּח in L zwar einen Circellus trägt, es aber keine Mp-Anmerkung dazu gibt.[25] An dieser Stelle war der Schreiber also nachlässig.

Die fragliche Mp-Notiz weist auf eine Auffälligkeit oder Unsicherheit bei der Schreibung des Ortsnamens Kirjat-Huzot hin, der wohl als "Stadt der Märkte" zu verstehen ist.[26] Dies ist insofern interessant, als

[21] Diese Angabe entspricht exakt der Formulierung der Mp zu Num 22,39 im MS Sassoon 507 (ohne eckige Klammern).

[22] G. E. Weil, *Massorah gedolah iuxta codicem Leningradensem B 19a, Vol. 1, Catalogi* (Rom, 1971).

[23] Die Tradition der zwei Vorkommen ist stabil, vgl. Ginsburg, IV, ח, 79,a+b; Frensdorff, *Massora Magna*, 60 mit Anm. 6. Die Mp in Or 4445 verweist auf 3 Vorkommen dieser Schreibung; diese sind allerdings nicht zuzuordnen.

[24] Auch das alternative Verständnis des *daleth* als Hinweis auf דין, so daß "mit Ausnahme dieser Stelle" zu übersetzen wäre (s. Frensdorff, *Massora Magna*, 14), ergibt hier m.E. keinen Sinn. In den mir zugänglichen Ausgaben von *BHK*[3] ist hier gar ׳ zu lesen; dies ist offenbar ein Druckdefekt, da auch die umliegenden Konsonanten nur schlecht lesbar sind.

[25] Diese müßte כ̇ב̇ lauten und wurde von G. Weil in *BHS* nachgetragen.

[26] So Milgrom, *Numbers*, und B. A. Levine, *Numbers 21–36* (AB 4A; Garden City, 2000), z.St., anders H. Seebass, *Numeri*, BK IV/3, 18: "Stadt der Gassen".

die alten Textzeugen die gleiche Problematik signalisieren: Smr liest חיצות;[27] G läßt möglicherweise von εἰς πόλεις ἐπαύλεων auf eine Vorlage חצרות "Höfe" schließen,[28] ebenso die Peschitta. Denkbar ist aber ebenso, daß auch G חוץ gelesen hat, da ἔπαυλις in der G-Num für eine ganze Reihe von Äquivalenten stehen kann.[29] T° ist mit לקרית מחוזוי "Stadt seiner Märkte / Bezirke" nahe am vermuteten Sinn des MT; *BHK/BHS* wollen dies als Hauptstadt verstehen. T^N deutet: לכרכה דמלכותה היא מרישה "in die königliche Stadt, das ist Marescha"; T^J scheint verschiedene Deutungen des hebräischen Textes zu kombinieren, wenn es heißt: "und sie kamen zu einer Stadt, die mit Mauern umgeben war (דמקפן שורין), zu den Plätzen der großen Stadt (לפלטיוון קרתא רבתא), das ist die Stadt Sichons, die Stadt Biroscha."

Eine weitere Differenz zwischen Masora parva und Text des Codex L ist in 23,1.29 zu beobachten. Das Wort אֵילִים in 23,1 trägt den Hinweis ד֗ מל בתור֗ (4 plene-Vorkommen in der Tora; vgl. *BHS* und Mm 879). Tatsächlich begegnet das Wort aber an 5 Stellen in plene-Schreibung: Gen 32,15; Lev 8,2; Num 23,1.29; Dtn 32,14. Allerdings lesen die Rabbinerbibel, Sassoon 507 und Or 4445 das Wort in Num 23,29 defektiv (אֵלִם),[30] in L trägt das Wort keine Mp-Anmerkung und die Mm-Liste auf Fol 79v nennt den Vers ebenfalls nicht. So ist erneut erkennbar, daß sich die Masora von L auf eine geringfügig andere Texttradition bezieht.

Ein vergleichbares Problem findet sich in 23,19. Hier ist mit dem Namen צִפֹּר die Mp-Notiz verbunden, daß das Wort dreimal defektiv geschrieben vorkomme. Tatsächlich begegnet der Name nur noch in 22,10 in defektiver Schreibung, daher wurde die Mp-Notiz in der *BHS* zu ב֗ korrigiert und mit der Anmerkung "Mp sub loco" versehen. Die Anmerkung des Codex L ist jedoch nicht einfach falsch, sondern nur unvollständig. Sie stammt offenbar aus einer auch bei Ginsburg, II, צ, 190 belegten Liste. Hier geht es zunächst um die beiden ausnahmsweise plene geschriebenen Vorkommen von הַצִּפּוֹר im Abschnitt Lev 14; hier wird das Wort ansonsten plene geschrieben. Die Liste führt dann zusätzlich die weiteren defektiv geschrie-

[27] Dies ist wohl nicht einfach Schreibvariante, so Seebass, BK, 18, sondern eher von חיץ / חיצה "Mauer, (Trenn)Wand" (vgl. HAL) abzuleiten.

[28] Mit *BHS*, J. W. Wevers, *Notes on the Greek Text of Numbers* (SBL.SCSS 46; Atlanta, 1988), 382, aufgrund der Beobachtung, daß ἔπαυλις etwa in Ex 8,9; Lev 25,31 für חֲצֵרֹת steht, vgl. Num 34,4, wo חֲצַר־אַדָּר mit εἰς ἔπαυλιν Αραδ übersetzt wurde.

[29] So G. Dorival, *Les Nombres* (La Bible d'Alexandrie 4; Paris, 1994), 431.

[30] Das ist auch der Auflistung in Ginsburg, *Massorah* IV, א, 369 zu entnehmen.

benen Vorkommen des Wortes auf, dies ist neben den beiden Numeri-Stellen noch Gen 15,10.[31]

Eine interessante Differenz zwischen Mm und Mp ist in 23,23 zu notieren. Hier verweist die Mp richtig darauf, daß es 6 Vorkommen des Wortes וּלְיִשְׂרָאֵל gebe. Die Mm auf der gleichen Seite (Fol 90r) verweist ebenfalls auf 6 Vorkommen, zählt aber nur 5 auf und übergeht dabei ausgerechnet das in Num 23! Die Zahl 6 ist in der masoretischen Tradition stabil, so daß es sich um ein Versehen beim Schreiben der Mm-Liste handeln muß.

Ebenfalls fehlerhaft ist die Liste der Mm zu Num 24,1 (Fol 90r). Hier werden die neun Vorkommen von לְבָרֵךְ aufgeführt (vgl. Mm 969). Für 1.Chr. 16,43 findet sich dabei kein *siman*, statt dessen ist der für 1.Chr. 17,27 (הואלת) doppelt gegeben.

Eine Besonderheit der Bileam-Erzählung ist der Wechsel der Gottesbezeichnungen zwischen dem Tetragramm und Elohim, der offenbar schon in der G Anlaß zu theologischen Überlegungen war (dazu unten). In der Masora spiegelt sich das Problem in einer Anmerkung zu רוּחַ אֱלֹהִים in 24,2. Die Mp von L vermerkt, daß es 9 Vorkommen dieser Wendung gebe (im Unterschied zur Formulierung mit JHWH), und daß der Ausdruck überall im Samuelbuch verwendet würde, dies mit 7 Ausnahmen. In der *BHS* ist dies zu 8 Vorkommen der Wendung und 5 Ausnahmen im Samuelbuch korrigiert worden; erneut trägt die Anmerkung den Hinweis "Mp sub loco". Die in der *BHS* gegebenen Zahlen stimmen mit dem Textbefund von L überein.[32] Auch die Mp des Codex Sassoon 507 zur Stelle hat die richtigen Angaben,[33] während Or 4445 mit L übereinstimmt. Erneut handelt es sich also um unterschiedliche Texttraditionen, wobei nicht mehr zu ermitteln ist, an welcher Stelle JHWH und Elohim vertauscht wurden, so daß man auf die Zahl "neun" kommt.

Außerdem sei ein Fehler mitgeteilt, der in *BHS* zu notieren ist: In 24,9 fehlt bei וְאֹרְרֶיךָ der Circellus; das ל am Rand bleibt daher ohne Gegenstück in der Zeile.

Für die textkritische Arbeit an der hebräischen Bibel sind Anmerkungen der Masora von Interesse, die mit andernorts bezeugten Varianten des hebräischen Textes Berührungen zeigen, insofern als sie den Text vor solchen Abweichungen schützen möchten. Hierzu einige Beispiele, wobei auffällt, daß häufig der Samaritanus tatsäch-

---

[31] Dies nach Mynatt, *Sub Loco Notes*, 171.
[32] Dazu ausführlich Mynatt, a.a.O., 91f.
[33] Vgl. auch die Liste in Ginsburg II, ר, 340, und Frensdorff, *Massora Magna*, 15.

lich die abweichende Lesungen bewahrt hat: In 24,6 gibt die Mp zu נִטָּיוּ an, daß es ein Hapaxlegomenon ist; Smr liest נָטוּי; was als Sg. nicht ursprünglich sein kann. Im gleichen Vers trägt auch das Wort כַּאֲהָלִים die Mp-Notiz ל׳, um das seltene "Eiskraut" (HAL, vgl. Seebass, BK, 22f) vor der Verwechslung mit אֹהָלִים "Zelte" zu schützen, das in 4QNum[a], G, S bezeugt wird. Auch בְּמַיִם in V. 7 wird durch eine Mp-Anmerkung vor der nahe liegenden Verwechslung mit עַמִּים (vgl. G, T) geschützt. Auch für אִיעָצְךָ in 24,14 findet sich eine sichernde Mp-Notiz samt zugehöriger Mm-Liste (Nr. 972); Smr liest dagegen ואאיעצך. In 24,17 wird das Hapaxlegomenon וְקַרְקַר angezeigt, Smr liest hier das allgemein bevorzugte קדקד.[34]

Faßt man die Beobachtungen zusammen, so wird zum einen der auch von anderen geäußerte Eindruck bestätigt, daß die Masora des Codex L etwas nachlässig geschrieben wurde[35] und zumindest in Teilen aus einer anderen Texttradition stammt. Zum zweiten ist festzuhalten, daß die Masora einige seltene Lesarten sichert, was besonders bei den poetischen Texten dieser Perikope von Bedeutung ist. Dies gilt umso mehr, als davon auszugehen ist, daß die masoretischen Listen deutlich älter als die erhaltenen Codices sind.[36] Damit ist m.E. deutlich, daß die in der *Biblia Hebraica Quinta* intensivierte Beschäftigung mit diesem lange vernachlässigten Element des Codex L lohnend und sinnvoll ist.

Qumran: 4QNum[b] und Zitate

Aus Qumran sind insgesamt sieben verschiedene Fragmente von Numeri-Texten erhalten: 1Q3; 2QNum[a–c]; 4QLev-Num[a]; 4QNum[b]; 4QLXXNum.[37] Die Fragmente aus 1+2Q sind so klein, daß sie für textkritische Zwecke nahezu unbrauchbar sind, so daß sich die Diskussion auf die drei Texte aus Höhle 4 konzentriert. Unter diesen ist 4QNum[b] der Text mit dem größten erhaltenen Textbestand, der zugleich auch den interessantesten Befund liefert. Von 4QLev-Num[a] sind dagegen nur Reste weniger Verse erhalten; dieser Text geht in der Regel mit dem MT.

[34] Zur Diskussion dazu s. Seebass, *Numeri*, 24, s. auch Milgrom, *Numbers*, Anm. 65, S. 323, und Levine, *Numbers 21–36*, 202, die ebenfalls mit Smr gehen.

[35] Vgl. etwa E. J. Revell, "The Leningrad Codex as a Representative of the Masoretic Text," in: Freedman, *Leningrad Codex*, S. xxix–xlvi: xlii.

[36] Dazu Kelley/Mynatt/Crawford, *Masora*, 16–29.

[37] Mit Pike, *Book of Numbers*, 171f., rechne ich 2Q9/2QNum[d] nicht hierher; vgl. DJD III, 1962, 59.

Das wichtigste Charakteristikum der Rolle 4QNum^{b} ist, daß sie zur Gruppe der präsamaritanischen Texte gehört, daß sie also Varianten aufweist, die man vor der Auffindung der Qumran-Texte nur aus dem Samaritanus kannte.[38] Das sind vor allem die Zusätze in den Büchern Exodus und Numeri, die als Harmonisierungen mit dem Deuteronomium zu verstehen sind. In 4QNum^{b} finden sie sich nach 20,13; 21,12 (2x); und 27,23; eine weitere ist in 31,21–24 zu vermuten.[39] Damit steht die Rolle zunächst einmal unter dem generellen Verdacht, gegenüber dem MT sekundär zu sein.[40]

Allerdings finden sich auch Lesarten, die als ursprünglich eingeschätzt wurden; dies etwa in 23,3: Hier ist am Versende vor den schwierigen Wörtern וַיֵּלֶךְ שֶׁפִי allein in 4QNum^{b} folgende umfangreiche Zufügung belegt: [ו]ילך ויתיצב בלק על ע[ו]לתו ובלעם; um den Satz zu vervollständigen hat N. Jastram als Herausgeber des Fragments außerdem נקרה אל אלוהים rekonstruiert, was zur Zeilenlänge des Fragmentes passen kann.[41] Dies wird unterstützt durch die Tatsache, daß die G ein Plus gegenüber dem MT bietet, das auf eine nahezu identische Vorlage zurückgehen wird: καὶ παρέστη Βαλακ ἐπὶ τῆς θυσίας αὐτοῦ καὶ Βαλααμ ἐπορεύθη ἐπερωτῆσαι τὸν θεόν. Gegenüber der Lesart aus 4QNum^{b} fällt auf, daß ein Äquivalent für das erste וילך fehlt, außerdem steht für נקרה* ἐπορεύθη ἐπερωτῆσαι. Letztere Übersetzung findet sich auch in 23,15 und ist folglich gut zu rechtfertigen.[42] Daß für וילך kein Äquivalent vorhanden ist, läßt sich leicht als *aberratio oculi* erklären, zumal direkt davor לך steht. Der Ausfall des gesamten Satzes ist ebenso leicht als Haplographie וילך/וילך erklärbar; 4QNum^{b} hätte demnach den älteren, längeren Text erhalten. Zwar ist theoretisch auch denkbar, daß die beiden Textzeugen unabhängig voneinander die Ausführung des in der ersten Vershälfte Beschriebenen erzählen,[43] doch die Übereinstimmungen der Formulie-

[38] Dazu einführend Tov, *Text*, 80–82.

[39] Dazu N. Jastram, "The Text of 4QNum^{b}," in: J. Trebolle Barrera, L. Vegas Montaner (eds.), *The Madrid Qumran Congress*, Vol. 2 (StDJ XI,2; Leiden/ Köln/Madrid, 1992), 177–198; 182–184; vgl. DJD VII (1994), 205–267.

[40] Vgl. Jastram, "Text," 184: "When 4QNum^{b} has a reading not shared by any of the other witnesses, the reading is usually secondary."

[41] DJD VII, 234f.

[42] Mit Jastram, "Text," 185.

[43] So Wevers, *Notes*, 385f. (ohne Hinweis auf den Qumran-Text); Seebass, *Numeri*, 19 (Ohne Hinweis darauf, daß 4QNum^{b} eindeutig die erste Hälfte des LXX-Textes belegt).

rungen lassen N. Jastrams Urteil als das angemessenere erscheinen, daß der Langtext aus Qumran tatsächlich die älteste Lesart ist. Allerdings ist er m.E. nicht vollständig "unique" (Jastram, a.a.O.), sondern wird durch die G gestützt.

Im gleichen Vers 23,3 ist eine weitere wichtige Übereinstimmung zwischen G und 4QNum^b zu notieren: Abweichend vom MT hat 4QNum^b nicht וָאֵלְכָה, sondern ואנוכי אלך, was dem ἐγὼ δὲ πορεύσομαι der Mehrheit der G-Handschriften entspricht. Das Bekanntwerden des Textes aus 4QNum^b hat den Herausgeber der Göttinger Septuaginta, J.W. Wevers, dazu veranlaßt, die Änderung des kritischen Textes in ἐγὼ δὲ πορεύσομαι statt bisher καὶ πορεύσομαι vorzuschlagen.[44] Über die Ursprünglichkeit auf der Ebene des hebräischen Textes sagt dies freilich nichts aus; hier scheint mir der kürzere Text des MT und Smr die bessere Lesung zu sein; 4QNum^b und G sind als stilistische Verbesserung zu bewerten, die sich am MT des Verses 15 orientiert.

Außerdem ist in diesem Vers 23,3 eine Übereinstimmung zwischen 4QNum^b, Smr und G zu sehen: Während der MT das Tetragramm liest, haben 4QNum^b, Smr אלוהים, und G liest ὁ θεός. Während die G im Bereich der Gottesnamen offenbar eine eigene Übersetzungsstrategie verfolgte (dazu unten), sind im Smr und 4QNum^b nur wenige Auffälligkeiten zu beobachten: So liest in 23,27 der Qumran-Text אלוהים ohne den sonst bezeugten Artikel; Smr hat einmal in 23,26 mit G האלהים gegen das Tetragramm des MT, was allerdings als Harmonisierung mit dem folgenden Vers gelten kann; dafür sprich besonders die ungewöhnliche Artikelsetzung. Daher scheint mir in 23,3 die Lesung אלהים die besser bezeugte und daher gegenüber dem MT vorzuziehende zu sein.

Am Beispiel des Verses 23,3 zeigt sich also, daß 4QNum^b durchaus ein wichtiger Textzeuge ist, vor allem dann, wenn er mit anderen parallel geht. Auch an anderen Stellen der Bileam-Erzählung lassen sich mit G und/oder Smr übereinstimmende Varianten feststellen. So entspricht das והואה יושב in 22,11 dem καὶ οὗτος ἐγκάθηται der LXX. In 22,20 ist ein מלאך zu rekonstruieren, das Smr ebenfalls bietet; allerdings ist diese Lesart kaum ursprünglich, s.u.

Gleichzeitig zeigt die Rolle aber auch eigenständige Varianten, die eindeutig sekundär sind. Für die theologische Interpretation der

---

44 *Notes*, 385.

Bileam-Orakel ist wohl die in 24,9 am ertragreichsten: Hier hat der MT כָּרַע שָׁכַב כַּאֲרִי "er ist geduckt, liegt wie ein Löwe". Im Qumrantext liest man dagegen: כער רבץ כא]ריה. Das erste Wort wird auf einen Schreibfehler (*transpositio*) zurückgehen. Die Variante רבץ allerdings ist von höchstem Interesse, da sie aus Gen 49,9 stammen muß; ein Beleg für die intertextuelle Lektüre dieser beiden durch die Löwenthematik verbundenen messianischen Weissagungen.[45] Interessanterweise ist diese auffällige Variante nur in einigen Smr-Handschriften erhalten; ein weiteres Indiz für die Richtigkeit der Zuordnung "präsamaritanisch".

Die Grenzen der Rekonstruierbarkeit von Qumran-Varianten zeigen sich schließlich im berühmten Vers 24,7. Hier liest der MT das gewiß ursprüngliche מֵאֲגַג; Smr hat das eschatologisierende מגוג, auf dem das ἢ Γωγ der G basiert. In DJD VII,236 wird nun die Lesung des Smr auch für 4QNum[b] in der Lücke rekonstruiert, obwohl der Breitenunterschied zu מאגג vernachlässigenswert gering ist. Eine Begründung dieser Rekonstruktion wird nicht gegeben; sie ist m.E. auch nicht zu rechtfertigen.

Diese kurzen Einblicke in die Problematik des für das Numeribuch wichtigsten Textzeugen aus Qumran mögen genügen. Es ist deutlich, daß 4QNum[b] einen eigenständigen Texttyp darstellt, der nicht einfach mit Smr oder der Vorlage der G noch dem MT gleichgestellt werden kann. Vielmehr ist jede einzelne Variante genau zu prüfen, wobei nur als allgemeine Richtlinie gelten kann, daß 4QNum[b] näher am Smr als am MT und der G steht.[46]

Der rezeptionsgeschichtlich besonders wichtige Inhalt der Bileamorakel bringt mit sich, daß sich in Qumran weitere Bezeugungen von Texten aus Num 22–24 finden, die textkritisch interessant sein können. So ist der berühmte Spruch vom Stern aus Jakob auch in der Damaskusschrift erhalten, sowohl in CD-A VII, 18–21, als auch in 4Q266, 3, iii, 20–22. Hier ist interessant, daß der Text des MT in der Zitation eindeutig belegt ist, vollständig im MS CD-A (10.Jh. aus der Kairoer Geniza), in kaum anzuzweifelnder Rekonstruktion in 4Q266:

[45] Dazu demnächst ausführlich M. Rösel, "Jakob, Bileam und der Messias," in M. Knibb (ed.), *Septuagint and Messianism*, Congress Volume Leuven 2004 (BETL, voraussichtlich Leuven, 2005).

[46] So das zusammenfassende Urteil von N. Jastram in DJD VII, 214; vgl seine Zusammenfassung in ders., "Text," 197f.

דרך כוכב מיעקב וקם שבט ישראל... וקרקר כל בני שת

Zum einen ist deutlich, daß die in den Versionen zu beobachtenden Varianten[47] von שבט sich offenbar deutender Übersetzung verdanken und nicht auf eine andere Vorlage zurückgehen. Weniger sicher – da in 4Q266 nicht erhalten – ist dagegen die Bezeugung von וְקַרְקַר, denn die Geniza-Version steht natürlich unter dem Verdacht der Beeinflussung durch den MT.

In 4QNum[b] ist das Stück leider nicht erhalten, allerdings existieren weitere Zitate von Num 24,17 in 1QM XI,6f. und 4Q175 (Testimonia), 12f. Auch hier ist וקרקר eindeutig belegt, so daß das וקדקד des Smr ohne weitere unterstützende Bezeugung bleibt. Damit sprechen nur inhaltliche Gründe – genannt werden v.a. der Parallelismus mit פַּאֲתֵי מוֹאָב und die Schwierigkeit der exakten Herleitung des קרקר – für das Vorziehen der Smr-Lesung gegen die breite und alte Bezeugung der MT-Version. Doch es ist festzustellen, daß in den in Qumran belegten Texten keine Erklärungen zu diesem Wort zu finden sind; es galt offenbar als verständlich. Im Parallelismus ist zudem m.E. eher ein Verbum als das Nomen קָדְקֹד zu erwarten. Daher scheint mir die Lesart des MT weiterhin vorzuziehen zu sein, zumal offenbar auch LXX und die Targumim ein Verbum gelesen haben.

Wichtig ist am Ende dieses Abschnittes, daß die in Qumran belegten Zitate aus Num 24,17 in der bisherigen textkritischen Diskussion nicht berücksichtigt wurden, obwohl sie wie im Falle von CD sogar ausdrücklich mit einer Zitationsformel כאשר כתוב eingeleitet wurden und folglich auf den Bibeltext zurückverweisen sollen. Auch andere Texte des Numeribuches wurden in Qumran zitiert, allen voran der aaronidische Segen aus Num 6.[48] Solche Bezeugungen sind neben den eigentlichen Bibelhandschriften unbedingt wahrzunehmen. Erneut zeigt sich demnach, daß die künftige *BHQ* einen deutlichen Erkenntnisfortschritt bringen wird.

Der Samaritanus

Die allgemeinen Kennzeichen des Samaritanischen Pentateuch (Smr) wurden schon häufiger beschrieben, so daß hier darauf verzichtet

[47] LXX: ἄνθρωπος; S: *ryš'*; T°: מְשִׁיחָא.
[48] Eine gute Übersicht findet sich bei D. Pike, *Book of Numbers*, 180–191.

werden kann.[49] Wichtig ist die prinzipielle Differenzierung zwischen vorsamaritanischen Varianten, die zumeist in eine Zeit zurückreichen, in der die Texttradition noch nicht stabilisiert war, und eigenen, zahlenmäßig relativ geringen Änderungen der Samaritaner.[50]

Textkritisch relevant ist, daß sich auch in Num 22–24 einige der typischen Charakteristika dieser Texttradition finden, die demnach nicht für die Ursprünglichkeit des Textes ausgewertet werden können. Das betrifft etwa die Verwendung von Synonymen, vgl. 23,1, wo statt des בְּנֵה־לִי des MT עשה לי steht,[51] oder phonologische Änderungen wie die Gutturaldifferenz in 24,6, wo statt נָטַע des MT נטה steht.[52] Daneben finden sich eine Fülle von Differenzen bei der plene und defektiv-Schreibung der Vokale, wobei Smr häufiger plene liest als MT und nur selten gegen MT die defektive Schreibung hat, vgl. etwa הלך in 24,14 gegen הוֹלֵךְ oder die Häufung in 22,26.

Interessant sind Fälle, an denen Smr einen eigenen Gestaltungswillen verrät. So steht hier der Beginn von 23,4 in einer deutlich veränderten Version: Statt des וַיִּקָּר אֱלֹהִים אֶל־בִּלְעָם "Und Gott begegnete dem Bileam" hat Smr: וימצא מלאך אלהים את בלעם "und der Engel Gottes fand den Bileam". Diese Variante wird von 4QNum[b] gestützt, gehört also zur ältesten Schicht der (prä)samaritanischen Überlieferung. Dennoch ist sie als Erleichterung aufzufassen, zum einen in sprachlicher Hinsicht wegen des ungewöhnlichen קרה . . . אל, zum anderen in theologischer Hinsicht: Die Aussage, daß Gott dem fremden Seher direkt begegnet, wird vermieden. Dies ist kein einmaliges Phänomen, ebenso wird in 22,20 und 23,5.16 ein zusätzliches מלאך in den Text eingefügt. Eine vergleichbare Tendenz der Distanzierung zwischen Gott und Bileam zeigt sich auch in der G (s.u.). Sie wird allerdings in der G an dieser Stelle (23,4) nicht ausgedrückt; die griechische Version folgt mit ihrem καὶ ἐφάνη ὁ θεὸς τῷ Βαλααμ dem MT.

Auch das Phänomen der Harmonisierungen teilt Smr mit G, dies auch über die großflächigen Vereinheitlichungen mit dem Dtn hinaus. So liest Smr in 22,35 statt des תְּדַבֵּר des MT תשמר לדבר; dem

[49] S. etwa Tov, *Text*, 69–80; knapper Schorch, *Vokale*, 18–23, vgl. auch oben zu 4QNum[b].

[50] Diese durch die Qumran-Funde deutlich gewordene Dimension fehlt in E. Würthwein, *Der Text des Alten Testaments* (Stuttgart, [5]1988), 53–56 noch völlig.

[51] Dazu Tov, *Text*, 77.

[52] Tov, a.a.O., 79.

folgt LXX: φυλάξῃ λαλῆσαι. Diese Variante ist wohl als Angleichung an Bileams Aussage in 23,13 zu verstehen, wo er Balak mitteilt, daß er nur sagen könne, was Gott ihm gesagt habe (אֶשְׁמֹר לְדַבֵּר). Anordnung und Ausführung der Anordnung werden also einander angeglichen.[53] Interessanterweise harmonisiert Smr ein weiteres Mal, wenn in 22,38 ebenfalls אשמר לדבר gegen MT אֲדַבֵּר steht; G liest hier allerdings nur λαλήσω.

Ein exegetisch bedeutsames Phänomen der Bileam-Erzählung ist der auffällige Wechsel der Gottesnamen zwischen dem Tetragramm und *Elohim*, der auch zur Bestimmung unterschiedlicher Quellen herangezogen wurde.[54] Hier ist besonders auffällig, daß Smr in 22,22; 23,3+26 vom MT abweicht: In 22,22 steht das Tetragramm statt אֱלֹהִים des MT; in 23,3 ist der Fall genau umgekehrt; in 23,26 steht האלהים statt des Tetragramms. In allen Fällen wird Smr durch andere Textzeugen unterstützt: In 22,22 durch T° und einige G-Handschriften, in 23,3 durch G und 4QNum^b, in 23,26 durch G und V. Leider sind 22,22 und 23,26 in 4QNum^b nicht erhalten. Wie unten noch dazustellen sein wird, hat die G in der Frage der Gottesnamen wenig textkritisches Gewicht, da sich hier interpretative Interessen spielen. Betrachtet man nun die Abweichungen des Smr im Kontext, fällt auf, daß in allen drei Fällen im jeweils folgenden Vers MT und Smr den Gottesnamen bieten, den Smr als Variante hat. Das ist im Fall von 23,26 besonders auffällig, da Smr hier ja das seltene האלהים liest, das in der Bileam-Erzählung nur noch in 22,10 steht. Von dieser Beobachtung her liegt also der Schluß nahe, daß sich die abweichenden Gottesbezeichnungen im Smr am ehesten als Kontextharmonisierungen erklären lassen, daß also MT die älteren Lesarten bewahrt hat.[55]

---

[53] Dieses Kennzeichen wird bei Tov, *Text*, 73, in umgekehrter Reihung (detaillierte Anordnung ist original, kurzer Ausführungsbericht wird sekundär aufgefüllt) beschrieben.

[54] S. dazu W. Gross, *Bileam: literar- und formkritische Untersuchungen der Prosa in Num 22–24* (SANT 38; München, 1974), 69–83, der dieses Vorgehen jedoch ablehnt.

[55] So – allerdings ohne weitere Begründung – auch Levine, *Numbers 21–36*, z.St. Milgrom, *Numbers*, 320, Anm. 58, zieht G als Zeuge für die Ursprünglichkeit des MT in 22,22 heran; dieses Argument nutzt auch N. Jastram, *The Book of Numbers from Qumrân Cave IV (4QNum^b)* (Diss. Harvard, 1990), 163. Im jüngsten Kommentar zum Numeribuch beurteilt H. Seebass, *Numeri*, 17–22, die Stellen unterschiedlich: In 22,22 zieht er Smr vor (obwohl er auf W. Gross und das Argument der Angleichung an 22,23 verweist), in 23,3 und 23,26 folgt er ohne weitere Begründung MT: "darf man an *M* festhalten", S. 22.

Beim eben diskutierten Problemfeld war davon ausgegangen worden, daß die Varianten der G unabhängig von denen des Smr zu sehen sind; in 22,35 konnte dagegen beobachtet werden, daß die griechische Übersetzung dem samaritanischen Text folgt. Tatsächlich ist das Verhältnis der beiden Versionen untereinander sehr komplex. So finden sich eine ganze Reihe von Fällen, in denen die G offenkundig auf eine Vorlage vom Smr-Typ zurückgeht (etwa in 22,4 mit der Zufügung von הזה oder in 22,32 in der suffigierten Form לשטנך). Daneben gibt es aber auch Fälle, in denen die G dem Smr nicht folgt, vgl. etwa den strittigen Befund in 22,5: MT: בְּנֵי־עַמּוֹ; Smr (S, V): בני עמון; G: υἱῶν λαοῦ αὐτοῦ.[56] Auch hier sind demnach stets Entscheidungen im Einzelfall nötig.

Abschließend sei kurz auf ein für die Rezeptionsgeschichte extrem folgenreiches Beispiel für die Bedeutung der Smr-Texttradition für die G hingewiesen: In 24,7 liest der MT, daß Israels König größer sein werde als Agag (מֵאֲגַג); das ist der Amalekiterkönig aus 1.Sam 15. Der Samaritanus liest hier מגוג, was auf den endzeitlichen Herrscher Gog aus Magog in Ez 38f. hinweist. Da gerade bei plene-Schreibung zwei Buchstaben verändert sind, ist hier wohl nicht mit einem Versehen zu rechnen, sondern mit eschatologisierender Deutung seitens des Smr.[57] Diese war dann wohl die Initialzündung für den griechischen Übersetzer, der das gesamte Orakel eschatologisch-messianisch umdeutete.[58]

---

[56] Hier bieten wohl Smr und S,V die im Kontext schwierigere Lösung, da die Ortsangaben "Ammon" und "Petor" geographisch nicht zusammen passen (Seebass, a.a.O., 72). Wenn das damaligen Schreibern bewußt gewesen ist, wäre MT/G als Erleichterung anzusehen. Denkbar ist auch ein Schreibfehler (Ausfall des *nun*) oder die Erleichterung der schwierigen Konstruktion des MT durch Identifizierung mit einem bekannten Gebiet, wozu eben nur ein *nun* hinzuzufügen gewesen wäre. Allerdings ist die Frage nach der Herkunft Bileams sehr umstritten (vgl. die Kommentare), so daß ein endgültiges Urteil kaum zu fällen ist.

[57] Nicht verständlich ist daher, wie Seebass, *Numeri*, 23, schreiben kann: "Schon daß nur *G* 'Gog' liest, spricht gegen sie."

[58] Dazu in Kürze ausführlich: Rösel, "Jakob, Bileam und der Messias" (oben Anm. 45); doch vgl. die abweichende Position von J. Lust, "The Greek Version of Balaam's Third and Fourth Oracles. The ἄνθρωπος in Num 24,7 and 17. Messianism and Lexicography," in: L. Greenspoon, O. Munnich (eds.), *VIII Congress of the International Organization for Septuagint and Cognate Studies*, Paris 1992 (SBL.SCSS 41; Atlanta, 1995), 233–257.

Die Septuaginta

Wegen der eben angesprochenen messianischen Deutung, die die G insbesondere dem dritten und vierten Bileam-Orakel gegeben hat, sind diese Abschnitte häufiger in der Sekundärliteratur verhandelt worden. Auch zur Übersetzungsweise des Numeri-Übersetzers liegen ausführliche Untersuchungen vor, vor allem die "Notes" von J. W. Wevers und die annotierte Übersetzung von G. Dorival im Rahmen der "Bible d'Alexandrie".[59] Als generelle Grunddifferenz zwischen den beiden Arbeiten ist zu notieren, daß G. Dorival geneigter als J. W. Wevers ist, eine abweichende Vorlage in Fällen anzunehmen, in denen es Differenzen zum erhaltenen MT gibt; dies auch, wenn die G nicht vom Samaritanus unterstützt wird. Eine Entscheidung in dieser Frage kann im Rahmen eines Aufsatzes nicht geleistet werden.[60]

Mitzuteilen sind jedoch einige Besonderheiten, die sich gerade in der Bileam-Perikope zeigen. So ist zunächst auffällig, daß der Übersetzer sich hier stärker als in anderen Teilen des Buches um ein flüssiges Griechisch als Ergebnis seiner Arbeit bemüht hat. Während er in den narrativen Abschnitten ab Num 10 den hebräischen parataktischen Erzählstil meist beibehält, werden in der Bileam Passage häufiger hypotaktische Konstruktionen durch Verwendung des Participium conjunctum verwendet. Als Beispiele sei die Wiedergabe des formelhaften וַיִּשָּׂא מְשָׁלוֹ וַיֹּאמַר in 23,7; 24,3.15.20 durch καὶ ἀναλαβὼν τὴν παραβολὴν αὐτοῦ εἶπεν genannt; vgl. auch 24,25, wo drei aufeinanderfolgende Narrative zu der Folge Partizip-finites Verb-Partizip übersetzt werden. In diesem letzten Vers der Perikope ist auch auffällig, daß sowohl שׁוב als auch הלך mit dem Verbum ἀπέρχομαι wiedergegeben werden; dem Übersetzer lag offenbar daran, für beide Aktanten einen identische Abschluß zu formulieren.[61] Schon

[59] S. oben Anm. 28 und 29. Als Überblick vgl. auch M. Rösel, "Die Septuaginta und der Kult. Interpretationen und Aktualisierungen im Buch Numeri," in: Y. Goldman, Chr. Uehlinger (Ed.), *La double transmission du texte biblique: Hommage à A. Schenker* (OBO 179; Fribourg/Göttingen, 2001), 25–40, und speziell zur Bileam-Perikope (ohne die Orakel) J. W. Wevers, "The Balaam Narrative According to the Septuagint," in: *Lectures et Relectures de la Bible.* FS P.-M. Bogaert (BEThL 144; Leuven, 1999), 133–144.

[60] Die Arbeiten am Kommentarband der Septuaginta-Deutsch haben aber als vorläufiges Ergebnis erbracht, daß die Annahme einer abweichenden Vorlage weniger häufig wahrscheinlich ist als die einer freieren Zugangsweise des Übersetzers.

[61] Zu den weiteren Differenzen in diesem Vers vgl. Wevers, *Notes*, 418.

diese wenigen Beispiele, die sich leicht zu großer Zahl vermehren ließen, zeigen, daß der Übersetzer nicht einfach mechanisch seine Vorlage wiedergab, sondern den griechischen Text bewußt gestalten wollte. Es ist unmittelbar einsichtig, daß solche Differenzen nicht textkritisch auszuwerten sind.

Das gilt auch für das bereits angesprochene Problem der Gottesnamen. Bei den Überlegungen zu 4QNum[b] konnte gesehen werden, daß in 23,3 offenbar Smr, G und 4QNum[b] gemeinsam die ältere Lesart אלהים gegen das Tetragramm des MT bewahrt haben. Die Verwechslung der Gottesbezeichnungen mag gerade wegen des in diesem Kapiteln häufigen Wechsels leicht möglich gewesen sein (vgl. auch oben zum Smr). Interessant ist nun, daß die G sich offenbar durch den differenzierten Gebrauch der Vorlage motiviert sah, ihrerseits eine interpretierende Übersetzungsweise auszuüben. So wird – wie J. W. Wevers überzeugend gezeigt hat –[62] die Gestalt des Bileam dadurch abgewertet, daß er nicht mit κύριος, sondern fast durchgängig mit θεός in Verbindung gebracht wird. Daher wird in diesen Kapiteln die sonst übliche Übersetzungsgleichung יהוה-κύριος immer dann aufgegeben, wenn nach dem MT der Engel JHWHs zu Bileam spricht.[63] Die einzige Ausnahme von dieser Konvention findet sich in 22,34; einem Sündenbekenntnis Bileams. Dies wird man nicht für einen Zufall halten können oder einer "allgemeinen Vorliebe (der LXX) für θεός",[64] sondern für eine theologisch motivierte Interpretation. Damit zeigt sich, daß die Differenzen im Gottesnamengebrauch nur dann Anspruch auf textkritische Signifikanz haben können, wenn sie von anderen Zeugen unterstützt werden.

Die wenigen, aber deutlichen Beispiele belegen, daß vor den nötigen textkritischen Entscheidungen im Einzelfall immer ein Gesamtbild des jeweiligen Textzeugen zu erstellen ist. Nur so läßt sich unter-

[62] *Balaam Narrative* (Anm. 59).

[63] Vgl. 22,13; 22,22.23.24.25.26.27.28.31.32.35; 23,5 u.ö. Aber s. 22,19, wo *kyrios* im Munde Bileams stehen bleibt. In 22,18 bleibt das Suffix von אלהי unübersetzt, um nicht aussagen zu müssen, daß *kyrios* der Gott Bileams ist.

[64] So Seebass, *Numeri*, 16, in Anschluß an W. Gross, *Bileam*, 73f. Allerdings wird man der Untersuchung von Gross nicht mehr zustimmen können, da er noch pauschal von einem LXX-Übersetzer ausgeht und nicht zwischen den einzelnen Büchern des Pentateuch differenziert. Meine eigenen Untersuchungen haben das Urteil von J. W. Wevers bestätigt; sie fügen sich zudem gut zu dem Bild, das in der Genesis erworben werden konnte: M. Rösel, "Die Übersetzung der Gottesnamen in der Genesis-Septuaginta," in: D. R. Daniels, U. Gleßmer, M. Rösel (Hg.), *Ernten, was man sät*. FS K. Koch (Neukirchen-Vluyn, 1991), 357–377.

scheiden, welche Variante als ursprünglich plausibel erscheinen mag und was sich einer bestimmten Tendenz der Version verdankt.[65] So ist etwa das Plus des λέγων in 22,10 keiner solchen Tendenz zuzuordnen, was dafür spricht, daß der Übersetzer es in seiner Vorlage fand. Da es nun in 4QNum[b] belegt ist, kann diese Annahme als gesichert gelten. Die im nächsten Vers 22,11 zu הָעָם הַיֹּצֵא belegte indeterminierte Variante λαὸς ἐξελήλυθεν ist zwar als Harmonisierung mit V. 5 verdächtig, doch wird sie durch Smr und 4QNum[b] gestützt (עם יצא), so daß sie ebenfalls als ursprünglich gelten kann.[66]

Erneut ließen sich die Beispiele problemlos vermehren; Textkritik lebt ja von dem Eindruck, der aus der Fülle von Einzelfällen und -entscheidungen entsteht. Im Rahmen dieses Artikels ist jedenfalls die Problematik deutlich geworden, die bei der Verwendung der G als Zeuge für den hebräischen Text entsteht: Einerseits ist ein eigener Gestaltungswillen des Übersetzers unverkennbar, andererseits ist er seiner Vorlage verbunden und trägt damit Varianten weiter, die entweder auf einer früheren hebräischen Überlieferungsstufe entstanden oder gar ursprünglich sind.

Zusammenfassung

Als Ergebnis dieser Übersicht lässt sich folgendes formulieren: Der hebräische Text des Numeribuches und damit auch der Bileamgeschichte ist vergleichsweise gut überliefert. Es gibt keine Indizien dafür, daß es prinzipiell abweichende Texttraditionen gab, wie dies bei den eingangs genannten Büchern Jeremia oder Könige der Fall ist. Dennoch gibt es eine Fülle von Varianten, die zumeist auf fehlerhafte Überlieferung oder Interpretationen der Überlieferer zurückgehen. Letzteres konnte bei den drei ältesten und wichtigsten Textzeugen 4QNum[b], Smr und G beobachtet werden, die je für sich eigene Interessen in die Textgeschichte einfließen ließen. Die Problematik für die Textkritik besteht nun darin, daß keiner dieser

[65] So ist m.E. der fragende Vorschlag W. Rudolphs in *BHS* zu 22,6 verfehlt, mit G die 1. Pers. Pl. נוכל statt des Sg. אוכל zu lesen (ähnlich Dorival, *Nombres*, 420), da die erleichternde, auf Ausgleich schwieriger Formen bedachte Tendenz des G-Übersetzers nicht genügend berücksichtigt wurde (mit Wevers, *Notes*, 363).

[66] Mit Wevers, *Notes*, 366; anders Seebass, *Numeri*, 16, der die Variante als Harmonisierung einschätzt. Allerdings ist die syntaktische Konstruktion im MT ganz ungewöhnlich, so daß ein Fehler wahrscheinlicher ist.

drei Zeugen pauschal ab- oder aufzuwerten ist, noch daß es prinzipiell gültige Abhängigkeitsbestimmungen untereinander geben könnte. Möglich sind nur Tendenzaussagen – etwa daß 4QNum[b] näher am Smr als am MT steht oder daß G oft dem Smr folgt –, diese sind aber stets am Einzelfall zu überprüfen. Dabei wird man oft – wie in einigen der hier gezeigten Falle – über Wahrscheinlichkeitsaussagen nicht hinauskommen.

Der große Vorteil der von Adrian Schenker in bewundernswerter Weise projektierten und betreuten *Biblia Hebraica Quinta* wird daher nicht darin liegen können, die Probleme endgültig zu lösen oder gar im Kommentarteil einen synthetischen Text vorschlagen zu können. Aber sie wird besser als die bisherigen hebräischen Bibelausgaben einen Eindruck von der Komplexität der Textüberlieferungen und der Vielfalt der bei textkritischen Entscheidungen zu berücksichtigenden Faktoren vermitteln und damit vorschnelle oder zu selbstsichere Urteile verhindern können. Schließlich wird sie auch einen besseren Eindruck von der Dynamik der Textentwicklung geben können, wenn die Lesarten der einzelnen Zeugen nicht nur in kritische Textangaben gezwängt werden, sondern auch herangezogen werden, um Bilder von den eigenen Überlieferungsinteressen der jeweiligen Versionen zu zeichnen. Die Grenzen zwischen Textgeschichte und Rezeptionsgeschichte biblischer Texte werden damit aufgeweicht, was hoffentlich dazu führen wird, daß die Beschäftigung mit der Textgeschichte aus dem Schattendasein bei wenigen Spezialisten heraustreten kann.

SOME REFLECTIONS ON THE USE OF *PASEQ* IN THE BOOK OF ESTHER

Magne Sæbø

1. The text history of the Hebrew Bible / Old Testament is basically a tradition and reception history. This affects not only the variegated history of its ancient versions but also the pre-history and history of the Masoretic text itself.

As for the Book of Esther its text history was very special. Compared to most Old Testament books, it is distinctive that the Greek text tradition in Esther is divided into two quite different versions, the so-called Old Greek and the so-called Alpha Text. Both versions also have six longer – similar but not identical – expansions. Moreover, the Aramaic Targum text tradition of Esther is divided and has developed two, if not three, different main forms of the book, viz., *Targum Rishon* and *Targum Sheni*, whereby the latter is definitely more paraphrastic than the former. Besides, there is in these traditions of Esther – as in all biblical books – a great variety of individual variant readings, as is also the case in its Syriac tradition of the Peshitta and its Latin ones of the Old Latin and the Vulgate. By all these diversities, then, it is evident that the textual transmission and reception of Esther is more than a simple – not to say 'neutral' – *traditio* of a textual *traditum*; rather the *traditio* represents a creative and formative activity over a longer period of time which has resulted in various textual *tradita*, received and further promoted in the framework of specific traditions.[1]

Though not to the same extent as the ancient versions, the Masoretic text also is the outcome of a complex tradition and reception history, as the many and various Hebrew divergences, for instance between

[1] See further M. Sæbø (ed.), "Esther," in A. Schenker, et al. (eds.), *General Introduction and Megilloth* (*Biblia Hebraica Quinta* 18; Stuttgart, 2004), 73–96, and esp. 20*–24*. On this special occasion, I would like to express my best thanks to the Jubilarian, Professor Adrian Schenker, for all the help and positive instruction that he, together with the other members of the Editorial Committee of the *BHQ*, especially Professors Jan de Waard and Richard Weis, gave me during the whole process of this edition of the Book of Esther. Also, I owe my best thanks to Dr. Lea Himmelfarb, of the University of Bar-Ilan, for her expert comments on the present essay.

the Eastern and the Western Masoretic traditions or between the Ben Asher and the Ben Naphtali traditions or 'schools', clearly show.[2] In all, the emergence of the Masoretic text was a long and complex tradition procedure from a proto-Masoretic to the Masoretic text, including varying Palestinian, Babylonian and Tiberian vocalizations.[3] More generally, it was a process moving from textual pluriformity to uniformity.[4]

To this textual tradition and reception history contributed not least the various Masoretic accentuation systems, which – like the vocalization – were threefold, i.e., the Palestinian, the Babylonian and the Tiberian. They had a common purpose, namely, to safeguard a standardized or 'fixed' text, not only with regard to its reading and cantillation, but also hermeneutically, i.e., for its exegetical-syntactic understanding and interpretation.[5] However, they did it in various ways and had their individual histories.[6]

The Tiberian accentuation system was the most elaborated one – and the best known.[7] Characteristic to this system was, moreover,

---

[2] See esp. P. Kahle, *Masoreten des Ostens* (Leipzig, 1913; repr. Hildesheim, 1966); idem, *Masoreten des Westens*, I–II (Stuttgart, 1927 and 1930); cf. also idem "Foreword III," in *BHK*[3] (Stuttgart, 1937), XXIX–XXXVII. Among recent studies see I. Yeivin, *Introduction to the Tiberian Masorah* (transl. and ed. by E. J. Revell; SBLMasS 5; Missoula, Mont., 1980), 138–144, §§152–157.

[3] See A. Dotan, "Masorah," *EncJud* 16, cols. 1401–1482, esp. 1433–1468; recently E. Tov, *Textual Criticism of the Hebrew Bible* (Assen/Maastricht & Minneapolis, 1992), 22–67. Cf. also P. Kahle, "Pre-Massoretic Hebrew," *Textus* 2 (1962), 1–7; and G. Kahn, "The Tiberian pronunciation tradition of Biblical Hebrew," *ZAH* 9 (1996), 1–23.

[4] See further M. Sæbø, "From Pluriformity to Uniformity: The Emergence of the Massoretic Text," in *Gillis Gerleman Festschrift* (ASTI 11; Leiden, 1978), 127–137, reprinted in M. Sæbø, *On the Way to Canon: Creative Tradition History in the Old Testament* (JSOTSup 191; Sheffield, 1998), 36–46; see also idem, "Traditio-historical Perspectives in the Old Testament," in Saebø, *On the Way to Canon*, 21–33.

[5] Cf. Tov, *Textual Criticism*, 68: "At the outset, the accentuation was probably intended to indicate the melodic pattern of the reading, although according to some scholars, its primary function was exegetical-syntactic. The tradition of the accents is ancient, as is apparent from *y. Meg.* 4.74d . . .".

[6] See Dotan, "Masorah," esp. "Vocalization and Accentuation," cols. 1433–1468; Yeivin, *Introduction*, 157–274, §§176–374; Tov, *Textual Criticism*, 22–79 and 155–197. See also P. Kahle, "Zur Geschichte der hebräischen Accente," *ZDMG* 55 (1901), 167–194, who refers to Greek and Syriac influences; and M. B. Cohen, "Masoretic Accents as a Biblical Commentary," *JANESCU* 4 (1972), 2–11.

[7] Cf. Dotan, "Masorah," col. 1447: "The Tiberian system [of accentuation], unlike the other two, was a consolidated, complete system of disjunctive accents and conjunctive accents with defined functions, complete orderliness, and a very uniform textual transmission. This is the result of improvement after improvement, and it can be considered the zenith of the development of the graphemes in Hebrew."

that it had three signs that were considered not to be part of the accentuation system proper. Recently E. Tov has explained this fact simply and clearly by saying,

> The system of accentuation also includes three signs that are actually not accents, since they do not have a musical function: *maqqeph*, a conjunctive sign, *paseq* or *pᵉsiq*, a sign denoting a slight pause, and *gaʿyah* (literally: 'raising' of the voice), also named *metheg*, a sign indicating a secondary stress.[8]

As for the *pāsēq*, however, a closer look easily gives one the impression that the state of affairs for this particular sign is considerably complicated. This may be due, first of all, to its variegated use, which has turned out to be very hard to systematize in spite of much investigation in this respect. On the present occasion it might be worthwhile to review the specific character of the *pāsēq* and its use in the book of Esther.

2. The Masoretic sign פָּסֵק *pāsēq* (פְּסִיק *pĕsîq*), meaning 'divider', is marked by a vertical stroke | (originally a small line) between two words. It may come after a word with a conjunctive accent and indicate a pause after that word. As for its occurrences in the Hebrew Bible they are listed in the Masorah, but the countings of various manuscripts – and by modern scholars – differ.[9] That may be due to several reasons, of which just some will be brought up here.

First, in addition to the *pāsēq* proper there are also cases where the vertical stroke | is part of an accent. That is the case with the disjunctive accent *šalšelet* that occurs only seven times (and none of them in Esther), and more often with the disjunctive accent *lĕgarmēh* when it comes before a *rĕbîaʿ*. This may have affected the actual counting of the *pāsēq*, as well as a precise understanding of its character. In modern Hebrew grammars it is often stated that *pāsēq* occurs about 480 times in the Hebrew Bible.[10] But in his classical *Treatise on the Accentuation*, W. Wickes – who according to Yeivin has an "accurate list"[11] – counted 415, and thereupon added "a list of the L'garmehs,

---

[8] Tov, *Textual Criticism*, 68.

[9] Cf. Dotan, "Masorah," col. 1459; Yeivin, *Introduction*, 215–216, §§280–282.

[10] Cf. GKC, §15*f*, n. 2; P. Joüon and T. Muraoka, *A Grammar of Biblical Hebrew* (Rome, 1996), §15*m*; R. Meyer, *Hebräische Grammatik* (Berlin, 1966), §16.3.

[11] See Yeivin, *Introduction*, 215, §280.

which take the place of Paseq before R'bhîa".[12] Recently, in her doctoral study L. Himmelfarb has made a list based on M[L] (the Leningrad Codex, EBP. I B 19a) that "includes 587 *paseqs*, of which 438 are *paseqs* and 80 are *technical munaḥ ləgarmeh* (*munaḥ* and *paseq* before *revîa*) in the (21) Prose Books, and 69 are *paseqs* in the (3) Poetical Books".[13] The relationship between the *pāsēq* and the *lĕgarmēh* seems to have caused over time some uncertainty in the counting although the differences may be explicable.

Second, just this rather fluid relationship between the *pāsēq* and the accent *lĕgarmēh* may contribute to a better understanding of the various uses and complex character of the *pāsēq*. As already stated, the *pāsēq* is usually not supposed to belong to the Tiberian accentuation system because of its lack of musical function. However, the relation of *pāsēq* to the *lĕgarmēh*, which is an integrated part of the accentuation system, andas such does have functions beyond the musical one, may help to explain the complex picture of the use of *pāsēq* that has remained so puzzling in spite of all examination of it in modern research.[14]

At this point, attention may be drawn to another side of the picture. It is generally claimed that *pāsēq* does not appear in the Babylonian Masorah but is idiosyncratic to the Tiberian system. However, L. Himmelfarb has in the Babylonian system recently "discovered a disjunctive accent, while in parallel situations in the Tiberian system, a *paseq* would appear". Furthermore, with regard to the Palestinian accentuation in this respect she adds: "In the Palestinian system, we found a dot or line indicating a pause, parallel to the Tiberian *paseq*". Finally, from these observations she concludes: "This indicated that

[12] W. Wickes, *A Treatise on the Accentuation of the Twenty-one so-called Prose Books of the Old Testament* (Oxford, 1887), 127–129; reprinted in *Two Treatises on the Accentuation of the Old Testament* (New York, 1970).

[13] L. Widawski, *The Paseq in the Hebrew Bible: Occurrences in Medieval Manuscripts, Characteristics and Relation to the Accentuation System* (Hebrew), (Ph.D. thesis, Bar-Ilan; Ramat-Gan, 1990), Abstract, p. I. (Dr. Himmelfarb's thesis, was written under her former name, Widawski, and so will be cited by that name.)

[14] Basic on the use of the *pāsēq* is the critical edition by A. Dotan of ספר דקדוקי הטעמים לר' אהרן בן משה בן אשר/*The Diqduqe haṭṭĕʿamim of Ahăron ben Moše ben Ašer* (Jerusalem, 1967), 135 (text) and 244–246 (commentary and analysis). For earlier research see first of all Wickes, *Accentuation of the Twenty-one*, 119–29; cf. GKC, §15*f*, esp. n. 2, with references to many older studies on the *pāsēq*. Among recent works see in particular Widawski, *The Paseq*; cf. A. Dotan, "Masorah," col. 1459; Yeivin, *Introduction*, 216, §283.

the *paseq* is not an invention of the Tiberian system, neither in its function, nor in its graphic realization".[15] Along these lines, then, one may maintain that the border between the systems should not be as exclusively defined as often seems to have been the case.

This may affect the much debated chronological problem of the *pāsēq* as well, for also with regard to its dating there have been great differences of opinion. On the one hand, some older scholars went for an early, pre-Tiberian date: so for instance, F. Praetorius who antedated the *pāsēq* in relation to the Tiberian system of accents; or E. von Ortenberg who used the *pāsēq* as part of a literary-critical argumentation in order 'to point out marginal glosses subsequently interpolated into the text'.[16] On the other hand, most scholars since W. Wickes, who called the *pāsēq* "the final touch, applied to the [Tiberian accentuation] system",[17] have assumed a late date, subsequent to the Tiberian system of accents. A modern scholar like I. Yeivin assumes – although with some reservation – that: "It seems probable that *paseq* was established after the system of conjunctives and disjunctives as it completes it. If so, the lateness of its introduction would explain the lack of system in its use". The matter is similarly expressed in the Hebrew grammar of Joüon/Muraoka.[18]

However, to this some critical questions may be raised. First, one may ask whether the dating of the *pāsēq* is as essential as has been the case in modern research, or whether the focus should be put on its function rather than on its assumed date. Second, as far as the chronological question really is relevant, one may, with fairly good reasons, raise the question whether arguments advanced for a late dating of it are fully convincing. One may indeed ask whether it is likely that the accentuators, who over a period of time created a complete system of disjunctive and conjunctive accents such as the Tiberian one, would add a sign with such multiform functions as the *pāsēq* presents. Would it not be more plausible that the *pāsēq* – like the *māqqep̄* – could be some old sign of disjunctive – resp. of conjunctive –

[15] Widawski, *The Paseq*, Abstract, I–II.

[16] So GKC, §15*f*, n. 2, with references to Praetorius and von Ortenberg and others.

[17] Wickes, *Accentuation of the Twenty-one*, 120.

[18] Yeivin, *Introduction*, 216, §283; cf. Joüon and Muraoka, *Grammar*, 69: 'Paseq was introduced at a late period and in a manner less coherent than other accents, as a result of which its use is not very clear'. On the other hand, Meyer, *Hebräische Grammatik*, §16.3, does not refer to the chronological question of the *paseq* at all.

character,[19] which in turn the sophisticated Tiberian system of accents had to cope with and try to integrate into its system in some useful way? In this respect further research may unquestionably be needed, but steps in a new direction have already been made. In an essay of 1981 A. Dotan has asked some – as he says – "'naughty' questions, as are all questions attempting to reopen issues which allegedly have long been settled by general consensus".[20] His new thesis is as follows: "vocalization and accentuation are originally *different* systems, instituted *not* at the same time, the accent signs having *preceded* the vowel signs".[21] He also includes the Palestinian and the Babylonian systems in this. In addition, he questions "the current assumption that the Syriac signs are earlier, and that some of them were the source and origin for the Hebrew signs". Of special interest on this occasionis his historical differentiation within the traditional material and his focal point that "the Tiberian *accentuation* system was not monolithic, and that it, too, consisted of several phases".[22] The recent studies of the *pāsēq* by Himmelfarb[23] contribute thoroughly to this differentiating approach to the history of the Hebrew accentuation made by Dotan.

Third, a systematization or classification of the uses of *pāsēq* was made relatively early on. One is found already in the *Diqduqe haṭṭĕʿamim* of Ahăron ben Moše ben Ašer,[24] and new ones have been added later, but many of them differ. Traditionally, one has classified the use of *pāsēq* by means of five 'rules' or categories. They may be summarized easily, as is done by the Gesenius-Kautzsch-Cowley grammar, in the following way:

> The purpose of *Paseq* is clearly recognizable in the five old rules: as a divider between identical letters at the end and beginning of two words; between identical or very similar words; between words which are absolutely contradictory (as *God* and *evil-doer*); between words which

[19] As for *gaʿyâ / meteg*, matters may stand differently since this sign always is used ahead of another accent.

[20] A. Dotan, "The Relative Chronology of Hebrew Vocalization and Accentuation," *PAAJR* 48 (1981), 87–99.

[21] Ibid., 92.

[22] Ibid., 98f. For the assumed Syriac influence see n. 6 above on the view of P. Kahle.

[23] See nn. 13–15 above.

[24] See esp. n. 14 above. Dotan points out that in the *Diqduqe haṭṭĕʿamim* 'a few rules for *paseq* were enumerated'; see his "Masorah," col. 1459; §5.3.3.3.1.1.

are liable to be wrongly connected; and lastly, between heterogeneous terms, as 'Eleazar the High Priest, and Joshua'.[25]

Evidently, the *pāsēq* refers to a given form or to the content of a text, and in both cases the concern for a correct reading as well as understanding of the text in question is imperative. Since these 'rules', however, do not cover all occurrences of the *pāsēq*,[26] other classifications have been made, the most prominent of which is that of Wickes. After having divided the occurrences of the *pāsēq* into two classes, the "ordinary" *pāsēq* (that 'separates *two* words that are kept together by the accents') and the "extra-ordinary Paseq" ('where *three* or *more* words are conjoined'), he has subdivided the first one into: '*distinctivum*', '*emphaticum*', '*homonymicum*' and '*euphonicum*', and the latter into '*distinctivum*', '*emphaticum*', '*homonymicum*', '*euphonicum*' and, in addition, '*euphemisticum*'.[27] These terms, partly referring to the 'five old rules', have often been cited in the handbooks, mainly in a simplified form. The latest examination and classification of the use of the *pāsēq* is made by Himmelfarb. She has examined old "compiled lists of *paseq*" and found that "they can no longer be considered reliable".[28] In her doctoral thesis she presents "a new version of the five generally accepted rules to explain the occurrences of a *paseq*" and calls them Rules A–E.[29] A and B are identical with the two first ones in GKC cited above. She defines C as "a *paseq* separating a Holy Name from an adjacent word". D refers to "a *paseq* separating between two words for reasons of meaning and comprehension". E refers to "a *paseq* dividing a unit containing two or more conjunctive accents", but does not refer to the *lĕgarmeh*.[30] In a manner somewhat like that of Wickes she divides the material into two main groups, but she calls them, on the one hand, a "final unit, i.e., a two-word unit",[31] and,

[25] GKC, §15*f*, n. 2; cf. Meyer, *Hebräische Grammatik*, §16.3.

[26] Cf. Joüon and Muraoka, *Grammar*, 69: "several hypotheses of varying degrees of likelihood have been put forward to account for these [i.e. the few instances not covered by the five rules]: e.g., that paseq is a diacritical symbol, or that it indicates an ancient abbreviation, or the insertion of a short gloss."

[27] Wickes, *Accentuation of the Twenty-one*, 122–127.

[28] It is about lists "such as those in the Final Masora of L and in the *Mikra'ot Gədolot* of Jacob Ben Ḥayyim, and of Ginsburg", Widawski [Himmelfarb], *The Paseq*, Abstract, III.

[29] Ibid.

[30] Ibid., IV.

[31] Ibid. In Ch. 3 she treats 213 cases.

on the other hand, "a non-final unit, i.e., a unit of three or more words".[32] She discusses all instances – including different manuscripts and printed editions – related to each of the individual 'rules'. It may be of special interest here that she has given explicit attention to the name list in Esth 9:7–9.[33] This leads us to the third and last section of this essay, which will offer a brief examination of the occurrences and use(s) of the *pāsēq* in the Book of Esther.

3. Against this background of an outline of the modern research on the Hebrew accentuation systems and in particular on the variegated use of the *pāsēq* in the Hebrew Bible, the specific use and character of the *pāsēq* in the Book of Esther may be brought into focus.

In all ten chapters of Esther, except for chapter six, there are in total 36 occurrences of a vertical stroke, but not all of them are to be classified as a *pāsēq* in the proper sense. A group of twenty-two cases may be distinguished from a smaller group of fourteen which comprises the instances of the *pāsēq* in the strict sense. The references of all thirty-six occurrences are: 1:2, 3, 5, 6 (*bis*), 8, 14, 15, 18; 2:12, 14; 3:1, 7, 12; 4:7; 5:1, 14; 7:8; 8:9, 11, 15; 9:7–9 (ten times, following after each ואת in the list of the names of the sons of Haman), 16, 27 (*bis*); 10:1, 3.

a. In the twenty-two instances of the first group the stroke | belongs to a unit of three words, which Himmelfarb has described as 'a non-final unit', and which follows a strict accentual pattern, as may be shown by 1:2, its very first instance:

כְּשֶׁ֣בֶת ׀ הַמֶּ֣לֶךְ אֲחַשְׁוֵר֗וֹשׁ

The sequence of the accents in this unit is as follows:

conjunctive *mûnāḥ* – stroke | – conjunctive *mûnāḥ* – disjunctive *rĕbîaʿ*

The stroke | divides here two words both having *mûnāḥ* and the last standing before a word with *rĕbîaʿ*. The combination of *mûnāḥ* with stroke | ordinarily represents the disjunctive accent *lĕgarmēh* – that regularly comes before a *rĕbîaʿ*. The unit at 1:2, moreover, comes first after an *ʾatnāḥ* and is in this respect the first unit of the second verse half. An initial position of this kind in a verse half is the case in twelve of the twenty-two instances. For the rest of them the posi-

[32] Ibid., VI. In Ch. 4 she treats 283 cases.
[33] Widawski, *The Paseq*, 229f.

tion of the individual units in their respective verse or verse half differs.[34] Except for its position in the verse the same accent pattern as in 1:2 is found at the following instances in Esther:

1:3	חֵ֣יל ׀ פָּרַ֣ס וּמָדַ֗י
1:5	וּבִמְל֣וֹאת ׀ הַיָּמִ֣ים הָאֵ֗לֶּה
1:6[1]	ח֣וּר ׀ כַּרְפַּ֣ס וּתְכֵ֗לֶת
1:6[2]	מִטּ֣וֹת ׀ זָהָ֣ב וָכֶ֗סֶף
1:8	כִּי־כֵ֣ן ׀ יִסַּ֣ד הַמֶּ֗לֶךְ
1:14	שָׂרֵ֣י ׀ פָּרַ֣ס וּמָדַ֗י
1:15	עַ֣ל ׀ אֲשֶׁ֣ר לֹֽא־עָשְׂתָ֗ה
1:18	תֹּאמַ֣רְנָה ׀ שָׂר֣וֹת פָּֽרַס־וּמָדַ֗י
2:12	לָב֣וֹא ׀ אֶל־הַמֶּ֣לֶךְ אֲחַשְׁוֵר֗וֹשׁ
2:14	בָּעֶ֣רֶב ׀ הִ֣יא בָאָ֗ה
3:1	אַחַ֣ר ׀ הַדְּבָרִ֣ים הָאֵ֗לֶּה
3:12	אֲשֶׁ֣ר ׀ עַל־מְדִינָ֣ה וּמְדִינָ֗ה
4:7	וְאֵ֣ת ׀ פָּרָשַׁ֣ת הַכֶּ֗סֶף
5:1	וַיְהִ֣י ׀ בַּיּ֣וֹם הַשְּׁלִישִׁ֗י
5:14	וּבַבֹּ֣קֶר ׀ אֱמֹ֣ר לַמֶּ֗לֶךְ
7:8	אֶל־בֵּ֣ית ׀ מִשְׁתֵּ֣ה הַfiיִן
8:9	אֲשֶׁ֣ר ׀ מֵהֹ֣דּוּ וְעַד־כּ֗וּשׁ
8:11	לַיְּהוּדִ֣ים ׀ אֲשֶׁ֣ר בְּכָל־עִיר־וָעִ֗יר
8:15	יָצָ֣א ׀ מִלִּפְנֵ֣י הַמֶּ֗לֶךְ
9:16	נִקְהֲל֣וּ ׀ וְעָמֹ֣ד עַל־נַפְשָׁ֗ם
10:3	כִּ֣י ׀ מָרְדֳּכַ֣י הַיְּהוּדִ֗י

At some of these twenty-two instances the vertical stroke |, resp. the combination of *mûnāḥ* – stroke |, occurs at (or after) words that in the text tradition have turned out to be problematic or uncertain to some degree. This is the case in 1:2, where the understanding of the infinitive form שֶׁבֶת and its preposition כ exhibits a certain ambivalence;[35] in 1:3, where the position of חיל is syntactically ambiguous;[36] in 1:5, where the infinitive form מלואת is grammatically uncommon.[37] This is especially so at the beginning of the puzzling verse 1:6, which differs syntactically from its context, the verse starting rather abruptly in a nominal and enumerating style;[38] also in 1:18, where the transitive verb form תאמרנה lacks an object, which has caused some perplexity among the witnesses in the text history.[39] In 3:1 and 3:12

[34] The ten instances are: 1:14, 18; 2:12; 3:12; 5:14; 7:8; 8:9, 11, 15; 9:16. Some of these are problematic in some way, and will be dealt with below.

[35] Cf. Sæbø, "Esther," 73, apparatus ad loc. and 137*, commentary ad loc.

[36] See ibid., ad loc.

[37] See ibid., 74 ad loc. and 137* ad loc.

[38] See ibid., 74 ad loc. and 138* ad loc.

[39] See ibid., 76 ad loc. and 139* ad loc.

the vertical stroke | has a *circellus masoreticus*, and in 4:7 the form | ואת, here after *ʾatnāḥ* and with *mûnāḥ*, recalls the special construction in 9:7–9 that will be discussed below. In 7:8 the stroke | after בית may indicate this word's difficult middle position, first, after the similar word ביתן and then nearest, after the preposition אל that also might refer to the following משתה היין. In other words, the stroke | may here point out a – perhaps unexpected – doubleness of ביתן and בית and in this respect disclose a possible contamination in the tradition of two different readings. Also 8:11 is syntactically 'hard', having two אשׁר-clauses and many different elements in an enumerating style (cf. also 8:9).[40] Furthermore, it may be observed that in some cases the stroke | comes after an indication of time (בערב, 2:14; בבקר, 5:14; אחר, 3:1; cf. also 5:1),[41] or that the combination of *mûnāḥ* – stroke | in 8:15, where it comes after יצא (ומרדכי) and before מלפני המלך, may have the same meaning and function as elsewhere the emphatic *pāsēq* has.

Considering the cumulative effect of these cases with their various problems, it seems hard to avoid the impression that the use of the combination of *mûnāḥ* – stroke | at instances normally denoted as cases of the accent *lĕgarmēh* may well coincide with the function of *pāsēq emphaticum* that Wickes has characterized as "the chief object of the ordinary Paseq", or with that of *pāsēq distinctivum* in its function of "a *nota bene* to the reader".[42] Consequently the border between the accent *lĕgarmēh* and the *pāsēq* in the proper sense should presumably not be drawn too sharply.

b. In the remaining fourteen instances – the same number and cases as Wickes has in his list of the occurrences of the *pāsēq*[43] – the vertical stroke | divides two words, and the whole of it constitutes a unit that Himmelfarb has described as a "final unit, i.e., a two-word unit". These instances are as follows:

---

[40] Cf. Wickes, *Accentuation of the Twenty-one*, 42–43, discussing the question of parenthesis in Hebrew and referring to Esth 2:12.

[41] Sæbø, "Esther," 84 ad loc. and 143* ad loc.

[42] See Wickes, *Accentuation of the Twenty-one*, 122–126; cf. Meyer, *Hebräische Grammatik*, §16.3, who on the diverse functions of *paseq* finally says: "gelegentlich zur Kennzeichnung einer auffallenden und schwierigen Textstelle, unseren Zeichen 'sic!' und '!' vergleichbar".

[43] Ibid., 129.

3:7		מִיּ֣וֹם ׀ לְי֗וֹם
9:(6)7–9	וְאֵ֣ת ׀	אִֽישׁ׃
	וְאֵ֣ת ׀	פַּרְשַׁנְדָּ֗תָא
	וְאֵ֣ת ׀	דַּלְפ֛וֹן
	וְאֵ֣ת ׀	אַסְפָּֽתָא׃
	וְאֵ֣ת ׀	פּוֹרָ֗תָא
	וְאֵ֣ת ׀	אֲדַלְיָ֗א
	וְאֵ֣ת ׀	אֲרִידָֽתָא׃
	וְאֵ֣ת ׀	פַּרְמַ֙שְׁתָּא֙
	וְאֵ֣ת ׀	אֲרִיסַ֔י
	וְאֵ֣ת ׀	אֲרִדַ֖י
		וַיְזָֽתָא׃
9:27 (*bis*)		הַיְּהוּדִ֡ים ׀ עֲלֵיהֶ֣ם ׀ וְעַל־זַרְעָ֗ם
10:1		אֲחַשְׁרֹ֥שׁ ׀ מַ֛ס

In the first instance, 3:7, the function of the *pāsēq* is a very common one, expressed in one of the 'five old rules' (Himmelfarb's Rule B): the *pāsēq* is here "separating two identical or similar words".[44]

The next ten instances, in the list of 9:7–9, are of a more special character; they represent a rare structure of stichometric arrangement in the Hebrew Bible, otherwise used only in the list of the defeated kings of Canaan, Josh 12:9–24. The specific method and name of this list is, with reference to *b.Meg.* 16b, described by E. Tov in the following way:

> 'a half-brick, אריח, over a half-brick and a whole brick, לבנה, over a whole brick,' i.e., a space above another space in the following line with the written text appearing above the written text in the following line.[45]

Together with this most special list composition, the ten instances of *pāsēq*, preceded and succeeded by varying accents – so also, with further differences, in Joshua 12, clearly have an emphasizing and distinguishing function when they focus on the name of each of the sons of Haman by indicating a pause and dividing each *nota accusativi* from its object. The intention is clearly to lay a negative emphasis on a defeated enemy of the people of Israel.

[44] See Widawski, *The Paseq*, Abstract, IV.

[45] Tov, *Textual Criticism*, 212; there are similar stichometric patterns in Exod 15:1–18, Deut 32:1–43 and Judg 5:2–30, cf. also J. M. Oesch, *Petucha und Setuma* (OBO 27; Freiburg & Göttingen, 1979), 121f.

In 9:27 there are two instances of *pāsēq*, that come one after the other in the clause of the same disjunctive accent, preceding and following the word עליהם. In a verse with an overloaded syntax and some grammatical problems,[46] the word עליהם, followed by the complex sequence of ועל־זרעם ועל כל־הנלוים עליהם, may perhaps have been felt superfluous. Anyway, these instances of *pāsēq* may indicate the contamination of a double tradition, having put 'a *nota bene* to the reader' around the 'suspicious' word of the overloaded text, which may be the result of a complex process of tradition.

The last instance, 10:1, has the *pāsēq* in a position that may be explained by 'the fifth rule' (Himmelfarb's Rule E, 'dividing a unit containing two or more conjunctive accents'), occurring parallel to a disjunctive accent in a similar combination (cf. 1 Kings 5:27). As for its function in a broader, hermeneutical sense it may mean 'a *nota bene* to the reader', coming after and thereby attracting attention to the doubly false writing of the name of the king, אחשרש, which otherwise has been corrected in the margin by the Qere אחשורוש.[47]

4. In conclusion, it may briefly be stated that in the book of Esther the *pāsēq* has various functions, related first of all to the specific meaning of single words and elements of the text, whereby it intends to secure a correct understanding and reading of the text. In particular, however, it seems to have an emphasizing and distinctive character. In this way the *pāsēq* is part of the creative tradition history of the book's Hebrew text.

What applies for the *pāsēq* in the proper sense, may also, in relatively many instances in the book, concern the cases where the stroke | is combined with the accent *mûnāḥ* and so constitutes the disjunctive accent *lĕgarmēh*.

[46] See Sæbø, "Esther," 95 ad loc. and 149* ad loc.
[47] See ibid., 96 ad loc. and 150* ad loc.

DER URSPRÜNGLICHE TEXT UND DIE POETISCHE STRUKTUR DES ERSTEN KLAGELIEDES (KLGL 1)

TEXTKRITIK UND STRUKTURANALYSE IM ZWIEGESPRÄCH*

Rolf Schäfer

Im biblischen Buch der Klagelieder sind fünf Dichtungen überliefert, denen als formales Gestaltungsprinzip mehr oder weniger deutlich das hebräische Alphabet zugrunde liegt. Bei Klgl 5 ist dieser Bezug verhältnismäßig lose, denn lediglich durch seinen Umfang von genau zweiundzwanzig Bikola ergibt sich eine Korrespondenz mit der Anzahl der hebräischen Konsonanten. Bei Klgl 1–4 handelt es sich dagegen um echte alphabetische Akrosticha, die mit den Buchstaben ihrer Versanfänge genau der Sequenz des Alphabets folgen. Innerhalb dieses formalen Grundschemas ist jedem Buchstaben des Alphabets eine Gruppe von zwei (in Klgl 4) oder drei (in Klgl 1–3) regelmäßigen Bikola zugeordnet; in Klgl 3 beginnen sogar alle drei Bikola jeder Gruppe jeweils mit dem gleichen Buchstaben.

Dies hohe Maß an formaler Geschlossenheit hat einerseits sicherlich dazu beigetragen, dass der Text der Klagelieder weitgehend einheitlich überliefert ist.[1] Andererseits lässt aber gerade die strenge gebundene

* Erst durch die Begegnung und Zusammenarbeit mit Adrian Schenker kam der Verf. dazu, sich eingehender mit Textkritik zu befassen; zuvor hat er sich wissenschaftlich neben Archäologie vor allem mit der Strukturanalyse von Weisheitsgedichten beschäftigt (*Die Poesie der Weisen* [WMANT 77; Neukirchen, 1999]). Die vorliegende Untersuchung bewegt sich methodisch am Schnittpunkt beider Gebiete. Sie ist Adrian Schenker in Dankbarkeit und Freundschaft zu seinem Geburtstag gewidmet. *Ad multos annos!*

[1] Alle alten Übersetzungen beruhen auf einem hebräischen Text, der mit der späteren masoretischen Textgestalt vielleicht nicht völlig identisch, ihr aber zumindest sehr ähnlich war. Es gibt zwar, wie die textkritischen Apparate vor allem in *BH3* und *BHQ*, aber auch in *BHS* dokumentieren, eine ganze Reihe scheinbarer Varianten, doch bei näherer Betrachtung zeigt sich in den meisten Fällen, dass es sich wahrscheinlich eher um Eigentümlichkeiten der betreffenden Übersetzung handelt oder um Versuche der Übersetzer, eine besondere Schwierigkeit des hebräischen Textes zu bewältigen; trifft das Erste zu, so sind die Abweichungen textkritisch bedeutungslos, trifft das Zweite zu, so bestätigt gerade die scheinbare Abweichung (sobald nämlich die Intention erkennbar wird, die den Übersetzer dazu veranlasste, von seiner Vorlage abzuweichen) indirekt wieder den MT.

Zum einheitlichen Bild der Textüberlieferung trägt entscheidend mit bei, dass die Septuaginta der Klagelieder, wie D. Barthélemy, *Les devanciers d'Aquila* (VTSup 10;

Form auch zwei Passagen besonders hervortreten, in denen das gestalterische Ebenmaß in höchst auffälliger Weise durchbrochen wird. Das ist in Klgl 1,7 und 2,19 der Fall, denn beide umfassen jeweils *vier* Bikola und heben sich durch diese irreguläre Länge deutlich vom Kontext ab, der sonst durchgehend aus Versen mit jeweils nur *drei* Bikola besteht. Angesichts dieses Sachverhalts stehen die beiden Verse seit jeher unter kritischem Verdacht, und es stellt sich die Frage, ob der überlieferte Text hier wirklich den ursprünglichen Wortlaut bewahrt hat.

Im Fall von 2,19 gibt es keinerlei textkritische Anhaltspunkte, die auf einen anderen als den im masoretischen Text überlieferten Wortlaut hindeuten, so dass die Beurteilung sich bisher ausschließlich auf literarkritische Argumente stützen musste. Immerhin ist das literarkritische Urteil beinahe einhellig: "V. 19d ist eine nach 2,11f. und 4,1 gebildete Glosse".[2]

Im Fall von 1,7 liegen die Dinge jedoch ganz anders, denn seit der Veröffentlichung der Handschrift 4QLam durch F. M. Cross,[3] ist eine Textvariante zu Klgl 1,7 bekannt, die zumindest die Möglichkeit einer texkritischen Lösung des Problems bietet und dadurch neue Gesichtspunkte in die bisher ausschließlich literarkritisch geführte Diskussion einbringt. Ob die textkritische Lösung aber wirklich trägt, hängt in beträchtlichem Maß davon ab, wie sich die Variante aus 4QLam in die poetische Gesamtkomposition des ersten Klageliedes einfügt.

Leiden, 1963), 33 und 158f, gezeigt hat, deutlich erkennbar die Charakteristika der kaivge-Rezension aufweist. Der hexaplarische Apparat der Göttinger Septuaginta verzeichnet dementsprechend in den Klageliedern keine einzige Theodotion-Variante und eine naheliegende Schlussfolgerung aus diesem Befund könnte sein, dass es sich beim überlieferten griechischen Text der Klagelieder gar nicht um die ursprüngliche Septuaginta handelt, sondern durchweg um die "Theodotion"-Fassung aus dem 1. Jh. n. Chr.

[2] O. Kaiser, "Klagelieder," in H.-P. Müller, O. Kaiser, J. A. Loader, *Das Hohelied – Klagelieder – Das Buch Ester* (ATD 16/2; Göttingen, 1992), 133; so auch U. Berges, *Klagelieder* (HThKAT; Freiburg, 2002), 163, der die einzelnen Bezüge zwischen den Versen 11f und 18f ausführlich beschreibt und damit das literarkritische Urteil erhärtet; Klgl 4,1 hält er jedoch umgekehrt für abhängig von 2,19d.21a, was bedeutet, dass die Glosse in V. 19d bereits Bestandteil des Textes von Klgl 2 gewesen sein müsste, als Klgl 4 entstand.

[3] F. M. Cross, "Studies in the Structure of Hebrew Verse: The Prosody of Lamentations 1:1–22," in: C. L. Meyers and M. O'Connor (eds.), *The Word of the Lord Shall Go Forth. Essays in Honor of David Noel Freedman in Celebration of His Sixtieth Birthday* (Winona Lake, 1983), 129–155. Nach dieser ersten Bearbeitung liegt seit 2000 auch die Endpublikation von 4QLam durch Cross in DJD XVI (Oxford, 2000), 229–237 vor.

In seinem jüngst erschienenen großen Kommentar zu den Klageliedern hat U. Berges unter anderem auch den Aufbau und die Struktur dieser Dichtungen eingehend untersucht und beschrieben. Bei der Frage nach dem Text von Klgl 1,7 verbindet er die textkritische Fragestellung mit seiner Strukturanalyse und kommt dabei zu dem Schluss, die Lesart von 4QLam widerspreche dem Aufbau des Gedichts und biete deshalb hier keinen besseren Text.[4] Diese These soll im Folgenden überprüft und mit einer Gegenthese konfrontiert werden. Dazu wird zunächst das relevante Material aus Qumran – vor allem das Fragment 4QLam und insbesondere dessen Textvariante zu Klgl 1,7 – vorgestellt, sodann die Aufbauanalyse von Berges nachgezeichnet und schließlich eine alternative Betrachtungsweise vorgestellt.

1. Der Text von Klgl 1 in den Handschriftenfragmenten 3QLam und 4QLam aus Qumran

Unter den bis heute bekanntgewordenen Handschriften aus Qumran befinden sich Überreste von insgesamt wahrscheinlich vier[5] verschiedenen Abschriften der Klagelieder. Es handelt sich um die Manuskripte 3QLam (3Q3), 4QLam (4Q111), 5QLam[a] (5Q6) und 5QLam[b] (5Q7). Zwei davon, 3QLam und vor allem 4QLam, überliefern bruchstückhaft Textpassagen aus Klgl 1.

Von der Handschrift *3QLam* sind nur zwei kleine Fragmente erhalten, geschrieben in einer winzigen, aber sehr sorgfältigen herodianischen Handschrift.[6] *Fragment 1* zeigt das Tetragramm in (neo-)paläohebräischer Schrift, in der Zeile darüber in Quadratschrift das Wort ב]קהל und in der Zeile darunter ebenfalls in Quadratschrift Reste des Wortes הונ[ה. Da בקהל als vorletztes Wort in Klgl 1,10 vorkommt, das Tetragramm als fünftletztes Wort in Klgl 1,11 und הונה als ebenfalls fünftletztes Wort in Klgl 1,12, kann das Fragment praktisch zweifelsfrei identifiziert werden. *Fragment 2* enthält die Reste

[4] Berges, *Klagelieder*, 89.

[5] Sofern die beiden Fragmente 3QLam zum selben Exemplar gehören – was aber so gut wie sicher ist – und es sich außerdem bei dem Hinweis auf 4Q241 im Companion Volume der Microfiche Edition (vgl. G. W. Nebe, "Qumranica I," *ZAW* 106 (1994), 307 Anm 7) nicht doch noch um Fragmente eines weiteren Klgl-Exemplars handelt. – 4QapLam kann hier unberücksichtigt bleiben.

[6] "Petite calligraphie hérodienne"; Höhe des *taw* ca. 1 mm, Zeilenabstand 4 bis 5 mm; siehe DJD III (Oxford, 1962), 95.

von vier Zeilen untereinander aus Klgl 3 die in unserem Zusammenhang unberücksichtigt bleiben können. Der erhaltene Konsonantenbestand von 3QLam stimmt völlig mit dem Masoretischen Text überein.[7] Mit der Einschränkung, dass 27 lesbare Zeichen nur eine äußerst schmale Basis sind, läßt sich also die Schlussfolgerung ziehen, dass es sich bei 3QLam um eine Abschrift des protomasoretischen Texttyps handelt.

3QLam trägt nach diesem Befund zwar für die Textkritik wenig aus, aber umso interessanter ist die Gliederung des Textes, oder genauer: dessen graphische Anordnung. Die Position der jeweils untereinander geschriebenen Wörter erlaubt nämlich bei beiden Fragmenten den Schluss, dass jede Zeile von 3QLam jeweils genau einen Vers aus Klgl 1 bzw. drei Verse aus Klgl 3 enthielt, d. h. durchschnittlich zwischen ca. 75 und 85 Zeichen (die Wortzwischenräume mitgerechnet), was einer Kolumnenbreite von etwa 9–10 cm entspricht. Sowohl bei Klgl 1 als auch bei Klgl 3 trat bei dieser Textanordnung das alphabetische Akrostichon als Gestaltungsprinzip augenfällig hervor, indem nämlich am rechten Rand der Kolumne von oben nach unten das hebräische Alphabet erschien.

Die Handschrift *4QLam* ist das am besten erhaltene,[8] umfangreichste und textgeschichtlich interessanteste Klagelieder-Fragment aus Qumran. Es umfasst einen großen Teil des Textes von Klgl 1 sowie ein einzelnes kleines Fragment aus Klgl 2,5, das hier aber nur der Vollständigkeit halber am Rande erwähnt sei.

Der in 4QLam enthaltene Abschnitt aus Klgl 1 war, wie noch deutlich zu erkennen ist, auf drei Kolumnen verteilt: Von Kolumne I (Klgl 1,1–6) ist nur noch ein schmaler (zwischen 0,5 und 2,5 cm breiter und ca. 9–10 cm hoher) Streifen vorhanden. Von Kolumne II (Klgl 1,6–10) ist die obere Hälfte gut erhalten (9 cm breit und

[7] Die Herausgeber vermuten allerdings, dass in Zeile 2 von Fragment 1 vor dem Tetragramm ein etwas längerer Text gestanden habe als im MT von Klgl 1,11, und sie stellen deshalb in ihrer Textrekonstruktion והביטה *vor* das Tetragramm (DJD III, 95). Da die Differenz von ca. 5–8 Zeichen gegenüber dem in Zeile 1 und 3 nach rechts vorauszusetzenden Text aber auch ganz andere Ursachen haben könnte (z. B. eine Streichung, eine Rasur oder auch nur einen etwas raumgreifenderen Duktus beim Schreiben), bleiben solche Überlegungen völlig spekulativ.

[8] Erstmals veröffentlicht im Jahre 1983 von Cross, "Prosody of Lamentations 1". Außerdem hat Nebe, "Qumranica I," 313–315, eine (allerdings durch mehrere Druckfehler beeinträchtigte) Liste der vom masoretischen Text abweichenden Stellen aus 4QLam erstellt. Die maßgebliche Edition von 4QLam hat Cross zuletzt in DJD XVI, 229–237, vorgelegt.

4,5 cm hoch, d. h. 5 Zeilen), die untere jedoch nur zu einem kleinen Teil (ca. 2 cm breit und 4 cm hoch). Kolumne III ist, abgesehen von einigen wurmzerfressenen Stellen am unteren und am linken Rand sowie einer größeren Fraßstelle im linken oberen Viertel, nahezu vollständig erhalten.

Die Kolumnen I und II enthielten je 11 Zeilen mit einer Länge von ursprünglich jeweils ca. 35 Zeichen (Wortzwischenräume mitgerechnet); beide Kolumnen waren in unversehrtem Zustand etwa 8 cm breit und 8 cm hoch. Kolumne III hingegen enthält nur 10 Zeilen, jedoch mit einer Länge von je ca. 60 Zeichen; sie ist etwa 15 cm breit und 7 cm hoch. Die Schriftrolle, von der die Fragmente stammen, war insgesamt etwa 10 cm hoch. Im Fundzustand waren Kolumne II und Kolumne III noch aneinandergenäht.[9]

Der Text ist – anders als in 3QLam – ohne erkennbare Gliederung fortlaufend geschrieben. Der Zeilenabstand beträgt ca. 7 mm, die Schriftgröße ca. 3,5 mm. Cross charakterisiert den Schriftduktus von 4QLam als "vulgar semi-formal" und datiert das Manuskript in die herodianische Zeit.[10] Ganz im Gegensatz zum Manuskript 3QLam, das ungefähr aus der gleichen Zeit stammt, ist bei 4QLam auf den ersten Blick zu erkennen, dass es sich um eine mit vergleichsweise wenig Sorgfalt hergestellte Abschrift des Klagelieder-Textes handelt, die wohl nicht für den offiziellen Gebrauch gedacht war.[11]

Im Vergleich mit dem masoretischen Text weist 4QLam – neben einigen morphologischen Unterschieden[12] sowie der für die "qumranische Schreiberpraxis"[13] charakteristischen *plene*-Schreibung – eine beträchtliche Anzahl von Fehlern und Varianten auf. Alle diese Abweichungen vom masoretischen Text wurden bereits an anderer Stelle hinreichend beschrieben[14] und müssen deshalb hier nicht nochmals einzeln aufgezählt werden. Nach Art und Anzahl der offenkundigen

[9] Siehe dazu z. B. die Photographie PAM 42.289.

[10] Cross, "Prosody of Lamentations 1," 133, und Ders., DJD XVI, 229.

[11] Cross, DJD XVI, 229: ". . . evidently not a public copy of Lamentations."

[12] היא[ה (4QLam I,5) vs. היא (MT V. 3); בלי (II,2) vs. בלא (V. 6); [פ]לאות (II,9) vs. פלאים (V. 9).

[13] Siehe dazu E. Tov, *Der Text der Hebräischen Bibel. Handbuch der Textkritik* (Stuttgart, 1997), 89–92.

[14] Cross, "Prosody of Lamentations 1," *passim*; Ders., DJD XVI, 229–237; Nebe, "Qumranica I," 313–315; R. Schäfer, "Der Masoretische Text der Klagelieder und die Handschriften 3QLam, 4QLam und 5QLam-a.b aus Qumran," in U. Dahmen, A. Lange, H. Lichtenberger (Hg.), *Die Textfunde vom Toten Meer und der Text der Hebräischen Bibel* (Neukirchen, 2000), 132–146.

Fehler kann kaum Zweifel daran bestehen, dass in 4QLam ein "sleepy scribe",[15] ein nachlässiger oder zumindest unaufmerksamer Schreiber, am Werke gewesen ist. Einerseits ist daher beim Beurteilen der kleineren Varianten (z. B. der Fälle einer zusätzlichen Kopula oder unterschiedlicher Pronominal-Suffixe) Vorsicht geboten. Andererseits macht gerade seine erkennbare Nachlässigkeit den Schreiber auch wiederum unverdächtig, was absichtliche größere Veränderungen betrifft, denn es ist wenig wahrscheinlich, dass solch ein nachlässiger Kopist gleichzeitig mit Absicht ändernd oder 'korrigierend' in den von ihm abzuschreibenden Text eingegriffen haben sollte. Somit wird es einzig und allein auf das hohe Alter des Manuskripts 4QLam zurückzuführen sein, dass sich darin einige Lesarten erhalten haben, die dem masoretischen Text möglicherweise vorzuziehen sind oder zusammen mit dem masoretischen Text die Rekonstruktion einer älteren Lesart ermöglichen.[16] An zwei dieser Stellen unterscheidet sich der Text von 4QLam so auffällig vom masoretischen Text, dass sich daraus Konsequenzen für die poetische Struktur des gesamten ersten Klageliedes ergeben; auf diese beiden Stellen konzentrieren sich darum die folgenden Überlegungen.

Der eine in die Struktur des Textes eingreifende Unterschied zwischen 4QLam und dem masoretischen Text betrifft die Reihenfolge der Verse 16 und 17: Nach dem masoretischen Text geht der mit dem Buchstaben *'ayin* beginnende V. 16 dem mit *pe* beginnenden V. 17 voraus, d. h., das alphabetische Akrostichon hat hier die Reihenfolge *'ayin–pe*, die auch der üblichen Abfolge im hebräischen Alphabet entspricht. In 4QLam dagegen finden sich die beiden Verse in der umgekehrten Reihenfolge *pe–'ayin*; auffälligerweise haben im masoretischen Text die Akrosticha Klgl 2, 3 und 4 ebenfalls die Reihenfolge *pe–'ayin*, sodass Klgl 1 in diesem Punkt seit jeher in einer gewissen Spannung zu den drei nachfolgenden Gedichten steht.[17] Es könnte sich daher bei der Abfolge *'ayin–pe* im masoretischen Text von Klgl 1 um eine nachträgliche 'Modernisierung' handeln,[18] doch ebensogut

[15] Cross, "Prosody of Lamentations 1," 139.

[16] Siehe dazu im einzelnen Cross, "Prosody of Lamentations 1," *passim*; Ders., DJD XVI, 229–237; Schäfer, "Text der Klagelieder," 132–146.

[17] Berges, *Klagelieder*, 77, argumentiert, nach dem heutigen Wissensstand sei "davon auszugehen, dass Klgl 2, das älteste Lied der Sammlung, die weniger gebräuchliche Alphabetfolge *(pe–ajin)* aufwies"; im chronologisch nachfolgenden Gedicht Klgl 1, das sich stark an Klgl 2 anlehne, habe man vielleicht absichtlich die umgekehrte Abfolge *'ayin–pe* gewählt, um "die beiden Gedichte besser von einander zu unterscheiden."

[18] Möglicherweise wollte man "die akrostichische Sammlung nicht gleich mit einer

könnte auch die umgekehrte Abfolge in 4QLam das Resultat einer nachträglichen Vereinheitlichung mit Klgl 2–4 sein. Da inhaltliche Indizien fehlen, läßt sich die Frage, welche Abfolge in Klgl 1 die urspüngliche war, rein textkritisch nicht beantworten.[19]

Zu erwähnen ist in diesem Zusammenhang noch, dass sich in 4QLam auch der Text von V. 17 durch eine hinzugefügte Glosse und einige Textvarianten vom masoretischen Text unterscheidet;[20] diese Unterschiede können aber hier mit einer Ausnahme unberücksichtigt bleiben, da die Glosse ohnehin ausscheidet und die übrigen Varianten sich nur unwesentlich auf die Struktur des ursprünglichen Gedichts auswirken. Die erwähnte Ausnahme besteht in der Lesart צפה anstelle von צוה am Anfang von V. 17b. Nach dem syntaktisch etwas unebenen masoretischen Text hat Jahwe "bezüglich Jakobs dessen Nachbarn befohlen, dass sie ihm zu Feinden würden"; nach 4QLam dagegen hat der Herr "Jakob aufgelauert:[21] Seine Feinde haben ihn umstellt." Die drastische Aussage, dass Jahwe Jakob "auflauert", fügt sich nach den Bildern פרשׂ רשׁת in V. 13b und נת דרך in V. 15c gut in den "Gerichts"-Kontext dieser Passage ein und der anstößiger Anthropomorphismus wäre ein gutes Motiv für eine spätere Änderung von צפה in צוה. Freilich könnte grundsätzlich jede der beiden Lesarten durch einen einfachen phonologischen Irrtum aus der anderen hervorgegangen sein. Unter syntaktischem Aspekt ist צוה,[22] unter theologischem Aspekt jedoch צפה die *lectio difficilior*. Der andere in die Struktur von Klgl 1 eingreifende und deshalb hier zu erörternde Unterschied zwischen 4QLam und dem masoretischen Text besteht in den beiden verschiedenen Fassungen von V. 7, die einander in der folgenden Synopse gegenübergestellt sind:[23]

ungewöhnlichen Alphabetfolge beginnen lassen" (Berges, *Klagelieder*, 77). Dieser Gesichtspunkt spricht m.E. eher dafür, dass die im masoretischen Text bezeugte 'gewöhnliche' Alphabetfolge erst bei einer Redaktion der Klagelieder-Sammlung hergestellt wurde, wohingegen Berges ihn anscheinend zugunsten der Authentizität der masoretischen Textabfolge anführt.

[19] Cross, DJD XVI, 236, bezweifelt, dass in dieser Sache überhaupt eine Antwort möglich ist: "I do not believe that the question can be answered."

[20] Siehe dazu Schäfer, "Text der Klagelieder," 143–144, und *BHQ, Megilloth*, 58 und 119*.

[21] Vergleiche zu diesem Gebrauch von צפה mit Präp. ל insbesondere Ps 37,32a.

[22] Cross hält die Syntax der masoretischen Fassung für "extremely awkward, if not impossible", die Lesart von 4QLam hingegen "makes admirable sense." DJD XVI, 237, und ebenso bereits in "Prosody of Lamentations 1," 147.

[23] Leerräume im Text sind durch die synoptische Darstellung bedingt; Fehlstellen im Text von 4QLam sind dagegen durch eckige Klammern gekennzeichnet.

MT (V. 7a.b)	זָכְרָה יְרוּשָׁלַםִ יְמֵי עָנְיָהּ וּמְרוּדֶיהָ כֹּל מַחֲמֻדֶיהָ אֲשֶׁר הָיוּ מִימֵי קֶדֶם
4QLam (II,2/3)	זכורה יהוה [כו]ל מכאובנו אשר היו מימי קדם
MT (V. 7c)	בִּנְפֹל עַמָּהּ בְּיַד־צָר וְאֵין עוֹזֵר לָהּ
4QLam (II,3/4)	בנפל [עמ]ה ביד צר ואין עוזר
MT (V. 7d)	רָאוּהָ צָרִים שָׂחֲקוּ עַל מִשְׁבַּתֶּהָ׃
4QLam (II,4/5)	צריה שחקו על [כו]ל משבריה

Der masoretische Text dieses Verses hat immer wieder zu literarkritischen Operationen angeregt, denn wie schon eingangs erwähnt bestehen alle übrigen Verse des Gedichts aus drei Bikola, wohingegen V. 7 als einziger *vier* Bikola umfasst und somit aus dem Rahmen fällt. Die Textzeugen, die vor der Entdeckung von 4QLam bekannt waren, helfen hier nicht weiter, weil sie alle bereits auf dem masoretischen Text beruhen.

Kaiser fasst in seinem Klagelieder-Kommentar von 1992 die Lage der Forschung kurz und bündig zusammen: "Als Ergänzungen kommen entweder V. b oder V. c in Frage. Die Mehrheit der Ausleger streicht V. 7b, der den Verlust ihrer einstigen Kostbarkeiten als Grund des Kummers nennt . . ."[24] – der Gedanke ist sinngemäß folgendermaßen zu ergänzen: . . . denn ein solch materialistischer Aspekt wird von den Vertretern dieser These als störend empfunden. Kaiser selbst schließt sich der alternativen Auffassung an: ". . . vermutlich verhält es sich genau umgekehrt: V. 7b konnte einem Späteren als zu materialistisch erscheinen, so dass er in V. 7c die Preisgabe ihres Volkes durch die Feinde und das Ausbleiben der Hilfe nachtrug".

Blickt man jedoch auf 4QLam, so trifft keine dieser beiden Auffassungen zu. Vielmehr spricht der hier überlieferte kürzere Text dafür, dass die vermutete Erweiterung in V. 7aß zu suchen ist; möglicherweise wurde sie in Anlehnung an die Wendung זכר־עניי ומרודי ("das Denken an mein Leid und Irrsal") aus Klgl 3,19 formuliert.

Neben dieser sich abzeichnenden textkritischen Lösung einer bislang ausschließlich literarkritisch verhandelten Frage, ist freilich nicht zu übersehen, dass 4QLam auch sonst in diesem Vers beträchtlich vom masoretischen Text abweicht: Das Subjekt des Satzes ist nicht Jerusalem wie in der masoretischen Fassung, sondern Jahwe, und das Verb steht nicht in der 3. Pers. f. sg. Perf., sondern im emphatischen Imperativ; also nicht "Jerusalem gedenkt . . ." wie im MT, son-

[24] *Klagelieder*, 125.

dern "Gedenke doch, Jahwe . . .".[25] Dieser gänzlich anderen Aussagerichtung entspricht als nächstes in V. 7b auch ein anderes Objekt und ein verändertes Suffix, nämlich מכאובנו "unseren Schmerz/unser Leiden" an Stelle von מַחֲמֻדֶּיהָ "ihre (f. sg.) Kostbarkeiten" im masoretischen Text.

In 4QLam fehlt am Ende von V. 7c die suffigierte Präposition לָהּ, also "niemand half" statt dem "niemand half *ihr*" des masoretischen Textes. Interessanterweise hat auch die Vulgata hier kein explizites Äquivalent für ein hebräisches לָהּ – der lateinische Text lautet: *cum caderet populus eius in manu hostili et non esset auxiliator.*

Im letzten Bikolon (V. 7d) fehlt in 4QLam das erste der beiden Verben, was die Syntax deutlich vereinfacht; gerade das Verb ראה ist jedoch ein markantes Strukturelement in den Versen 7–11. צריה mit Suffix 3. f. sg. weicht ebenfalls vom MT ab, hat aber überraschenderweise eine Entsprechung sowohl in der Septuaginta (G) (οἱ ἐχθροὶ αὐτῆς ἐγέλασαν), obwohl diese sonst beinahe sklavisch dem MT folgt, als auch in der Peschitta (S) (ܐܠܘ̈ܨܝܗ̇).

Auch beim letzten Wort des Verses scheint die S (ܬܒܪܗ̇) die Lesart von 4QLam (משבריה) zu stützen; möglicherweise handelt es sich aber auch um eine etwas freiere Wiedergabe des *hapax legomenon* מִשְׁבַּתֶּהָ "ihre Vertilgungen", mit dem sich alle alten Übersetzungen mehr oder weniger erfolglos abmühen (z. B. G: κατοικεσίᾳ αὐτῆς via ישׁב; Vulgata rätselhaft: *sabbata eius*). Die Lesart von 4QLam könnte aber auch leicht durch ein Versehen des Kopisten aus der graphisch sehr ähnlichen Form des masoretischen Textes entstanden sein. Das in 4QLam dem משבריה vorangehende ל[..] ist wohl mit Cross[26] eher zu כול zu ergänzen, könnte aber auch eine Dittographie von על sein; ein Urteil wird durch den allgemein etwas nachlässigen Charakter der Handschrift erschwert.

Als Zwischenergebnis ist zunächst festzuhalten: Unabhängig davon, wie man die abweichenden Lesarten im Detail bewertet, bezeugt 4QLam für V. 7 einen sinnvollen, kürzeren und eigenständigen Text.

Die beiden ersten Worte dieses Textes, זכורה יהוה, stellen nach textkritischen Kriterien gegenüber dem זכרה ירושלם der masoretischen Fassung die ursprünglichere Lesart dar. Der emphatische

[25] Ein ähnlicher Wechsel der Redeperspektive finden sich auch in den Versen 11c und 13c.
[26] DJD XVI, 233.

Imperativ זכורה kann als *lectio difficilior* angesehen werden, denn besonders in der defektiven Schreibweise זכרה lag auf dem Hintergrund der zahlreichen feminen Formen des Kontexts die Fehlinterpretation als 3. fem. sg. nahe; eine Verwechslung der beiden Verbformen in umgekehrter Richtung ist dagegen eher unwahrscheinlich. Als das zur 3. fem. sg. passende Subjekt befand sich zudem ירושלם in V. 8a bereits in unmittelbarer Nähe; in Manuskripten mit einer Textanordnung wie 3QLam stand ירושלם etwas links von זכרה in der folgenden Zeile und konnte durch einfache *aberratio oculi* leicht mit זכרה verbunden werden.

Schwieriger zu beurteilen ist das Verhältnis zwischen dem in 4QLam folgenden Objekt [כו]ל מכאובנו und dem ימי עניה ומרודיה כל מחמדיה der masoretischen Überlieferung. Auffällig sind vor allem in 4QLam das Suffix der 1. Person pl. aus stilistischen und im masoretischen Text das Substantiv מחמדיה, ‘ihre Kostbarkeiten’, aus inhaltlichen Gründen.[27] Und noch zwei weitere Beobachtungen sind mit zu bedenken: Zum einen kommen sowohl die Wendung כל מחמדיה (V. 10a; vgl. außerdem מחמודיהם in V. 11b) als auch das Substantiv מכאוב (zweimal in V. 12b und nochmals in V. 18b) im nachfolgenden Kontext vor, und zum anderen hat offensichtlich die Deutung des seltenen ומרודיה, ‘und ihre Heimatlosigkeit/ihr Umherirren’, allen antiken Übersetzern Schwierigkeiten bereitet.[28] Die bisher m. E. plausibelste Deutung dieses komplexen Befunds hat Cross vorgetragen.[29] Demnach ist davon auszugehen, dass weder die knappe Lesart von 4QLam noch das wortreiche Pendant im masoretischen Text den ursprünglichen Text bewahrt hat. Am Anfang stand vielmehr מרודיה oder כל מרודיה. Wie der Blick in die alten Übersetzungen belegt, lagen bei diesem seltenen Wort Missverständnisse oder Umdeutungen sozusagen in der Luft. So entstand zunächst – wahrscheinlich durch einen Abschreibfehler, der zur Vorwegnahme dieser gleich darauf in

[27] “The inappropriateness of מחמדיה, ‘her delights’, in this context is evident.” Cross, DJD XVI, 233.

[28] Nach heutiger Auffassung ist מרודיה der suffigierte Abstraktplural eines von der Wurzel רוד abgeleitetes Nomens (vgl. Gesenius[18] III, 737, und HALAT II, 598 *s.v.* *מָרוּד sowie Rudolph, *Text*, 101); die Vulgata (*et praevaricationis*, “und [ihrer] Untreue”) ebenso wie Aquila (καὶ ἀποστάσεων [αὐτῆς]) und das Targum (ומרדא) deuten es dagegen von der Wurzel מרד her; die Peschitta verwendet den phonetisch nächstliegenden syrischen Ausdruck ܘܡܪܕܘܬܗ, ‘ihre Züchtigung’, der jedoch semantisch zur Wurzel רדה gehört.

[29] DJD XVI, 232–233; vgl. auch Cross, “Prosody of Lamentations 1,” 140.

V. 10a vorkommenden Wendung führte – die Variante כל מחמדיה. Der masoretische Text hätte folglich in den Worten מרודיה כל מחמדיה eine Doppellesart aus ursprünglichem Text plus Variante bewahrt; das vorausgehende עניה dürfte hinzugekommen sein unter dem Einfluss von 3,19, wo ein zweites Mal innerhalb der Klagelieder das seltene מרוד vorkommt, und zwar neben עניה und verbunden mit dem Imperativ זכר. Der Eintrag von ימי schließlich ist wohl ein Versuch, die Syntax zu "retten", wobei vielleicht מימי aus dem nachfolgenden Kolon als Anregung diente.

Bei der Lesart [כו]ל מכאובנו (vielleicht zunächst מכאובה und dann nachträglich verschrieben zu מכאובנו) in 4QLam handelt es sich entweder um eine andere Variante zu כל מרודיה oder wahrscheinlicher – so Cross – bereits um einen frühen Versuch, das verderbte כל מחמדיה unter Aufnahme der Vokabel מכאוב aus V. 12b.18b zu emendieren.

Folgt man diesen Überlegungen, so stand mit hoher Wahrscheinlichkeit an Stelle von V. 7a.b des masoretischen Textes ursprünglich ein einzelnes Bikolon von normaler Länge; dieser V. 7a* lautete:

זכרה יהוה כל מרודיה   אשר היו מימי קדם

Ausgehend von diesem rekonstruierten Text des Verses 7 sowie der in 4QLam belegten umgekehrten Abfolge der Verse 16 und 17 soll nun im Folgenden untersucht werden, wie sich der veränderte Wortlaut auf die poetische Struktur von Klgl 1 auswirkt.

2. *Die Struktur des masoretischen Textes von Klgl 1*

Eine umfassende und detaillierte Strukturanalyse des masoretischen Textes der Klagelieder hat Berges in seinem unlängst erschienenen Kommentar vorgetragen.[30] Die wichtigsten Einsichten zur Struktur von Klgl 1 seien zunächst kurz skizziert: Als erstes und grundlegendes Gestaltungselement fällt ins Auge, dass in V. 1–11 von Jerusalem fast nur in der 3. Person die Rede ist, wohingegen in V. 12–22 die personifizierte Stadt fast durchgehend in der 1. Person spricht. Bemerkenswerte Ausnahmen, sind 9c und 11c (1. Person im 3. Person-Kontext) sowie V. 17 (3. Person im 1. Person-Kontext). Dieser Befund legt nahe, dass der Text zwischen V. 11 und V. 12 eine *Mittelachse* besitzt.

[30] Berges, *Klagelieder*: zur Struktur von Klgl 1 insbesondere die Seiten 90–92.

Die beiden sich daraus ergebenden “Sektionen” untergliedert Berges im Anschluss an Renkema[31] in vier “Stanzen” mit jeweils zwei “Sub-Stanzen”:

1. Sektion (V. 1–11)

Stanze I (V. 1–6)	Sub-Stanze (1–3)	3 + 3	11 Verse
	Sub-Stanze (4–6)		
Stanze II (V. 7–11)	Sub-Stanze (7–9)	3 + 2	
	Sub-Stanze (10–11)		

2. Sektion (V. 12–22)

Stanze III (V. 12–16)	Sub-Stanze (12–13)	3 + 2	11 Verse
	Sub-Stanze (14–16)		
Stanze IV (V. 17–22)	Sub-Stanze (17–19)	3 + 3	
	Sub-Stanze (20–22)		

Diese Gliederung lässt sich anhand vieler einzelner Kompositionselemente (Wortfeldgruppen, Inklusionen, Wechsel der Redeperspektive) belegen, wie die folgende Auswahl der auffälligsten Merkmale zeigt.

Stanze I: Die erste Sub-Stanze (V. 1–3) wird durch eine Wiederholung von ישׁבה (1a // 3c) und בגוים (1b // 3b) sowie durch die beiden zum selben Wortfeld gehörenden Begriffe מס (1c) und רב עבדה (3a) gewissermaßen von einer dreifachen Inklusio zusammengehalten. In der zweiten Substanze (V. 4–6) hat die Wiederholung von ציון bzw. בת־ציון (4a // 6a) dieselbe Funktion. Die Einheit der Stanze zeigt sich an einer dreifachen Entsprechung in den Versen 3 und 6: גלתה יהודה (3a) // ויצא מן בת־ציון (6a); לא מצאה (3b) // לא־מצאו (6b) und רדפיה (3c) // רודף (6c).

Stanze II: Die erste Sub-Stanze ist durch die Wiederholung von ירושלם (7a // 8a) und durch eine doppelte Inklusio mit זכרה (7a) // לא זכרה (9a) und עניה (7a) // את־עניי (9c) gekennzeichnet. Die kürzere zweite Sub-Stanze wird durch das Begriffspaar כל־מחמדיה (10a) und מחמודיהם (11b) zusammengehalten. Die Einheit der Stanze zeigt sich am fünfmaligen Gebrauch des Verbums ראה, das in allen fünf Versen je einmal vorkommt (7d, 8b, 9c, 10b, 11c), und insbesondere an der zweimaligen Bitte ראה יהוה (9c // 11c), durch welche die beiden Sub-Stanzen im jeweils letzten Bikolon auf ähn-

[31] J. Renkema, “The Literary Structure of Lamentations (I),” in: W. van der Meer und J. C. de Moor (Hg.), *The Structural Analysis of Biblical and Canaanite Poetry* (JSOT.S 74; Sheffield, 1988), 294–320, bes. 305; ähnlich bereits A. Condamin, *Poèmes de la Bible. Avec une Introduction sur la Strophique Hebraïque* (Paris, 1933), 48–49.

liche Weise miteinander verklammert sind wie die beiden Sub-Stanzen der ersten Stanze (V. 1–6) aufgrund der Entsprechungen in den Versen 3 und 6.

Stanze III: Die Verse 12–16 sind ganz als Rede Zions gestaltet. Sie wendet sich hier nicht an Jahwe wie zuvor (9c und 11c), sondern an außenstehende Dritte (כל־עברי דרך), die sie gewissermaßen als Zeugen aufruft (12a). "Die direkte Anrede an Passanten ... zu Beginn des zweiten Hauptteiles stellt eine wichtige Leserlenkung dar."[32] על־אלה am Beginn von V. 16 "hat konkludierenden Effekt."[33] Nach Ansicht von Berges heben sich die beiden Sub-Stanzen durch unterschiedliche thematische Schwerpunkte voneinander ab: Die erste (V. 12–13) "konzentriert sich auf den Zorn JHWHs, die folgende (V 14–16) auf das völlige Unvermögen Jerusalems, sich aus ihrer Lage angesichts der übermächtigen Feinde zu befreien (V 14c.16c)."[34]

Stanze IV: Der Beginn der vierten Stanze (V. 17–22) ist erneut durch einen Wechsel der Redeperspektive markiert. V. 17 ist eine kurze Klage des Sprechers, welche "die Szenerie für die anschließenden Zionsworte (V 18ff) vorbereitet."[35] Die "überraschende Rückkehr des Sprechers in V 17"[36] unterbricht die Rede Zions in der zweiten Sektion des Gedichts genau in der Mitte. Die Einteilung in zwei Sub-Stanzen ergibt sich aus der jeweils unterschiedlichen Redeperspektive: V. 17–19 sind Rede über Jahwe, V. 20–22 dagegen Rede zu ihm.[37] Die letzte Sub-Stanze ist außerdem durch die beiden Bitten "Sieh ..." (20a) und "es komme ... vor dich" (22a) sowie die Wiederholung des Motivworts "Herz" (20b // 22c) eingefasst. Das Verb עלל (12b, 22a.b) schließlich bildet eine Inklusio um die ganze zweite Sektion des Gedichts: Was Jahwe Jerusalem antat, soll er auch ihren Feinden antun.[38]

Über diese Gliederung in vier Stanzen hinaus gibt es, wie Condamin schon 1933 entdeckt hat, in Klgl 1 eine ganze Reihe von auffälligen symmetrischen Wiederholungen einzelner Textelemente;[39] diese scheinen sozusagen an der zwischen V. 11 und V. 12 verlaufenden Mittelachse

[32] Berges, *Klagelieder*, 89.
[33] Ebd., 92.
[34] Ebd., 92
[35] Ebd., 92
[36] Ebd., 117
[37] Ebd., 117.
[38] Ebd., 92.
[39] Condamin, *Poèmes*, 47: "répetitions symétriques d'un ou de plusieurs mots".

gespiegelt zu sein, sodass eine *konzentrische Struktur* entsteht. Im Text von "außen" nach "innen" fortschreitend nennt Condamin die folgenden Entsprechungen:[40]

רבתי	(1)	//	רבות	(22)
אין לה מנחם . . . לאיבים	(2)	//	אין מנחם לי . . . איבי	(21)
המצרים	(3)	//	צר	(20)
כהניה	(4)	//	כהני	(19)
יהוה . . . הלכו שבי	(5)	//	יהוה . . . הלכו בשבי	(18)
ציון	(6)	//	ציון	(17)
פרשׂ	(10)	//	פרשׂ	(13)
ראה . . . והביטה	(11)	//	הביטו וראו	(12)

Zu 6 // 17 ist anzumerken, dass in V. 6 genaugenommen von בת־ציון die Rede ist und ציון auch noch in V. 4 genannt wird; dieses Paar gehört demnach zu den weniger signifikanten. In den Verspaaren 7 // 16, 8 // 15 und 9 // 14 scheint es überhaupt keine näheren Entsprechungen zu geben. Renkema, der Condamins Beobachtungen ein halbes Jahrhundert später eigenständig wiederholt hat, ergänzt zwar:[41]

צר ואין עוזר	(7)	//	רחק מנחם . . . אויב	(16)
מכבדים	(8)	//	אבירי	(15)
יהוה	(9)	//	אדני	(14)

Aber die Korrespondenz liegt bei diesen drei Paaren längst nicht so klar auf der Hand. Die eindeutigen symmetrischen Entsprechungen bestehen demnach einerseits zwischen den beiden innersten, jeweils nur zwei Verse umfassenden Sub-Stanzen und andererseits zwischen den Stanzen I und IV.

3. *Offene Fragen zur Struktur von Klgl 1*

Die im vorigen Abschnitt nachgezeichnete Analyse der poetischen Einheiten und die sich daraus ergebende Gliederung erscheinen in hohem Maße plausibel und sind weithin überzeugend. Dennoch bleiben einige auffällige Details, die zumindest die Frage aufwerfen, ob in dem skizzierten Bild nicht noch die eine oder andere Modifikation nötig ist.

[40] Ebd., 48.
[41] Renkema, "Literary Structure," 296.

Erstens hat sich, obwohl das Geflecht der strukturierenden Elemente in Klgl 1 erkennbar dicht und planvoll angelegt ist, daraus keinerlei Hinweis ergeben, der verständlich machen würde, weshalb in V. 7 ein zusätzliches viertes Bikolon vorhanden ist; jedenfalls scheint es sich dabei nicht um ein Strukturelement zu handeln.

Und zweitens kommt insbesondere die spiegelbildliche Architektur des Gedichts (6+5 // 5+6 Verse) – und damit zusammenhängend seine von Condamin und Renkema beschriebene konzentrische Struktur –[42] zumindest in dem von Berges entworfenen Gesamtbild m. E. noch nicht genügend zum Tragen. So werden zwei bedeutsame Störungen der konzentrischen Struktur nicht als solche wahrgenommen. Bezeichnenderweise sind es gerade die Verse 16 und 17 von denen diese Störungen ausgehen.

V. 16 nimmt auffallend deutlich Bezug auf V. 2; nicht weniger als vier[43] Motive kehren in derselben Reihenfolge wieder:

בכו תבכה	(2a)	//	אני בוכיה	(16a)
דמעתה על לחיה	(2a)	//	עיני ירדה מים	(16a)
אין־לה מנחם	(2b)	//	רחק ממני מנחם	(16b)
היו לה לאיבים	(2c)	//	גבר אויב	(16c)

Die daraus sich ergebende starke Korrespondenz zwischen diesen beiden Versen, bzw. zwischen Stanze I und Stanze III wurde zwar wahrgenommen, aber anscheinend nicht in die Überlegungen zur Struktur des Gedichts einbezogen, obwohl (oder weil?) sie nicht mit der der offensichtlich auch von Berges angenommenen konzentrischen Struktur bzw. der "Spiegelbildlichkeit" der beiden Gedichthälften[44] in Einklang zu bringen ist.

Anders als V. 16, bei dem sämtliche Bezüge genau auf einen einzigen korrespondierenden Vers fokussiert sind, nimmt V. 17 mit breiter gestreuten Verbindungen, die aber dennoch genauso deutlich zu erkennen sind, Bezug auf Stanze II. Dies geschieht durch eine ganze Reihe *sprachlicher* Anklänge, insbesondere an die Verse 8 und 10, aber auch an V. 9:

[42] Condamin, *Poèmes*, 47–48; Renkema, "Literary Structure," 296–297.

[43] Berges, *Klagelieder*, 117, fasst die beiden zuerst genannten Entsprechungen zusammen und zählt folglich nur drei Motive, die auf V. 2 zurück weisen.

[44] "Die Symmetrie, die auf der Ebene der Sektionen notwendigerweise verloren geht, da elf nicht regelmäßiger zu teilen ist als in sechs zu fünf Strophen, wird durch die Spiegelbildlichkeit beider Hälften (6,5 // 5,6) wiederhergestellt." Berges, *Klagelieder*, 92.

ירושלם	(8a)	//	ירושלם	(17c)
לנידה היתה	(8a)	//	היתה . . . לנדה	(17c)
אין מנחם לה	(9b)	//	אין מנחם לה	(17a)
ידו פרש	(10a)	//	פרשה . . . בידיה	(17a)
צויתה	(10c)	//	צוה[45]	(17b)
צר	(10a)	//	צריו	(17b)

Außerdem besteht darüber hinaus noch eine *thematische* Verbindung mit V. 9:

טמאתה בשוליה	(9a)	//	היתה . . . לנדה	(17c)

Es gibt also neben dem Rückbezug von V. 16 auf V. 2 auch eine ebenso deutliche Korrespondenz zwischen V. 17 und den Versen 8–10. Auf der Ebene der Stanzen wären demnach Stanze I und Stanze III sowie Stanze II und Stanze IV aufeinander bezogen, sodass man annehmen müsste, in Klgl 1 werde die konzentrische Grundstruktur noch von einer *parallelen* Struktur überlagert. Solch ein komplizierter Befund kann zwar nicht grundsätzlich ausgeschlossen werden, bliebe aber angesichts der sonst sehr klaren und strengen Gestaltung des Gedichts doch überraschend.

4. Die Struktur des rekonstruierten ursprünglichen Textes von Klgl 1

Die oben im zweiten Abschnitt vorgestellten Textvarianten aus der Handschrift 4QLam stellen sozusagen eine Minimalauswahl der Daten dar, die für eine einigermaßen gesicherte Rekonstruktion des vormasoretischen Textes von Klgl 1 zur Verfügung stehen. Übernimmt man nun an Stelle von V. 7a.b des masoretischen Textes den oben nach 4QLam rekonstruierten V. 7a* und vertauscht man außerdem 4QLam entsprechend die Reihenfolge der Verse 16 und 17, so zeigt sich bei einem erneuten Blick auf die Struktur, dass die im vorigen Abschnitt beschriebenen Störungen ganz und gar behoben sind.

V. 7* besteht nur noch aus drei Bikola und fällt damit nicht länger aus dem Rahmen, sondern entspricht stichometrisch nun genau dem Maß der übrigen einundzwanzig Verse des Gedichts. Berges hat die Annahme dieses kürzeren Textes nach 4QLam aus zwei Gründen abgelehnt, die sich bei näherer Betrachtung aber als nicht stichhaltig erweisen. Sein erster Grund ist eine von ihm in 4QLam vermutete

[45] Nach dem masoretischen Text! 4QLam liest hier צפה; vgl. dazu oben S. 245.

ideologische Tendenz: "Gegen die Lesart von 4QLam spricht . . ., dass Jerusalem gezielt in den Hintergrund tritt, da weibliche Formen (זוללה "verachtet" 11c; שֹׁממה "verachtet" 13c; דוה "krank" 13c) bewusst in männliche umgesetzt wurden."[46] Die Beobachtung, dass an den genannten Stellen in 4QLam männliche statt der im masoretischen Text bezeugten weiblichen Formen verwendet werden, ist selbstverständlich zutreffend, doch dahinter steht nicht etwa das Bemühen, Jerusalem in den Hintergrund treten zu lassen, sondern ein schlichtes Missverständnis: Das in den Versen 11c und 13c auftretende "Ich" ist irrtümlich als das "Ich" des Dichters – nach überlieferter Auffassung[47] Jeremia – verstanden worden.[48] Aller Wahrscheinlichkeit nach dürfte ein vorausgehendes "Gedenke Jahwe ihrer Heimatlosigkeit . . .", das ja offensichtlich nicht von der personifizierten Stadt selbst gesprochen sein kann, dieses Missverständnis durchaus gefördert haben; gerade die maskulinen Formen in 11c und 13c könnten demnach auch als Indiz dafür gewertet werden, dass in V. 7a seit jeher schon ein זכרה יהוה stand.

Das andere und offenbar für Berges ausschlaggebende Argument gegen die Variante von 4QLam basiert unmittelbar auf der oben dargestellten formalen Analyse: "Ein solcher Imperativ [sc. 'Gedenke, Jahwe . . .'] widerspricht . . . dem Aufbau der Stanze, in der die Bitten Jerusalems jeweils am Ende der Sub-Stanzen stehen (9c.11c)."[49] Bei leicht veränderter Betrachtungsweise kann man aber auch zum genau entgegengesetzten Schluss kommen: Ohne dass die Untergliederung in 3+2 Verse deswegen hinfällig würde, erweisen sich die Verse 7–11 nicht nur durch das in jedem Vers einmal vorkommende ראה[50] als eine Einheit, sondern eben auch durch die dreifache Anrufung Jahwes, die wie ein Dreiklang am Anfang (זכרה יהוה, 7a*), in der Mitte (ראה יהוה, 9c) und am Ende (ראה יהוה, 11c) der Stanze steht. Der Imperativ זכרה יהוה bereitet außerdem die beiden Hilferufe Zions ראה יהוה in V. 9c und V. 11c vor.

V. 16 steht nun nicht mehr am Ende von Stanze III, sondern am Beginn von Stanze IV und leitet hier mit dem "konkludierenden"[51]

---

[46] Berges, *Klagelieder*, 89.

[47] Vergleiche die Präskripte vor Klgl 1,1 in Septuaginta und Vulgata.

[48] So auch Cross, DJD XVI, 235: "Evidently in the textual tradition that these readings represent, the 'I' of personified Zion has been incorrectly taken as the 'I' of the poet."

[49] Berges, *Klagelieder*, 89.

[50] Siehe oben S. 250 zur Struktur von Stanze II.

[51] Vergleiche Berges, *Klagelieder*, 92.

על־אלה die letzte entscheidende Wendung des Gedichts zur Gerichtsdoxologie (V. 18a) und zur abschließenden Bittklage ein. Außerdem stellt V. 16 in dieser neuen, d. h., seiner mutmaßlich urspünglichen, Position nicht länger einen Fremdkörper innerhalb der konzentrischen Struktur dar, sondern fügt sich ihr völlig ein: Erstens ergibt sich inhaltlich eine starke symmetrische Entsprechung zwischen ילכו בלא־כח לפני רודף in V. 6c und היו... שוממים כי גבר אויב in V. 16c, und zweitens unterstreicht V. 16 durch die sprachliche und motivische Wiederaufnahme von V. 2 die rahmende Funktion der Stanzen I und IV.

Die Stanzen II und III in der Mittelposition sind allein schon durch ihren Umfang von 3+2 und 2+3 Versen (gegenüber den jeweils 3+3 Versen der Stanzen I und IV) aufeinander bezogen. Dieser enge Bezug kommt auch in weiteren strukturierenden Textelementen zum Ausdruck. Wie Condamin und Renkema übereinstimmend beobachtet haben, schließt unmittelbar an der Mittelachse des Textes der Beginn von Stanze III (הביטו וראו . . .; V. 12a) sprachlich unmittelbar an das Ende von Stanze II (ראה . . . והביטה . . ., V. 11c) an;[52] diese Entsprechung gehört zu grundlegenden Indizien für die konzentrische Struktur des Gedichts.[53] Inhaltlich korresponiert das Thema "Sünde/Unreinheit Jerusalems" von Stanze II mit dem Thema "Gerichtszorn Jahwes" von Stanze III; als Kernaussagen stehen einander gegenüber חטא חטאה ירושלם (8a) und גת דרך יהוה לבתולת בת־יהודה (11b).

Indem V. 17 an die Stelle von V. 16 rückt und somit den Schlussvers von Stanze III bildet ergeben sich zusätzliche Entsprechungen, die das Gesamtbild weiter abrunden. Die starken sprachlichen Anklänge in V. 17 an die Verse 8–10 (insbesondere die durch ירושלם . . . לנידה היתה in V. 8a und היתה ירושלם לנדה V. 17c gebildete Inklusio) wurden bereits genannt.[54] Darüber hinaus ist aufgrund der neuen, d. h. auch in diesem Fall wohl ursprünglichen Position von V. 17 die dreigliedrige Motivkette mit dem Verb פרשׂ (Verse 10a, 13b, 17a) ganz in den Mittelteil des Gedichts eingeholt. Vor allem aber zeigt sich nun, dass "die überraschende Rückkehr des Sprechers in V 17",[55] d. h., der zwischenzeitliche kurze Rückfall der Rede in die 3. Person, formal exakt der Vorwegnahme der Rede in der 1. Person in V. 9c

[52] Das Verb הביט kommt sonst in Klgl 1 nicht vor, was der Beobachtung noch zusätzlich Gewicht verleiht; vgl. Condamin, *Poèmes*, 48.

[53] Renkema, "Literary Structure," 296.

[54] Siehe oben S. 254.

[55] Berges, *Klagelieder*, 117.

und V. 11c entspricht. Dabei fungiert das eindrückliche Bild vom Kelter tretenden Herrn (15c) als Überleitung, in der das Objekt, die "Jungfrau Tochter Juda" bereits wieder in der 3. Person erscheint, sodass der anschließende Wechsel in die 3. Person mit "Zion" als Subjekt (V.17a) weich vonstatten geht. Die drei Bikola von V. 17 entfalten das vorausgehende Bild und fassen die Aspekte der Verwüstung nochmals zusammen: Es gibt keinen Tröster, weil es Jahwes Gerichtshandeln ist, das Jerusalem erleidet; er selbst hat den Feind geschickt und Jerusalem der Verachtung preisgegeben.

Die beiden nachfolgend abgedruckten Schemata sind ein Versuch, die hier beschriebene poetische Struktur des rekonstruierten Textes von Klgl 1 nochmals zusammenfassend zu veranschaulichen.

Schema 1 zeigt die innerhalb des Gedichts auftretenden Entsprechungen und die sich daraus ergebende Textstruktur. Elemente, die den Zusammenhang der einzelnen Untereinheiten (d. h. der Stanzen und Sub-Stanzen bzw. des Korpus) signalisieren, sind im Schema grau hinterlegt. Elemente, die zur konzentrischen Struktur gehören, sind eingerahmt bzw. unterstrichen und durch verbindende Linien einander zugeordnet.[56] Bei dieser Darstellungsweise tritt deutlich zutage, wie einerseits ein dichtes Geflecht von Textbezügen das Korpus (Verse 7–15.17) des ersten Klageliedes zu einer durchgeformten Einheit verbindet und wie andererseits die Entsprechungen zwischen den Versen 1–6 und den Versen 16.18–22 einen vollkommen symmetrischen "Rahmen" bilden, der das Korpus umschließt.

Schema 2 zeigt, wie sich auf der inhaltlichen Ebene die Betrachtungsweise im Verlauf des Gedichts sozusagen von außen nach innen[57] bewegt und wie parallel dazu die theologische Deutung des Geschehens von der Diagnose des zerbrochenen Gottesverhältnisses über die Schilderung der kollektiven Unreinheit und das darüber ergehende Gericht schließlich zur Annahme des Gerichts führt und sogar zu einem ersten zaghaften Versuch, die Gottesbeziehung jenseits des Gerichts wieder anzuknüpfen:

[56] Die Entsprechungen zwischen den Versen 3 und 6 (גלתה 3a // ויצא ... כל־הדרה 6a; לא מצאה 3b // לא מצאו 6b; כל־רדפיה 3c // רודף 6c) sowie zwischen V. 18 und V. 20 (כי פיהו מריתי 18a // כי מרו מריתי 20a) wurden im Schema nicht verzeichnet, um die ohnedies komplexe Darstellung nicht vollends zu überfrachten; diese Entsprechungen binden das erste und das letzte Sub-Stanzen Paar zur Stanze I bzw. Stanze IV zusammen. Am Gesamtbild ändert sich dadurch nichts.

[57] In der linken Spalte des Schemas ist die in der betreffenden Stanze jeweils dominierende und *explizit* genannte Bezeichnung für Jerusalem hervorgehoben; etwas eingerückt sind die flankierenden Synonyme aufgeführt; dabei steht "Juda" für das Umland Jerusalems und "Jakob" für die Bevölkerung.

Schema 1: Die Struktur und die tragenden Strukturelemente von Klgl 1

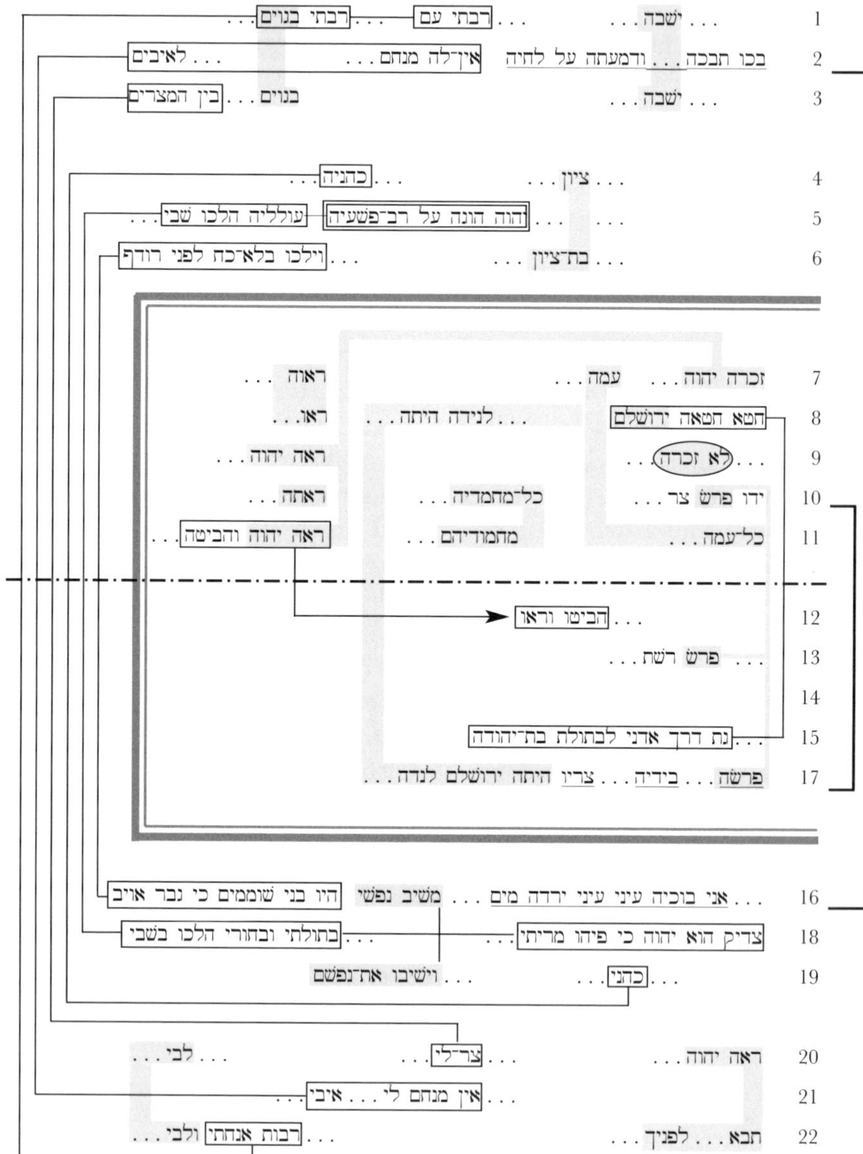

*Schema 2: Die inhaltliche Entwicklung in Klgl 1**

	Perspektive		*Gottesbeziehung*	
	sachlich			
1	העיר	*DIE STADT*		
2				
3	יהודה	Juda		
4	ציו	Zion		
5			רב־פשׁעיה	Verfehlungen
6	בת־ציון	Tochter Zion		
	persönlich		*Jerusalems Unreinheit*	
7	עמה	Bevölkerung		
8	ירושלם	*JERUSALEM*	חטא חטאה	Sünde
9			טמאה	Unreinheit
10			גוים באו מקדשה	Heiligtum entweiht
11	עמה	Bevölkerung		
			Jahwes Gericht	
12			חרון אפו	Zornesglut
13			אשׁ, רשת	Netz, Feuer
14		Jungfrau	נתנני . . . בידי. . .	Preisgabe an den Feind
15	בתולת בת־יהודה	Tochter Juda	גת דרך	"tritt die Kelter"
17	ירושלם	*JERUSALEM*	צפה* ליעקב	"lauert Jakob auf"
	ציון, יעקב	Zion, Jakob		
	individuell-vertraut		*Ergebung*	
16	אני	*ICH*	צדיק הוא יהוה	Gerichtsdoxologie
18			פיהו מריתי	Schuldbekenntnis
19				
20	לבי בקרבי	mein Herz in	מרו מריתי	Schuldbekenntnis
21		meinem Innern		
22			תבא ... לפניך	Vergeltungswunsch

Als Resultat kann festgehalten werden: Das erste Klagelied besitzt eine konzentrische Grundstruktur, bestehend aus einem Mittelteil oder Korpus (V. 7–15.17) und einem darum gelegten Rahmen (V. 1–6 und V. 16.18–22). In diese poetische Struktur fügen sich die aus 4QLam gewonnenen Textkorrekturen harmonisch ein, sodass insgesamt ein stimmigeres Bild entsteht, als es der masoretische Text bietet. Es spricht demnach vieles dafür, dass 4QLam in den hier untersuchten Fällen tatsächlich den ursprünglichen Text des Gedichtes besser bewahrt hat.

LEXICAL IGNORANCE AND THE ANCIENT VERSIONS OF PROVERBS

Jan de Waard

In the critical apparatus of the forthcoming *BHQ* edition of Proverbs the abbreviation "ign-lex", standing for "ignorance of lexical information", will sometimes be used to characterize a rendering of one or several of the ancient versions. The use of this term implies a judgment that the origin of the reading is to be found in the copyist's or translator's lack of data or understanding concerning their *Vorlage*. Ignorance can be specified with regard to cultural or geographic information and, linguistically, in reference to stylistic, syntactic, grammatical or lexical information. The limits of a paper oblige us to select only one specific instance of ignorance and for this the last one has been chosen.

It is, of course, inconceivable to deal in one paper with all the cases in Proverbs in which a lack of understanding of one of the ancient translators could be at stake. There also is no necessity to attend to all cases. Some, such as the hapax יַחֲרֹךְ in 12:27, can be excluded straightforwardly because both the ancient and the modern lack of understanding of its meaning are total. Others can be omitted because of their little interest. For example, in 25:11 the *hapax* form אָפְנָיו, "at its appropriate occasion" or "in a suitable way", has been correctly translated by Aquila, Theodotion, Symmachus, Vulgate and Targum, but it is left untranslated in the G and S, no doubt because of a lack of understanding of the Hebrew form on the part of the translators. Evidently, non-translation of a lexical item often is a normal confession of ignorance.

It is tempting to establish a relationship between lexical ignorance and the *hapax* nature of certain lexemes. One should, however, not lose sight of the fact that the rare occurrence of words and forms may be haphazard and due to the limited size of a written corpus of texts with specific features. It is remarkable to see that even in the case of so-called absolute *hapax legomena*, to use Greenspahn's classification, the ancient versions sometimes have no problems of understanding at all.[1] For example, they all know the meaning 'leech' of the absolute *hapax* עֲלוּקָה in 30:15. The same is true of the absolute *hapax* מְפַנֵּק in 29:21 even if a different vocalization of the consonantal form, a different reading of the last word in the first half line, and a different syntactical option may have led to the related meanings 'to pamper' and 'being spoiled'. Most remarkably, the Greek translator seems to know perfectly the meaning 'truth' of the absolute *hapax* קֹשְׁטְ in 22:21, although it is always possible that ἀληθῆ is the result of a good guess in view of the parallel אֱמֶת. More likely קֹשְׁטְ was known as an Aramaic loan in Hebrew. In V's translation *firmitatem*, "steadfastness", even the etymological meaning of the Aramaic verb קְשַׁט, 'to establish', shines through. Strangely enough, the Syriac rendering ܫܠܝܐ, 'peace' or 'quietness', seems to have been obtained through the Hebrew metathesis שֶׁקֶט, as already seen by Pinkuss.[2] This is the only case I know of in which one absolute Hebrew *hapax* (קֹשְׁטְ) has been replaced by another absolute Hebrew *hapax* (שֶׁקֶט) found only in 1 Chron 22:9. Or was the Syriac translator victim of a metathesis in his *Vorlage* or in his mind?

Finally, it is unavoidable for the modern researcher to be guided by ancient and modern lexicographical insights and by the glosses and definitions presented in recent lexicons. Nonetheless, the notion of lexical ignorance should be handled with great care because of the greater closeness of some of the original translators to the source language and to competent informants.

Taking into account the restrictions stated above, those texts of Proverbs will be selected in which lexical ignorance on the side of the ancient versions can best be defended. Priority will be given to multiple occurrences of the same word in the Hebrew parent text which remains without equivalent in the versions. Major focus will always be on G as the most important ancient witness which has frequently been used as model text by S, which in turn seems to function as the *Vorlage* of T. The particular, sometimes contrastive, position of V will occasionally be illustrated.

A good example is the rather rare word קֶרֶת, 'city', almost all occurrences of which are found in the book of Proverbs: 8:3; 9:3, 14 and 11:11. In fact, the only instance outside Proverbs is Job 29:7.

[1] F. Greenspahn, *Hapax Legomena in Biblical Hebrew* (Chico, Calif., 1984), 183–86.
[2] H. Pinkuss, "Die syrische Übersetzung der Proverbien," *ZAW* 14 (1894), 197.

In 8:3 G has not rendered the Hebrew word. Where M literally translated reads: "beside the gates in front of the town", G reads: "by the gates of princes she sits". It seems that the Greek translator ignored the meaning of the Hebrew lexeme. However, compensation for the loss was provided in two different ways: (*a*) by the procedure of double translation of the second word in 8:3a, reading once שְׁעָרִים, "gates", and once שָׂרִים (δυναστῶν), "princes"; and (*b*) by introducing from the parallel 1:21b the verbal form παρεδρεύει, "she sits", which he had been using there. The Syriac translator is also unaware of the meaning, but he stays closer to his Hebrew parent text. His rendering ܩܪܝܐ, "crying", clearly shows, as already has been seen by Pinkuss,[3] that he guessed a derivation from the Hebrew root קרא, 'to cry'. The Targum translator simply copies his Syriac base text with קָרְיָא. Remarkably, only V with its rendering *civitatis*, "of the town", shows knowledge of the word.

In 9:3b the Greek translator is confronted with the same problem. However, the differences between M and G are here even greater as the two literal translations of Hebrew and Greek reveal: M, "(the highest places of) the town"; G, "(calling with a loud) proclamation to the drinking-vessel saying". The unknown Hebrew word קָרֶת has been replaced by a triple paraphrase: κηρύγματος ἐπὶ κρατῆρα λέγουσα. The first and the last Greek word are independent attempts to relate the incomprehensible word to the Hebrew root קרא, and the translation κρατῆρα is an ingenious, partial phonetic transcription of the unfamiliar lexeme. It is at the same time an indirect confirmation of the formal presence of the word in the Hebrew *Vorlage* of the Greek translator. The translator seems to overcompensate for ignorance by three guesses as if three are better than one! The phonetic transcription, so frequent in Proverbs, seems to stem from a fundamental need to present at least the form of an unknown Hebrew term. At the same time, mnemotechnical purposes are served by an agreeable alliteration and rhythm, another beloved device in the Greek Proverbs. No such surprises present themselves in S where an equivalent of the word is simply lacking and where a logical solution has been found on the basis of the parallel structure of the stich. It is hard to find an explanation for the problematic rendering עֲשִׁינְתָא, "mighty", in T. The correct translation is, again, only

[3] Pinkuss, "Die syrische Übersetzung," 138.

found in V with *civitatis*. Is this an indication of a particular acquaintance of the Latin translator with Hebrew? Conclusions should not easily be drawn. For the very fragmentary texts of Symmachus and Theodotion have πόλεως in this text, and it is a well-known fact that V has frequently found correct solutions in Hexaplaric materials.

In 9:14 the foolish woman is depicted in M as being "on a seat at the high places of the town", whereas in G she is located "on a seat openly" ἐν πλατείαις (in the streets/on the squares). Although ἐμφανῶς, "openly", could be an interpretation of "the heights" and "squares" a *pars pro toto* rendering of "town" and therefore a synecdoche, it is more likely that the Greek translator has been led by lexical ignorance, and that he has found his inspiration again in the contrastive example of wisdom in 1:20ff.: "on the squares she speaks boldly". It should also be noted that πλατεῖα in Proverbs always renders Hebrew רְחֹב. The Peshitta translator knows that his Greek model is wrong, but, being uncertain with regard to the meaning of קָרֶת, he prefers to leave a blank in his Syriac text. Being deprived of his Syriac base text, the Targum translator is totally lost and he decides to copy his "solution" in 9:3 in the form of וַעֲשִׁינָא, "and strong", "upon her high and mighty seat". I have considered the possibility of a derivation of the Hebrew root קרה[II], 'furnish with beams', but the semantic links are not too evident. One is again left with V as the only right translation, this time in the form of the stylistic variation *urbis*.

Looking briefly at the last case, 11:11, it seems that vv. 10b and 11a are totally lacking in G. A closer look shows, however, that this is not the case. The Hebrew of v. 10a could be rendered with "When righteous men prosper, a city rejoices",[4] but a translation of the Greek would be, "Through the well-being of righteous men a city prospers". In the Greek translation κατώρθωσεν, "prospers" or "is established", does not match Hebrew תַּעֲלֹץ "rejoices" in v. 10, but, as already noted by Mezzacasa, Hebrew תָּרוּם, "is raised up" in v. 11a.[5] The strong parallelism between vv. 10a and 11a made it possible for the Greek translator to telescope the information contained in both half verses. By translating only v. 11b of M, a better antithesis was obtained, a beloved device of this translator. My main hypothesis, however, is that such a facilitation had become necessary because

[4] W. McKane, *Proverbs* (London, 1970), 227.
[5] G. Mezzacasa, *Il libro dei Proverbi di Salomone* (Rome, 1913), 139.

the Greek translator was unfamiliar with the meaning of קֶרֶת in 11:11a. By contrast, he knew the meaning of קִרְיָה, "a city", in 11:10, correctly rendered with πόλις, which he could make the grammatical subject of the verb in 11:11b, "but through the mouths of ungodly men it (i.e. a city) is overthrown". It is, of course, true that in comparison with the Hebrew parent text the verbal subject in the end is correct. However, this argument does not take away the exactitude of my main thesis, which is based upon cumulative evidence. It is certainly remarkable that 11:11 is the only instance in which S correctly translates קֶרֶת with ܡܕܝܢܬܐ. This fact should, however, not be overstressed. S had already provided the same translation in the case of קִרְיָה just before in v. 10 and the Greek model of S had already guessed a possible identity in meaning of the two words. T is without surprise since it had only to copy its Syriac base text to arrive at the same result. V professes his knowledge again with the rendering *civitas*. However, the Latin translator may have had access to Greek manuscripts with the asterisked text of vv. 10b and 11a, probably to be attributed to Theodotion, in which πόλις figured at the end of 11a.

There is an interesting extension of lexical ignorance with regard to the pausal form קָרֶת, or its base form קֶרֶת beyond the primary versions in Saadia's Arabic translation which uses everywhere a singular or plural noun with the meaning 'roof'. Quoting J. Derenbourg and M. Lambert in their French translation, one has in 8:3 "(sur) les toits", in 9:3 "(sur le sommet) des toits (les plus élevés)", in 9:14 "(au plus haut) du toit" and in 11:11 "le toit (s'élève)".[6] Is "roof" an extended meaning based on a Hebrew defective reading קֹרֹת, 'beams', 'rafter'? This is not to be excluded since the root קרה[II] in Middle Hebrew has the meaning 'supply with a roof' or 'being supplied with a roof'.[7]

Lexical ignorance may be related to the rather limited distribution of the form known from Hebrew in other Semitic languages. The same form with the same meaning is in fact only attested in North Western Semitic. It is found in the Phoenician Karatepe inscription

[6] J. Derenbourg and M. Lambert, *Version arabe des Proverbes de R. Saadia ben Iosef Al-Fayyoûmî* (Paris, 1894), 12, 14, 15, 18.

[7] HAL, 1062a; and G. Dalman, *Aramäisches-Neuhebräisches Handwörterbuch zu Targum, Talmud und Midrasch* (Hildesheim, 1967), 389a.

at II 9.17 and III 5.7.15.[8] Moreover, on the authority of Donner-Röllig, IV 17 should certainly be added to these references and most probably IV 6 as well.[9] It is further attested in Ugaritic as can be seen from the glossary items 2278 and 2284 in Gordon's *Ugaritic Textbook*.[10] Fisher has pointed out the interesting fact that the same parallel בית // קרת of 9:14 also occurs in the texts Krt: 81–82 and 172–173, and that the same applies to the parallel קריה // קרת of 11:10–11 found in the text Aqht: 163–164.[11]

Another case in which a plurality of occurrences make the conclusion of lexical ignorance almost inevitable is found in the triple presence of the *hitpael* of the root גלע. In Tanak this root and this conjugation are only attested in three texts of Proverbs: 17:14, 18:1, and 20:3. The uniform dictionary glosses are 'burst out',[12] 'losbrechen'.[13] In 17:14 the reference is to a conflict and in 18:1 and 20:3 to a person.[14] The very limited distribution of the root, as well as its presence in reputedly difficult proverbs, are certainly responsible for lack of knowledge with regard to meaning. If early translators ever had access to extant word lists containing rare expressions of the Pentateuch, they would have found no solutions for Proverbs. For a seemingly correct translation only Aquila can be singled out in 20:3 where he renders יִתְגַּלָּע with ἐξυβρισθήσεται, "he breaks out in insolence". As the verse by verse treatment will show, all other versions ignore the correct meaning.

A literal rendering of the Hebrew text of 17:14b would run as follows: "and before the quarrel break out, quit". It is hard to detect any relationship with the Greek, προηγεῖται δὲ τῆς ἐνδείας στάσις καὶ μάχη, "but sedition and strife precede poverty". With certainty one can only say that προηγεῖται δέ corresponds with וְלִפְנֵי in M and μάχη with הָרִיב. However, ἐνδείας is highly problematic. Schleusner's suggestion that the Greek would have read a *hitpael* of גלה could be considered,[15] but the link between *nudum fecit*, "is naked", and "poverty" seems rather strained. Jaeger, although remarking in his commen-

[8] *DISO*, 267.
[9] *KAI*, 26.
[10] C. Gordon, *Ugaritic Textbook* (Rome, 1965), Glossary, 480b and 481a.
[11] L. Fisher, *Ras Shamra Parallels* (Rome, 1972), 1:499f., 503.
[12] *DCH*, 2:356a.
[13] *HAL*, 187a.
[14] *BDB*, 166b.
[15] J. Schleusner, *Novus Thesaurus philologico-criticus sive lexicon in LXX et reliquos interpretes graecos ac scriptores apocryphos Veteris Testamenti*, 5 vols. (Leipzig, 1820), 2:354.

tary on ἐνδείας· *quamquam haec quoque litigiosos homines saepe consequitur*, considers the possibility of an inner-Greek corruption of an original ἀναιδείας, "shamelessness".[16] He bases himself on Schultens, who taught that a meaning *conviciorum obscenitas* could be found in התגלע. This semantically rather impossible reading has been taken over as a certainty by de Lagarde.[17] It seems more likely that הִתְגַּלָּע remains untranslated in G. There is no lexical element corresponding to the Hebrew in S and in T and it seems to be a normal practice that lexical ignorance leads to non-translation. The only rendering is found in V, *patiatur contumeliam*, "(before) he suffers injury", in which *patiatur* should be based upon a reading of the *hitpael* of גלה with the meaning "expose oneself to".[18] This translation of V should be related to its rendering in 20:3, *miscentur contumeliis*, "they will be mingled with injuries". In both cases *contumelia* is a badly needed object, and it may not be haphazard that *contumelia* is a synonym of *injuria* which is a frequent translation of Greek ὕβρις present in 20:3 in Aquila's translation ἐξυβρισθήσεται.

One of the possible English glosses of M in 18:1b could be, "he breaks out against all sound judgment". The translation of G runs as follows, ἐν παντὶ δὲ καιρῷ ἐπονείδιστος ἔσται, "but on every occasion he will be liable to reproach". Although, technically speaking, the Greek translation focuses on the result of the action of bursting out, one should not project such a consideration into the mind of the Greek translator. In all his ignorance he made not too bad a guess which even convinced the translator of the Vulgate, *erit exprobrabilis*, "he will be worthy of reproach". On the other hand, the Peshitta renders with ܡܡܝܩ, a *pael* participle of ܡܝܩ, "mocking". Therefore, as has already been noted by Pinkuss and by Cappell before him, the Syriac translator has read a form of the Hebrew root לעג, 'to mock' on the base of metathesis.[19] Most probably, this permutation has not occurred accidentally in the Hebrew *Vorlage* of S, but in the translation process. In fact, the *hitpael* of the root לעג is nowhere attested in Hebrew. Moreover, the conscious application

[16] J. Jaeger, *Observationes in Proverbiorum Salomonis versionem alexandrinam* (Leipzig, 1788), 127.

[17] P. de Lagarde, *Anmerkungen zur griechischen Übersetzung der Proverbien* (Leipzig, 1863), §56.

[18] *DCH*, 2:352a.

[19] Pinkuss, "Die syrische Übersetzung," 186; and L. Cappell, *Critica Sacra* (Halle, 1775–1786), 267.

of metathesis of root consonants seems to have been one of the means of "hiding" lexical ignorance. The same metathesis is adopted in T which, according to the best manuscripts, renders with מְצַטְרֵי, "he mocks (with all advice)", a rendering which with Levy certainly has to be corrected into מְצַטְדֵי.[20]

In 20:3 the Greek translator is again confronted with the problem how to translate the unknown form יִתְגַּלָּע. However, this time he tries to solve it in a different way by exploiting the antithetic structure of the two half lines. He chooses an antonym of the verb from the first half verse, ἐποστρέφεσθαι, 'to turn aside (from railing)', by translating יִתְגַּלָּע with συμπλέκεται: τοιούτοις συμπλέκεται, "(with such matters) he will be entangled". V has partly been influenced by the Greek solution in its version *miscentur*, "they will be mingled", whereas the explicit object which follows, *contumeliis*, "with injuries", may show some influence from Aquila as noted before. The revision of Symmachus, ἀποκαλυφθήσεται, which can hardly be translated because of the total lack of context, can only be related to the Hebrew root גלה like the rendering of V in 17:14. Finally, S and T simply copy the metathesis לענ, already applied in 18:1.

These two selected cases are presented to honour Adrian Schenker, the inspiring leader of the *BHQ* project.

[20] J. Levy, *Chaldäisches Wörterbuch über die Targumim und einen grossen Theil des rabbinischen Schriftthums* (Leipzig, 1866–67), 2:316a.

THE TEXTUAL SITUATION IN THE BOOK OF JEREMIAH

Richard D. Weis

It is a privilege to present these reflections to my colleague Adrian Schenker on the occasion of his sixty-fifth birthday. I am delighted to offer him a consideration of the textual situation for the book of Jeremiah, a discussion to which he has contributed.[1] This essay reviews the textual situation in the book of Jeremiah, discusses the particular method it requires, and illustrates the method from chs. 37–38 (G 44–45).

The Overall Situation

As is well known, the textual situation for the book of Jeremiah is dominated by the question of the relation between two quite distinct text forms, each attested by multiple witnesses. The longer text form is attested in Hebrew in the Masoretic Text and in the fragments of 2QJer, 4QJer[a] and 4QJer[c], and in various ancient translations, i.e., the Targum, various fragmentary Hexaplaric witnesses, the Peshitta, and the Vulgate.[2] The other, shorter by a seventh, is attested

[1] A. Schenker, "Nebuchadnezzars Metamorphose vom Unterjocher zum Gottesknecht: in beiden Jeremia-Rezensionen," *RB* 89 (1982), 498–527; idem, "La rédaction longue du livre de Jérémie doit-elle être datée au temps des premiers hasmonéens," *ETL* 70 (1994), 281–293; idem, "La liberazione degli schiavi a Gerusalemme secondo Ger 34,8–22," *RivB* 41 (1993), 453–458; idem, "Der nie aufgehobene Bund: Exegetische Beobachtungen zu Jer 31,31–34," in E. Zenger (ed.), *Der neue Bund im alten: Studien zur Bundestheologie der beiden Testamente* (QD 146; Freiburg im Breisgau, 1993), 85–112.

[2] The Coptic versions of Jeremiah appear to be dependent on G rather than a Hebrew *Vorlage* (cf. F. Feder [ed.], *Biblia Sahidica: Ieremias, Lamentationes (Threni), Epistula Ieremiae et Baruch* [TUGAL 147; Berlin, 2002], 74–78). P.-M. Bogaert has argued that, where it exists, the Old Latin version of Jeremiah preserves the earliest text of G, and in turn witnesses through G to the earliest stage of the Hebrew text of the book (most recently in P.-M. Bogaert, "La *vetus Latina* de Jérémie: texte très court, témoin de la plus ancienne Septante et d'une forme plus ancienne de l'hébreu (Jer 39 et 52)," in A. Schenker (ed.), *The Earliest Text of the Hebrew Bible: The Relationship between the Masoretic Text and the Hebrew Base of the Septuagint Reconsidered* [SBLSCS 52; Atlanta, 2003], 51–82). However, Bogaert does not argue for La as a *direct* witness

in Hebrew in the fragments of 4QJer[b] and 4QJer[d], and in translation in the Old Greek of Jeremiah.[3] A sixth fragmentary witness from Qumran, 4QJer[e], is unable to be assigned to one text form or the other.[4]

The relation between these two text forms has been a central question in the study of the text of Jeremiah since the nineteenth century. Before discovery of the Qumran witnesses the debate was whether G reliably translated its *Vorlage*, meaning that there were once *two* distinct *Hebrew* text forms for the book, or engaged in a high degree of editing and adaptation in the course of translating the *one* Hebrew text form we have received through M. Ultimately the second option seemed more persuasive until the discovery of the Qumran witnesses.[5] The appearance of 4QJer[b] and 4QJer[d] among the fragments from Qumran altered the scholarly consensus dramatically. Today the preponderant view is that as far back as our witnesses to the text of Jeremiah reach, there were two distinct Hebrew text forms of the book existing side by side.[6]

This then raises the issue of the relation between these two Hebrew text forms. Two questions are central here. The first concerns the origin of the divergences between the two text forms since at the level of individual variations they often appear to be text transmissional in nature, but when one considers the book as a whole, the magnitude of the differences suggests a redactional process or processes. The second occurs in the event that redactional activity is posited, and asks after the nature of that activity. For both questions there is not

to a Hebrew *Vorlage*. Based on my evaluation of La readings I tentatively agree with Bogaert that La renders a G *Vorlage*, but I more often agree with Ziegler's evaluation of its testimony ("Oftmals bringt La[W] freie, umschreibende und erweiternde Wiedergaben," J. Ziegler, *Jeremias, Baruch, Threni, Epistula Jeremiae* [2d rev. ed.; *Septuaginta: Vetus Testamentum Graecum*, XV; Göttingen, 1976], 18) than Bogaert's. Here too we are faced with a versional witness to G.

[3] E. Tov, *The Text Critical Use of the Septuagint in Biblical Research* (2nd rev. ed.; Jerusalem, 1997), 243.

[4] This is the judgment of its editor, E. Tov (E. Ulrich, et al., *Qumran Cave 4, X, The Prophets* [DJD XV; Oxford, 1997], 207).

[5] For a review of the history of this discussion see J. G. Janzen, *Studies in the Text of Jeremiah* (HSM 6; Cambridge, Mass., 1973), 2–7.

[6] P.-M. Bogaert offers a thorough review of the discussion in "Le livre de Jérémie en perspective: les deux rédactions antiques selon les travaux en cours," *RB* 101 (1994), 363–406. See also the somewhat more recent review of the discussion in B. Huwyler, *Jeremia und die Völker: Untersuchungen zu den Völkersprüchen in Jeremia 46–49* (FAT 20; Tübingen, 1997), 48–64.

yet a settled answer although in each case one might speak of a majority opinion.

Assessments of the divergences between the longer and shorter text forms as text transmissional or redactional in nature fall into three main camps: those positing only text transmissional origins for the differences, those positing only redactional origins, and those positing some mixture of the two processes.[7] Positions attributing the differences solely or mostly to text transmissional processes must face the reality that the scale of difference is beyond what is typical of these processes unless a significant interpretive agenda is present. Since both text forms existed in Hebrew, the further question arises how one differentiates between redactional intervention in the formation of the book and significant interpretation in the subsequent process of transmitting a settled form of the book. Positions that attribute the differences between the two text forms entirely or mostly to redactional intervention simply are not realistic since both text forms were copied and translated, making typical text transmissional changes inevitable. Positions in the third group, attributing the divergences to both text transmissional and redactional processes, seem the most reasonable explanations of the evidence, but they are faced with the need to discriminate case by case between a text transmissional change and a redactional intervention. This question is especially pressing since the specific textual phenomena resulting from these two processes often are similar.

The question of the nature of the redactional activity that accounts for a significant share of the differences between the two text forms

[7] Examples of positions attributing the differences only to textual processes are (albeit in quite different ways): G. Fischer, *Das Trostbüchlein: Text, Komposition und Theologie von Jer 30–31* (SBB 26; Stuttgart, 1993); Janzen, *Studies in the Text of Jeremiah*; J. R. Lundbom, *Jeremiah 1–20* (AB 21A; New York, 1999), 57–62; S. Soderlund, *The Greek Text of Jeremiah: A Revised Hypothesis* (JSOTS 47; Sheffield, 1985), 193–248. Examples of positions that attribute the G/M differences purely to redactional processes are: H. Migsch, *Jeremias Ackerkauf: Eine Untersuchung von Jeremia 32* (OBS 15; Frankfurt am Main, 1996); L. Stulman, *The Other Text of Jeremiah: A Reconstruction of the Hebrew Text Underlying the Greek Version of the Prose Sections of Jeremiah with English Translation* (Lanham, Md., 1985). Examples of positions attributing the differences to a mixture of redactional and textual processes are: A. Aejmaleus, "Jeremiah at the turning-point of history: the function of Jer. xxv 1–14 in the Book of Jeremiah," *VT* 52 (2002), 460–461, 479–480; A. G. Shead, *The Open Book and the Sealed Book: Jeremiah 32 in its Hebrew and Greek Recensions* (JSOTS 347; London and New York, 2002); E. Tov, "Exegetical notes on the Hebrew Vorlage of the LXX of Jeremiah 27 (34)," *ZAW* 91 (1979), 73–93; R. D. Weis, *A Definition of the Genre Maśśāʾ in the Hebrew Bible* (Ph.D. diss., The Claremont Graduate School, 1986), 416–475.

also receives various answers. On the one hand, there is a proposal that the redactional process takes the form of a "rolling corpus," which produces the two text forms out of the accumulation of thousands of small scale changes without a single over-arching design.[8] Of course, one may ask why this should be thought of as a redactional process since it looks rather like a text transmissional process. On the other hand, many hold positions that either posit a single redactional intervention that produces the longer text form (Edition 2) out of the shorter (Edition 1), or posit a small number of redactional stages leading to the same eventual result.[9] Among these scholars, there are also diverse views on the date and location of the redactional interventions.[10]

Methodological Implications

This complex of open questions concerning the two text forms of the book of Jeremiah calls for a particular method if one is to establish the text (or texts) of the book with some measure of confidence. Among the witnesses for a single text form the normal text critical procedures for evaluating testimony are valid, of course. It is in

[8] H.-J. Stipp, "The Prophetic Messenger Formulas in Jeremiah according to the Masoretic and Alexandrian Texts," *Textus* 18 (1995), 84–85; W. McKane, *Introduction and Commentary on Jeremiah I–XXV* (*A Critical and Exegetical Commentary on Jeremiah*, vol. 1; Edinburgh, 1986), l–lxxxiii, esp. lxxxiii.

[9] Aejmaleus, "Jeremiah at the turning-point"; P.-M. Bogaert, "Jérémie 17,1–4 TM, oracle contre ou sur Juda propre au texte long, annoncé en 11,7–8.13 TM et en 15,12–14 TM," in Y. Goldman and C. Uehlinger (eds.), *La double transmission du texte biblique* (OBO 179; Fribourg & Göttingen, 2001), 59–74; Y. Goldman, *Prophétie et royauté au retour de l'exil: Les origines littéraires de la forme massorétique du livre de Jérémie* (OBO 118; Fribourg & Göttingen, 1992); idem, "Juda et son roi au milieu des nations. La dernière rédaction du livre de Jérémie," in A. H. W. Curtis and T. Römer (eds.), *The Book of Jeremiah and Its Reception – Le livre de Jérémie et sa réception* (BETL 128; Leuven, 1997), 151–182; B. Huwyler, *Jeremia und die Völker*; Y.-J. Min, "The Case for Two Books of Jeremiah," in S. Crisp and M. Jinbachian (eds.), *Text, Theology and Translation: Essays in honour of Jan de Waard* (Reading, 2004), 109–124; Schenker, see works cited in n. 1; Shead, *Open Book and the Sealed Book*; E. Tov, "L'Incidence de la critique textuelle sur la critique littéraire dans le livre de Jérémie," *RB* 79 (1972), 189–199; R. D. Weis, "A Conflicted Book for a Marginal People: Thematic Oppositions in MT Jeremiah," in D. Ellens, et al. (eds.), *Reading the Hebrew Bible for a New Millennium: Form, Concept and Theological Perspective*, vol. 2, Exegetical and Theological Studies (Philadelphia, 2000), 290–301.

[10] The proposed dates range from the late sixth century B.C.E. to the first half of the second century B.C.E. For a convenient résumé of the options see Huwyler, *Jeremia und die Völker*, 63.

assessing the significance of the differences between the two text forms that the usual text critical procedures are not enough. In my view recent discussions of both text and redaction have seldom employed a satisfactory method.[11] Text critically focused discussions have primarily remained focused at the word- and phrase-levels, which means that they are not likely to detect redaction in a controllable way since redaction necessarily operates from the level of pericopes up to the whole book even though its concrete interventions may be implemented at the word- and phrase-levels.[12] Redaction critical discussions have mostly ignored the evidence of G, which raises questions about the validity of their results, as A. Aejmaleus has pointed out.[13]

A satisfactory method must be able to detect the presence of redaction. If redaction is judged to be a factor in the differences between the text forms, the method must be able to differentiate redaction from a large-scale exegetical agenda on the part of a translator or copyist,[14] and to differentiate specific textual variations that are due to redactional intervention from those due to the vicissitudes of text transmission. Where the text forms are judged to differ redactionally, they should not be treated as witnesses to the same text, but rather as two co-existent texts of the book. On the other hand, where the text forms are judged to differ text transmissionally, they are implicitly judged to have shared the same text and thus are related witnesses to a portion of text they hold in common.

Thus the method pursued for *Biblia Hebraica Quinta* begins with parallel redaction critical analyses of each pericope in M and in G. A form critical approach to redaction criticism is used since the questions under investigation have to do with the possibility of detecting different overall designs and intentions for the passage, and of detecting different settings in life – pointing to different social and historical

[11] The monographs of Goldman, *Prophétie et royauté*, Huwyler, *Jeremia und die Völker*, and Shead, *Open Book and the Sealed Book*, are notable exceptions.

[12] H.-J. Stipp's results (e.g., as in "Prophetic Messenger Formulas in Jeremiah," and *Das masoretische und alexandrinische Sondergut des Jeremiabuches* [OBO 136; Fribourg & Göttingen, 1994]) are essentially a product of this lack of a "higher level" redactional focus.

[13] Aejmaleus, "Jeremiah at the turning-point," 460–461, 479–480. The study by B. Boyle on our two illustrative chapters ("Narrative as Ideology: Synchronic (Narrative Critical) and Diachronic Readings of Jeremiah 37–38," *Pacifica* 12 [1999], 293–312) is an example of the sort of approach Aejmaleus criticizes.

[14] A. van der Kooij has shown the presence of such phenomena in Isaiah (see *The Oracle of Type: The Septuagint of Isaiah XXIII as Version and Vision* [VTSup 71; Leiden, 1998]).

locations for each text form.[15] Substantive variations in form and intention are evidence for the presence of redactional or large-scale interpretive agenda. Variations in the implied audience (and hence social location) are clues to the sequence between the two text forms, and to whether the one represented in the Old Greek is redactional in origin, or the result of an interpretive agenda on the part of the Greek translator.

Analysis of translation technique in the versions constitutes the next step. This is of particular importance because the shorter text form is witnessed completely only in translation. Thus analysis of the translation technique of G is a key feature of method for the text critic of Jeremiah in order to establish G's *Vorlage* with any degree of probability.[16] Analysis of the translation technique of the other versions, of course, is also necessary to establish which divergences might be due to variant *Vorlagen*.

Based on this preparatory work we proceed to the consideration of individual textual variations. Individual differences between the two text forms that conform to a confirmed redactional agenda are most simply explained as the result of redaction. The differences that have a parsimonious explanation as a text transmissional change (including any exegetical agenda confirmed in G by the redactional analysis), and have no impact on redactional shape, are regarded as text transmissional in origin. Differences among witnesses to the same text form are self-evidently text transmissional in nature. Where the two text forms diverge due to redaction, they should not be used to correct each other in text critical terms. Since *Biblia Hebraica Quinta* aims at the reconstruction of the earliest attested reading for the text form that survives in M, this means that G readings due to redactional differences will not be used to establish the text for *BHQ*.[17] Divergences that are text transmissional in nature – whether between

[15] The approach exemplified by the Forms of the Old Testament Literature series is well suited for this task. The volumes by M. A. Sweeney (*Isaiah 1–39 with an Introduction to Prophetic Literature* [FOTL 16; Grand Rapids, 1996]) and M. H. Floyd (*Minor Prophets, Part 2* [FOTL 22; Grand Rapids, 2000]) are especially valuable exemplars of the approach.

[16] For a thorough discussion of the considerations involved in the reconstruction of G's *Vorlage* see Tov, *Text-Critical Use of the Septuagint*, 57–121. On the essential difficulty of reconstructing the *Vorlage* for any ancient version see E. Tov, *Textual Criticism of the Hebrew Bible* (2nd rev. ed.; Minneapolis & Assen, 2001), 129–133.

[17] Such readings will, however, be reported in the apparatus of *BHQ* with the characterization "lit", i.e., literary in origin.

the two text forms or among the witnesses to the longer one – must, of course, be weighed and evaluated in order to establish the earliest attested reading.

An Illustration of the Method: Jeremiah 37–38 (44–45)

We will illustrate this approach using Jeremiah 37–38 (G 44–45). The discussion necessarily has been abbreviated, but it should suffice for the purpose of illustrating the method. We will begin with the parallel redactional analyses, continue with an overview of translation techniques, and conclude with a few examples of the treatment of individual cases of variation among the witnesses based on these analyses.

The Redactional Shape of the Masoretic Text

The passage in the Masoretic Text begins with Jer 37:1 and ends with Jer 38:28a. Jer 38:28b is part of the introductory formula for the narrative in chapter 39. Although chapters 37 and 38 are commonly regarded as two separate, albeit similar, narratives, I do not think that interpretation can be sustained in the end. Instead the narrative segmentation between the two chapters is best explained as the segmentation of two episodes within a single coherent narrative, rather than as marking two discrete narratives.[18]

Two structures shape the narrative in Jer 37:1–38:28a: the linear structure of plot, and the structure of relationships among the characters who move through the plot. The plot structure organizes the narrative, but the structure of relationships among the characters is crucial to questions of genre, intention and setting.

The account begins in 37:1–2 with a summary assessment of the reign of Zedekiah. This introduces the coming narrative and orients the reader to a particular way of reading it. Then the plot unfolds

[18] See also C. Seitz, "The text of these two chapters [i.e., 37 & 38] as we now have them is certainly meant to be read as an organic whole, as a continuous narrative" ("The crisis of interpretation over the meaning and purpose of the exile: a redactional study of Jeremiah xxi–xliii," *VT* 35 [1985], 86). So also R. P. Carroll, *Jeremiah: A Commentary* (OTL; Philadelphia, 1986), 672; and M. C. Callaway, "Exegesis as Banquet: Reading Jeremiah with the Rabbis," in R. D. Weis and D. M. Carr (eds.), *A Gift of God in Due Season: Essays in Scripture and Community in Honor of James A. Sanders* (JSOTSup 225; Sheffield, 1996), 223–226.

in six episodes. The first four alternate between accounts of Zedekiah inquiring of Jeremiah and Jeremiah responding (37:3–10; 37:17–21), and accounts of Jeremiah's imprisonment by the *śarîm* (37:11–16; 38:1–6). The fifth episode (38:7–13) recounts Ebed-Melek's petition to the king and his subsequent rescuing of Jeremiah. The final episode (38:14–28a) includes both Zedekiah's inquiry with Jeremiah's response, and an attempt against Jeremiah by the *śarîm*, which this time is foiled.

Of the cast of characters who act out the plot of this narrative four are significant for the structure of relationships among the characters of the story: Jeremiah, Zedekiah, the *śarîm*, and Ebed-Melek. The other individuals mentioned are essentially adjuncts to Zedekiah, Ebed-Melek or the *śarîm*. Among the four protagonists there are two significant patterns of relationships.

The first pattern centers on Zedekiah as facing a choice between two construals of the universe. These are espoused respectively by Jeremiah and the *śarîm*. Each construal entails a corresponding understanding of the fates of Zedekiah and Jerusalem, and of the actions that lead to a future of safety for both king and city. The *śarîm* of Judah in this narrative are a voice for resistance to Babylonian power, a voice for maintaining Judahite independence at all costs. They are the voice for the survival of the Judahite community on the terms under which it has survived up until the moment, i.e., as a quasi-independent polity in which they exercise autonomy and dominance. Implicitly they rely on YHWH's "wonderful deeds" as the basis for a communal future in the face of Babylonian power.

Jeremiah articulates an alternate construal of the world, which is a paradoxical understanding from the point of view of the traditional theology implied by the construal associated with the *śarîm*. Surrender leads to survival. Acceptance of Babylonian dominance and the consequent loss of independence lead to the survival of individuals and city. The humiliation of submission results in the dignity of autonomy. In the last resort, after the destruction of the city, this course of action leads only to the survival of autonomous individuals, but that potentially is a basis for communal survival.

The plot structure of the narrative places the choice between the competing construals before the reader by alternating between episodes in which Zedekiah inquires of Jeremiah about his and the city's future and receives Jeremiah's responses, and episodes in which the *śarîm* try to contain what they perceive as the threat Jeremiah poses to the city's ability to persist in its resistance to Babylonian dominance. The final episode, in which Zedekiah's inquiry of Jeremiah is enmeshed in the opposition between Jeremiah and the *śarîm*, makes clear that within the narrative the choice is before Zedekiah. As that episode makes clear, the alternative that Jeremiah poses is fearful indeed because it appears to mean a loss of autonomy and dignity (38[45]:19). Zedekiah epitomizes the difficulty of the choice that the reader also sees in his or her own context.[19]

The second pattern centers on Ebed-Melek as a model for how marginal persons can exercise influence on the holders of power in a dominant culture to protect a marginal or outsider community. Whereas the alternating pattern of most of the episodes in the narrative cues the reader to the first pattern of relationships, the fact that the episode with Ebed-Melek does not fit that pattern of alternating episodes calls the reader's attention to the second pattern. Although Ebed-Melek is the focus of this pattern, it includes Zedekiah, the *śarîm*, and Jeremiah in a set of power relationships that parallel those among the principal characters of the book of Esther. In Jeremiah 37–38 Zedekiah is the ultimate human source of power in the polity of Judah, as can be seen from his being the object of various petitions from the *śarîm*, Jeremiah, and Ebed-Melek. The *śarîm* seem to hold day-to-day operational responsibility for what happens in the city, as can be seen from the fact that Irijah brings Jeremiah to them, not the king. Jeremiah's case is only brought to the attention of the king at a later stage by the *śarîm* themselves. As the repeated conclusion of episodes with a note about Jeremiah's location in prison, and the concern about his possible death in prison show, Jeremiah – even though he represents YHWH and is the object of repeated inquiries from Zedekiah – is vulnerable to the exercise of power by those dominating his society. Indeed he is under threat

[19] This evidence has often been construed as a portrayal of the historical Zedekiah as vacillating, or as the product of redactional layering of the text whereas the reading proposed here sees this as part of a careful literary shaping that results in the engagement of the reader in the choice between the two construals of the world. See especially Boyle, "Narrative as Ideology"; M. C. Callaway, "Telling the truth and telling stories: an analysis of Jeremiah 37–38," *USQR* 44 (1991), 253–265; idem, "Exegesis as Banquet," 218–230; idem, "Black Fire on White Fire: Historical Context and Literary Subtext in Jeremiah 37–38," in A. R. P. Diamond, K. M. O'Connor, and L. Stulman (eds.), *Troubling Jeremiah* (JSOTSup 260; Sheffield, 1999), 171–178; H.-J. Stipp, "Zedekiah in the Book of Jeremiah: On the Formation of a Biblical Character," *CBQ* 58 (1996), 627–648.

of death. Ebed-Melek the Cushite is both insider (a member of the king's court with access to the royal person and power) and an outsider (a Cushite). His marginal status is emphasized by the repeated labeling of him as a Cushite – in a Judahite court. He has only derivative power within the structures of this story world, but he manages to use his rhetorical skill to deploy royal power on behalf of the vulnerable. This is very much the set of power relations and roles that one encounters in the book of Esther, as Sidnie White Crawford has shown.[20]

In spite of reporting "a historically plausible event" (a characteristic of the genre PROPHETIC STORY), this narrative most likely should be classified as a PROPHETIC LEGEND since it seems designed to instruct concerning correct conduct.[21] Among the sub-types of prophetic legends this complex narrative does not fit easily into one, but shows characteristics of two. It certainly has characteristics of PROPHETIC HISTORIOGRAPHY in that "the adherence to or rejection of that word is frequently the cause of the success or failure of major characters" (in this case Zedekiah).[22] The narrative also conforms to the character of an EXEMPLUM insofar as it aims "to teach moral lessons or proper conduct."[23] A notable aspect of this narrative's individuality is seen in the fact that Ebed-Melek is the figure who models proper conduct, not the prophet as would ordinarily be the case for this genre.

The setting for this narrative is probably to be found in the social location where Zedekiah's choice, and Ebed-Melek's position and choices have some reality in the life of the narrative's audience. Thus it seems likely that the setting for this narrative is to be found among the elite in Jehudite society, i.e., those in Jehud who can exercise power and come from families that once exercised power "independently" (i.e., under the Davidides before 587). A Persian Period date for the setting is thus also implied. Under the Persians submission to the dominant power could still lead to communal and cultural autonomy and survival, unlike the situation under the Seleucids.

---

[20] S. A. White, "Esther: A Feminine Model for Jewish Diaspora," in P. L. Day (ed.), *Gender and Difference in Ancient Israel* (Minneapolis, 1989), 161–177; Zedekiah=Ahasuerus; *śarîm*=Haman; Jeremiah=Mordechai; Ebed-Melek=Esther. Note also the related discussion in L. Wills, *The Jew in the Court of the Foreign King: Ancient Jewish Court Legends* (HDR 26; Minneapolis, 1990).

[21] For a definition of the genres 'Prophetic Story' and 'Prophetic Legend' see Sweeney, *Isaiah 1–39*, 535.

[22] For a definition of the genre 'Prophetic Historiography' see Sweeney, *Isaiah 1–39*, 21.

[23] For a definition of the genre 'Exemplum' see Sweeney, *Isaiah 1–39*, 534.

The Redactional Shape of the Old Greek

In G the passage also embraces both chapters (44 and 45), and displays a continuous, coherent, unifying narrative thread. Here too the plot unfolds in six episodes (44:3–10, 11–16, 17–21; 45:1–6, 7–13, 14–28).

However, there are two key differences between the two sets of six episodes. In the fourth episode of the story in M it is clearly the *śarîm* who are responsible on their own for Jeremiah's imprisonment. In the story in G it is Zedekiah who authorizes their action. They are only his instruments. In the fifth episode in M Ebed-Melek petitions Zedekiah to prevent Jeremiah's death without implicating Zedekiah in the action. In the same episode in G Abdemelech rebukes Zedekiah as an evildoer with sole responsibility for Jeremiah's death. Thus whereas in M the opponents and persecutors of Jeremiah are the *śarîm*, in G it is Zedekiah, who indeed is set up as YHWH's opponent. The focus is still on Zedekiah, but not as having to choose between two construals of the world, rather as offered a last chance to save Jerusalem. This he stubbornly refuses to take, choosing instead to persecute YHWH's prophet and thus resist YHWH. Moreover, Abdemelech's Cushite identity is not emphasized repeatedly as in M, so his marginal status is de-emphasized. These differences have consequences for the force and impact of the narrative as a whole.

In G the narrative is also best classified as a PROPHETIC LEGEND, but here more specifically a POLITICAL LEGEND, rather than PROPHETIC HISTORIOGRAPHY.[24] It is, as is characteristic of the POLITICAL LEGEND, an account of opposition to the prophet and what he endures at the hands of his enemies. However, it departs from the typical pattern of the genre in that the narrative does not show us a clear-cut victory of the prophet over his enemies. Instead the reader sees the prophet's endurance in the face of persecution, and his vindication in the vision report at the end of the narrative, as well as his escape from confinement in the cistern. This departure from the typical political legend gives the narrative something of the flavor of an EXEMPLUM, with Jeremiah as an example of faithfulness to κύριος under great duress. Moreover, the figure of Abdemelech is certainly also a figure worthy of emulation, especially as an effective protector of the righteous while serving a king who is hostile to their fate.

[24] For a definition of the genre 'Political Legend' see Sweeney, *Isaiah 1–39*, 534.

The lack of a clear cut victory for the prophet shifts the focus to opposition to the prophet. Focus on opposition to Jeremiah supports an intention to explain the destruction of Jerusalem by the Babylonians. Even in the face of the imprisonment and ill treatment of God's messenger, κύριος continued to offer the leadership of Jerusalem a possibility for saving the city to the very end. Their refusal to take the option means that the destruction of Jerusalem is not the fault of its protective deity, but of its human leaders, especially Zedekiah. Since surrender to the Babylonians would not only save the city, but Zedekiah and his household, the same narrative also accounts for the loss of royal power by the Davidic house. Κύριος has not broken the promise to David; David's descendants threw away the opportunity presented them through Jeremiah.

Another departure from what is typical for the genre, the use of a non-prophet, Abdemelech, as a secondary focal figure of the EXEMPLUM, signals another intention. Here the aim is to model right action in a changed context. In the absence of God's "wonderful deeds" the protection of the righteous depends on the initiative of individuals who, although they may have little power in their own right, are willing to challenge the actions of YHWH's opponents.

These intentions point to a setting among the deported elites in Babylon. Necessarily this is the setting for the Hebrew text underlying G, rather than the setting for the Old Greek translation itself. Differences between G and M contributing to the difference between their redactional shapes will be regarded in the first instance as the result of intervention by the editor who produced Edition 2. In these instances G will not be regarded as a witness to the text witnessed by M, etc.

Translation Techniques of the Versions

The following section profiles the translation technique for each versional witness for which my research suggests some nuancing of the accepted picture for that witness. In keeping with the illustrative character of this presentation, I document these nuances with data from chapters 37–38 (44–45), rather than present a comprehensive picture. The witnesses are discussed in a sequence corresponding to an approximate chronology.[25]

---

[25] Dating G to the early second century B.C.E. (Tov, *Textual Criticism of the Hebrew*

(a) Old Greek

Two themes dominate discussion of G's translation technique in Jeremiah, the two translators question, and the striking literalness (i.e., consistent conformity to the presumed source text) of the translation.[26] Discussion of the "two translators" question has been re-opened in two recent articles by A. Pietersma.[27] No particular evidence that emerges from an examination of our illustrative chapters helps address that question. Thus we will discuss only the second issue, the basic character and norms of G as a translation.

There is ample evidence within G Ieremias 44–45 to corroborate the view that in Jeremiah G is concerned to achieve consistent equivalence of form between source text and target language.[28] It is clear

Bible, 137), Targum Jonathan to before 135 C.E. (P. S. Alexander, "Jewish Aramaic Translations of Hebrew Scriptures," in M. J. Mulder [ed.], *Mikra* [Assen/Maastricht & Philadelphia, 1988], 247), the Hexaplaric witnesses from the early second century C.E. to the fifth century C.E. (N. Fernández Marcos, *The Septuagint in Context: Introduction to the Greek Versions of the Bible* [Leiden, 2000], 109–173), Peshitta to 150–200 C.E. (M. Weitzman, *The Syriac Version of the Old Testament: An Introduction* [Cambridge, 1999], 258), and Vulgate to the late fourth century (by 392) C.E. (B. Kedar, "The Latin Translations," in M. J. Mulder [ed.], *Mikra* [Assen/Maastricht & Philadelphia, 1988], 320).

[26] On "the two translators" question see H. St.J. Thackeray, "The Greek Translators of Jeremiah," *JTS* 4 (1903), 245–266; E. Tov, *The Septuagint Translation of Jeremiah and Baruch* (HSM 8; Missoula, Mont., 1976); Soderlund, *Greek Text of Jeremiah*, 153–192; Stipp, *Das masoretische und alexandrinische Sondergut*, 17–19. On the "literal" or formal equivalence character of G as a translation see H. St. J. Thackeray, *A Grammar of the Old Testament in Greek according to the Septuagint I* (Cambridge, 1909), 12–13; R. A. Martin, *Syntactical Evidence of Semitic Sources in Greek Documents* (SBLSCS 3; Missoula, Mont., 1974), 16–43; R. Sollamo, *Renderings of Hebrew Semiprepositions in the Septuagint* (AASF 19; Helsinki, 1979), 286–287; E. Tov and B. G. Wright, "Computer-Assisted Study of the Criteria for Assessing Literalness of Translation Units in the LXX," *Textus* 12 (1985), 181–187.

[27] A. Pietersma, "'Επίχειρον in Greek Jeremiah," *JNSL* 28 (2002), 101–108; idem, "Greek Jeremiah and the Land of Azazel," forthcoming in the Ulrich *Festschrift*. See also J. Smith, "Jeremiah 52: Thackeray and Beyond," *BIOSCS* 35 (2002), 55–96.

[28] This may be documented with the following examples from the list of items encountered in Jeremiah 37–38(44–45): βασιλεύω: except in 41(34):5 this always (ten times) corresponds to an M verb form from the root מלך; except for two minuses וַיֹּאמֶר is rendered always by καὶ εἶπε(ν) except 37(44):17; לֵאמֹר is rendered eighty-three times out of eighty-six by the present active participle of λέγω; חטא is rendered eleven times by ἁμαρτάνω, once by ἐφαμαρτάνω, once not at all, and only in 37(44):18 by ἀδικέω; אַל is rendered seventy-five times by μή, has no G equivalent twice, and is rendered once each by οὐ, τί (in 37[44]:20 – absolutely exceptional!), μὴ δή, and εἰς (via אֶל); מַטָּרָה: all eleven times in Jer-M are rendered in Jer-G with φυλάκη; in 37(44):21 ἔξωθεν οὗ πέσσουσιν for מִחוּץ הָאֹפִים; עַל־כֵּן: rendered with διὰ τοῦτο thirteen times, καί once, and in 38(45):4 there is no G equivalent for the M text; כָּל־הָעָם: of the thirty-five times in Jer-M six times have minuses in G, twenty-six times there is a correct formal equivalence rendition of the expression, always

that for this translation unit of G the primary norm guiding the translation is the consistent one-to-one sequential representation of the form of the source text. It is equally clear that although this is the primary norm, it is not the only norm.

A number of interesting contextual adaptations observable in G for these chapters demonstrate that this translator worked with a couple of important subsidiary norms, without departing from one-to-one, sequential representation of the items in the source text. Some contextual adaptations indicate that the translator was unwilling to pursue formal equivalence to the extent of sacrificing essential semantic equivalence.[29] Other contextual adaptations betray a concern to ensure a certain perception of the content. This is not an actualizing or contemporizing interpretation, however, but rather a concern for a correct portrayal of figures in the text (and thus in the past).[30] The basic norm concerning representation of the source text means, however, that instances of contextual adaptation, or consistent semantic rather than formal equivalence, do not lead to omissions, so that minuses should be regarded as potential variants in G's *Vorlage*.[31] In

forms of πᾶς + article + λαός; in three loci (34[41]:8; 38[45]:1; 44[51]:24) only article + a form of λαός; שׁלח: ἀποστέλλω sixty times, ἐξαποστέλλω sixteen times, and ἐπαποστέλλω, ἐκτείνω, βάλλω, χαλάω, and ῥίπτω once each, no equivalent nine times; οἰκία renders בַּיִת twenty-nine times, and ערבות, חצר, and מָבוֹא once each.

[29] The rendition of הלך is a good example of this. In G for Jeremiah it is rendered forty-nine times by πορεύω, twenty times by βαδίζω, nine times by οἴχομαι, twelve times by compounds with ἐκ and ἀπό, and once each by seven other verbs. This pattern is consistent across both "halves" of G. The considerable predominance of non-directional forms in G's usage might suggest that the use of compounds would signal a variant *Vorlage*. However, these appear to be contextual adaptations in instances where a stereotyped rendition would lose some significant nuance, e.g., in 37(44):9.

[30] The rendition of נפל in these chapters is a good example of this. In Jeremiah G renders נפל in the expression נפל על/אל הכשדים with προσχωρέω in 21:9, and with φεύγω in 37(44):13, 14; 38(45):19. Otherwise, it renders נפל mostly with πίπτω (twenty-two times), and then with a number of individual (or nearly individual) equivalents: πτῶσις (twice), ἐμπίπτω (once), εἴμι (once), and ἐπιρρίπτω (once). It uses φεύγω mostly for forms from the root נוס: twice with the nouns and ten times with the verb. There are four exceptions: one time for סחף, and the three for נפל. However, in Jeremiah נוס is used only in the OAN, so that its usage in the *Vorlage* for 37–38 seems unlikely. Instead this appears to be a contextually specific rendering of נפל that is designed to ensure that Jeremiah is not portrayed as treasonous since the first two occurrences of the expression in 37–38 (44–45) refer to his departure from the besieged city.

[31] The rendition of כִּי provides a nice example of this. The word occurs 403 times in M Jeremiah. G renders it with ὅτι 298 times, with διότι twenty-eight times, with ἀλλά eighteen times, with ἐάν eleven times, and with ὅταν eight times. These

matters of syntax and grammar there are necessarily differences due to the differences between the languages, but G's emphasis on consistent formal representation of the source text extends to these matters as well even if the rendition is not truly equivalent in either syntax or grammar, but only a kind of approximation.[32]

This picture of the norms that shape G's translation has a number of consequences for the assessment of this witness's testimony. First, the norm of formal representation of source text elements essentially on a one-to-one basis means minuses and pluses must be taken seriously (but not automatically!) as likely *Vorlage* variants. Second, attention must be paid in each case whether the translation technique for any particular item follows the norm of formal equivalence or semantic/syntactic equivalence. In the case of formal equivalence formal variation in the rendition more likely signals a variant *Vorlage* than semantic/syntactic variation. Correspondingly, in the case of a norm of semantic/syntactic equivalence substantive variation in semantic or syntactic value more likely signals a variant *Vorlage* than formal variation.

(b) Targum

The fundamental norm guiding the Targum rendering of Jeremiah is the expression of the meaning the text holds for the Targum's target audience. The specific techniques that implement this norm are well known and have been described elsewhere.[33] R. Hayward offers the following single sentence summary in the introduction to his translation and commentary for Targum Jeremiah, "Targum not only translates the Hebrew Bible; it also gives its *meaning* by means of interpretation, commentary, supplying of missing details, the making precise of what may appear vague, and by the introduction of

---

all correspond to typical semantic values for כִּי, as perhaps do seven other Greek equivalents that occur only once each. In twenty-five occurrences G has no correspondent for כִּי, in seven instances the correspondent is καί, and once it is ὡς. This eight percent of the total number of occurrences is so at variance with the translation technique for G that these thirty-three cases probably should be regarded as having variant *Vorlagen*.

[32] For example, in G לֵאמֹר is rendered eighty-three times out of eighty-six by the present active participle of λέγω, and the number of the participle is matched to the number of the speaker(s).

[33] Alexander, "Jewish Aramaic Translations," 225–228; R. Hayward, *The Targum of Jeremiah* (ArBib 12; Wilmington, Del., 1987), 21–26.

aggadah."[34] Jeremiah 37–38, however, provide ample testimony of a notable variation in the usual pattern for effecting the basic translational norm of Targum Jonathan. These chapters show strikingly little aggadic expansion of the text. Moreover, renditions of individual items are much less often contemporizing. The result for these chapters is a translation that follows a set of norms very similar to those for S and V.

(c) Hexaplaric Witnesses

For the Hexaplaric and related witnesses N. Fernández Marcos has provided excellent summaries of the current state of our understanding of these witnesses in *The Septuagint in Context.*[35] These witnesses, so far as they occur in our illustrative chapters, conform to the descriptions of their translational character offered by Fernández Marcos.

(d) Peshitta

The norms governing the Peshitta translation are neatly summarized by M. Weitzman in the following remarks, "an idiomatic, though faithful translation. The translators aim primarily to convey the plain sense,. . . . However, broadly following the classical ideal, they convey not the words but the content."[36] On the whole, these norms and the specific translation techniques discussed by Weitzman for S as a whole, and by G. Greenberg for Jeremiah in particular, are good explanations of the textual phenomena encountered in S in our illustrative chapters.[37] The consequences of this for the assessment of the testimony of S in Jeremiah are largely similar to those drawn for V below.

(e) Vulgate

In V the fundamental norm governing the translation is the consistent creation of semantic and syntactic equivalence between the translation and the source text. Consistency in formal representation, either lexically or grammatically, is subordinated to this norm.[38]

---

[34] Hayward, *Targum of Jeremiah*, 21.

[35] Fernández Marcos, *Septuagint in Context*, 109–173.

[36] Weitzman, *Syriac Version*, 61.

[37] Weitzman, *Syriac Version*, 15–62; G. Greenberg, *Translation Technique in the Peshitta to Jeremiah* (Monographs of the Leiden Peshitta Institute 13; Leiden, 2002).

[38] I find this a more helpful way to describe the phenomena that B. Kedar

Formal consistency in rendition does indeed occur in V, especially with lexical items, but only as an incidental by-product of its consistent semantic and syntactic equivalence. So nouns typically are used to render nouns, verbs to render verbs, etc. because in these cases consistent grammatical equivalence correlates with consistent syntactic equivalence. A secondary norm is the stylistic preference for formal variety, but this also is subordinated to the achievement of consistent semantic and syntactic equivalence. As far as the sequence of items in the text is concerned, V will follow the sequence of the Hebrew source text so long as this does not interfere with the fundamental norm of adequately representing the meaning of the source text, as B. Kedar has observed.[39] The fairly consistent modernization of toponyms and gentilics perhaps also is related to these norms.

These norms are easily illustrated from a variety of items in V's rendition of Jeremiah 37–38. For example, in these chapters as elsewhere in the book the Hebrew conjunction ו, when it joins clauses, is rendered with a wide variety of Latin conjunctions. There is no consistent formal equivalence, but the Latin conjunctions consistently make explicit the logical relation that actually obtains between the conjoined clauses.[40] For lexical items the common pattern of representation in V for a Hebrew word is the predominant use of one Latin item as the equivalent for the Hebrew item with a variety of less frequent Latin renditions.[41] The total group of equivalents nicely

describes when he suggests that Jerome, in apparent contradiction, enunciates principles of translation that emphasize the target language (dynamic equivalence) and that emphasize the source language (formal equivalence) ("The Latin Translations," 323–24). As far as formal equivalence is concerned, it is indeed as Kedar suggests ("The Latin Translations," 324–25). V displays great variability in whether it sticks to standard equivalences or not, but that misses the point that V aims instead at semantic equivalence.

[39] Kedar notes that books translated earlier (e.g., Prophets) "exhibit adherence to the linguistic structure of the source language" ("The Latin Translations," 326).

[40] When joining clauses in chs. 37 and 38, the conjunction ו is rendered by V with "*et*" sixty-three times; with "*autem*" ten times; with "*ergo*" nine times; with "*ut*" or "*ne*" three times; twice with "*itaque*"; twice with a relative pronoun; twice with the enclitic "*-que*"; once each with "*igitur,*" "*enim,*" "*sed,*" "*porro,*" "*vero,*" and "*quam ob rem*"; and twice with a combination of participle plus finite verb rather than two finite verbs joined by a conjunction. Six times V does not render the conjunction at all (as, for example, when it introduces the apodosis of a condition).

[41] As noted by B. Kedar ("The Latin Translations," 325), who observes that V's rendering of lexemes sometimes shows a strong pattern of concordant rendering, but more frequently exhibits the use of a standard equivalence with frequent and relevant contextual adaptation.

maps the semantic range of the Hebrew word. The less frequent Latin forms occur in those contexts where the predominant equivalent does not cover part of the semantic range of the Hebrew term.[42]

[42] E.g., for נתן V predominantly uses *do* (104 times in Jeremiah), but in thirty-nine other instances it uses other verbs (*pono, tribuo, mitto, redo, curvo, trado* [esp.]). V renders הלך with sixteen different verbs. *Abeo* (twenty-three times) and *ambulo* (twenty-two times) are the most frequent, then *vado* (seventeen times) and *eo* (seventeen times). נפל in Jer-V is rendered twenty times with *cado*, five times with *corruo*, three times with *ruo*, twice with *perfugas*, and once each with *inruo, ruina, valeo*, and *concido*. In Jeremiah V does not render נָא at all except at 37:20(19) (*obsecro*), 38:4 (*rogamus*), and 38:20 (*quaeso*). These are all pleas addressed to the king. This seems to be a technique confined to this context within the book, and perhaps is intended to convey the emotion of Jeremiah's plea. For עלה *hifil* in Jer V follows a translation technique of contextual adaptation, rather than lexical consistency. It uses the following equivalents: *educo* six times (mostly recitals of the Exodus), *adduco* four times, *offero* three times (offering a sacrifice), *levo* twice, and once each *elevo, obduco*, and *ascendo*. In Jer-V פקד *hifil* is rendered three times with *commendo*, three times with *praepono*, twice with *praefacio*, and once each with *trado* and *constituo*. V seems to choose an equivalent for this Hebrew verb according to the nuance that needs to be expressed in the particular context (as also does G). Of the more than seventy occurrences of אוֹצָר in the Bible V renders most of them with *thesaurus*, but it also uses four other words when the Hebrew term refers to a storehouse of some kind, rather than a treasury per se. These are: *horreum* five times, *apotheca* twice, *cellarius* once, and *cella* once. Thus the rendering with *cellarius* in Jer 38:11 can be said to conform to V translation technique. V is thinking of the אוֹצָר as the wine cellar, rather than the treasury. In Jeremiah V renders יכל with *possum* eleven times, *praevaleo* four times, and *valeo, invalesco, sustineo, infirmus esse* (לא יכל), and *fas esse negare* (38:5) once each; מאן with *nolo* seven times, and with *renuo* three times; יצא *hifil* by *educo* ten times, *eicio* three times, *profero* twice, and once each by *separo, intro*, and *produco*. In Jeremiah V renders נפל *hifil* with *prosterno* twice, and with *averto, mitto, subverto*, and *praecipito* once each. Of the thirty times לִפְנֵי occurs in Jeremiah V renders it fifteen times with *coram*, seven times with *in conspectu*, three times with *ante*, twice with the dative case and once each for three other options. V renders חרשׁ in these ways: in Jeremiah with *cesso* at 38:27, and with *taceo* at 4:19; in the Bible with *taceo* twenty-three times, *sileo* six times, *cesso* twice (1 Sam 7:8 and Jer 38:27), *parco* once, a phrase once, and no equivalent twice. The use of *cesso* at Jer 38:27, while rare in V, is quite an apt contextual adaptation whereas *taceo* would be a poor choice there. In the Bible V renders נשׂג with *adprehendo* fifteen times, *conprehendo* eleven times, *invenio* twice, *occupo* twice, and seven other words once each.

For an example of syntactic equivalence implemented through grammatical diversity see V translation technique for וְהוּא: Jer 20:1 *qui constitutus erat* = וְהוּא פָקִיד; Jer 33:1 *cum . . . clauses erat* = וְהוּא עָצוּר; Jer 38:7 *qui erat* = וְהוּא; Jer 40:1 *vinctum* = וְהוּא אָסוּר. Note also: וְהוּא + participle = *qui* + finite verb (Gen 14:12, 13); or = cj + finite verb (Gen 14:18; 18:8; 24:62; 32:22, 32; 34:19); or = participle (Gen 18:1). The use of *respondit autem* for וַיֹּאמֶר in Jer 38:20 is an example of V's contextual adaptation in regard to both verb and conjunction.

In Jeremiah V's technique for rendering retrospective pronouns in relative clauses seems actually to be *not* to render such forms (e.g., Jer 7:10, 11, 14; 8:2; 9:13; 11:11; 14:16; 39:17). This should probably be attributed to the capacity of the relative pronoun in Latin to be declined.

In Jeremiah, when a finite verb is accompanied by an infinitive absolute of the same root, V uses the same verb to render the infinitive as the finite verb fifteen

The desire for formal variety, even while maintaining semantic consistency, can be seen in the rendition of Hebrew ולא, which is rendered in V for Jeremiah mostly by *et non, nec,* or *neque.* A number of lexical equivalences occur in these chapters that are instances of consistent renderings that are both formally and semantically equivalent.[43] In chapters 37–38 the modernization of toponyms and gentilics is seen in the consistent rendition of הַכַּשְׂדִּים with *Chaldaei,* and of כּוּשִׁי with *Aethiopicus.* The frequent occurrences of renderings that make implicit information explicit and that make substitutions probably should also be considered evidence for V's translation norms.[44]

The consequences for textual criticism of this understanding of the norms guiding V are fairly straightforward. Variation from a predominant pattern of using a particular grammatical or lexical form in the target language for a given form in the source language does not by itself make the presence of a variant *Vorlage* arguable. On the other hand, a substantive difference between the semantic or syntactic value of V and that of M would in itself tend to make a variant *Vorlage* at least arguable if not finally probable. The exact reconstruction of the *Vorlage* will have a higher degree of uncertainty attached to it even where regarded as probable if the semantic/syntactic consistency of V is not matched by a formal consistency.

---

times, two different verbs for the infinitive and finite verb fifteen times, and omits an equivalent for the infinitive absolute thirteen times. In 39:18 the use of *eruens* for מַלֵּט seems intended to emphasize the context within which the action of the main verb takes place since *eruens* is not semantically equivalent to מלט.

In Jer 38:27 there seems to be a notable V "paraphrase." M has כִּי לֹא־נִשְׁמַע הַדָּבָר׃. V has *nihil enim fuerit auditum,* rendering both לֹא־ and הַדָּבָר׃ with one word. Perhaps actually this should be thought of not as a paraphrase, but as a translational adjustment since this is certainly an adaptation to normal Latin style.

[43] The use of *custodia* for מִשְׁמָר/מִשְׁמֶרֶת is consistent enough to be regarded as stereotyped (*custodia*: twenty-one times מִשְׁמֶרֶת, five times מִשְׁמָר, twice פְּקֻדָּה, once בֵּית מִשְׁמֶרֶת, once בֵּית הַסֹּהַר, once מַטָּרָה). All eleven occurrences of מַטָּרָה in Jer-M are rendered in V with *carcer,* but then this consistent formal equivalence also produces consistent semantic equivalence. The rendition of נכה *hifil* is strikingly consistent, twenty-eight times with *percutio,* and only once (37:15) with *caedo,* which appears to be introduced to make explicit a specific nuance of the Hebrew text at that point (see below); of the twelve occurrences of חָיָה in Jer, V renders all but one (38:17; *et salvus eris* for וְחָיִתָה) with forms of *vivo.* For all seven occurrences of דאג in the Bible V uses *sollicito.*

[44] Making implicit information explicit: 37:4 וְלֹא־; 37:9 הָלֹךְ יֵלְכוּ . . . יֵלֵכוּ׃ (= G T); 37:12 אֶרֶץ (= G S T ιω'); 37:15 וְהִכּוּ (= S ιω'); 37:15 וְנָתְנוּ (= G); 37:15 בֵּית הָאֵסוּר (= σ' α'-θ'); 37:20 בֵּית (= G S T); 37:20 וְלֹא (= σ' S); 37:21 וְנָתֹן; 38:20 יִתְּנוּ (= G S); 38:22 אָחוֹר׃ (= G σ' S); 38:27 צִוָּה (= G S); Substitution: 37:13 בַּעַל פְּקִדֻת; 37:13 נֹפֵל׃ (= G S); 37:14 נֹפֵל (= G S); 37:15 לְבֵית; 37:19 לֵאמֹר; 37:20 תִּפָּל־; 38:10 בְּיָדְךָ (σ' S T); 38:11 בְּיָדוֹ (= S T); 38:17 וְחָיִתָה.

Examples of the Treatment of Cases

In the light of the differing redactional shapes of the two text forms and the translational norms guiding the versions, we now proceed to the examination of the individual cases of textual variation among the witnesses. In keeping with the illustrative intention of this essay, we will present summaries of the total picture for Jeremiah 37–38 and then examine a few selected cases.

(a) Examples of Cases of Redactional Variation

After examining each of the M/G differences in Jeremiah 37–38 (44–45) in the light of the redactional agenda of the two text forms, I conclude that many of the differences are redactional in nature. Of 139 instances of difference that have consequences for translation and/or exegesis seventy-two (52%) are due to redactional features proper to these two chapters. Another nine (6%) are due to redactional features proper to the whole book. Here are some examples:

38:9 הֵרֵעוּ הָאֲנָשִׁים הָאֵלֶּה θ' V S T | 'Επονηρεύσω G (lit) •
38:9 עָשׂוּ לְיִרְמְיָהוּ הַנָּבִיא θ' V S T | ἐποίησας G (lit) •
38:9 אֵת אֲשֶׁר־הִשְׁלִיכוּ אֶל־הַבּוֹר θ' V S T | > G (lit) •
38:9 וַיָּמָת תַּחְתָּיו θ' V T | τοῦ ἀποκτεῖναι τὸν ἄνθρωπον τοῦτον G (lit)
| ܘܗܐ ܡܐܬ S (abbr) •

These four cases combine to yield two dramatically different versions of what Ebed-Melek says to Zedekiah. In Edition 1, witnessed by G, Zedekiah is the sole perpetrator of evil against Jeremiah, seeking to kill him. Ebed-Melek's speech is a rebuke, challenging Zedekiah's wrong-doing. In so doing Ebed-Melek models faithfulness to YHWH in the midst of a context that is hostile to YHWH. In Edition 2, witnessed by M θ' V S T, it is the *śarîm* who are the perpetrators of evil. Ebed-Melek's speech is a petition, more precisely a complaint, that seeks to deploy royal authority and power on behalf of Jeremiah. In this Ebed-Melek models how to effect righteousness from a marginal location where one does not hold sufficient actual power for the task. These two versions of Ebed-Melek's speech fit exactly into the two different redactions for these chapters, indeed they are central components in them. Thus G offers us real variants, but they are redactional in origin, not textual.

37:12 לַחֲלִק α' σ' θ' <α'-θ'> | τοῦ ἀγοράσαι G (lit) | εἰς τὸ νειμᾶσθαι τὸν κλήρον ιω' V S (interp) | לפלגא אחסנתא דאית ליה T (interp) •

This is the only occurrence of this verb in M Jeremiah. As G. Greenberg points out, this could either refer to a division of property, if based on חלק^II^, or to Jeremiah "slipping away" if based on חלק^I^.[45] The unvocalized text can bear either meaning. This is an example of what P. Raabe has designated a parasonantic pun, wherein a word with one clear meaning (in this case, "to make a division") suggests another (in this case, "to slip away").[46] The result is a text that at the same time describes Jeremiah's intention and the way that intention is perceived by others. All the versions except G resolve the ambiguity in favor of the meaning associated with חלק^II^. The Hexaplaric witnesses correspond to the vocalized text of M, but do not have the capacity to hint at the second meaning that remains even in the vocalized M text.

The use of ἀγοράζω in G is likewise its only occurrence in Jeremiah. In the Pentateuch this verb renders שָׁבַר, "to buy grain." Perhaps the verb should be understood with that nuance here. If so, it fits perfectly into the context. There is no apparent explanation for this G reading unless it is the earlier text. It could not arise from an error, and goes in a rather different direction from the obvious options for resolving any perceived ambiguity. On the other hand, the M text makes good sense as a redactional creation from the *Vorlage* of G. The double perception of Jeremiah's action corresponds to the dilemma faced by Zedekiah and the ancient reader, namely, that which Jeremiah says is the path YHWH has provided for life looks like disaster and treason.

Thus we have two cases in one. There is the question whether the G and M readings differ due to redactional intervention. Having determined that this is the case, there are still the two other variants, which given the witnesses involved, necessarily constitute a text critical case for the text of Edition 2. However, these readings seem more likely to be secondary readings, resolving the bi-valent sense of the text found in M (hence "interp" in *BHQ* nomenclature).

(b) Examples of Textual Cases Relevant to Edition 2

Once we have identified the cases where the variation is the result of redactional processes, we are left with a set of cases where presumptively the difference is the result of text transmissional processes

[45] Greenberg, *Translation Technique*, 185.

[46] P. R. Raabe, "Deliberate Ambiguity in the Psalter," *JBL* 110 (1991), 217–218.

in the handing on of Edition 2. Indeed, in more cases than one might expect the difference between G and M is not redactional (fifty-eight times=42%). In the majority of these cases where G and M differ textually, i.e., stand as differing witnesses to what originally was shared text, M appears to preserve the preferable (i.e., earliest) text. In some cases it does so alone. In many it has the company of witnesses from the proto-Masoretic period. Secondary readings in G or its *Vorlage* arise for a variety of reasons, the most common being traits shared with other versions (especially V and S): explicitation, facilitation, modernization, and substitution.[47] Also noteworthy are the occurrences of homoioteleuton (37:1) and homoioarcton (37:15; 37:17) in G's *Vorlage.*

In an important minority of cases G is the better witness to the text G and M have in common, thus preserving the reading that should be preferred as earliest, even for Edition 2. Not surprisingly, G often stands alone in these instances, but it does not always do so.[48] In chs. 37–38 I do not believe that any other witness preserves the earliest text except when it agrees with either M or G.

The thirteen cases where the text of M is a secondary formation from an earlier text preserved in G seem to arise for one of three reasons. In seven cases the M reading arises from assimilation to a more common pattern of expression. Three result from an intention to make an expression more emphatic, and two result from a desire to create a more structured narrative scheme.[49] The prevalence of assimilation is noteworthy since for the whole Bible M is rightly characterized as a heterogenous text that preserves considerable diversity.[50] Here are seven cases of the reduction of textual heterogeneity

---

[47] Explicitation: 37:4 בֵּית (= α' T); 37:9 הָלֹךְ יֵלְכוּ . . . יֵלֵכוּ׃ (= V T); 37:12 אֶרֶץ (= V S T ιω'); 37:15 וְנָתְנוּ (= V); 37:15 בֵּית ; 37:20 בֵּית (= V S T); 37:21 וְנָתֹן (= S T); 38:20 יִתְּנוּ (= V S); 38:22 אָחוֹר׃ (= σ' V S); 38:27 צִוָּה (= V S). Facilitation: 38:23 וְאֶת־הָעִיר הַזֹּאת תִּשְׂרֹף (= S T). Facilitation-syntactic: 38:4 יוּמַת נָא אֶת־הָאִישׁ הַזֶּה (= V S T). Facilitation-stylistic: 38:4 עַל־כֵּן (= S). Modernization: the rendering of הַכַּשְׂדִּים in 37:5, 9, 10, 11, 13, 14; 38:2, 19, 23 (all = V S). Substitution: 37:13 נֹפֵל׃ (= V S); 37:14 נֹפֵל (= V S); 38:4 דֹּרֵשׁ לְשָׁלוֹם.

[48] 37:8 הַכַּשְׂדִּים; 37:10 כִּי אִם־; 37:13 וּשְׁמוֹ; 37:16 כִּי (= σ' θ' S V); 37:17 וַיֹּאמֶר¹; 37:17 וַיֹּאמֶר²; 37:21 כָּל־הַלֶּחֶם; 38:1 כָּל־; 38:4 אַנְשֵׁי הַמִּלְחָמָה (= V S); 38:8 לֵאמֹר׃; 38:16 אֵת (= M[qere] V S); 38:23 בָּאֵשׁ׃; 38:26 לִפְנֵי.

[49] Assimilation to the usual form/pattern: 37:8 הַכַּשְׂדִּים; 37:13 וּשְׁמוֹ; 38:1 כָּל־; 38:4 אַנְשֵׁי הַמִּלְחָמָה; 38:8 לֵאמֹר׃; 38:23 בָּאֵשׁ׃; 38:26 לִפְנֵי. Increasing emphasis: 37:10 כִּי אִם־; 37:16 כִּי; 37:21 כָּל־הַלֶּחֶם. Narratization: 37:17 וַיֹּאמֶר¹; 37:17 וַיֹּאמֶר². The motivation for the change at 38:16 אֵת remains elusive.

[50] J. A. Sanders, "Text and Canon: Concepts and Method," *JBL* 98 (1979), 26–27.

in two chapters. I am not ready to draw final conclusions, but it seems reasonable to suppose that Edition 2 of Jeremiah, with its many doublets and frequent use of stereotyped expressions, may be a textual environment that encourages assimilation.

Here are some examples of cases where G and M differ for text transmissional reasons rather than redactional ones:

37:13 וּשְׁמוֹ֙ α' σ' V S T (assim-usu) | > G || pref *omit* וּשְׁמוֹ֙ see G •

In Jer 11:19 G renders the reading found in M, וּשְׁמוֹ, with καὶ τὸ ὄνομα αὐτοῦ. In Jer 14:9 it uses καὶ τὸ ὄνομά σου for וְשִׁמְךָ, and in Jer 52:1 uses καὶ ὄνομα for וְשֵׁם. This suggests that the absence of the expression here is because it was lacking in G's *Vorlage*. The presence (M) or absence (G) of the expression serves no particular redactional agenda, so the change is likely to be text transmissional. It is common in the Hebrew Bible, when a new character appears in a story, to introduce his or her name in a clause that begins with וּשְׁמוֹ or וּשְׁמָהּ. That M, etc. assimilate to this common pattern is an easier explanation than any for the absence of the expression in G.

38:4 אַנְשֵׁ֣י הַמִּלְחָמָ֗ה T (assim-usu) | τῶν ἀνθρώπων τῶν πολεμούντων G V S || pref הָאֲנָשִׁים הַנִּלְחָמִים see G V S •

Translation technique for both G and V (*virorum bellantium*) strongly suggests a variant *Vorlage* behind their readings. In Jeremiah the noun מִלְחָמָה occurs twenty-seven times. Twice it has no equivalent reading in the text of G; once (8:16) it is rendered with χρεμετισμός, suggesting a *Vorlage* מִצְהָלָה. Twenty-three times it is rendered with a noun or adjective from the root πολεμ-; *only once* (here) is it rendered with a verb form. The *nifal* participle of לחם occurs six times in Jeremiah, and on every occasion in G the corresponding form is a form of the verb πολεμέω. The expression אַנְשֵׁי הַמִּלְחָמָה occurs seven times. Twice it has no equivalent in G. Four times it is rendered with οἱ ἄνδρες οἱ πολεμισταί (or other case); the G reading found here is found only here. In V מִלְחָמָה is always rendered with a noun; this case is the only exception. The use of a participle in the rendering of אַנְשֵׁי הַמִּלְחָמָה is likewise limited to this case. In V the *nifal* participle of לחם is always rendered with a participle.

Between the reading of M and T, אַנְשֵׁי הַמִּלְחָמָה, and the *Vorlage* implied by G, V and S, הָאֲנָשִׁים הַנִּלְחָמִים, the G V S reading appears preferable. The expression would be unique in Jeremiah since, except for its use in 21:4, the *nifal* participle of לחם typically is used to refer to those fighting *against* Jerusalem and Judah, not *for* them. On the other hand, אַנְשֵׁי הַמִּלְחָמָה is a common expression in the book. The M T reading could easily arise from the G V S reading by assimilation to the more common usage in the book. That G and two proto-Masoretic witnesses agree is also significant weight for their reading.

37:1 מֶּלֶךְ V S T | > G (homtel) •

There is no clear motivation for an intentional change either from the M V S T reading to the G reading, or vice versa. Instead this is a text book example of homoioteleuton. This is clearly the most parsimonious explanation.

37:13 נֹפֵל: α' σ' T | φεύγεις G V S (substit) • (Cf. a second, parallel case in 37:14.)

The translation techniques established for G, V and S make a Hebrew variant arguable in this case.[51] The difficulty with a reconstruction with some form of נוס, which is the indicated *Vorlage* in each case, is that that verb is otherwise used only in the OAN of Jeremiah. Moreover, in both G and V the use for נפל of verbs describing flight is a distinctive technique for rendering the root when referring to desertion to the Chaldeans. The renditions offered by G, V and S avoid two extremes, a mechanical rendition with a verb describing falling, and a contextually exact rendition referring to treason. Instead they appear to have carefully substituted a contextually appropriate, but gentler, rendition referring to flight, not desertion. The resulting perspective on Jeremiah's action would fit well with Edition 1, and the perspective inherent in the M text would fit well with Edition 2, but neither do the redactional agendas of those editions *require* those particular readings. For that reason, the fact that the reading occurs also in two proto-Masoretic versions known for contextual adaptation of their renditions (i.e., V and S), and the pattern of

[51] In Jer-G φεύγεις occurs sixteen times, twelve of them rendering forms from the root נוס. All three times when it appears to render נפל occur in Jeremiah 37–38. In V *cado* is the predominant term used to render נפל. However, there is a subset of renderings using compounds of *fugio*, which with other minority renderings seem to be the use of contextually appropriate alternatives to *cado*. In the Pentateuch S ܥܪܩ renders נוס twenty-nine times out of forty-one, and five other roots for the remaining twelve times, but it is never used for נפל.

usage for נוס in M, treating the G reading as redactionally different from M is a more difficult explanation than understanding it as a text transmissional difference that arose in G or its *Vorlage*.

37:20 בֵּ֖ית | εἰς οἰκίαν G V S T (explic) •

The preposition need not be explicit for the Hebrew to make sense. Were it in M's *Vorlage* there would be no reason to delete it although haplography cannot be ruled out. On the other hand, it would be much more common, both in Hebrew and the versional languages to use the preposition to make explicit the relationship between "house" and the verb. Thus the M reading is to be preferred as the more difficult even though that witness stands alone against the agreement of G and the three proto-Masoretic witnesses besides M.

BIBLICAL INDEX

Biblical loci are entered in this index only for those pages where they are actually discussed, rather than merely being referenced.

AUTHORS INDEX